COGNITION IN
SCHIZOPHRENIA AND PARANOIA:
THE INTEGRATION OF COGNITIVE PROCESSES

*an integration of past theories of schizophrenia and
an information-processing explanation that applies current
behavioral, developmental, and hemispheric research*

PETER A. MAGARO
University of Maine

LEA LAWRENCE ERLBAUM ASSOCIATES, PUBLISHERS
1980   Hillsdale, New Jersey

Lawrence Erlbaum Associates, Inc., Publishers
365 Broadway
Hillsdale, New Jersey 07642

Library of Congress Cataloging in Publication Data

Magaro, Peter A.
  Cognition in schizophrenia and paranoia.
  Bibliography: p.
  Includes indexes.
  1. Cognition disorders.   2. Schizophrenia.
3. Paranoia.   I. Title.   [DNLM: 1. Cognition.
2. Paranoia—Psychology.   3. Schizophrenic
psychology.   WM203 M188c]
RC553.C64M33   616.89'82   80-13870
ISBN 0-89859-028-0

Printed in the United States of America

Contents

Preface

The effort to provide a scientific understanding of schizophrenia has been immense. Bellack (1958)[1] estimates that 7000 papers have been published on the subject between 1936 and 1956, a brief 20 years. Grinker (1969)[2] believes that there has been more time, money, and energy spent on schizophrenia than all other psychiatric problems combined. This large expenditure of resources has mainly stemmed from an attempt to answer the many statements of theory with some empirical facts. However, such research efforts have not appeared to be overly successful.

The past 30 years have yielded a continuing parade of theories containing empirical support followed by conflicting evidence and eventually diminishing interest. In effect, each theory has produced an experimental task to support its hypothesis, but it is at the task level where the research enterprise has faltered. The instruments were not available to demonstrate the effects demanded by the theory. In this sense, it can be considered that the past decade has produced a plateau in the understanding of schizophrenia, and this has mainly been due to a methodology that could only produce an inexact application of the scienfific method.

Such a history might create an inclination to be pessimistic about the efficacy of the scientific approach in the study of schizophrenia. However, if one looks closely at our present level of understanding, it can be seen that we have gradually progressed and that there is a consensus in regard to the focus

---

[1]Bellack, L. *Schizophrenia: A review of the syndrome.* New York: Logos Press, 1958.

[2]Grinker, R. R. An essay on schizophrenia and science. *Archives of General Psychiatry,* 1969, *20,* 1–24.

of interest in schizophrenia. Following the direction of psychology in general, we have come to place a priority on examining cognitive processes.

The research during the present decade has focused upon cognitive mechanisms, beginning with gross descriptions of cognitive styles and progressing to the processes inherent in information theory. Although specific mechanisms within this frame of reference are hotly debated, there is a uniting interest in the cognitive processes that create meaning from external events. Within the framework of a focus upon cognition, there have been three major developments, which encourages an optimism in creating a more accurate description of the uniqueness of schizophrenia.

The first is the relatively clear mandate to specify the type of schizophrenia one is studying. We show that the distinctions that have been formed allow us to distinguish between levels of disorganization and types of schizophrenia. Of crucial importance has been the distinction between the schizophrenic and the paranoid. This distinction does not only come from clinical experience but also from performance on laboratory tasks. The second major development involves the development of a methodology that allows us to begin the specification of the interacting psychological mechanisms unique to each personality. Information theory has produced a body of research that now allows an examination of individual differences. It is the prevailing conceptualization of schizophrenia, mainly, because it offers a means to operationalize the multiple processes that determine behavior. We review this work in schizophrenia and operationalize our terms within that framework. The third development evolves from the research in hemispheric functioning. As with information theory, enough is known about the type of functions performed in each hemisphere to allow us to generate hypotheses about the schizophrenic and the paranoid. In fact, the information-processing mechanisms observed to be distinct in both groups are readily translatable into neurological terms and, hence, provide a much more complete explanation than previously generated in the past.

The first task is to combine previous theories of schizophrenia into a coherent whole. We hope this section will be of help in understanding where we have evolved from in developing our current interests in the particular psychological mechanism considered present in schizophrenia. For this we delve into the theory-building process as used in psychology to demonstrate that we have stressed too much the operationalism phase to the neglect of the ordering of higher theoretical constructs. We attempt to show that there has always been a need for a unification of theoretical terms, just as there has been the requirement to tie our terms to the operations residing in our observations. When past schizophrenic theories are marshaled together within the structure of a unifying model, we begin to see that all were correct in what they found, and incorrect in terms of what they inferred. In fact we contend that the theories of schizophrenia that emerged through the 1960s

were supported by the loose sands of an epiphenomena. The findings of differences between schizophrenics and others were due not to the particular process that was investigated, such as motivation, preception, or conceptualization, but to a requirement inherent in every task, no matter what its label: the demand to integrate different psychological processes. The behavioral data, therefore, will tell us that the deficit on any one task is not related to the empirical construct operationalized by that task, but to that process which is not operationalized but present and active in determining the resulting performance deficit.

The chapters are organized so that one can read individual chapters without being severely hampered by not reviewing the previous chapters. It is expected that the reader may have specific interests and would not wish to review material with which he is acquainted. Chapters 1 and 2 deal with research strategies in schizophrenia; Chapters 3 and 4 are a review of past work. These four chapters are recommended for someone who is looking for an overview of the research in schizophrenia. I would expect that they would be especially valuable for the student beginning the serious study of the field. The rest of the chapters are addressed to the researchers in the field who already have a grasp of prior literature. They attempt to provide arguments for new conceptions of schizophrenia and the means to study it. Chapter 5 argues for separating paranoid from nonparanoid schizophrenics. Chapter 6 presents an extensive review of the research using an information-processing methodology. Chapter 7 is an overview of schizophrenia as it can be considered in terms of integration theory. This chapter may be read first to gain a sense of the theme of the book, which again may be helpful to the scholar beginning to derive a synthesis of the field. Chapters 8 and 9 are speculative formulations that are intended to chart new research directions. In each case, the hope is that the material is complete and ideas for further scholarship are stimulated. Chapter 9 is intended for those who are interested in applying laboratory research to treatment. Although the procedures suggested are rather speculative, the attempt is made to provide a direction for treatment that is prescriptive in the sense that the treatment is aimed at specific psychological mechanisms.

In more detail, Chapter 1 deals with the use of the scientific method, especially the process of operationalizing a construct, and provides a means to define terms more rigidly and exactly. The operationalizing process, which is used to examine past work, is unconventional and possibly more restricting than necessary but is offered to distinguish between the real and the imagined differences of the processes specified by each theory.

Chapter 2 develops the means to organize our empirical past by using Hullian Theory as a model. Hullian terms are offered to correspond to theoretical terms used in past work. In this manner, it is hoped that a historical perspective will be gained and the value of past work will be seen.

We hope to demonstrate that past research strategies that have investigated one theoretical term in isolation from all others has produced an experimental impasse.

Chapters 3 and 4 critically examine the dominant theories and operations leading to our present conceptions. The third chapter is a review of the major performance deficit theories interested in cognitive processes. The fourth chapter reviews those theories that are motivational in interest or are concerned with enduring habitual response tendencies.

Chapter 5 is a detailed examination of our subject dimensions, notably the paranoid as separate from the schizophrenic. Here, we make what we believe to be the crucial discrimination in the schizophrenic population, the distinction between paranoids and schizophrenics with the former not considered to be a subset of the latter. We marshal the evidence to demonstrate that schizophrenics and paranoids use completely different cognitive styles having a common tie only in their history of belonging to the same classes in the Kraeplinian classification system. The crucial task, therefore, is to designate the psychological process characteristic of paranoids and schizophrenics. We contend that the schizophrenic has difficulty creating an organization of conceptual material, while the paranoid has a difficulty with common perceptual-type tasks. Underlying both problems, however, is the need to integrate both processes, and that distinguishes both groups from others. This last process is the most difficult to demonstrate, as it involves the observation of the interaction of two separate processes as they create another separate and different state—that of integration. Hence, at a higher theoretical level, the integration process is introduced to unite the two conditions.

Chapter 6 presents an information-processing model and reviews existing work testing schizophrenics within such a model. The chapter progresses through the work on icon strength, encoding, recognition memory, recall, and the organization of assemblies and schemata. The intent is to pinpoint the stage where the paranoid and schizophrenic exhibit their specific deficit. The information-theory work is just beginning; hence, there is not the completeness one would wish, but enough of the promise is evident to advance some hypothesis about the processes active in schizophrenics and paranoids.

Chapter 7 begins the explanation of the integration term. Since it is a higher-order term, a metaphor in terms of existing experimental observations, we discuss the construct in terms of its relationship to other terms in the literature. We conceive of integration as the crucial element in creating a consensual reality. Piaget is used as the theoretical vehicle to relate integration to the developmental process, because he provides a framework for the normal and deviant integration of perceptual and conceptual processes. We closely follow his stages of development and consider what

would be the resultant behavioral effects if the resolution of perceptual and conceptual processes does not proceed as found with average children. From such an analysis, we speculate upon the stages of development that are prone to produce childhood schizophrenia or paranoia and adult schizophrenia and paranoia, all as a product of not forming the differing age-related integrational demands of childhood. Thus, from a developmental perspective, we reach the same conclusion as in the experimental task literature; that it is necessary to conceptualize behavior in terms of interacting processes, especially that of perception and conceptualization.

Chapter 8 carries our thesis into recent neurological theory concerning hemisphere dominance. We note the coresspondence between hemispheric functioning and the cognitive processing of paranoids and schizophrenics; hence, we localize the dominant hemisphere for both groups. The lack of integration of the two processes is localized in the connecting neurological link between the two hemispheres, so that each functions independently without the modulating effects of the other. Although the metaneurological quality of this construct will be recognized, its importance will not be minimized as it explains, at a neurological level, what has been offered on a developmental and behavioral level. What is most important, however, is that this work provides us with another methodology to examine the dominant cognitive processes of our groups of interest, as well as the integration of the two processes. If we are correct that each group processes material in a unique manner and that each processing style is hemisphere specific, we will have begun a novel and exciting view of schizophrenia. The implications aim toward specific cognitive styles with a neural substitute that may not imply any form of disease.

Out total effort is a theoretical framework that relates three fields of psychology: the experimental research in psychopathology, the developmental literature on intellectual growth, and the literature on hemispheric specialization. The specifications of the separate processes and their integration provides the means to reanalyze our empirical operations and theoretical terms in order to provide a more complete level of understanding, or at least to alert us to additional possibilities in research strategies. Admittedly, at times we enter into speculative hypotheses to draw the correspondence between diverse areas of research. We justify this approach by our attempt to develop postulate sets that bring together what are usually divergent areas of interest. We intend to present the focus of current research interests. We will be pleased if we are able to encourage efforts to put this research strategy to the test.

The data presented and interpreted by the Integration Theory, as well as the therapeutic implications discussed in Chapter 9, are not considered definitive but are presented as an indication of the experimental and therapeutic actions that could occur with a shift in the current experimental paradigm. Possibly the value of this treatise lies not in the presentation of a new theory but in the manner of viewing past theories and considering future directions. It does seem that we are developing a new epistemology that has to be a subject of concern as we begin a new era of investigation. Certainly, as we develop a more accurate methodology, the possibility of providing an understanding that may diminish the rule of faith in determining the cause and care of schizophrenia is increased.

Possibly what gives one the impetus to want to write a book about a topic that seems to defy a rational solution is the encouragement from students and colleagues. The writers of the past and present have provided the ideas that are developed here. I especially want to thank Brendan Maher for his invaluable encouragement and the time and patience to shepherd this work through to publication. The greatest thanks and appreciation, however, are to my students. They criticized when needed and provided solutions when required. Mr. David McDowell was a major contributor to Chapters 5 and 7. Ms. Ann Pic'l was instrumental in organizing Chapters 6 and 8. Mr. Ivan Miller, along with helping with the development of Chapter 7, contributed to Chapter 9. Mr. John Vojtisek and Mr. Ross St. Germaine contributed to Chapter 4, and Mr. Victor Des Maris contributed to Chapters 5 and 9. Ms. Nancy Hasenfus aided in the material presented in the appendix. I do hope the experience will become as valuable for them as it has for me. Praise and thanks also must go to the secretaries and especially Marian E. Perry here in the psychology office for performing the long arduous job of typing and at times rephrasing to present some needed clarity. Last, I want to thank the many patients who have expended their efforts in order to help me understand. An early version of the Hullian model was presented in the *Progress in Experimental Personality Research,* Vol. 7, 1974. The initial discussion of Integration Theory in Chapter 7 was presented in the proceedings of the conference on Psychiatric Problems of Childhood, 1974.

Orono, Maine

PETER A. MAGARO

1 Research Strategies and Theory Building

Up on Cold Mountain
the devil has roared by
searing my soul with his cold fire
his white angels
have stabbed me with their
icy glass daggers
tied me down with white cloths
locked me in a white cell
yet my mind was not imprisoned
with his pain and poison
it roamed from Siberia
to the Enchanted
listened to whale chants
and
tasted forbidden wine
You put me on Cold Mountain
You are paid by Cold Mountain
Cold Mountain is your master
Cold Mountain is my prison

you intend to build terraces
and plant soil holding trees
to preserve Cold Mountain
so you can continue
to offer up our bodies
I intend to tunnel under Cold Mountain
and plant charges
to call on wind and river
to wear Cold Mountain away
if my mind still wanders
it is still escaping from Cold Mountain
I pray you understand this
and why I must tear your altar down
and you must give us up
as your sacrifice
and go back to tilling the fields
while we, your prisoners,
carry Cold Mountain away
on our backs

INTRODUCTION

This poem by Kendall A. Merriam (1976) is his statement of the experience of schizophrenia. As contrasted with other examples given in the literature which display a great amount of disorganized thought, we have here the thinking of the schizophrenic in a normal or even creative state. Merriam states the contrast between the usual and psychotic state and begins the presentation of the riddle. If we can accept that schizophrenic behavior can be normal as well as pathological, what is the process common to both states? We are beginning to answer that question by exploring the cognitive processes of different types of schizophrenics and other individuals. The question is then what is the common process, not what is the pathological process. Hence, now we propose to study schizophrenia not as a deficit but possibly as a cognitive process that is different from other groups and that possibly has beneficial qualities, both to the individual and the society. We do not deal with questions of value although we think they are important. We intend to pursue the question of the process through theories developed from experimental investigations of schizophrenia.

The work of David Shakow in the Worcester State Hospital Schizophrenia Research Service during the 1930s formalized the search for an experimental explanation of schizophrenia. The common medical or psychoanalytic explanations of the time were not accepted by the behavioral emphasis in psychology. Shakow therefore carried the procedure prevalent in the laboratory into the hospital and began the first systematic description of schizophrenic behavior. The reaction-time task was the instrument chosen to reliably measure behavior. Differences were observed that differentiated schizophrenics from other groups. Further manipulations of the parameters involved in the task produced the empirical laws from which a set of closely tied experimental hypotheses was generated. From these testable hypotheses, a theory of schizophrenia was formed that not only focused on cognitive processes but also a deficient cognitive process, a perceptual mechanism, inherent in schizophrenia. At the same time, Norman Cameron was using a card-sorting task to develop rather extensive theories of the type of conceptualization unique to schizophrenics and especially paranoids. This basic strategy of devising a task that was considered to mirror the operation of one psychological process became the dominant research model up through the 1960s. Unfortunately, this approach has bred a field of inquiry that contains as many different experimental operations as there were theories, all tending to conflict.

Surveying theories of schizophrenia, therefore, can be a confusing and frustrating enterprise. Isolated bits of information and segments of theories may be interesting, and even fascinating, but a meaningful progression through the theories and empirical work is difficult, if not impossible. One reason for this difficulty is that there are many conflicting theories of schizophrenia. If some common thread were found either in the theories or the empirical studies generated from them, it would illuminate our understanding of schizophrenia. In an effort to maximize our grasp of the research data, the beginning chapters organize the theories that have shaped our current understanding into one systematic framework. Theory structure is discussed first. It provides the framework in which each theory can be analyzed in relationship to others and in terms of empirical verification of its constructs. Thus, our first goal is to construct a system, using Hullian theory as a model, by which to compare and contrast theories of the schizophrenic deficit.

Our main purpose is to offer an explanation of schizophrenia that focuses on the cognitive processes and specifically on the interaction between them. Borrowing a term from Kuhn (1970), we argue for a paradigm shift by presenting a cognitive framework and techniques to be used in the performance deficit research. It is our contention that past research paradigms have produced the traditional image of conflicting results because of their neglect of the interactional relationship between psychological processes. Hence, we discuss new constructs explaining schizophrenic performance that are based on a recognition of the importance of the interaction between psychological processes. Research in information processing is introduced to define the operation of such psychological processes. Neurological concepts are then introduced to support the utility and relevance of the approach.

The study of behavior, not just limited to schizophrenia, has progressed from molar theories such as the inclusive learning theories of Hull, Tolman, Guthrie, and others to more micro-theories concerned with one specific aspect of behavior such as rote learning, simple discrimination, and partial reinforcement. In the literature on schizophrenia, the same progression has occurred, resulting in theories of verbal behavior, concept formation, size estimation, form discrimination, response dispositions, etc. All theories present some confirmatory evidence and implicitly or explicitly state the mechanism or process hypothesized to explain schizophrenic behavior. Such theoretical statements are at various levels of sophistication and range from highly complex psychoanalytic explanations to very specific statements of causal factors related to experimental operations. Our first goal is to provide a historical overview of the field by integrating previous causal explanations tied to experimental operations as contrasted to those explanations derived from clinical observations. In effect, we construct a molar theory by organizing the theoretical constructs advanced in the literature of experimental psychopathology. We also examine the empirical base of these constructs. Although the varieties of tasks utilized seem infinite, they share the common purpose of operationalizing a theoretical construct. This construct is the psychological process responsible for a deficit in performance. We argue that such measures are too imprecise to operationalize any construct properly.

The many studies that have been reported in support of or against a particular theoretical position are not fully reviewed. The research generated within the schizophrenic performance deficit framework has been organized in relatively general reviews (Arieti, 1955; Buss, 1966; Buss & Lang, 1965; Hunt & Cofer, 1944; Lang & Buss, 1965; Psychological Deficit Chapters in the Annual Review), and from a particular theoretical vantage point (Broen, 1968; Chapman & Chapman, 1973; Neale, Held, & Cromwell, 1969; McGhie, 1970; Pavy, 1968; Payne, 1966; Rodnick, 1967; Rodnick & Garmezy, 1957; Shakow, 1962; Silverman, 1964; Venables, 1964; Yates, 1966). Each specific review permits an analysis of the experimentation supporting a theoretical position.

The focus here in our review of the literature is upon an analysis of the different theoretical constructs offered to explain the mechanism hypothesized to function differently in psychopathological groups. Each theory has its own set of confirmatory data derived from the use of dependent variables. These variables are usually quite different, depending on the particular theorist's interest and explanation. In short, each theorist develops a specific experimental operation which discriminates between the performance of schizophrenics and other groups and at the same time defines a theoretical construct with psychological or physical referents to explain the schizophrenic deficit. The task of organizing these constructs into one framework may seem rather simple, involving no more than a listing of theoretical terms. Further, an assessment of the strength of a theory would then involve only an examination of the supporting research. However, such a view assumes that the many posited causes of the deficit fit into one nomological net, tied to specific definable operations, and confirmed by demonstrable observables. Such an ideal condition does not exist. There are problems in the comparability of theoretical constructs because of their distance from empirical constructs as well as in the actual definition of terms. Therefore, before proceeding on to our first goal of organizing theoretical constructs into one theoretical framework, the process of theory building itself will be discussed briefly. We will attempt here to clarify the nature of the terms that are employed in building a theory. Hopefully, this effort will aid us in classifying the theories which are used or misused in the explanation of schizophrenia.

THEORETICAL STRUCTURE IN THE SCHIZOPHRENIA LITERATURE

Empirical Event

Figure 1.1 schematically illustrates the different aspects of a theory. At the bottom level is the actual empirical event, the experiential base from which an operation is derived. This level is divided into two classes of empirical events, antecedent and consequent. The classes are further arranged into

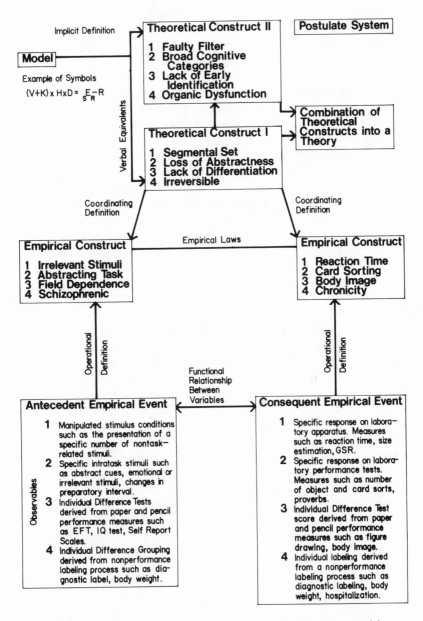

FIG. 1.1.   Terms and relationships in theory construction from a model as applied to the performance deficit literature.

types to clarify the means of deriving theoretical terms. In Type 1, the antecedent event refers to the manipulation of some variable external to the task such as presenting specific "noise" stimuli, or by shocking incorrect responses. The consequent event refers to a reliable response produced under specified well-known laboratory task conditions such as reaction time. The Type 1 antecedent event is usually conceptualized in terms of an independent variable that is experimentally manipulated, and the Type 1 consequent event is usually the dependent variable that is measured.

Type 2 is similar to Type 1 in that an independent variable is usually introduced, except that in this case an intratask variable is manipulated. An example of the antecedent event in a reaction-time study is varying the length of the preparatory interval or the intensity of the warning signal instead of introducing external stimuli as in Type 1. Another is varying the abstractness, emotionality, irrelevant cues, etc., of the stimulus cards in an object-sorting task. Thus, the antecedent event is the additional qualities that are manipulated in the task and operationally define a construct. The consequent event is the actual sorting of the cards having the differentially defined stimulus attributes. The difficulty with the Type 2 event is that the independent variable cannot be as clearly manipulated as in a Type 1 event. Hence, it is never completely clear if the variable of interest is not confounded by another intratask variable. We will also tend to find that Type 2 events sometimes are postulated to have occurred in a Type 1 experimental situation and are used as ad hoc explanations of results.

Bridgman (1938) considers operations derived from Type 1 and Type 2 events to be instrumental operations and distinguishes them from paper and pencil operations which are our Type 3 event. In this case, the antecedent and consequent events are similar to paper and pencil tests, which usually reveal individual differences and allow assignment of individuals to groups. Examples of this type of empirical event are scores on IQ Tests, a Draw-a-Person Test, achievement tests, diagnostic scales, etc. There is no manipulation, as such, at this level but the correlation between events is important.

The Type 4 event is the customary labeling of subjects in some non-task performance procedure such as the use of hospital admitting diagnosis, body shape, residence in a hospital or neighborhood, etc. Although this event is usually an antecedent event that is then related to other consequent events, there are theories which relate two Type 4 events such as number of hospitalized schizophrenics and social class to infer a causal relationship. The types of operations presented in Fig. 1.1 do not suggest that a particular antecedent type always operates with the same numbered consequent type. Rather it is the particular combination of antecedent and consequent types that seems to characterize the research strategy of different theorists.

The Type 4 events are crucial in the study of schizophrenia since these operations define the category of schizophrenia and what is most important, the subclass or type of schizophrenia. Here the lack of control over diagnosis or of long-term institutionalization becomes crucial. The Type 4 event is usually one arm of the empirical function. Schizophrenics are compared to normals or other controls and this Type 4 event is then related to task scores. If the subclassification is not accurate or fine enough, it is because we are in effect plotting functions that relate to another dimension besides that of schizophrenia. Or we are adding multiple functions together to derive a composite function not related to any schizophrenic group. An example of the first problem is where long-term institutionalized schizophrenics are compared to normals. It cannot be determined by this grouping whether the resulting performance function is due to long-term institutionalization or schizophrenia. An example of the second problem is grouping all subtypes of schizophrenics such as good-premorbid–poor-premorbid or paranoid–non-paranoid into one group labeled schizophrenic and comparing them to normals. In either case, the resulting functional relationship, the relationship between the Type 4 antecedent event and a consequent event, has dubious meaning. The constructs inferred to explain this relationship are of even less value since they are explanations of a relationship mistakenly applied to schizophrenia. The effort is now being made to treat schizophrenia as a Type 3 antecedent event and hence reduce the confounding that could occur with a less precise Type 4 procedure.

The relationship between the antecedent and consequent events is a functional relationship between variables. With instrumental operations, specific stimulus conditions are related to specific responses usually in the form of functions which could be specified in precise mathematical terms. What is more common, especially in Type 3 and 4 events, is that the function is a relationship between two classes of events. Questions raised at this level of observation are those of experimental control in the actual determination of the data. In other words, it is at this level that we have to become concerned with confounding variables in the research design. Moreover, it will become clear that possibly the greatest source of confounding is that the task itself may contain a multitude of dimensions that could never be considered one operation. Chapters 3 and 4 attempt to organize theoretical constructs derived from the empirical events and raise questions of experimental control especially about the use of Type 4 designations of schizophrenia. Chapter 5 further discusses this issue and provides a means to raise the classification of schizophrenia from a nominal to an interval scale of measurement.

Empirical Construct

We have been speaking of the data itself, the observables. Now we move to how we develop short-hand notes for these operations. The next level in Fig. 1.1 depicts the empirical construct. The empirical construct states the "what it is" in the experimental situation by defining the experienceable subject matter through the rules of operationalism. In the words of Bridgman (1927): "In general, we mean by a concept nothing more than a set of operations: The concept is synonymous with the corresponding set of operations [p. 5]." In our use of empirical constructs, this definition is adhered to with a vengeance. Each set of observations serves as the definition for one empirical construct. This procedure often elevates terms previously considered as empirical constructs to the levels of theoretical constructs. As a result, a major problem with operationalism in the schizophrenic performance deficit literature is confronted. What have passed as operations are really open-ended theoretical constructs. Such operations only partially interpret a concept, thereby leaving the meaning open. We attempt to close such openings by fully stating the meaning of the empirical construct. In short, an empirical construct in this volume is rather molecular in that it refers to one specific operation and does not refer to a relationship between operations.

Empirical Laws

The functional relationship between the antecedent and consequent events at the observable level leads to the relationship between empirical constructs which are the empirical laws. In Fig. 1.1 the empirical constructs are defined by the actual experimental operations. For example, the manipulation of stimulus conditions can serve as the operational definition for the empirical construct "irrelevant stimuli," while the immediate response to a stimulus serves as the operational definition of reaction time. The relationships between the empirical constructs are the empirical laws which explain the functional relationship between the empirical constructs. Following our example, the empirical law could state that reaction time increases with the number of irrelevant stimuli.

An empirical law therefore is the statement which describes the function between measurements. They also are the law-like statements that are the initial postulates of a theory. Turner (1965) states: "Laws are generalizations of relations and conformal patterns from which we may infer individual events, providing the individual events fulfill the conditions of the law's applications. Laws have become the instruments of classification and inference. They have become 'inference tickets' by which we categorize physical process and inferentially exploit our experience [p. 251]." By specifying the relationships formed by empirical constructs, laws clarify operational definitions. However, for clarity to be enhanced by the empirical laws, the empirical constructs themselves cannot blend different or subsequent operations into one empirical construct. If any law is formed with such blending, the crucial next step of developing theoretical constructs may refer to a completely different process than that which is intended. For example, in the Type 4 event, schizophrenia is now clearly recognized to be unacceptable as a subject grouping. Size estimation is clearly a multiple process operation as we will demonstrate in a later chapter. Relating the two empirical constructs, schizophrenia and size estimation with an empirical law is, therefore, devoid of any real meaning. Furthermore, using empirical laws to generate further theoretical constructs moves us further from reality and hinders the construction of meaningful theory. If our empirical terms were as unambiguous as those in the physical sciences, (e.g., weight being operationalized by units on a number of equivalent scales), our empirical laws might explain the functional relationship of variables. However, when one examines the usual relationship such as the function of schizophrenics and normals on a size estimation task, it is obvious this is not the case.

Semantical Construct Invention

There are two main processes that introduce ambiguity into the empirical construct and hence the empirical laws. They are the semantical construct invention and the operational dynamism. Both problems occur at the level of operationalization and call into question what operation defines what empirical construct. The "semantical construct invention" occurs when two constructs have labels implying different processes but are empirically equivalent. To illustrate, the Embedded Figure Test defines the same empirical construct of field dependency that the Rod and Frame Test defines. At this point, there is no problem because the actual measures are closely related. However, suppose one of the field dependency measures also correlates with another operation defining, let us say, the construct of size estimation. In this case, one of the empirical constructs must be redefined or lose its identity and merge with the more dominant construct; that is, size estimation must be seen as identical to field dependency and be labeled as such even though the task involves estimating sizes. Of course, these two measures do not correlate highly. However, other supposedly different operations do seem to be similar and hence could be seen as empirically equivalent. The point is that differences suggested by two empirical constructs and their resultant theories may be differences only in semantics. If the initial operations are highly related, the inferred constructs, which may have widely different implications and different specifications about the psychological mechanism deficient in schizophrenia, may be mere exercises in fruitful imagination. In short, two operations may exhibit the same degree of concordance, yet be labeled as different empirical constructs, and be the basis of competing theories of schizophrenia. We illustrate this process in Appendix A, where we conpare the empirical constructs of creativity and schizophrenia and conclude that the two processes may involve a semantical invention. Creativity may be a semantic invention for schizophrenia. The empirical construct of each are presented, and the conclusion is reached that as far as the empirical terms are considered, the two constructs of creativity and schizophrenia as defined in terms of thought processes are equivalent. Such an analysis calls for measures that can discriminate between the two processes if such a distinction is theoretically demanded.

Operational Dynamism[1]

A more serious problem is produced by the inverse of this procedure, when the empirical construct is the same but the operations are different and unrelated. We call this "operational dynamism." To illustrate, size estimation is an empirical construct that defines the relationship between the subjective judgment of a physical stimulus and the actual physical size of that stimulus. A common method of defining the construct is to present a standard and a variable stimulus simultaneously. The subject is required to adjust the variable stimulus until he judges it to be identical in size to the standard. When this operation was incorporated into the performance deficit studies, various modifications were introduced, such as performing the task by memory, presenting modified stimuli such as those including emotional content, creating distances between the comparison and the standard, etc. (e.g., Neale 1969). The introduction of different conditions produced differing operations and consequently different empirical constructs. An "operational dynamism" occurred when the operation was borrowed from the experimental laboratory and then slightly varied by each of a succession of researchers until the operation was essentially different but still bearing the original name.

Differences in empirical constructs due to the variety of operations employed produce confusion in understanding the performance deficit research. The solution suggested—the standardization of experimental operations—has not been adopted (Garmezy, 1966; Lang & Buss, 1965). We argue that the solution is not simply a matter of finer experimental control but involves an issue of theoretical structure. Processes such as operational dynamisms and semantical inventions do not produce valid theoretical constructs. We return to this issue after we discuss the problem of clearly defining the terms introduced to explain the relationships between empirical constructs.

Theoretical Constructs I and II

The next level in Fig. 1.1, the Theoretical Construct I, is the initial causal explanation of the empirical laws and attempts to answer the question of "How does it work?" The posited hypothetical psychological mechanism explains how an empirical law operates. Other more distant causal

---

[1]I wish to thank Dr. Colin Martindale for suggesting the term to describe the process.

explanations constructed to answer the "Why does it work" question are at the Theoretical Construct II level which is even more speculative and hypothetical. The use of both types of theoretical constructs, Theoretical Construct I and Theoretical Construct II, is similar to first- and secondary-order theories used in different levels of explanation in science (Koch, 1941). Distinguishing between two levels of theory is necessary in order to clarify the distance between theoretical and empirical constructs.

Illustration

We should attempt to illustrate the elements involved in theory building especially in relation to the schizophrenic literature. Consider a typical procedure in schizophrenia research. The schizophrenic is instructed to move a lever as quickly as possible in response to a light. The time elapsed between the presented stimulus and the response is conceptualized as reaction time. One could also present a tone and require the subject to press a button. If the same result occurs, one could infer that different classes of operations lead within certain ranges to the same result. Hence, we have an acceptable operation to define the empirical construct of reaction time. Now, if one introduces another empirical construct, let us say a Type 4 operation labelling schizophrenics and nonschizophrenics, and a relationship is stated between the two constructs, such as schizophrenics exhibit slower reaction times, the function is stated as an empirical law which could be further explained by a Theoretical I level construct of, let us say, disordered set. Now, if one introduces a new empirical construct of preparatory interval, by varying the time between the warning stimulus and the reaction time stimulus, it may be found that the reaction time function of the different experimental groups varies with the length of the preparatory interval. A new dimension is added to the disordered set construct, or a completely new term can be introduced if this function conflicts with previously established postulates.

In the reaction time example, the empirical law is the specified relationship between two empirical constructs. On the next level, a theoretical construct is postulated to explain *how* the law operates. Disordered set explains how each empirical law is formed. To further test the validity of Theoretical Construct I, a new variable may be introduced such as an increasing number of non-task-related stimuli that defines a new empirical construct of irrelevant stimuli. If Theoretical Construct I is correct as defined, the predicted function should occur with the new empirical construct as with the previous empirical construct of preparatory interval. If not, the theoretical construct could be modified or the operation of the new empirical construct could be questioned.

The theoretician does not stop there, however, but may also introduce a higher level theoretical construct to explain *why* the schizophrenic does not have the same process or mechanism as others have. Such higher level explanation could take the form of positing historical conditions such as a previous learning history or a damaged neurophysiological mechanism which produces the disorder set mechanism. The theoretical constructs create the postulate system. All that is required of such postulates or constructs is that they have testable consequences. If the experimental hypothesis stating these consequences is confirmed, we could have a greater degree of faith that the postulates, the theoretical constructs, are plausible (Turner, 1965).

Theory Building

We have been speaking of the steps involved in theory building beginning with the experimentation that produces empirical laws. After the law is stated, the experimenter infers a theoretical construct to explain the psychological process responsible for the observed function. Since the schizophrenic usually differs from a control group, their performance is explained by the inverse of the construct defined by the operations. For example, if the relationship between two empirical constructs is explained by a theoretical construct of attention then the differential function exhibited by the schizophrenic would be explained by a lack of attention. The difference between two functions is conceptualized in terms of the first level theoretical construct and, therefore, describes how the performance deficit occurs. Other theoretical constructs at the Theoretical Construct II level are then inferred to explain the mechanism responsible for the operation of the initial construct. This process permits the development of a theoretical framework, possibly leading to the formation of an extensive theory. It should be clear that theoretical constructs in the performance deficit literature are hypothetical constructs rather than intervening variables. It is tempting to consider the empirical laws as intervening variables. However, even at this level there is not the definability required by MacCorquodale and Meehl (1948). Also there is much more meaning inherent in the theoretical terms of performance deficit theory than would be expected in an intervening variable.

   The building of such a clear theoretical structure as in our illustration is seldom realized. Most theorists find that their theoretical constructs are at a relatively large deductive distance from empirical constructs. This distance produces rather vague constructs whose implicit definitions suggest differences in theory that may not exist. To illustrate, let us take another example from size estimation research. An experimenter devises a size estimation task in which the inferred empirical construct of size estimation is stated and a function is determined with schizophrenics and other groups. After the empirical construct is established, a theoretical construct is introduced to explain the psychological mechanism accounting for the relationship between the empirical constructs. The theoretical construct of scanning, for example, could be applied to explain size estimation performance with predictions of high scanning leading to one extreme of size estimation for one group and low scanning to the opposite pole of size estimation for the other group. However, when the scanning construct is described in terms of eye movement and examined in relation to size estimation, little relationship is found. This finding is evidence of the distance between the theoretical construct, scanning, and the empirical construct, size estimation. In short, there are at least two weaknesses found in theories of schizophrenia: The distinction between theoretical and empirical constructs could be blurred, or a Theoretical Construct I is omitted and a Theoretical Construct II is presented to explain the whys of an empirical law, often assuming that the empirical construct has enough surplus meaning to serve also as a Theoretical Construct I. Probably the most conside statement of this problem as related to the schizophrenia literature is by Kopfstein and Neale (1972), which is quoted here in its entirety:

> In one prevalent means of organizing this literature, the deviant performance of schizophrenics on various tasks is *assumed* to reflect an underlying deficit in some single process such as attention (Silverman, 1964; Venables, 1964). For example, the long reaction time (RT) found especially in chronic schizophrenics has been ascribed to an inability by these patients "to select the material relevant for optimal response (Shakow, 1962, p. 9)." Likewise, the size under-estimation found in acute good premorbid and paranoid patients has been attributed to extensive scanning (or sampling of environmental cues), while the size overestimation found in acute poor premorbid and nonparanoid patient has been attributed to minimal scanning (Silverman, 1964). In a similar vein, the poor performance of schizophrenics on object sorting and proverb interpretation tasks has been viewed as a reflection of a breakdown in the mechanism which usually functions to screen out irrelevant stimuli (Payne, 1966). Thus, a wide variety of schizophrenic performances has been interpreted by constructs which all appear to be related to attention.
>
> While interpretations such as the foregoing are reasonable, they have not been empirically validated (Neale & Cromwell, 1970). It would have been desirable, for example, to first assess the factor structure of the tasks that purportedly index attention and then investigate schizophrenics using the best measure of each factor. However, such information is lacking and the interrelationships among the tasks supposedly reflecting attentional deficits have not been examined. Hence, one cannot determine whether deviant attentional response dispositions, in fact, are applicable to a variety of schizophrenics' performance deficits. Indeed, the tasks may be empirically distinct and require different input processing mechanisms [p. 294].

Such conditions have prevented us from merely listing the theoretical terms used by different theorists in our review of the theories of schizophrenia and compelled us to examine each theory in terms of its theoretical terms to demonstrate that the theories involve a common process. Our argument is not with theoretical terms but with their use.

Theoretical Construct or the Interaction Between Theoretical Constructs

In addition to the problem of the distance between empirical and theoretical terms, a more serious problem is that most theories explaining the schizophrenic performance deficit have only one or two theoretical constructs, and hence, lack the necessary transitional statements. Admittedly, a single theoretical construct is valuable when it consolidates our factual gains by providing a basis of classification. However, if the construct does not logically relate to other constructs to form a sound theory, such classification is useless. The parameters of one construct are not tested against the parameters of another. In considering the role of the theoretical constructs in theory building, Hempel (1960) states our intent in examining the crucial interrelationships between theoretical constructs:

> The entire history of scientific endeavor appears to show that in our world comprehensive, simple and dependable principles for the explanation and prediction of observable phenomena cannot be obtained by merely summarizing and inductively generalizing observational findings. A hypothetico-deductive-observational procedure is called for and is indeed followed in the more advanced branches of empirical science: Guided by his knowledge of observational data, the scientist has to invent a set of concepts—theoretical constructs, which lack immediate experiential significance, a system of hypotheses couched in terms of them, and an interpretation for the resulting theoretical network; and all this in a manner which will establish explanatory and predictive connections between the data of direct observation [p. 119].

In addition to being an explanation because it is tied to observation through the empirical construct, the theoretical construct should relate to other theoretical constructs in a systematic logical fashion. Thus, an important function of a theory is to exhibit systematic connections between experimental laws. Statements made as a theory or a hypothesis function as means to effect: "transitions from one set of statements to other set, with the intent of controlling natural changes and of supplying predictions capable of being checked through manipulating directly experienceable subject matter" (Nagel, 1939, p. 75).

Koch (1941) differentiates between operationism and a postulational technique in stating that the latter generates a purely formal language system while the former makes such terms meaningful. Both processes are essential in building scientific theory. As mentioned earlier, psychology in moving away from "grand" theories, those employing large postulate systems, presently relies on the small single mechanism theory having constructs resting on one or two operations. It is our contention that this aproach has produced many "small" theories and no consensus on the psychological process inherent in the schizophrenic condition. There is a need for greater use of a postulational technique.

The operationalizing of one construct and using it as the totality of the theory is partially because research in schizophrenia is an applied science. Most of the constructs used in an explanation of the performance deficit are borrowed from theories in other areas such as information theory, learning, motivation, which are supported in more "basic" science laboratories. The construct, which at times is perceived more as a principle than a hypothetical construct, is then applied to the more practical problem of the performance deficit. But, only specific constructs are applied and the postulate system of the theory is neglected since the other theoretical terms are not seen as relevant to an explanation of schizophrenic behavior. For example, a drive construct is borrowed from learning theory to explain the delusional system of schizophrenics in terms of the drive-reducing quality of remote associations. However, drive can only predict response strength when other factors such as habit strength, incentive, stimulus intensity, etc., are known or kept constant. The meaning of a construct is diminished when a construct is borrowed and separated from the postulate system because the postulate system in asserting relations between terms adds meaning to terms:

> Terms of this kind (theoretical construct) are not introduced by any piecemeal process of assigning meaning to them individually. Rather, the constructs used in theory are introduced jointly, as it were, by setting up a theoretical system formulated in terms of them and by giving this system an experimental interpretation which in turn confers empirical meaning on the theoretical constructs [Hempel, 1960, p. 115.]

Since the theoretical constructs are used outside the context of the original theory, they are suspect as explanatory statements of the mechanism responsible for the schizophrenic performance deficit.

Positing single theoretical constructs without fitting them into a more complete theoretical system also introduces a problem of discontinuity. That is, the construct tends to be discarded with the theoretical fads of the day. To explain the schizophrenic performance deficit, statements have been made about schizophrenic motivation, concept formation, response, limitations, habits, etc., all specifying some operation with accompanying observational data. Systematic connections between divergent subject matter are usually lacking in such statements. The explanation usually proposed seems to coincide with the theory most popular in psychology at that time. The borrowing of constructs in fad, while providing a great deal of operational information, encourages the neglect of whole areas of research while the utility of new constructs are explored. This process leaves the field in disarray and is counterproductive when past functional relationships are ignored because of their irrelevance to the current construct. As Dallenback (1966) observed, rather than being disproven by evidence or logic, theories tend to fade away by being superseded or bypassed. Theoretical constructs in the schizophrenic literature suffer a similar fate. A synthesis of theoretical constructs into one theoretical system may reduce the vagueness of such constructs and rescue valid data which have been dismissed along with unpopular constructs.

To summarize, we contend that the principles of theory-building have not been followed in previous theories of the schizophrenic performance deficit. A variety of operations has been used to define the empirical constructs which have not been checked for independence. The explanatory theoretical construct stating the "why" of the deficit is inferred from a distant theoretical construct stating the "how" of the deficit. The latter is inferred from vague empirical constructs defined by a multitude of operations, some of which are given the same name. Under such conditions, the explanatory second-level theoretical constructs allow such a wide range of predictions, some even contradictory, that they are virtually useless. A theory as a specific formula based on facts for the purpose of explaining given phenomena (Dallenback, 1966) is relatively rare. The rarity of such a well-developed theory is due not so much to the absence of facts but to the absence of an explanation of a wide group of phenomena, that is, the failure to apply a postulational technique to clear empirical constructs.

The task, therefore, involves not only the clarification of the empirical constructs but the development of a postulate system which clarifies theoretical terms. We propose an information-theory explanation of schizophrenia because the empirical constructs only involve one process, and they could be specified in terms of their relation to one theoretical construct and not to another, or if they are related to more than one empirical construct, the interrelation between the two could be specified.

A greater specification of postulates and their relationships also could be met by the use of a more general and more inclusive model than usually employed. We do not contend that we have completed that model, but we demonstrate a possible move toward such a state of affairs by first developing a postulate set using a Hullian model and then developing a complete theory using information theory. Our intent in the following chapters is to relate the constructs in the realm of cognition with a postulational technique while also tying the constructs to specific operations.

2 The Hullian Model and Redefinition of Terms

INTRODUCTION

The theories presented in the schizophrenic performance deficit literature are theoretical constructs in that they are highly abstract terms derived from a specific set of operations. Since their focus is on empirical terms and the multiple factors operating in man, it should be possible to use their terms to generate a theoretical system that is coherent and comprehensive, permitting meaningful explanation and prediction. We organize the schizophrenic performance deficit research by a theory that is, in a sense, horizontal. Meaning is derived by drawing relations between constructs with a postulational technique while at the same time deriving meaning from operations.

We use Hullian theory to compare and contrast the dominant theories, because the Hullian terms can provide us with a common language that gives order to the multitude of theoretical constructs employed in the literature. As each theory is classified in terms of its use of one or several components of the model, its relationship to other theories should be more clearly positioned. It is recognized that the Hullian terms may be familiar neither to the student beginning his study of schizophrenia nor possibly to the seasoned researcher who has not found any reason to explore past learning theories. In that case, a new language has to be learned. The reason for such a demand upon the reader is the need to develop a full symbolic language to adequately incorporate widely discrepant theories into a coherent whole. Hopefully, the effort will be rewarded with a unified picture of our past empirical efforts.

We translate each of the hypothesized schizophrenic processes into one language—that used in the Hullian learning theory. This procedure should not do any disservice to the Hullian theory, although some of the Hullian concepts will be modified. Recognizing that the use of analogy has been very fruitful in the physical sciences (Nagel, 1961), we use Hullian theory as an analogy in developing a theory of the schizophrenic performance deficit. The purpose is not to expand the Hullian theory but to integrate the differing schizophrenic deficit hypotheses by the use of one model that allows a more general and integrated view. As stated by Hull (1943): "the use of logical constructs thus probably in all cases comes down to a matter of convenience in thinking, i.e., an economy in the manipulation of symbols [p. 111]." Past research in schizophrenia is in need of a convenient manner of organization in order to clarify our understanding of it. The Hullian learning concepts integrating the theoretical constructs of the different major performance deficit theories into a coherent holistic theory serve this purpose. It is assumed that the empirical constructs and their operations are methodologically sound and only need further differentiation. Hull (1943) recognized the need for a science to derive meaning from expansion of the theoretical along with the empirical:

> The empirical procedure consists primarily of observation, usually facilitated by experiment. The theoretical procedure, on the other hand, is essentially logical in nature; through its mediation, in conjunction with the employment of the empirical procedure, the range of validity of principles may be explored to an extent quite impossible by the empirical procedure alone. This is notably the case in situations where two or more supposed primary principles are presumably operative simultaneously. The logical procedure yields a statement of the outcome to be expected if the several principles are jointly active as formulated; by comparing deduced or theoretical conclusions with the observed empirical outcome, it may be determined whether the principles are general enough to cover the situation in question [p. 381].

We hope that by demonstrating the relationship between theories, we will be closer to recognizing the possibility that all theories are correct at the function level but need clarification at the theoretical level. We also argue that some theories are more correct than others, in that some theoretical terms may be more susceptible to confounding variables while others may be closer to explaining the schizophrenic condition. At the least, we provide a means to organize previous theories of schizophrenia so that they can be compared and understood in relation to one another. If they are not perceived as part of a total scientific explanation, they may easily be lost in our scientific progress.

A MODEL

We use Hullian theory as a model to develop the postulate sets that can elucidate the relationship between theoretical terms. The upper left blocks in Fig. 2.1 depict the theory and postulate system from which the theoretical constructs to be presented are implicitly defined. These theoretical constructs are verbal equivalents of constructs in the Hullian learning theory. Through implicit definition we will convert a learning theory into a theory of the schizophrenic performance deficit. The use of implicit definition is consistent with the overall emphasis of the present discussion in exploring the benefits of examining the relationships between postulates. Through implicit definition, the meaning of constructs are enlarged when added to the system and their unique contingency upon the whole system of postulates is specified (Mac-Corquodale & Meehl, 1954). The coordinating definitions in this case would correlate empirical constructs to the formal terms of the postulate set (see Fig. 1.1), thus transforming an abstract system into an empirical one (Koch, 1941).

Since we are in the uncommon position of treating the Hullian theory as a model, a definition of a model would clarify our purpose. Marx (1970) defines a model as "a conceptual analogue that is used to suggest how empirical research on a problem might best be pursued. That is, the model is a conceptual framework or structure that has been successfully developed in one field and is now applied, primarily as a guide to research and thinking, in some other, usually less well-developed field [p. 11]."

Although there may be some question of how successful Hullian theory is in predicting behavior or in stating postulates precisely (Koch & Hull, 1954), there should be little question of its conceptual strength especially when compared to theory in the less developed area of the schizophrenic performance deficit. Turner (1965), in his definition of a structured model, also states our intention:

> A structured model, therefore, is taken to be one such that not only is it a realization of a theory, but the realization is such that some of its nonlogical terms are interpretable in an existential medium different from that of the thing modeled. By "existential medium" I mean some uniquely classified domain of prediction in the observation language [p. 238].

Moreover, the Hullian theory fits Achinstein's (1965) view of a model. The four attributes of a model described by Achinstein are:

1. A model presents a set of assumptions about a system which specify some of the attributes of the system.
2. The assumptions are organized to imply properties.

3. The model claims an approximation to the "true" state of affairs in comparison to other models.
4. The model is an analogy to another system.

In regard to the first attribute, the Hullian theory provides a definite set of assumptions concerning the learning process as well as providing specific interrelated attributes and conditions for the prediction of behavior. As exemplified by those performance deficit theorists who have employed Hullian terms and hypotheses, the Hullian system also allows additional derivatives of properties as specified in attribute 2. In regard to attribute 3, the use of a Hullian model implies a bias toward a learning view of behavior which according to current theories and practice in psychopathology reflect a "truer" state of affairs than the older dynamic analytic or medical models. As the terms in the present paper become more clearly defined, the final attribute of a model as analogous to another system is specified.

Another advantage of using Hullian learning theory as a model is that the theory is relatively common and has been found to facilitate explanation in many diverse areas. For example, it has been recently applied to the area of social facilitation (Weiss & Miller, 1971). Also, and probably most important, the Hullian system has elements which are similar to the disparate schizophrenic performance deficit constructs. In view of the many separate theoretical constructs explaining the schizophrenic deficit and the sparcity of relations being posited between them, a model which primarily aims to formulate the relationships between constructs and to experimental operations could be very helpful. For thorough and interesting discussion of models beyond the scope of the present paper the reader is directed to Turner (1965).

In Fig. 2.1, a simplified revised version of the Hullian Learning Theory (Hull, 1943, 1952) with some modifications relating the Hullian concepts to perceptual phenomena (Campbell, 1967) has been connected to various constructs used in schizophrenic research. Each term explained in a previous work (Magaro, 1974) is defined below. In the following section, theories of the performance deficit are classified according to one of these terms. When a dual or interactive focus is hypothesized, it is categorized as such.

Our use of Hullian theory may be criticized because it is not a clear axiomatic position. But since we are not engaged in reductionism, this factor is not detrimental to our purpose. What is important is that the mediating variables, the hypothetical constructs, such as drive, reaction potential, etc., are similar to the hypothetical constructs in the schizophrenic literature. The defined relationships of the Hullian terms such as $_sH_r = 1-10^{-aN}$ will not be part of the present discussion since such operations will be replaced by the operations employed by the schizophrenic performance deficit theorists. In response to the familiar objection that Hullian terms are intervening variables

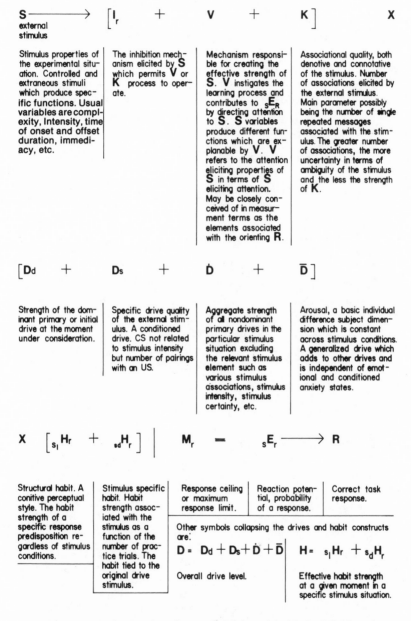

FIG. 2.1.   A schizophrenic performance deficit model with the definition of terms from the Hullian Learning Theory.

that are not available in the performance deficit theory, making correspondences impossible, we side with the position (Turner, 1965) that:

> Even $_sH_r$ is regarded as being something more than a convention. We sense that effects of reinforcement and trial repetition bring about changes in the structure of the organism which are what $_sH_r$ *intends* to measure. In other words, $_sH_r$ is not just a convenient invention but is semantically tied to a state of the organism which we might better regard as a habit *structure* predisposing the increased probabilities of certain response patterns [p. 313].

Using the Hullian terms that have the same meaning beyond a set of definitive operations permits us to develop a correspondence with the performance deficit constructs. We extract at the theoretical level, and Hull provides clear denotative meanings of such terms.

As mentioned above, a problem with using Hullian theory is that the theory has passed out of common usage, and as such, the terms employed are not readily understandable or seen as applicable to our task of organizing the theories of schizophrenia. We are using the theory to focus upon different components of the S–R bond, so to speak. Each theory of schizophrenia attempts the same task. How can schizophrenic behavior be explained in light of specific stimulus conditions? Are there defects in the perception of a stimulus (the stimulus dynamism term used by Hull), the derivation of conceptual meaning (the associated links between the stimulus and the response), motivation (drive), prior patterns of behavior previously reinforced and now habitual (habit), or the inability to inhibit an inappropriate response (inhibition)? All of these aspects of normal functioning provide a catalog of the possible weak links in the bond between stimulus and response.[1]

Psychologists have historically conceptualized the processes active in schizophrenia as a variation of normal psychological functioning. The use of the Hullian system does provide the list of such processes and, more importantly, demonstrates the interrelationship between such interests. The symbols employed to notate the system may be foreign to the present generation of readers, hence, the following pages attempt to define each symbol and the process it defines. We should keep in mind, however, that we are not interested in explaining schizophrenia in terms of Hullian theory, but only wish to use the theory to provide a framework for multiple explanations to interact. We want to review past work and the framework is intended to only facilitate the task. I do not intend to produce added difficulty. In fact, it is hoped that if one solely wants to review past work without relating it to other

---

[1] I am indebted to Professor Brendan Maher for suggesting this explanation of the use of a Hullian model in the organization of this material.

theories, they can skip the Hullian terminology and examine each theory in terms of its own focus of interest.

DEFINITION OF TERMS

S. *S* refers to the external stimulus such as a physical dimension at the moment of consideration. In terms of the theories of the schizophrenic deficit *S* includes the characteristics of the total experimental situation including the experimental task. As argued earlier, although the operations carry the same label such as reaction time, size estimation, etc., discrepancies between two tasks may be such that quite different processes are involved. For instance, as discussed earlier in terms of operational dynamism, a scanning construct has been operationalized by size estimation tasks that have differed in terms of the concomitant stimulus display such as the size of the comparison stimulus, the distance between the standard and the comparison, the amount of illumination, etc. It is these differences which may elicit the operation of another process besides the intended psychological mechanism. In Hullian (1943) terms, differences that exist in S_a, such as differences in apparatus, many times are interpreted to indicate the variations in the operation of a theoretical construct as defined by the various performance functions of specific subject groupings. However, such discrepancies may be present in the experimental situation in terms of the experimenter or the testing laboratory which may have as strong an effect. When a great number of extraneous stimulus variables are active, the psychological processes active may be quite disparate from the process allegedly being studied. In design terms, *S* calls attention to the problem of experimental control and comparability of results across studies. These problems have been discussed extensively. Hicks (1971) discusses the effects of both the experimenter and the experimental situation in eliciting varying degrees of conformity behavior which are as important in determining task performance as the subject. Cole and Bruner (1971), in a discussion of the deficit concept as applied to intellectual functioning of different cultural subgroups, question the use of a deficit term and conclusions which do not recognize the "situation-bound" quality of such findings. One could argue in a similar way about the schizophrenic deficit work. However, besides considering what variables should be controlled before the operation of a hypothesized psychological process can be inferred from a specific task, we will discuss one theory which views *S* as the cause of the deficit.

V. *V* is the effective strength of *S* (Campbell, 1967), which contributes to $_sE_r$ in terms of initiating the learning process by directing attention to the relevant stimulus at the moment of consideration. In Hullian (1952) terms, *V*, the stimulus-intensity dynamism, refers to a stimulus intensity component or the response evocation condition of the reaction potential—the elements in S which affect attention and contribute to $_sE_r$. The Hullian stimulus-intensity dynamism sets up the conditions for other factors to enter into the complete equation. Hull, in defining V within the hypothetical-deductive model, specified those stimulus elements determining the V function in terms of an operation and related V to other theoretical constructs, especially $_sE_r$. (Hull also considers V to enter into the learning process, but this usage is not intended here.)

In the present framework, V is a perceptual construct usually specifying a mechanism within the organism which produces the S-V function unique to schizophrenia as well as the S-V functions common to normals. The V theoretical construct, therefore, deals with that aspect of the organism that is subject to the attention-eliciting properties of S. These properties of S, when manipulated, would show a different function for schizophrenics as compared to other groups because of the inferred perceptual-organismic mechanism specified by the V theorists. We are especially interested in the V-type theories, because they deal with an aspect of cognition.

To avoid confusion in developing the present theory using the Hullian theory as a model, the relation between the Hullian and the present usage of the V construct should be elaborated. Our concern in the present chapter is to organize the psychological processes or mechanisms that are hypothesized to account for the schizophrenic performance deficit. We are thereby concerned with specifying the psychological process or mechanism that accounts for the prediction or determination of $_sE_r$ under specific S conditions. The theoretical construct posited in a schizophrenic deficit theory describes the mechanism that is faulty. Therefore, we are using the V term as a theoretical construct and not as an operational empirical construct as in the Hullian model. However, the V theorists in the schizophrenic literature utilize an operational construct which is at the same level of analysis as V in the Hullian model. But the empirical events are very different and the focus is upon inferring a theoretical construct from the relation between two empirical constructs. Thus, the present usage of V is analogous to the Hullian usage on a horizontal plane, specifying the relationship between constructs. The specific advantage in using the Hullian model is to relate V type constructs to K, D, and H type constructs. All of these proposed first-level theoretical constructs state how a mechanism operates to explain the empirical function.

V in the present usage consequently defines a process within the organism which is inferred to mediate or transmit S conditions into a specific response. Both theory and model are dealing with inferred processes, but in the process of creating the analogy, V becomes a theoretical construct that does not depend on the same empirical constructs used in the Hullian theory. This should become clearer when the various theorists are presented. Since we want to develop a system with a group of highly related postulates that specify the relationship of different constructs about behavior, we must interrelate the single constructs that have their own empirical systems. The Hullian model seems to be an appropriate vehicle for this purpose.

K.   The K construct refers to the associational or mediating process that is elicited by a stimulus. It is assumed that stimuli elicit varying amounts of associations, both denotative and connotative, and such associations form a hierarchy of a greater or lesser degree of associative strength. The K construct focuses on the type of associative links between S and $_sE_r$. The value of K is determined by the probability of eliciting the dominant association at the moment under consideration. Therefore, K is the probability of S eliciting a specific dominant association. The greater number of associations at a given moment elicited by S, the lower the strength of K since the dominant association observed as response would be lowered. The lesser the number of associations, the greater the number of repeated single associations, and the higher the strength of K. The more practice (the greater number of times one specific associational meaning is emitted) the higher K value of S. The extreme case of a high K would probably be a constant repetition of a response when presented with a particular stimulus regardless of other conditions. A low K would indicate little probability of any specific response being elicited by S. Such a case is probably the response elicited by an ambiguous stimulus such as an inkblot or a nonsense syllable.

K, therefore, is a construct that indicates the informational quality of S and derives its strength from repeated single associations to S. The present K concept deviates from the Hullian (1952) use of K, which refers to an incentive component of $_sE_r$ related to the magnitude of the reinforcement. K used by Campbell (1967) also has the same incentive meaning in terms of its strength being determined by past associations with reinforcement. However, the present K is similar to the Hullian K in that it is a function of number of associations. While the Hullian usage defines K as the number of associations with reinforcement, the present theory defines K solely in terms of the number of conceptual associations. Therefore, in the present theory, the strength of K is not a motivational construct dependent upon the quality of reinforcement (Hull, 1952), but a conceptual construct determined by mediating concepts elicted by S. Therefore, K, as with V, is a function of S and enters into the determination of $_sE_r$ through the parameters of S rather than as a function of reinforcement.

The use of K focuses on the conceptual process of attaching meaning to a stimulus. It should be noted that the process here is not the degree of attending to S, which is the property of V, but rather the process of deriving meaning from S once V has occurred. The schizophrenia theories that make use of the K construct consider the problem to either be the case of rigid stereotyped conceptual categories or of multiple random conceptual associations. The first explanation would predict that performance will improve when a dominant meaning response is required by a task and will diminish when an associational flexibility is necessary. In contrast, the second type of theory would describe the schizophrenic as being subject to multiple associations. S elicits numerous associations with none being dominant. Hence, there is an inability to complete a task that requires at least some ordering of associations. In each case, the K theorist would view the schizophrenic deficit as caused by the associational quality of S.

I_r. The Inhibitory Potential is an unobservable logical construct which is operationalized by the amount of work performed on a response and which diminishes as a function of time (Hull, 1943). The inhibitory potential acts as a motivational state with a physical substrate that increases with the strength of the response. It explains the extinction process in that the extinguished response does not increase its reaction potential but increases its inhibitory potential in an inverse linear function. For Hull, the inhibitory potential is operationalized by the number of responses and the amount of work involved in a response.

Our use of I_r differs from Hull's in that it will not be a function of R but rather of S. Hence, a stimulus not only possesses an S and K quality, but also an inhibitory quality. The theorist who will use this construct will be concerned with the schizophrenic's ability to inhibit either attention or conceptual process to allow a particular set of perceptions or associations to occur. Hence, the position of I_r with V and K is a set acting in an additive fashion as shown in Fig. 2.1.

$_sE_r \rightarrow R$. A distinction has to be made between the stimulus demands of the tasks and the response demands of the tasks. We usually assume that a particular task "calls for" a particular set of responses. However, what is elicited by the task and what is demanded by the task in terms of a response may not coincide. Obviously, the requirements of the task are crucial in determining if a low or high K would improve performance or create a deficit. Some tasks require a single dominant response for successful performance as in the usual signal detection task, while other tasks require a multitude of associations as in tests of creativity. A high or low K value in itself does not necessarily relate to the number of correct task responses, R. $_sE_r$ and not R is a function of K, as well as V or any of the other factors. As diagrammed in the model in Fig. 2.1, $_sE_r$ and R are not necessarily identical. $_sE_r$ refers to the probability of a specific response depending upon the parameters of S, K, or V and does not necessarily predict the strength of R, the correct response as defined by the task. Using this distinction, the performance deficit may be seen as an inability to narrow the differences between $_sE_r$ and R, the processes elicited and the response demanded. The deficit would be the difference between the response required by the task and the dominant response or process provided by the schizophrenic.

D.   The following set of drive terms attempts to specify the various motivational states that are hypothesized to explain the schizophrenic performance deficit. All *D* constructs are viewed as being responsible for motivating the organism into action and eliciting those habits which have been learned on the basis of the drive of interest or of different drives. *D* itself as shown in Fig. 2.1 refers to the total overall drive level during performance and is therefore in agreement with the Hullian usage. The *D* theorists characterize the schizophrenic process as determined by a motivational deficiency which either does not motivate the schizophrenic to perform to the level of normals or increases activity to such a high level that task performance cannot be completed. They also postulate that the drive-eliciting stimuli for the schizophrenic are so different from those for normals that the drive-reducing or eliciting aspects of the experimental situation are only applicable to normals and not to schizophrenics. That is, the schizophrenic is viewed as not having the same drives as others or if they are the same, they are either too high or too low. The deficit in performance is a function of this different drive state which does not activate the habit structures to the same degree as in other groups. Although all drive theorists emphasize a drive deficit, usage of the drive concept varies from theorist to theorist. Drive constructs may be used interchangeably and substantial differences in the constructs such as being causative factors in themselves or in interaction with other processes are ignored. Moreover, there is an instance in which the same theory uses at least two different drive concepts without any attempt to offer a differentiation of terms either experimentally or theoretically.

Dd.   *Dd* refers to a specific internal drive that is dominant at the moment under consideration. In this usage, *Dd*, is an energizer concept which activates the total organism, is specific to a certain type of deprivation, and is not dependent upon learning. The concept as usually used refers to a primary drive state because the drive is observed early in development. While *Dd* is usually considered to be due to a state of deprivation, the deprivation does not have to refer to a physical need state with its *Sd* stimuli as in the Hullian model. Nor does it have to be experimentally induced such as in the hours of food deprivation procedure, but rather it can refer to an imbalance or deficiency in any system such as a perceptual or sensory system. It should be noted that, although *Dd* can be manipulated by certain deprivations, it is nondirective and can therefore facilitate or inhibit all behavior independent of the particular antecedent condition of which it may be a function at the moment.

Ds. *Ds* refers to a specific drive elicited by an external stimulus as contrasted with the internal *Dd* construct that is unlearned and related to deprivation. Although both drive constructs are energizers, this construct refers to a conditioned stimulus which has taken on secondary drive properties through pairing with an unconditioned stimulus. The essential quality is that *Ds* has acquired a conditioned tendency to evoke an associated reaction (Hull, 1943). *Ds*, therefore, usually has both *S* and *R* components and is consequently not as nondirective as *Dd*. Rather it is more directive and dependent upon past learning. Therefore, in terms of drive being activated, the construct calls for more specific situational conditions. *Ds* thereby assumes a learning process in which specific stimuli have taken on drive-evoking properties to which the schizophrenic, and not others, respond. The schizophrenic in this case is not considered to have a basic deficit but only exhibits the deficit in those situations which have taken on, through stimulus generalization, the drive-producing properties of the original unconditioned stimulus.

Ḋ *Ḋ* refers to the aggregate strength of all the nondominant drives in the experimental situation. As such, *Ḋ* is more a problem of experimental control than a specification of a proposed schizophrenic mechanism. The incidental drives may be primary or secondary drives. Within any experimental situation, the subject may be in states such as uncertainty, thirst, transient emotional states, etc. Such drive states would be alien to the experimental situation and the dominant drive under consideration. *Ḋ* could share with *Dd* the quality of deprivation or imbalance and contribute to the total state. But whereas *Dd* is the drive under consideration, *Ḋ* is more incidental and uncontrolled, possibly elicited by elements extraneous to the experimental situation and by conditions present in the specific environment of the schizophrenic. An example of an incidental drive in a schizophrenic performance deficit study would be the amount or type of tranquilizing medication that may contribute to the total drive state in either a positive or negative fashion. The evocation properties of drive with the habit system may therefore be modified by *Ḋ* and tend to distort the strength of a particular task response under a set of specified experimental conditions. As in the Hullian model, *Ḋ* is additive. With lower animals, such residuals may account for 20% of the reaction potential (Hull, 1943). In more complex organisms that may be disorganized such as the schizophrenic, such residuals may be more important than the relevant drive in that the reaction potential may be mainly determined by this drive component. *Ḋ*, therefore, may blur the effect of an independent variable since the performed response may be more a function of the irrelevant drive. Differences between schizophrenics and normals in terms of amount of *Ḋ* could produce differences in task performance incorrectly inferred to be due to an experimental manipulation.

$\bar{D}$. $\bar{D}$ refers to a state of generalized drive that is relatively constant across stimulus conditions and differs from individual to individual. $\bar{D}$ is therefore a subject dimension as embodied in the concepts of arousal or activation (Malmo, 1959). $\bar{D}$ in the Hullian system refers to the effective drive or a combination of Dd and $\dot{D}$. The present volume deviates from this usage by considering $\bar{D}$ as a basic level of activation upon which all other drives are added and which could consequently influence the effective strength of other drive states. $\bar{D}$ is also seen as independent from various emotional states and from Dd (Walker, 1970). $\bar{D}$ has some similarities to the V component in that it can be related to the attention-eliciting qualities of the stimulus situation. However, $\bar{D}$ in the present usage is conceptualized more as an internal construct not affected by S. Tecce and Cole (1972), dealing with this problem in distinguishing between arousal and attention, conceptualize arousal as a dynamogenic factor that is devoid of steering properties. It energizes behavior, unselectively affecting only the intensity of response. Attention, on the other hand, is conceptualized as an organismic process facilitating the selection of relevant stimuli. Tecce and Cole's (1972) review of other authors stating the same distinction lends justification to the present usage of arousal as a drive state and attention as a V process. That is, $\bar{D}$ is mainly viewed as a motivational concept in that it activates the habit system. The essential quality of $\bar{D}$ used here is its organismic dimension that would be reflected in inter-subject variability as commonly measured by the various psychophysiological basal level measures. The increment or decrement in skin conductance, GSR, in relation to environmental conditions would relate to the Ds concept while changes in basal level related to deprivation conditions such as sleep or activity would be assumed under the Dd concept. $\bar{D}$ in the present paper refers to the resting basal level, the basal level devoid of stimulus conditions, which varies between individuals. It reflects a drive level to which other drive components are added and which can interact with attentional components in increasing $_sE_r$.

$_sH_r$. $_sH_r$ is the total effective habit strength at a given moment in a specified stimulus situation. Its two components are $_{s_1}H_r$ and $_{s_d}H_r$. In each case, the emphasis is on past learning, which establishes a predisposition to emit specific responses depending on the position in the habit hierarchy. The Hullian notion of habit strength being a function of the number of previous reinforced trials (Hull, 1952) is not essential to either component.

$_{s_1}H_r$. $_{s_1}H_r$ in the Hullian model refers to the effective habit loading of the non-drive component of the stimulus complex (Hull, 1943). In accounting for the complexity of stimulus elements in an experimental situation that have various habit strengths, $_{s_1}H_r$ symbolizes that component of $_sH_r$ that is due to reception-discharge perseverations active during reinforcement of the to-be-conditioned reaction. In a sense, $_{si}H_r$ may be viewed as the component of $_sH_r$ that is irrelevant to the actual S situation and could be used to indicate the predisposition to respond in individualistic unique ways which are not stimulus-dependent. Although this concept is of minor usage in the Hullian system, it takes on major importance in considering the views of the schizophrenic performance deficit. We will use this concept to indicate specific habits which are structural in being habitual ways of responding to any stimulus situation. According to a $_{si}H_r$ theorist, the schizophrenic has a very rigid habit hierarchy with a specified habit being dominant. Consequently, the degree of successful task performance is a function of how well the task requirements match the specified dominant habit (i.e., how similar R is to $_sE_r$). The more task requirements match the response elicited by dominant habit, the less the deficit. Some theorists view the schizophrenic deficit solely in terms of this concept while other combine it with a drive component in the traditional Hullian fashion.

$_{sd}H_r$. $_{sd}H_r$ is the habit tied to the original drive stimulus that has been associated and conditioned to a specific stimulus. The specific stimulus could be a conditioned stimulus or a drive stimulus, S_d. It is the stimulus experimentally manipulated, excluding the non-drive stimulus component, which contribute to $_{si}H_r$ as discussed above. In effect, $_{sd}H_r$ is the habit strength component usually considered in the $_sH_r$ construct. The present usage basically conforms to the original Hullian usage in considering $_{sd}H_r$ to be the portion of habit strength that is a function of the number of reinforcements. It is a predisposition to respond depending on past experience with a specific stimulus be it a drive stimulus or a conditioned stimulus. The schizophrenic deficit theorist who utilizes this explanation of deficit performance focuses upon the specific cues in the schizophrenic environment that evoke a specific response.

M_r. M_r is a response ceiling concept similar to the drive ceiling concept in the Hullian model. It is not necessarily a physiological limit but can be influenced by specific stimulus conditions and varies between individuals. The limiting response condition can limit the effect of D and H in determining the strength of $_sE_r$. It is the maximum response strength which cannot be increased by other factors such as D or H that can increase the probability of $_sE_r$.

We must now begin to apply the terms in categorizing the theories of schizophrenia. We start in the next chapter with the cognitive theories that become the basis for our theoretical presentation. We then follow with the inhibition, drive, habit, and response theories. The measures used in most theories are examined, and the conclusion is drawn that the latter theories are not as promising as the former theories in explaining the schizophrenic performance deficit. Since we view behavior from a cognitive bias, it would be expected that we would favor discussions of percepts and concepts. However that is not the sole reason we favor the cognitive theories. It is more that the major drive and habit theories are not given much credence today. Their measures are inadequate, and they have confounded their measure of schizophrenia with irrelevant dimensions.

3

S, V, K, and I_r Theories of the Schizophrenic Performance Deficit

This chapter is the first of two that attempt to examine the more comprehensive theories of the schizophrenic performance deficit. Each theory we will review has posited a type of psychological mechanism to explain schizophrenic behavior and has generated an extensive amount of research. Our purpose here is to present a historical understanding of current methods as well as to demonstrate the points of convergence with current theoretical efforts. Hopefully, by focusing upon the empirical constructs derived from tasks and subject classifications, we can also begin to suggest the specific psychological process common to each schizophrenic subgroup. This is of central concern when we discuss Information Theory.

S THEORISTS

There is one theory that may be considered an S-type theory since the deficit is conceptualized in terms of stimulus elements without any reference to a psychological mechanism. This position, advocated by Salzinger, Portnoy, and Feldman (1966), states that the performance deficit is caused by a prepotency of immediate over remote stimuli. In examining the speech patterns of schizophrenics, the authors concluded that verbal deficits are due to the schizophrenic's inability to remember the initial words in a sentence that are necessary to establish the contextual meaning of a subsequent word. The schizophrenic responds to the immediately presented word, the last stimulus, and does not incorporate the remote verbal stimuli which are necessary for complete understanding.

The theory was developed from three models for measuring speech samples: a reconstruction technique, the method of unitization, and the cloze procedure. As shown in Fig. 3.1, all three speech measures operationalized empirical constructs that were explained by the theoretical construct I of communicability. The theoretical construct II of immediate stimulus potency explained why communicability produced such relationships. It was inferred that a greater communicability would be achieved if there is a retention of the meaning of past as well as present speech stimuli. It was hypothesized that the lesser degree of communicability exhibited by schizophrenics was due to a greater potency of immediate speech stimuli than would be experienced by nonschizophrenics. The theoretical construct I of communicability is related to other theoretical constructs I, such as conceptualization and conditioning.

In terms of the present model, the strength of $_sE_r$ is determined by stimulus potency or the immediacy of S in space or time. There is a similarity between this construct and the original Hullian construct of V, the stimulus intensity dynamism. The difference is that Hull defines V as a function of the intensity of S while Salzinger et al. (1966) define the function in terms of the immediacy

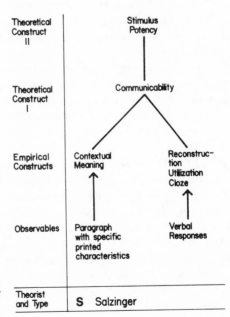

FIG. 3.1. Schematic representation of the theoretical structure of stimulus theories.

of *S.* For this theory to be considered a V theory in our framework, a theoretical construct would have to be offered describing the psychological mechanism within the individual which is responsible for the empirical laws.

A later elaboration of the theory (Salzinger, 1971) is quite explicit in considering that the immediacy hypothesis describes a principle that can be best described in behavior theory terms. Since the schizophrenic is more affected by immediate stimuli, he is more likely to be conditioned by immediate stimuli which would lead to unusual associations. The normal would allow other stimuli other than immediate ones to enter into associative relationships. Why or how this occurs is not addressed. What is clear is that the empirical law is between the stimulus and the response, and the parameter of the stimulus which is of most relevance is its intensity as determined by space or time. The stimulus response bond is what is investigated and other terms requiring the operation of an internal state are to be dismissed. It is a clear operant definition a la Skinner. Behavior is to be explained by the discriminative stimulus and the reinforcement without the need of any intervening variable. Within such a framework, the justification is established for an *S* type theory.

It should be noted that Salzinger et al. (1966) mention an internal process, that of memory to explain why previous words are not included in the context of speech. However, the type of memory process (short-term, iconic, recognition, recall, the access to memory or the encoding into memory) is not discussed. In fact, memory is seen more as a correlative phenomenon to the potency of immediate stimuli since the latter also explains problems in memory (Salzinger, 1971).

The Salzinger position, therefore, uses a theoretical construct where most *V* theorists use an empirical construct. An *S* construct of stimulus prepotency is usually operationally defined by the *V* theorists as an empirical construct and explained by a theoretical construct which is organismic, a mechanism within the organism which predicts the effects of other *S* variables such as stimulus intensity, delay of stimulus presentation, number of stimuli presented, etc. The reason for this difference is that the Salzinger et al. (1966) position developed from the study of speech which led to the theoretical construct of communicability. However, the cause of the deficit was eventually considered to reside beyond the communicability measures. Therefore, the construct introduced at the theoretical II level sought to explain speech differences with an *S* explanation. It is a circuitous and questionable procedure to infer the effects of stimulus conditions by a method that measures a language process. It would be much more direct to manipulate empirically the stimulus conditions defining stimulus potency and relate them to other empirical constructs on the response side such as communicability, and then explain the empirical laws. At least the parameters of the proposed terms could be directly studied.

Later work (Salzinger, 1971) did explain a variety of experimental situations which varied stimulus conditions and found a schizophrenic deficit. However, to explain that the variation of a stimulus causes a deficit while most investigators, as we will see, aim at varying specific psychological processes with the particular stimulus condition, does create a breadth of explanation but very little depth. In effect, much is explained but little is understood about the schizophrenic. There is an attempt to explain the schizophrenic's symptoms in terms of past reinforcement history where he is conditioned almost randomly because he is responding so actively to immediate stimuli while the normal is responding to immediate and past stimuli and hence is reinforced more appropriately. However, it is never explained why the schizophrenic should be reinforced for inappropriate behavior, assuming that responses to immediate stimulation without an awareness of context produce inappropriate responses. If the problem is in the reinforcement system, then the use of the unusual discriminative stimulus is not really needed. The explanation that most of his behavior is inappropriate because of the inappropriate responding to immediate stimuli does not answer why the inappropriate response is not negatively reinforced and hence only appropriate behavior is learned through positive reinforcement.

In short, the theory of Salzinger et al. (1966) can be viewed as an operational nontheoretical position which has advantages especially in terms of parsimony. However, the transformation of an empirical construct into a theoretical construct is not necessary since it introduces theoretical constructs at a level on which empirical constructs are possible and required. In contrast, the perceptual theorist utilizes a more direct test of the same empirical construct and hence, manipulates the experimental condition defining stimulus potency as an empirical construct rather than as a theoretical construct.

The present analysis of the relationship between theoretical and empirical constructs suggests that the Salzinger position should be relegated to the irrelevant category. It can be easily incorporated into a perceptual theory but the effect may be one of adding a superfluous note to an already complex fugue. Another criticism of the theory is made by Pavy (1968) who dismisses the position because of a lack of attention to linguistic structure. The underlying language model may be inadequate as a theory of natural language and is questionable as a theory of the schizophrenic deficit. Finally, empirical evidence against the position is found in a recent study by Davis and Blaney (1976), in which associations were examined in relation to the immediate physical stimulus. They did not find any effects of an immediately presented distractor which would have been expected by Salzinger. Also Rutter, Wishner, and Callagher (1975) used the same Cloze Procedure with acute schizophrenics predicting schizophrenic and normal speech. Although schizophrenics did not predict speech as well as normals, there were no differences between groups on the type of speech. The authors make the point that with an increase in context, there should not be a corresponding increase in performance for schizophrenics since according to the Immediacy Hypothesis, the schizophrenic speaker is less influenced than the normal by what he has said. Also, the end of a passage of schizophrenic speech should be less predictable than the beginning. The results did not support these hypotheses. Normals and schizophrenics gave more unpredictable end passages as compared to the beginning, and schizophrenic material was predicted as accurately when the end word or when the next-to-the-end word was omitted. The authors also question the Cloze Procedure itself because it requires a presentation of written material which is interpreted to represent spoken material. In effect, the dependent variable may be measuring something akin to visual perception rather than auditing speech.

The stimulus potency position, however, stresses the importance of the perceptual system by focusing on how the schizophrenic initially processes incoming information. By explaining schizophrenic attention to stimuli in terms of potency, the position suggests that at least one schizophrenic subgroup can be differentiated from others by their manner of approach to a stimulus field. This is the main interest of the V theorists.

V THEORISTS

The V construct is relevant to those theories that focus on the schizophrenic's inability to "maintain attention"—that is, to focus upon a specific stimulus. The clinical material supporting this view include changes in perception such as constancies being lost, objects changing hues, and stimuli being random and fluctuating. The schizophrenic is seen as being bombarded by stimulation. The deficit in this case is viewed as perceptual since he is affected by a multitude of perceptual stimuli which he doesn't order. Irrelevant properties of the stimulus situation dominate his attention and lead to responses which are incorrect. Variations in the stimulus complex that are attention-eliciting override those stimulus elements necessary for task performance. In effect, the schizophrenic is reality-bound in the sense that he views the world as it is in all of its fluctuating aspects without ordering it into a consensually meaningful fashion by excluding the irrelevant aspects of the moment. Problems such as the difficulty in forming concepts, illogical or loose association, are seen as secondary effects of this primary cause.

Shakow

Historically Shakow (1962) is the most dominant V theorist. In the development of the concept of segmental set, he emphasizes the schizophrenic's inability to maintain a major set because of his distraction by those minor sets which are elicited by irrelevant aspects of the S situation. In other words, the schizophrenic is unable to discriminate between the relevant and irrelevant aspects of S, and attends to whatever comes into view. In this sense, there is always a stimulus that interferes with the reponse to another stimulus. Shakow manipulates some measureable variable which operationalizes an empirical construct such as length of preparatory interval, PI; the constancy of the preparatory interval, Pc; the length of the preceding preparatory interval, Pp; or the number of extraneous stimuli presented within the preparatory interval, Pe. With the introduction of the antecedent empirical event, reaction time R_1 defines specific functions, which in the simplest form could be presented as $R = f(PI, Pc, Pp, Pe)$. Each of the different stimulus variables in relation to the response shows a specific function that forms the basis of relationship between empirical constructs. These empirical laws are explained by the theoretical construct of segmental set, defined as the inability to maintain a major set (Shakow, 1950). This theoretical construct is then employed to explain the relationship between other empirical constructs such as tapping speed, word association, etc. This position is presented in Fig. 3.2. Shakow (1962) explicitly states that such a level of explanation is at the "how" rather than the "why" understanding of the schizophrenic disorder. When introducing "why" type constructs, the speculative level of the theoretical explanation is duly noted and a theoretical construct II of a "filter mechanism" is introduced and acknowledged to reside far from the initial operations. An interference or inhibition construct could also be substituted for the filter term. However, the filter term is explicitly stated and interference is the condition which exists when a major set is not maintained.

In discussing the stimulus situation and the psychological process postulated to interact with S, Shakow (1962) states:

> Another source is the stimulus situation itself which, of course, contains, in addition to the focal stimulus, many less relevant, and even irrelevant aspects, whether these are provided by the experimenter or by the nature of the situation. The normal person deals with these irrelevancies as ground against which the figure is seen, as noise against which the signal is perceived. For him the irrelevancies are kept in their proper place. The mere presence of these irrelevant factors, however, seems to lead the schizophrenic to give them focal rather than ground significance, signal rather than noise import. Of course, the normal subject too has a slight tendency to do the same thing, but manages to keep down the prominence of these peripheral stimuli. His persistent maintenance of the relevant figure in the foreground makes adaptive response possible [p. 9].

As the experimental situation is manipulated to allow for the introduction of extraneous external or internal stimuli, the schizophrenic deficit increases. Each empirical law relating any of the antecedent empirical constructs to the

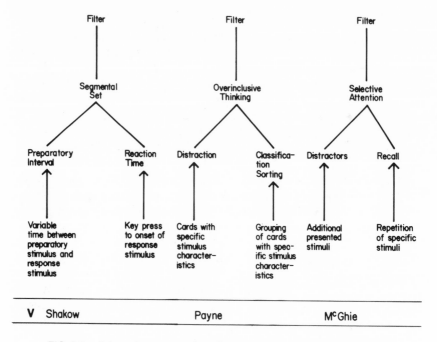

FIG. 3.2. Schematic representation of the theoretical structure of perceptual theories.

response empirical construct could be explained by the causal theoretical construct I of segmental set. As postulates are added such as the disability of segmental set increasing with chronicity or diagnosis, other prediciton can be made about differential functions by patient groups. Also, performance on other tasks can be predicted, if they seem to require the same process. Shakow (1962) mentions other constructs such as motivation and thought disorder which could also be responsible for performance of schizophrenics. However, these are seen as secondary factors which should be controlled by the experimenter so that only the function of the causal perceptual factor will be observed.

Shakow's (1962) results mainly applied to nonparanoids, with paranoids performing like normals, as shown in Fig. 3.2. In fact, the paranoids were considered to be "overconceptualizers" in that the irrelevant stimulus paradigm produced so few effects. This was one of the first indications that perceptual deficits was unique to nonparanoid schizophrenics.

McGhie

McGhie (1970) and Chapman (McGhie & Chapman, 1961) present another perceptual theory. Working with conceptual and perceptual materials in different modalities, McGhie (1970) postulates a filter mechanism and considers the deficit to be due to an inability to process selectively:

> In order to function effectively, the individual is forced to perform a selective operation on the input to ensure that his limited capacity is not overloaded. McGhie and his colleagues interpret their finding as indicating that in schizophrenia this normal filtering process has broken down so that the patients are less able to attend selectively and to process only relevant information. This defect may be expected to have varying effects depending upon the nature and demands of any task. In dealing with a situation requiring a response to simple predictable stimuli, overloading will be less likely and the patient's deficit is less obvious. In tasks demanding the monitoring of a range of stimuli involving more complex decision making and fully occupying the limited decision channel, the failure in selective attention is more likely to lead to overloading and consequent breakdown in performance [p. 11].

In using more of an information-processing model than the other V theorists, McGhie focuses upon an information overload caused by the schizophrenic's inability to filter out irrelevant messages. The schizophrenic cannot exclude the redundant aspects of speech nor group words into phrases but rather he perceives messages word by word with no inhibition of redundant or irrelevant units.

McGhie (Lawson, McGhie, & Chapman, 1966; McGhie, Chapman, & Lawson, 1965) used an experimental situation in which a number of non–task-related stimuli were introduced, sometimes in the same and sometimes in a different sensory modality, which operationalized the empirical construct of distracting stimuli. Changes in performance were observed on various tasks such as stimulus detection and recall that operationalized such empirical constructs as shown in Fig. 3.2. A common task was to present to separate ears letters or digits interspersed with irrelevant information. Another task was to present information through two different sensory modalities. The greatest deficit occurred in the latter case when two modalities had to be integrated (McGhie, 1970). The differential functions with distracting–nondistracting stimuli in the performances of schizophrenics and normals were explained by the theoretical construct I of selective attention. This term is further explained by the theoretical construct II of defective filter. The theoretical construct I of selective attention explains the empirical law relating the empirical construct of distraction operationalized by the introduction of irrelevant stimuli and the empirical constructs of recall, detection, or whatever is the task. McGhie emphasizes that this deficit may be related to specific schizophrenic subtypes. He asserts that the deficit is found mainly with the *nonparanoid schizophrenic,* as in the work of Shakow. Also Goldberg, Schooler, and Mattson (1968), with a large sample of acute schizophrenics, found that *RT,* in a detection task was correlated with schizophrenic symptoms and not paranoid symptoms. Hence for both a simple detection task and a selective attention task, the deficit may be more relevant to schizophrenics and not paranoids. In either case the difference between schizophrenics and paranoids in attention-type research has led McGhie to propose that paranoids should be removed from the schizophrenic category (McGhie, 1970).

The first-level theoretical construct of selective attention is comparable in terms of theoretical structure to the segmental set construct of Shakow and, as we will discuss, the overinclusive construct of Payne. Again, the second-level theoretical construct used to explain the distraction is the filter. There is the added postulate that the inability to "filter" or select out irrelevant material tends to overload the short-term memory system. However, problems in the memory system are secondary and a result of the initial handling capacity of the decision-processing channel. What is of relevance to our interest is that most operations used by McGhie are perceptual in nature, and in this case, the deficit is allegedly found with nonparanoid schizophrenics. Also, his use of an information-processing theory marks a path that we attempt to follow.

Although McGhie has conducted studies which seem to support his position, others have found evidence against it. One reason for the conflicting results is that there are problems with the McGhie procedure. The most noteworthy is that there is no control for response strategies (Korboot & Damiani, 1976). The McGhie work assumes that the response to the distractions reflect the effect of the distraction rather than a strategy of low risk in identifying the target. Clark (1966) and Vojtisek (1975) found that response strategies were quite different for schizophrenics and others. When the response strategy or distraction versus just straight data input was controlled, there was no support for the McGhie hypothesis. We will see that in any detection tasks there are different strategies which affect rate of search and detection.

Korboot and Damiani (1976) found that paranoids, not nonparanoids, were affected by distraction. They used a dichotic shadowing task with a signal detection analysis to compare levels of distraction. In comparing acute groups, there were no differences between schizophrenics and controls over distraction conditions. In addition, there was also no difference in rate of processing once the "old reliable" chronics were removed from the analysis. An interesting finding that emerged was that schizophrenics were able to detect the stimulus with the masking as well as controls but paranoids showed the greatest difference from controls in all distraction conditions. Hence, the results failed to support McGhie in that rate of presentation or degree of distraction differentially influenced performance but not just for schizophrenics. The significant finding was that paranoids were not able to detect the relevant cue while schizophrenics detected as well as controls. We further discuss this study when we direct attention to the stages of data processing in the information theory chapter.

Another study providing evidence against the McGhie hypothesis is that by Royer and Friedman (1973). The task was to detect a target that was presented in a set of equivalent designs varying in mirror reflection and 90° rotation. There were two comparison sets, one having a greater number of distractions than the other. The relevant result here is that schizophrenics (no subtype designation) performed as well as controls in terms of time taken to identify the target and number of errors:

> The task requires that in order to make a correct response, the subject must observe during 350 msec. interval so as to be able to encode the presented stimulus, must store the stimulus information over a period of about 560 msec., must hold the information while scanning an array of related or unrelated figures, and must make a comparison of the stored target information and the array of information. Attentional deficit theories such as that of Chapman and McGhie (1962) would suggest the relevant information would be lost during several of these periods through distraction. Being unable to screen out irrelevant incoming sensory data, short-term memory might become overloaded and result in loss of stored information. Thus, errors should be greatest with schizophrenics and particularly with the process schizophrenics. The error data do not support this interpretation in any way [p. 218].

Schizophrenics were slower than controls across all conditions, but considering the probable inclusion of chronic patients, that result is not surprising. The slowness detected does not necessarily apply to the performance of nonchronic schizophrenics. Another study failed to support the McGhie hypothesis and in fact found the opposite of what would have been predicted. Berg and Leventhal (1977) studied retention in a free-recall, short-term memory task and found that not only did distractors increase performance for schizophrenics and controls, but that psychiatric controls were more affected by distractors than schizophrenics as measured by the amount of intrusive errors. Hence, in this study schizophrenics were clearly able to filter out distractors. However, although the study used non-paranoids, they were all chronic and, as we have seen, McGhie has mainly developed his position with acute patients. In summary, the lack of support of the McGhie hypothesis in terms of the effect of distractions in these studies suggests that the McGhie position is questionable on a basic empirical level irrespective of the ambiguity associated with the theoretical construct II of a filter.

Although in a recent update of the theory, McGhie (1977) reviews some evidence which further supports the distractability construct, especially in terms of auditory information, the effects of distraction in visual information processing are not as well supported. A clue to another problem with McGhie's position is found in an interesting study (Dykes & McGhie, 1976), reviewed by McGhie, which compares schizophrenics and creatives on a dichotic shadowing task. It was found that acute nonparanoid schizophrenics and normals were able to switch information channels when there was a high association between messages. However, only schizophrenics were able to switch when there was low association. As elaborated in later sections, we hypothesize that schizophrenics do not impose a conceptual schema on a stimulus field and hence are not as affected by the associational quality of the task. This finding suggests that the McGhie position is really a low K position, since conceptual associations, characteristic of the nonparanoid, may be the source of the deficit. As such, the dichotic listening tasks are not measuring a V process (distraction) but are measuring the use of conceptual categories. In our discussion of attention in Chapter 6, we show that the "leaky filter" concept of attention has been replaced by an explanation stressing the effect of conceptual categories. Also, there seems to be a growing consensus that the attentional deficit in schizophrenia may be more the inability to use concepts to organize information rather than their inability to select relevant information. In that case, the perceptual deficit proposed by McGhie may be discarded in favor of the conceptual explanations offered by the K theorists.

McGhie should be applauded for beginning the analysis of the performance deficit in terms of specific processes as contained in an information theory model. The deficit is found in those conditions where there is much material to handle. The filter term is a convenient construct to explain the data but too broad to provide much meaning in its present experimental form. One question is left unanswered. Which process is influenced by the noise, the decision process, or the perceptual or feature extraction process? As discussed in a later chapter, later work has attempted to specify deficits at the levels of threshold, icon, detection, or memory as well as with an attenuated filter. Bjork and Murray (1977) propose that filter effects, not detecting a cue from noise, are more a feature-specific inhibition and that there are many hierarchically organized limited-capacity feature detectors and inhibitors. A generalized filter concept is too general a term to provide information about specific deficits at this time.

In summary, the V theorists offer first-order theoretical constructs such as segmental set and selective attention with their own set of empirical operations. All theorists propose a similar higher level theoretical construct of a filter to explain the lower level theoretical constructs. However, all tests to demonstrate the effect of the common filter have been negative. The operations are not comparable, which should not be surprising since the different operational definitions of each construct do not coincide. The different operations will be examined in more detail later.

K THEORISTS

Cameron

Cameron (1938a,b, 1939, 1951) is an early K theorist, who was especially influential in the development of the later K and V theories. Cameron (1938a) compared the sequential stages of reasoning involved in developing a concept of causality (Piaget, 1928) for the schizophrenic and the child. He argued that the schizophrenic exhibited a reasoning deficit that was at a later rather than an earlier stage of intellectual development. From these studies and from other studies that examined the reasoning defects of senile patients (1938b), Cameron (1951) developed the concept of an overinclusive–overexclusive equilibrium to characterize the major cause of the schizophrenic deficit:

> Overinclusion—a failure to exclude the irrelevant and inconsequential leads initially to behavior disruption. A common defense in such situations is that of meeting the initial disorganization with prompt overexclusion; and this usually results in a simpler and more restricted perceptual reorganization [p. 285].

Overinclusion is considered to be a disturbance in symbolization resulting from a failure to eliminate conflicting and irrelevant elements and to maintain clear boundaries (Cameron, 1938a). The schizophrenic is characterized as having a loose cognitive structure which does not selectively eliminate concepts. Such a state leads to problems in social communication which in turn prohibit functional social behavior since the schizophrenic cannot develop consensually validated social concepts needed for interpersonal role playing.

The characterization of the looseness of association is not different from Bleuler's (1950) view that an underlying weakening of the associative process is fundamental to schizophrenia. Cameron's contribution is his emphasis on the defense or reaction to this looseness of thought which is a tightening of all concepts into one all-inclusive expectancy or belief system.

Cameron (1951) develops related constructs such as reaction sensitivity, progressive reaction sensitization, etc. that are manifestations of the basic deficit in forming clear conceptual boundaries. In other words, the schizophrenic does not maintain any dominant associations but has a multitude of competing associations. For him, thinking is a pattern of loosely related ideas that occur together and, at best, form inexact approximations to the thought appropriate for the stimulus situation. He reacts to this disorganization by overexcluding stimuli. Since only limited stimuli are attended to, his dysfunction appears to be perceptual. However, this state is a consequence of the initial state of overinclusion, which is a conceptual process. In addition, there is also a second state or a return to the initial state of overinclusion after the perceptual restriction stage, which is overinclusion with disorganization. It is at this stage in which delusions are most prominent since a dominant concept or expectancy begins to determine all perceptions.

Translated into our framework, where the potency of K is associated with the probability of a dominant association, Cameron (1938a) proposes that the schizophrenic is at a low K. Very little specific meaning is ever attributed to S. The low strength $_sE_r$ is always a function of the cognitive disability. The more a task involved a conceptual process and more specifically a process requiring a certain class of responses, the lower is R and the greater the deficit.

As presented in Fig. 3.3, the usual experimental procedure used by Cameron was to present incomplete sentences which required the subject to complete the causal relationship or state the exception. The antecedent event was the incomplete sentence that operationalized an incomplete causality

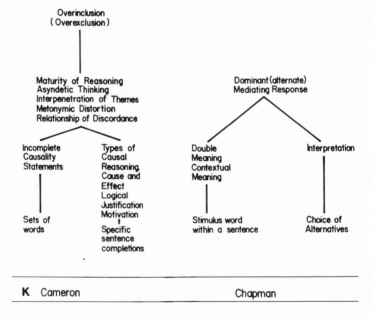

FIG. 3.3.   Schematic representation of the theoretical structure of conceptual theories.

statement. The consequent event was the specific sentence completion furnished by the subject that operationalized different classes of causal thinking. The categories of causal thinking employed by Cameron (1938a) were motivation, logical justification, and cause and effect. The particular relationship between the empirical constructs, the empirical laws, are explained by the theoretical constructs I of interpenetration of themes, asyndetic thinking, metonymic distortion, relationship of discordance, and maturity of reasoning. Overinclusive thinking is considered the basic cause of the schizophrenic disorganization and is defined as a failure to exclude the irrelevant and inconsequential which would lead to the problems specified at the theoretical I level. Overexclusive thinking is also a theoretical construct II and is vaguely related to certain constructs at the theoretical construct I level. However, the main K construct is that of overinclusion which describes the schizophrenic as operating with an equivalence of concepts. Any stimulus elicits numerous loosely organized concepts which are marginally related to the correct concept.

Cameron, like Shakow, made a clear ad hoc distinction between paranoids and nonparanoids. In his discussion of the pseudocommunity, Cameron made it clear that at both the operational and theoretical level, paranoids respond differently, in fact almost in the opposite way, from schizophrenics. However, since this division was not operationalized in the experimental situation, the findings were applied to schizophrenia in general with an ad hoc explanation of the performance differences of paranoids. In fact, the pseudocommunity concept of Cameron (1951) specifically argues that the delusional schizophrenic is not suffering from disorganization but is organizing perceptions and concepts in terms of a consistent conceptual expectancy. Such an individual conceptualizes his role and the role of others in life and fits all perceptions and meaning into that theory. At that point, he is totally overinclusive and distinctly different from the nonparanoid who is still in a state of perceptual disorganization where association are loose and shift with the stimulus field. In our terms, Cameron thus considers the paranoid to be at a high K while the nonparanoid is at a low K. In this case, the paranoid would be expected to be overinclusive while the nonparanoid would be at an average level of overinclusiveness or be underinclusive. We will find this result when we examine the work on overinclusion.

Chapman

In direct contrast to the Cameron position is the K theory advocated by Chapman (Chapman & Chapman, 1965, 1973; Chapman, Chapman, & Miller, 1964) to explain the verbal behavior of schizophrenics. This theory argues that the schizophrenic consistently responds with dominant meanings instead of the associations which are most relevant to the total stimulus context. The contextual cues in verbal stimulus material are insufficient for the schizophrenic. The deficit is a response bias in that the most dominant aspect of meaning is consistently emitted regardless of the contextual cues which would make an alternative response more appropriate.

Chapman is mainly concerned with the denotative meaning of words and considers the meaning of a word a hypothetical internal event which mediates the behavioral response to a word (Chapman et al., 1964). The schizophrenic deficit, at least in verbal behavior, arises from the schizophrenic's misinterpretation of verbal cues. While the normal is able to interpret words with both weaker and stronger meaning, schizophrenics neglect weaker meaning responses. In our terms, Chapman considers the schizophrenic to exhibit a high K. When the task requires a high K, the schizophrenic does as well or better than normals. When the task requires a low K, the deficit is exhibited. This position is the inverse of the position proposed by Cameron, as shown in Fig. 3.3.

In the common experimental situation used by Chapman (Chapman & Chapman, 1965; Chapman & Chapman, 1973), a word that has more than one meaning is presented within a sentence which suggests the correct definition. The subject has to choose the correct meaning from a number of choices. It is usually found that normals and schizophrenics exhibit a similarity in their choices when the dominant response is correct but schizophrenics make more errors when the weaker alternate response is correct (i.e., when the context suggest a less common definition). Essentially the same results occurred for a word-sorting task (Chapman et al., 1964). The antecedent empirical event is usually the double-meaning words which are presented within a context which defines the correct meaning. The stimulus event, therefore, is the stimulus complex operationalizing the empirical construct of double meaning, contextual meaning, etc., depending on the particular experiment. On the consequent side, the responses to the multiple choice situation could be the dominant or secondary meaning which defines the empirical construct of dominance. That is, the responses are usually choices reflecting the strength of association of the word and the responses and either a correct or incorrect interpretation of the stimulus. One class of responses could, therefore, be considered an interpretation and one class considered a misinterpretation.

The relationship between the empirical construct of double meaning operationalized by the antecedent events and the empirical construct of interpretation, or misinterpretation operationalized by the consequent events, creates the empirical laws which are explained by the theoretical construct of dominant mediating response. This construct is defined as the high-strength association of a stimulus which is commonly made by normals but which is not modified by schizophrenics when the alternate less strong associate is appropriate.

Chapman (Chapman et al., 1964) does not think that the theory offers any theoretical constructs but rather that it is a description of relationships:

> Also, this theory does not go beyond description to attempt an explanation of the etiology of the disorder. Nevertheless, the usual first step in understanding a disorder is to describe it, and the chief attraction of the present theory is the promise that it holds for reducing the number of principles necessary for that description [p. 76].

Chapman, in our terms, believes that the theory only describes the functional relationship between variables. The present analysis, however, indicates that the theory goes beyond description with the use of the dominant meaning construct. Chapman et al. (1964) argued that when there is no attempt to explain "why" the dominant mediating response is always emitted (a theoretical II level construct) by the schizophrenic, there is no theorizing. However, the dominant mediating response construct is a theoretical construct explaining the "how" of an empirical law. The postulation of a theoretical construct I, answering the "how" of a process, is entering into theoretical waters although certainly not to the depth of other theorists. To quote Chapman et al. (1964) again:

> It should also be noted that the theory offers no exact specifications of the nature of the interaction of schizophrenia with mediating responses. The hypothesized excess in schizophrenia of overt responses mediated by the strongest mediating responses could be accounted for by several alternative formulations concerning the corresponding interval events. It could be explained by a strengthening of the strong mediating responses, or by a weakening of the weak mediating responses, or by a multiplication of the strength of both strong and weak mediating responses, or by a selective failure to respond to weak mediating responses, or by some selective inhibitory process. There is no evidence at present for choosing among these alternative explanations [pp. 56–57].

Although it is true that much more theorizing beyond the theoretical I level is relatively speculative, specification of the operation of the dominant mediating response would provide some theoretical clarity. For example, is the dominant response present because the dominant response cannot be inhibited or was it never learned? Is the function due to a lack of recognition of contextual cues or to the power of the dominant response? Is there a perceptual problem as discussed by the V theorists? Or is a new direction being suggested by the use of an inhibition construct? There is a possibility that the theory is moving toward an inhibition explanation. While the chronic schizophrenic is still the focus of the Chapman theory, in an update of this position (Chapman, Chapman, & Miller, 1977), there is a tendency to move toward an "editing" explanation of the dominant meaning bias. In moving the theory closer to an inhibition of screening deficit explanation, they open new avenues for research and answer the criticism discussed earlier, by explaining why the dominant meaning bias occurs. Support for the Chapman position now must come from studies using a paradigm that allows for screening or nonscreening of the dominant and alternative meaning responses.

Broen (1968) notes that the Chapman position may be a V position since the lack of attention to contextual cues may be the deficit. Since both context and the stimulus word are joint determinants of performance, it is as much the lack of attention to contextual cues as the consistent dominant meaning response that creates a deficit. However, this point is not developed by Chapman, and the theory clearly takes a conceptual position in terms of dominant mediating associations.

There is some evidence that the Chapman measures do not relate specifically to schizophrenia. Hamsher and Arnold (1976), using a Chapman measure, found that schizophrenics did not differ from controls when they were acute, were rigidly defined as schizophrenic, and were compared to more appropriate controls (other hospitalized patients such as neurotics, personality disorders, and alcoholics). Chapman and Chapman (1973) argue against this result by asserting that other patients are not appropriate controls since they may share the same pathology. As noted by Hamsher (1977) this reasoning is difficult to follow. If the condition applies also to other patients, it cannot be considered unique to schizophrenia as proposed by Chapman. Furthermore, other studies have demonstrated that the strong meaning bias is not solely found in schizophrenics. Harrow and Quinlan (1977) found that the Chapman predictions held only for the most disorganized chronic schizophrenics. Acute schizophrenics performed like control psychiatric patients on the Chapman measures. Klinka and Papageorgis (1976) found that the strong meaning bias is a function of hospitalization and applies to any group that experiences extensive hospitalization. Marshall (1973) found that the Chapman matching measure is a function of age which would add to the chronicity effect since the longer the time in the institution, the older the individual becomes. Neuringer, Fiske, Schmidt, and Goldstein (1972) found a trend for a weak meaning bias for schizophrenics and a weak meaning bias when homographs had affective strong meanings but neutral weak meanings (Neuringer, Kaplan, & Goldstein, 1974). Miller's (1974) failure to find the dominant bias in a test which excluded affective material suggests that there is an affective component to the Chapman task which facilitates the dominant response set. Hence, evidence for the thought disorder as described by Chapman may be a function of a select schizophrenic sample or a select control group which is a possibility discussed by the Chapmans themselves (Chapman & Chapman, 1973). They concluded that their overinclusion measure elicits a deficit mainly with chronic schizophrenics while Payne's measure, which we will next discuss, is more informative for acute schizophrenics.

The major problem is that while the task performance is measured with great care, subject groups are not precisely distinguished. Controls are compared to unmedicated chronics uncategorized by paranoid or premorbid status. The lack of clear group distinctions, especially the failure to study acutes, leaves considerable doubt that the strong meaning bias is specific to schizophrenia, or to one subgroup of schizophrenics, or to psychopathological groups in general.

In summary, the Chapman theory has as its strengths a precision in making predictions, a completeness with which hypotheses are being tested, and a utility in clearly organizing much material (Chapman & Chapman, 1973). Final evaluation must await the specification of subject groups to determine whether or not the dominant meaning effect is a result of extensive hospitalization as has been found with other measures.

Payne

Payne (1966) applied Cameron's overinclusive thinking concept to measure the schizophrenic performance deficit. He maintains that the schizophrenic is unable to maintain conceptual boundaries because internal ideational stimuli or stimuli external and irrelevant to the concept are not incorporated. Any particular stimulus produces an excessive degree of stimulus generalization so that relevant and irrelevant elements cannot be discriminated. The theoretical construct II is that of a filter mechanism which does not inhibit irrelevant cues.

In analyzing the theoretical structure developed by Payne, the overinclusive construct which is derived from performance on various conceptual tests such as the object classification test (Payne & Hewlett, 1960) must be examined closely. Though a previous analysis (Magaro, 1974) placed Payne with the *V* theorists because of his use of a perceptual filter term at the theoretical construct level, we will now classify Payne as a *K* theorist because we will focus upon his operations and the overinclusive term applied to the theoretical I level construct. Such a change is further justified by the disappointing results of Payne's attempts to demonstrate the operation of the filter term which has apparently led to a gradual disinterest in the term (Payne, 1971).

The overinclusive term and the measures developed by Payne have received an extensive amount of attention. The observables are elicited by the presentation of stimuli which can be sorted into categories of various breadth.

The sorting of the specific stimuli presented at a consequent Event 2 level are considered the operational definition of classification, abstract sorting, etc. Other card stimuli having a specific quality such as scratches, number of non–task-related marks, etc., are introduced at an antecedent Event 2 level and define the empirical construct of distraction. The theoretical construct I of overinclusive thinking explains the functions or relationships between the sorting of distracting and nondistracting stimulus cards and the two empirical constructs of distraction and classification. The basic empirical constructs are those of "sorting" or "classification type." The function between the construct distraction or abstraction, defined by the stimuli presented, and the response construct of classification, defined by the specific task behavior, produces an empirical law which is the basis of all further explanation. Overinclusive thinking is the first level of explanation.

The similarity of the theoretical constructs employed by Payne and Shakow is striking, because although Shakow used simple perceptual tasks and Payne used conceptual tasks, either theorist could have written the following:

> Here we see particularly the various difficulties created by *context*, the degree to which the schizophrenic is affected by irrelevant aspects of the stimulus surrounding—inner and outer—which prevent his focusing on the "to-be-responded-to" stimulus. It is as if, in the scanning process which takes place before the response to a stimulus is made, the schizophrenic is unable to select out the material relevant for optimal response. He apparently cannot free himself from the irrelevant among the numerous possibilities available for choice. In other words, that function, which is of equal importance as the response to stimuli, is abeyant [Shakow, 1962, p. 25].

> ... that overinclusive thinking might be regarded as due to a defect in some hypothetical control "filter" mechanisms, the function of which is to screen our irrelevant data, both internal (in the form of irrelevant thoughts and associations) and external (in the form of irrelevant stimuli) to allow for the most efficient processing of incoming information [Payne, 1966, p. 79].

Both theorists consider the organization of *S* elements through attention to specific relevant elements and the exlusion of others to be the main factor related to the performance deficit. However, at the theoretical I level, Shakow posits a segmental set construct while Payne employs an overinclusive thinking concept. As can be seen in Fig. 3.2, both the overinclusive thinking and segmental set constructs are at the same level of analysis. The sorting operation used by Payne is comparable at the observable level to the reaction time operation. The introduction of the operationalized empirical constructs on the antecedent side, such as distraction and preparatory interval, are also comparable. The explanation of the relationships of the antecedent and consequent terms by the theoretical term, overinclusive thinking, corresponds to the use of segmental set. The theoretical construct of a filter is identical. Therefore, in terms of level of theoretical explanation, the positions are comparable. However, it is clear that the empirical operations are quite different since Shakow is examining perceptual processes, and Payne is examining conceptual processes. The fact that the operations used by each differ becomes a crucial point when the results of subgroup differences are examined.

Payne (1966) also noted the relationship between overinclusive thinking and segmental set, but when he examined the relationship, little in common was found between the operational measures of each construct. It was expected that the two first-level theoretical constructs would be related, and thus the second-level theoretical construct of a filter could be justified as an explanation of the relationship between segmental set and overinclusion. However, when the theoretical level II filter construct and its operations were tested, the results were found to be both ambiguous or contradictory to predictions concerning the operation of a filter. The filter term was abandoned when later studies indicated that empirical confirmation of the overinclusive term did not support the higher level construct of a filter. The first-level theoretical constructs of segmental set and overinclusive thinking seem to be quite different terms although Payne at one point suggested that they both involved a perceptual process and hence could be considered as an example of our "semantical construct invention." In saying (Payne, 1966) that "overinclusive thinking is basically not a thinking disturbance at all [p. 965]," he expresses a desire to abandon the conceptual construct for a perceptual explanation. It would seem that if that is the case, the next step would be to abandon the conceptual operations and employ perceptual ones. This was not done, and, hence, becomes the central problem with the Payne theory.

In summary, Payne is a *K* theorist if one stops at the theoretical I level, the overinclusion term. Yet, he has abandoned the stance of a perceptual theorist by not finding any evidence for the effect of a filter term. The foundation for the theory, therefore, rests upon the overinclusive term and its operations. We will examine the overinclusion term in some detail, since the results of the overinclusion studies do provide us with an excellent vehicle to indicate paranoid–nonparanoid differences and to suggest at what level each group exhibits a unique process. However, we first briefly review another *K* theorist who has followed in Cameron's theoretical footsteps but has been guided by a more recent empirical operation.

Bannister

Bannister (1960) used the personal construct system to examine the conceptual structure of schizophrenics. He employed a task in which schizophrenics had to check one pole of several bipolar adjective pairs in reference to several pictures of people. He hypothesized, in the same vein as Cameron, that thought-disordered schizophrenics had a loose cognitive structure. This was operationalized by a measure of the variability of concepts in a test–retest situation. That is, the schizophrenic would check different sets of adjectives for a given person at two different testings. The hypothesis was confirmed. In addition, however, some schizophrenics without a thought disorder (mainly paranoids) were found to have maldistributed constructs. By this, he meant that they did not employ the optimum 50–50 split in using their concepts; rather, almost all objects were placed at one end of the pole and almost none at the opposite end. For example, if almost every object is seen as good and only a few are seen as bad, the construct is classified as maldistributed. The distinction between variability of concepts and maldistribution is useful in our description of the schizophrenics as having unstable concepts and paranoids as having stable rigid concepts, being maldistributed. Bannister (1962) later reported results that support this hypothesis. He found that paranoid schizophrenics (non-thought-disordered) have tight constructs that are invariable in intensity. Paranoids also tend to allocate elements at one pole rather than contrast them on each construct dimension.

Some further evidence for our hypothesis about the two subgroups is provided by Foulds, Hope, McPherson, and Mayo (1967a). They found in a direct comparison of paranoids, and nonparanoids that nonparanoids had lower intensity scores and lower consistency scores than paranoids. Intensity of relationship represents the degree of correlation between the subject's usage of different bipolar adjective pairs. If the usage of all adjective pairs correlates perfectly (for example, if all "good" people were also seen as "likable," "sincere," "unselfish," etc.), then the subject would be seen as using only one construct. All of these words would mean the same thing, which is an extreme case of high intensity of relationship. If there is no relationship between adjective pairs, there is no relationship between various concepts, thus yielding a low intensity score. Nonparanoids had lower intensity scores than paranoids or were more inconsistent in their application of adjectives to objects.

A follow-up study by Gamble (1975) tested later thinking by Bannister (1971) that paranoids are expected to have tighter construct systems than nonparanoids. He found that paranoids did have a greater consistency across concepts then nonparanoids when the means of diagnosing paranoids was improved on the Foulds et al. (1967a) procedure. Paranoids did not exhibit less construct intensity, which reflects the looseness of associations, but they related these constructs in an overly consistent manner.

A severe problem with the Bannister work is discussed by Haynes and Phillips (1973). In reviewing the work supporting the Bannister hypothesis, they noted that consistency scores and intensity scores were related and that differences found in intensity were more a function of consistency. In effect, inconsistency, the inconsistent use of categories over time, is more characteristic of schizophrenics than intensity, the tendency to group categories together. Bannister (1971) proposed that the schizophrenic exhibited a "loose construing," which is a weakened conceptual structure reflected in low intensity scores; attributional categories would not relate to one another. Haynes and Phillips (1973) found that schizophrenics were inconsistent rather than nondiscriminate in their use of categories. In effect, this result states that the schizophrenic has a conceptual structure similar to others as also reported by Chapman and Chapman (1973), but he is inconsistent in the application of categories to events. He tends to assign different meanings to the same stimulus over time, possibly reflecting an attention to different elements of the same stimulus.

The Bannister type of measures are quite different from the Payne measures. When a subject arranges a set of photographs of people on a number of dimensions such as good, kind, mean, etc., the relationship between the dimensions is supposed to demonstrate a consistency of conceptual categories. The process is different from the process involved in grouping objects into categories. One difference is that the dimensions are provided by the experimenter, whereas in the overinclusion task of categorizing objects in as many ways as possible, the categories are not provided for the subject. The Bannister consistency measure involves an external structured organization; the Payne sorting measure involves more of a personal conceptual organization. Results follow this interpretation of the the task. Paranoids are quite able to follow the evaluative dimensions and assign consistent categories on the Bannister measure, whereas nonparanoids perform poorly. Nonparanoids although able to sort objects on the Payne object classification test were not able to construct consistent evaluative dimensions (Foulds et al., 1967b). It is not clear if the problem is in the construction classification system per se or the use of an evaluative system. The results suggest that it is the construction that is most difficult as elements ranged within dimensions, whereas normals kept them quite consistent (i.e., if one photograph was rated as kind, it would not be rated as mean). Also Foulds et al. (1967b) found that those who performed poorly on the Bannister measures were in the range of thought disorder as defined by the Bannister test. Paranoids were also found to be more idiosyncratic in this study indicating that they create many conceptual categories. The paranoid organized the Bannister photographs and was consistent. He also overorganized an object-sorting task and admitted more elements than necessary.

Besides the difference in conceptual structure demanded by the two tasks, it may be that the Bannister test, because of its complexity and relevance, could offer more distractors than the colored chips or objects in the Payne measure.

This interpretation would support the result that nonparanoids performed poorly since previous work has indicated that perceptual distractors are more relevant to the performance of nonparanoids than paranoids. In this interpretation, the Bannister task is simply a more distracting stimulus condition. In terms of the Harrow, Himmelhoch, Tucker, Hersh, and Quinlan (1972) analysis of the overinclusive construct, the Bannister test is a measure of stimulus overinclusion rather than conceptual overinclusion. As such it is more relevant to the problem experienced by the nonparanoid. The nonparanoid does not attempt the conceptual organization and organizes in a similar way to normals on a Payne task but is inconsistent on a Bannister task where consistency is measured. Most of the stimulus world for the nonparanoid is a distractor or a greater reliance is placed upon perceptual processes. Before pursuing this thought, we more closely examine the overinclusive measure and then discuss the role of such constructs within the context of recent work in the complexity of cognition.

The foundation for the Payne theory, rests upon the overinclusive term and its operations. We now examine the overinclusion term in some detail as we focus on the conceptual deficit in schizophrenia. The results of overinclusion studies provide us with an excellent vehicle to indicate paranoid-nonparanoid differences and to suggest at what level each group exhibits a unique process. This is helpful for our own analysis of the conceptual and perceptual processes in paranoia and schizophrenia.

OVERINCLUSION

The Measure of Overinclusion

Overinclusion has been measured by many different tests, but the major tests are those used by Payne and his associates. Payne and Friedlander (1962) operationalized the construct by a composite score based upon the number of words used in explaining Benjamin's Proverbs, the number of incorrect sortings in four trials on the Goldstein–Scheerer Color–Form Sorting test (The Object Classification Test), and the number of objects included in four trials on the Goldstein–Scheer Object Sorting test. The Object Classification test used by Payne (1962) provides two scores. One score is the A response score which designates the number of correct sortings, those based upon shape, size, thickness, color, etc. This score was the original measure of concreteness as used by Goldstein and Scheerer (1941). The Non-A score is defined by a repetition of a sort or an unusual sort, one not based upon the attribute of the objects. The non-A score is the measure of overinclusive thinking and could consist of sortings based on the scratches on the objects, uses of the objects, or preferences for certain objects which would be "screened-out" by the normal (Payne, 1962). The Non-A score by itself may not be an adequate measure of overinclusion. Payne (1962) found that the Non-A score differentiates acute schizophrenics from normals, but that only half the acutes were out of the normal range. Chronic schizophrenics did not differ from normals on this measure although they did produce more A scores. However, Payne and Hewlett (1960) reported that the intercorrelations of the three overinclusion measures were substantial enough to combine them into a total composite score, and this composite score is used to determine overinclusion.

Later work, especially that done in other laboratories, did not find high correlations between the overinclusion measures to justify it as a unitary construct. In particular, the proverb measure seems to be measuring a separate process. Payne, Hochberg, and Hawks (1970), who report some of the sparse reliability data in this area, found that the test–retest reliability of all measures including the proverb test is substantial but that the proverb test did not correlate highly with object-sorting measures. The proverb test also did not differentiate between overinclusive schizophrenics, non-overinclusive schizophrenics, and normals. Goldstein and Salzman (1967) compared the proverb performance of delusional and nondelusional schizophrenics as well as paranoid and nonparanoid schizophrenics who had been found to be overinclusive and nonoverinclusive respectively (Payne, Caird, & Laverty, 1964). They found no between-group differences on the proverb test. Foulds, Hope, McPherson, and Mayo (1967b) found a relationship between delusions and proverbs for chronics but not acutes while the Object Classification test showed significant correlations for both groups. Hence, measures of overinclusion at least should be separated from a proverb measure since it appears to have little of the common variance of the other sorting measures.

The reason for the lack of strong correlation between the proverb measures and other sorting measures may be because the sorting measures are less verbal than the proverb measure. Such a possibility is suggested in the following studies. Johnson and Bieliauskas (1971) directly compared verbal (Chapman test of grouping words) and nonverbal (Payne type sorting test of objects) tests of overinclusion. They found that chronic schizophrenics showed greater overinclusion on the Payne test than the Chapman test; however, the correlation between the tests was not reported. It should be noted, however, that in contrast to this finding, Chapman and Chapman (1973) conclude that their test separates overinclusive from nonoverinclusive schizophrenics only in a chronic population while Payne's measure separates overinclusive from nonoverinclusive acutes.

Both studies indicate that the Chapman verbal overinclusion measure is not related to the Payne object sorting measures and each scale has different effects on subgroups. This is further confirmed by Knight, Sims-Knight, and

Petchers-Cassell (1977) who compared overinclusion to recognition memory. The more overinclusive schizophrenics performed better than the less overinclusive schizophrenics on pictures but they did not differ on words. They concluded that since memory for pictures involves processing many attributes of a stimulus, it would differ from verbal memory which would focus on the categorization of common meanings. The point relevant to our discussion is that a verbal task produces different results than a nonverbal task, and it is a nonverbal task which is related to overinclusion. Hence, from those results we can conclude that a verbal measure of overinclusion is not the same as a nonverbal measure neither in terms of the correlation between measures nor in terms of separating the same schizophrenic groups into overinclusive and nonoverinclusive groups.

Not only the proverb measure but the composite score of overinclusion has also been challenged. Hawks (1964) compared the object-sorting task, the proverb test, and the total composite score used by Payne and Hewlett (1960). Only one sorting score correlated with the total score and all correlations were much lower than those previously reported. Such results suggest that each test is an independent measure of overinclusion.

Furthermore, the validity results were more damaging. The composite score did not differentiate schizophrenics from other groups, paranoids from nonparanoids, patients with delusions from those without, or any other clinical groupings. A similar conclusion is reported by Watson (1967) who found no relationship between the Goldstein object-sorting scores, proverbs, and the over- and underinclusion scores from the Epstein overinclusion test (Epstein, 1953). None of the Payne measures interrelated, casting doubt on the validity of the overinclusion measures especially in the form of a composite score. Watson (1967) questioned the unitary value of the construct: "However, as is the case in any such validational investigation, a second hypothesis—that clinical overinclusion is, in fact, multidimensional should be considered in view of the present findings [p. 519]."

A systematic investigation into the dimensions of overinclusion was conducted by Harrow et al. (1972). They hypothesized that overinclusion contains at least three phenomena which they labeled as behavioral overinclusion, conceptual overinclusion, and stimulus overinclusion. Behavioral overinclusion refers to the Payne Non-A measure. Conceptual overinclusion was scored by the experimenter who judged whether or not the concepts used as a basis for the sorting exhibited a process of overinclusion. Stimulus overinclusion is a perceptual term which refers to the difficulty in attending selectively to relevant stimuli and a tendency to be distracted by irrelevant stimuli. The last term was that used by McGhie. Harrow et al. (1972) state that "it is suggested that stimulus overinclusion is primarily a disorder of attention rather than of concept formation [p. 162]." Hence, Harrow et al. (1972) provide theoretical support for the empirical findings indicating that overinclusion is not a unitary measure and reflects both conceptual and perceptual processes. When the assumption is made that overinclusion measures reflect the same process, there is not only the inevitable confusion in terms of conflicting results, but the determination of which schizophrenic sample exhibits the particular overinclusion, and to what degree surely becomes obscured.

Who Is Overinclusive

When Cameron discussed overinclusion, especially when he developed the idea of the pseudocommunity, he spoke mainly of the paranoid. Others have followed his lead and compared paranoids or delusional schizophrenics to nonparanoids and nondelusional schizophrenics. For example, Payne (1961, 1962) tested Cameron's hypothesis and found that overinclusion is unique only to a subclass of schizophrenics—those showing delusions. This finding was confirmed later by Payne and Caird (1967) who found twice as many paranoids in an overinclusive group than in a nonoverinclusive group. Payne and Hewlett (1960) found that schizophrenics, as compared to depressives, exhibited more overinclusion, and it was only acute schizophrenics with delusions who exhibited the Non-A type of overinclusion. Chronic schizophrenics performed in the normal range (Payne, 1962). However, Foulds, Hope, McPherson, and Mayo (1967a) used the Payne measures and found that for both acutes and chronics, delusions were related to overinclusion on the Object Classification measure. Another report by the same authors (1967b) supports the relationship of overinclusion and diagnosis. They found that paranoids diagnosed clinically and on a Symptom Sign Inventory were more overinclusive than nonparanoids.

Though the findings relating overinclusion and delusions seem consistent, there are serious problems with some of the Payne studies. First, in their correlations, Payne et al. used the total sample including those who were nonschizophrenics. It may well be that the resulting relationships between overinclusion and delusion were due to the presence of manics or other pathological groups who were exhibiting delusions. Any conclusion from such analysis about overinclusion and delusions would then be of questionable relevance to the issue of overinclusion and paranoia. Doubt is further increased by the disquieting fact that one third of the clinically diagnosed paranoids was not found to be delusional. Second, once the total population is split into delusional and nondelusional groups, the less disturbed patients would probably be placed in the nondelusional group. Hence the relationship between delusion and overinclusion could easily be between greater pathology and overinclusion. Third, it should also be noted that the overinclusion studies of Payne and Caird (1967), and Payne, Caird, and Laverty (1964) who found the overinclusion–delusion relationship used a proverb measure. Since the proverb measure is more an indicator of verbosity rather than overinclusion in the usual meaning of the term (Chapman & Chapman, 1973), the Payne results are of questionable relevance. Fourth, in two Payne studies (Payne & Caird, 1967; Payne, Caird, & Laverty, 1964) paranoids and nonparanoids were matched on IQ. As Chapman and Chapman (1973) point out, since the paranoid has the higher IQ, this control has the effect of eliminating the higher-IQ paranoids and the lower-IQ nonparanoids. By that process of selection, the more typical paranoid is eliminated. Hence, it is not surprising that Payne and Caird (1967) found that overinclusives had a slower reaction time than nonoverinclusives. It has repeatedly been shown that paranoids exhibit a faster reaction time than nonparanoids. The selection process and the finding of slower reaction time for overinclusives then suggest that the overinclusive group consisted of the more pathological paranoids. Once again, the particular procedure used by Payne et al. may have invalidated the results by producing a biased sample.

It must be stressed that samples used in overinclusion studies can also be biased in the other direction. A sample can be biased to include more pathological subjects in either the overinclusive or underinclusive groups. For example, the Payne groups seem to include the more pathological subjects in the overinclusive group. On the other hand, studies by Knight, Scherer, and Shapiro (1977) and Knight, Sims-Knight, and Petchers-Cassell (1977) used a sample in which the overinclusives were less pathological (as defined by the process–reactive measure) than the underinclusives. In this case it was the underinclusives who exhibited the deficit and not the overinclusives who performed like normals. In short, there is a consistent indication that overinclusion is more indicative of pathology then of any thinking process characteristic of specific groups. Rather, the type of thinking exhibited in the overinclusion measure seems to reflect a level of disturbance that can be exhibited by any group, schizophrenics, paranoids, or others.

Other studies seem to support this inference. Harrow, Harkavy, Bromet, and Tucker (1973) in studying overinclusion in different acute pathological groups as well as schizophrenics, found that overinclusion relates to degree of pathology rather than schizophrenia. Davis and Blaney (1976) found the same result. However, certain problems in the later study considerably overlapped the measure of delusional thinking. Seven times as many delusional than nondelusional subjects were rated as showing more pathology and six times as many nondelusional subjects than delusional were in the low pathology groups. There was no relationship between overinclusion and delusion in the low pathology group. Second, there was no relationship between the two overinclusion measures, one presented under a free-response format and one administered using a multiple-choice format. Therefore, it is unclear what was measured in this study and whether paranoids or the more pathological are the overinclusives.

The findings of Harrow et al. (1972) also support the inference that overinclusion is a function of pathology. In distinguishing between behavioral and conceptual measures of overinclusion, they found only the conceptual measure related to the presence of delusions. When this operational distinction is made, delusional thinking was found to be related to overinclusion. However, since this overinclusion measure is also related to the amount of idiosyncratic thinking—an indication of greater pathology— these findings also suggest that conceptual overinclusion is a pathology measure (I thank Lloyd Abrams for calling my attention to this distinction).

There is some other evidence which indicates that overinclusion is not related to delusions or paranoid diagnosis. Hawks (1964) did not find schizophrenics to differ from other patients groups nor did he find differences between schizophrenics and paranoids. However, his sample is very select because subjects were only those referred for psychological examination due to problems in differential diagnosis. Eliseo (1963) found a potentially more damaging result when he reported that schizophrenics, process and reactive, were no different on overinclusion, using the verbal Epstein measure, than medical patients with chronic physical illness. In fact the trend was for the medical patients to be more overinclusive. Goldstein and Salzman (1965), using a verbal proverb measure, also found no difference between delusional and nondelusional schizophrenics or between paranoid and nonparanoid schizophrenics. However, as discussed above, a verbal measure of overinclusion may not be comparable to the object-sorting measures. Andreason and Powers (1974) who used the Payne sorting measures found no differences between paranoids and hebephrenics, but what is more, they found that manics were substantially more overinclusive than schizophrenics on all measures. In summary, not only are paranoids not found to be more overinclusive than nonparanoids, but other pathological and normal groups demonstrate equal or greater overinclusion.

The emerging conclusion from our analysis at this point is that overinclusion may relate to the degree of pathology since the more pathological the individual, the more disorganized at the time of testing, and the greater the overinclusion score. On the other hand, high overinclusion does not necessarily have to represent greater pathology. A particular sample, due to unusual sampling or matching procedures, may produce a low overinclusion group that is of greater pathology as in the Knight study (Knight et al., 1977). In either case the level of task performance on many types of conceptual tasks does seem to relate to pathology rather than overinclusion as a thought process.

Until the two Type 4 events, diagnosis and pathology, are directly compared, our inference about overinclusion and pathology is only speculative. There are other possible explanations. For example, Gathercole (1965) suggests that the Payne test measures mainly excessive responding.

Overinclusives say too many words on the proverb test or hand over too many objects on the Goldstein Object sorting test. Hawks and Payne (1971) found some evidence for this hypothesis. They found the test measures over-responsiveness, and this was especially true for delusional patients. Payne (1971) also concluded that the overinclusive measure may not be reflecting a conceptual process but may reflect verbosity. But a relationship between pathology and overinclusion is also implied by this alternative. Those who are pathological also talk more especially if they are conceptual individuals like paranoids. Hence, it may be that the most pathological of the delusional patients are those who are overinclusive. Perhaps the most pathological paranoids are more overinclusive because they are not as secretive or guarded and, hence, provide many more responses as well as expressions of their delusions. If this is the case, it would explain why delusions and pathology are related to overinclusion. To test this hypothesis, research should focus on the delusional patients with high pathology who should be the most overinclusive.

The multidimensional nature of the measure involving the quantity of the response insures such results without indicating if a similar process is involved with different groups. For instance manics may produce a high overinclusive score by a large number of creative associations rather than idiosyncratic associations while paranoids may produce the opposite. Only further refinement of the measure can provide evidence of a common process independent of pathology if such exists. The finding of a relationship between other pathological groups and overinclusion does not lend much credence to the belief that overinclusion is characteristic of paranoids or even schizophrenics, although there seems to be some relationship. We continue to look at the question of who is overinclusive as we discuss what overinclusion is. At this point, we might possibly conclude that some paranoids are overinclusive. In dealing with the construct, we may find further evidence that the more pathological (paranoid and nonparanoid) are the overinclusives.

What Is Overinclusion

In closely examining the nature of overinclusion, Payne proposed that overinclusion was an inability to filter out irrelevant stimuli (Payne & Caird, 1967). Such an inability would result in a longer reaction time, and hence Payne predicted a positive relationship between overinclusion and reaction time. Since some schizophrenics were found to be slow in response time (retarded), this factor was also hypothesized to affect reaction time. Therefore, it was hypothesized that the overinclusive schizophrenic would be most affected by distracting stimuli, which in the Payne and Caird (1967) study ranged from tones to background conversation. In this study, they concluded that overinclusion measured by the Benjamin proverb test consistently correlated with reaction time. Overinclusive schizophrenics had significantly slower reaction times in all conditions, whether or not distractors were present. Closer analysis revealed that the nonoverinclusive schizophrenics, although showing a faster reaction time in all conditions, were affected by the distractors in twice as many conditions than the overinclusive schizophrenics. That is, although overinclusive schizophrenics always had slower reaction times than the nonoverinclusive schizophrenics, the nonoverinclusive schizophrenics significantly decrease their reaction time when presented with distractors. However, the differential effect of the distractors on the two groups wasn't significant. The only significant result was that overinclusive schizophrenics were slower over all conditions. We argue that Payne's analysis is questionable.

The one significant result relating overinclusion to reaction time was obtained only when overinclusive and nonoverinclusive schizophrenics were incorporated into a correlational analysis of overinclusive scores and reaction time. There was a significant low correlation (range .28 to .45) between reaction-time distraction scores and average words per proverb. But, this may be as much the result of the low distraction scores of some of the nonoverinclusive schizophrenics as the high distraction score of some of the overinclusive. Hence, contrary to Payne's interpretation of his data, if one follows a strict interpretation of the significance in the results presented, opposite conclusions can be drawn. Nonoverinclusive patients are affected by distractions in a reaction-time situation at least as much as overinclusive schizophrenics, contrary to Payne's hypothesis. The two empirical dimensions of overinclusive scores and distraction scores correlate, sharing around 20% of common variance at the most, but provide little information about which group contributes to this common variance.

When the data is analyzed by paranoid–nonparanoid diagnosis the results yield conclusions contrary to the overinclusion analysis. The paranoids are significantly affected by distractors in five of the six distraction conditions while the nonparanoid is affected by the distractor in one of the six distractor conditions. The distractors affected the paranoids and underinclusive subjects in a similar way. In the overinclusion analysis, the overinclusive subjects were only significantly affected in the two most severely distracting conditions while the nonoverinclusive schizophrenics were affected in the four conditions, two of which were mild or moderate distraction conditions. In short, although the usual expectation is that paranoids will be overinclusive, they performed more like the underinclusive subjects. Although paranoids were slower overall, an analysis of variance indicated that they were not differentially affected by distractor conditions. In short, the results could be interpreted as indicating that both paranoids and nonparanoids are affected by distractors but paranoids are affected in a way similar to underinclusives, not overinclusives.

Overinclusive schizophrenics are less affected than nonoverinclusive schizophrenics when comparing the reaction time with distractors to reaction time without distractors. Overinclusive scores and reaction-time distractor scores correlate, but this may be due to the inclusion of nonoverinclusive schizophrenics in the analysis. In summary, the relationship of overinclusion, reaction-time distraction, and diagnosis is not clear from the Payne data. The two dimensions, overinclusion and paranoid status, do not coincide as expected by Payne.

The results indicate, however, that one aspect of overinclusion is related to distractability. That is, a proverb test score is related to reaction-time distractibility—the less the overinclusion on the proverb test, the greater the effect of the distractor and the greatest overall retardation. In other words, the more verbal the individual, the less the effects of distraction and the faster the reaction time. But the significance of this finding is uncertain because of some problems in the study. The use of the proverb test as a measure of overinclusion is questionable since it seems clear that the test does not relate to other overinclusive measures. Another problem is the validity of clinical diagnosis, which was used to determine paranoid status since both paranoids and nonparanoids were found to be overinclusive.

Payne, Hochberg, and Hawks (1970) continued to test the filter term by employing the same design in examining overinclusion and distraction but using a dichotic stimulation task. The filter term was again used but discarded when the measures of conceptual overinclusion did not relate to measures of perceptual overinclusion as predicted from a generalized filter process. This study used an auditory shadowing technique to assess the amount of interference that occurs when one message is presented to one ear and distractors are presented to the other. The overinclusion measures were object sorting and proverbs. As in the previous study, there is a large difference between Payne's interpretation of the results and the actual data. The presentation of irrelevant words into the word list through the opposite ear caused the overinclusive group to produce more errors in repeating the list of words than when no distractions were present. Payne et al. (1970) note that they made "30 times as many errors when the distracting words were presented in the other ear [p. 189]."Nonoverinclusives made 48 times as many errors and controls made 50 times as many errors. Payne concluded that the overinclusive group made more mistakes since they began at a higher baseline. He argued that the higher error rate in the baseline condition of the overinclusive is further evidence of their susceptibility to distractors, such as distraction caused by internal thoughts or being in the testing situation. But since the distracting condition was the operational definition of the effect of the distractor, the ratios of errors in the distracting condition are the data relevant to Payne's original hypothesis. Based on such data, the overinclusives were found to be less distracted than the nonoverinclusives.

When the material presented was prose passages rather than isolated words, there were differential effects. Overinclusion and nonoverinclusion group differences disappeared although both groups differed from normals. The trends revealed that normals decreased their errors with distractors while overinclusives doubled their errors. Nonoverinclusive schizophrenics were at the same approximate high position as in the nondistraction condition. In short, a prose passage (a message with context) had its greatest effect on the overinclusives.

The results of the study, however, are limited by certain methodological problems. For example, the overinclusive status of the subjects was clinically determined, but in actual tests of overinclusion, the non-A measure and the Object Sorting test, the overinclusive did not differ from the nonoverinclusive schizophrenic. There is a strong possibility that through the clinical designation of the overinclusive group, the degree of pathology was the basis of determining overinclusion. If such was the case (Harrow et al., 1973), the findings are not informative of overinclusion as usually defined.

What is useful is Payne's theoretical distinction between perceptual overinclusion and conceptual overinclusion. The shadowing tests are designed to measure the former and the overinclusion tests to measure the latter. Tests measuring perceptual overinclusion do not correlate with tests of conceptual overinclusion. But since both concepts relate to the clinical judgment of overinclusion, although not in any clear or predictable fashion, all measures probably reflect degree of pathology. Harrow et al. (1972) also distinguish between types of overinclusion. They found that conceptual overinclusion was a more powerful measure for separating schizophrenics from nonschizophrenics and predicting the presence of delusions. On the other hand, the behavioral overinclusion measure, the Non-A score which is the quantity measure used by Payne, did not significantly relate to delusions. Their results indicate that conceptual overinclusion is related to idiosyncratic thinking while behavioral overinclusion is related to the number of rich associations, a measure indicative of originality and creativity.

These findings are confirmed in an analysis of two overinclusion measures. Foulds et al. (1967a) investigated the Proverbs and Object Classification tests and found little relationship between them. Furthermore they found four different types of sorting responses in the Non-A score. Two of these measures account for 75% of the responses and, according to the authors, had little to do with Payne's description of overinclusion. Their analysis suggests that the overinclusion score is multidimensional and one factor is concrete bizarreness or repetitiveness, which is distinctively different from overinclusion as a measure of broad conceptual categories.

In summary, the Payne sorting measure seems to relate mostly to pathology and idiosyncratic thinking rather than category–width as intended.

Overinclusion and Strength of Association

In light of the findings that question the measure and its referents, it is not surprising that other investigators who have used other experimental tasks to operationalize overinclusion have been more successful in relating overinclusion to paranoia. For example, Craig (1965) described overinclusion as overincluding concepts, a definition similar to Payne's and Cameron's. He used a verbal breadth of association test in which the subject had to judge whether the word was an essential element of the concept, or a close or remote association. Inclusion of remote associations was labeled breadth of association. Craig found that the paranoids more often chose the more close or remote associations as essential. This result was repeated in a study by Gonen (1970) who used a Chapman (1958) measure. Subjects were required to select, from three choices, the word which together with the presented word formed a concept. One choice was irrelevant and one was an associate, some creatively linked with the initial test word. Good paranoids chose more "creative" associates than good nonparanoids, indicating that they more often ignored the common associate and chose more remote and possibly more interesting associations. In both studies in which overinclusion refers to an incorporation of objects into a conceptual category, the results indicate that paranoids have the broadest width.

The studies reviewed to this point suggest that there are at least two possible factors in the usual overinclusion measure, each related to different types of associations, one idiosyncratic and one creative. Associations may appear more idiosyncratic because the conceptual categories are more personal or because they are loose. Or as described by Payne, they appear idiosyncratic because there are so many more associates in the category than normal.

Evidence for idiosyncratic categories due to loose association is available. The relationship of overinclusion as a process of disorganization which relates to degree of pathology or to a condition of stress has been discussed by Harrow et al. (1972, 1973). Eliseo (1963) found that medical patients under stress exhibited greater overinclusion. Koh, Kayton, and Schwartz (1974) found that idiosyncratic responses in sorting mainly increased under time pressure, and noted that overinclusive performance could be a function of task difficulty. They found that by increasing the time demands to complete the task, nonparanoid schizophrenics became disorganized, becoming less constrictive and more idiosyncratic. With no time pressure the nonparanoid schizophrenic organized material in the same way as normals. The suggestion here is that the determining factor of disorganization is the drive state induced by the experimenter. It must be noted in this case that the effect was found with nonparanoid schizophrenics, so that these results are not informative of overinclusion and paranoia.

Although the work with overinclusion does lead to interesting speculations, it should be apparent that the measure is too broad to provide any real clarity in regard to the cognitive processes in schizophrenia. In effect, the progression from Cameron to Payne seems to raise more questions than confirm any of the initial propositions. The Bannister construct of loose construing, meaning an inconsistency of category usage, is just as vague as the overinclusive term mainly because it is so one-dimensional. The idea of reducing cognition to one process seems to be a bit too wishful at this time mainly because we are beginning to understand the complexity involved in cognition.

Scott (1969) describes a model which demonstrates the interacting dimensions required to assess differences in conceptual structure. There are three types of personal attributes: affective, evaluative, and descriptive. There is only one affective component—an emotional good–bad reaction. Evaluative attributes also contain a good–bad component, but also an objective component such as kind–cruel. Descriptive attributes such as small–large are purely objective and tell you nothing about how the speaker feels about an object. Whether an attribute is descriptive or evaluative depends upon how it is used. If the usage of a bipolar adjective pair correlates with the usage of the good–bad dimension, then the attribute is evaluative. If the usage of a bipolar adjective pair is independent of the affective attribute, it is descriptive.

The particular relationship of the attributes and the manner in which adjectives are applied to a number of objects provide specific cognitive elements comprising cognitive complexity. One concept in the system is *Dimensionality*—the number of independent dimensions a person is capable of applying to a set of objects. It corresponds to the number of factors which would result from a factor analysis of the way a person described and sorted objects. If two attributes are highly correlated, such as pretty–ugly and sophisticated–unsophisticated, they do not represent independent dimensions but rather are grouped on the same dimension for that individual. Another element is *Articulation,* which is the number of reliable distinctions that a person can make between objects on a given attribute. For example, if the objects were colored, an unarticulated individual would find that colors were indistinguishable. However, an individual with a more articulated color dimension would be able to make many discriminations between colors.

A person's cognitive system may be organized in a variety of ways. If evaluative attributes are highly correlated with the affective attribute, Affective–Evaluative Consistency will exist with objects being liked to the extent that they are seen as possessing desirable traits, or objects are seen as possessing desirable traits to the extent that they are liked. In Affective–Evaluative Consistency, the evaluative attributes will be highly correlated with each other and with the affective attribute. Domain–Ambivalence exists if objects are seen positively on one evaluative attribute and negatively on another. In domain ambivalence, the evaluative attributes will not correlate with each other. A person's cognitive space also may be organized by making one attribute central—applying one attribute to many objects. Centralization is the proportion of objects to which the most-used attribute is applied minus the average proportion of objects other attributes apply to. Centralization would vary from all objects being seen in terms of one and only one attribute to the condition where a different attribute is applied to each object. A person's most central attribute could presumably be either affective, evaluative, or descriptive. Rather than having just one central attribute, a person could use a set of attributes to judge all objects. This method of cognitive organization is classified as Image-Comparability. All objects are evaluated in terms of a specific set of relatively independent attributes.

A cognitive model such as that of Scott (1969, 1974a) demonstrates the complexity involved in studying conceptualization. None of the research in schizophrenia has followed this lead and investigated multiple interacting conceptual processes. Interestingly, Scott (1974b) has moved toward examining the manner in which the various conceptual processes are integrated and has presented some evidence that deviance is related to the degree that specific cognitive dimensions lack integration (Scott, 1974a). This work on the integration of conceptual processes parallels our conception of the integration of cognitive processing in schizophrenia, discussed in Chapter 7.

Although our analysis of conceptual theories may have enlightened us about some of the processes involved, it hasn't fully described the cognitive processes unique to schizophrenia or schizophrenic subgroups. In a later chapter, we look more closely at the information-processing results to specify more clearly the stages or levels of conceptualization involved in such an endeavor, but first we discuss the inhibition theorists.

I, THEORISTS

I, theories emphasize the inhibitions required in order for *V* or *K* process to proceed correctly. The *V* theorists are interested in how the schizophrenic is distracted by the properties of *S*—that is, by the inordinate number of perceptions received. The *K* theorists are concerned with conceptual problems in the sense of too few or too many associations being elicited by *S*. An emphasis upon the process that modulates the *V* and *K* processes permits the development of an inhibition theory. In previous discussion (Magaro, 1974), this type of theory was considered a combination of *V* and *K*. We modify that position to focus on the implied theoretical construct I, which is hypothesized to underlie both perceptual and conceptual processes. I_r theoretical positions attempt to explain how the schizophrenic fails to inhibit S properties either at the perceptual or conceptual level.

Buss and Lang

Buss and Lang (Buss & Lang, 1965; Lang & Buss, 1965) in their general literature review of schizophrenia present a broad interference theory, which seems to be an inhibition theory focusing upon the effect of I_r on V:

> Interference theory has focused mainly on association and attention-set. The associations of schizophrenics are idiosyncratic and deviant, and they deteriorate performance because they serve as distractors. Schizophrenics have difficulty in focusing on relevant stimuli, in maintaining a set over time, in shifting a set when it is necessary, in instructing themselves and in pacing themselves, and generally in performing efficiently.... The generality of interfering effects suggest a fundamental sensori-motor defect.... The locus of the sensori-motor defect is a matter for speculation. It seems clear that the defect is not at the level of the peripheral sensors or effectors, although feedback from the musculature and the ANS may contribute to the disturbance.... This raises the interesting possibility that the motor and perceptual symptoms of schizophrenia are related to defects in this carotid–cortical mechanism.... External stimuli, associational and biological "noise," routinely suppressed by normal subjects, intrude, and responses to the appropriate stimuli are not made. These facts suggest that researchers in schizophrenia should concentrate on the processes by which stimuli adapt out or habituate and response competition is resolved. The ascending reticular activating system is the neurological site of greatest relevance.... The data on the schizophrenic deficit are consistent with the hypotheses that such sensory inhibition centers are defective [Lang & Buss, 1965, pp. 97–98].

The external competing stimuli in the experimental situation are not inhibited by the schizophrenic, thus disrupting his performance. The internal stimuli are idiosyncratic associations which are also not inhibited, interfering with performance. The explanation of the effect of external stimuli is, therefore, similar to the formulations of the V theorists while the explanation of the effect of internal stimuli is similar to the K theorists. There is some suggestion in the use of a sensory inhibition construct and in the emphasis upon attentional problems leading to conceptual deficits (Buss & Lang, 1965) that the basic problem is perceptual inhibition, $V \times I_r$:

> Excessively broad attention should lead to overinclusive concepts; excessively narrow attention should lead to overexclusive concepts; alternating between too-broad and too-short attention should lead to both overinclusive errors and

overexclusive errors. This second variant of the interference hypothesis appears to be a promising explanation of schizophrenic deficit in the conceptual area [p. 17].

Although it is never explicitly stated, the weight of the statements implies that interference is the result of the lack of stimulus inhibition. Therefore, the use of V and K constructs are secondary to an inability to inhibit irrelevant stimuli. The research evidence used by Buss to support the perceptual interference position is the same as used by the V theorists while the evidence used to support the conceptual interference position is the same as that used by a K theorist. However, the K concept used by Buss and Lang (1965) is not the highly dominant associational process by Chapman but rather the highly variable number of associations of Cameron. Lang and Buss consider the problem to be a low K, a great number of associations elicited by S which interfere with performance. In summary, the authors accept the empirical constructs and research of the K and V theorists and offer the more intangible inhibition concept to explain the process basic to both.

As with the V and K terms, I_r is a theoretical term that must be tied to observation. Hull (1943) states that:

> Inhibitory potential (I_r) is an unobservable and so has the status of a logical construct with all the advantages and disadvantages characteristic of such scientific concepts. In this connection it will be recalled that the prime prerequisite for the proper use of the unobservables in scientific theory is that they be anchored in a quantitatively unambiguous manner (a) to observable antecedent conditions or events, or (b) to observable consequent conditions or events [p. 278].

Unfortunately the I_r term used by Buss and Lang is never tied to independent empirical observations. That is, it is never defined independent of K or V operations, and the same data and empirical constructs are used to infer the effects of the inhibition process. Without an attempt to define it independently of and in contrast to the opposing V or K process, there is no empirical justification for introducing a new construct to explain the same empirical laws.

In our terms, the observables and empirical laws of Shakow, Payne, McGhie, and Cameron are used by Buss and Lang to support an inhibition construct. As shown in Fig. 3.4, the construct is a theoretical level I construct. The empirical constructs which have produced such theoretical constructs I such as segmental set, overinclusive thinking, selective attention, etc., have been reinterpreted by the new theoretical construct I. The substitution of one

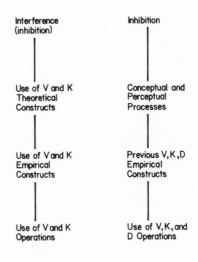

FIG. 3.4. Schematic representation of the theoretical structure of inhibition theories.

construct for all other terms would be a theoretical advance if the other empirical constructs and their operations were all highly correlated. In effect, the Buss and Lang position asserts that previously proposed constructs are measuring the operation of the same process, employing in our terms, a massive semantical construct invention. A strong relationship between the different operations has rarely been found (Payne et al., 1970; Weckowicz & Blewett, 1959), hence, we agree that the different constructs may be measuring different processes and support the Buss (Lang & Buss, 1965) analysis:

> In many instances the range of tasks used to study the deficit is not sufficient to sustain the broad conclusions of the investigators. For example, on the basis of demonstrated deficiency on conceptual tasks, some researchers have concluded that the basic problem of the schizophrenic deficit is an inability to handle concepts. Taken at face value, this conclusion is an overgeneralization because of the absence of evidence that schizophrenics show no deficit on nonconceptual tasks. In light of the evidence with conceptual tasks, the conclusion is patently false. Generalizations about schizophrenic deficit require a sampling of tasks that tap a variety of psychological functions. It would be considerable help if we knew more about what various task are measuring and their relations to each other [p. 99].

Buss (1966) also posits a construct beyond the theoretical level I. The neurophysiological sensori-motor deficit explains why the inhibition occurs in terms of specific neurological functions. At this level, he recognizes the speculative nature of his construct.

In summary, Buss incorporates *V* and *K* theories into one theory and calls for further research to examine the relationships between operations to see if the differences in present theories are more than a case of semantic inventions. We follow Buss's direction in our attempt to integrate terms but go further and specify what process or term is appropriate for schizophrenics and paranoids. We also differ from Buss by focusing on the process of integration rather than inhibition.

Maher

Another *I,* theorist is Maher (1972), who explains the performance deficit from the vantage point of schizophrenic language:

> The central feature of this hypothesis is that the attentional disturbance believed to affect the processing of sensory input also underlies the failure to inhibit associations from intruding into language utterances.... From this point of view, the utterance of normal, coherent speech may be seen as the result of the successful and instantaneous inhibition of associations to elements in the utterance [p. 12].

Like Buss, this position asserts that inhibition fails to operate in both the perceptual and conceptual areas. However, emphasis is upon the conceptual associations that are reflected in language. Each sentence is a chain of stimuli which produce many associations. While irrelevant associations are inhibited in the normal, associations compete with the relevant associations in the schizophrenic to produce what is sometimes considered a confusion of semantics. The schemata of this position is presented in Fig. 3.4.

As with Buss and Cameron, Maher considers the resultant conceptual state to be at low *K*. Evidence of looseness of thought or speech would be indirect evidence for a lack of inhibition. A recent study by Reilly, Harrow, Tucker, Quinlan, and Siegel (1975) is relevant to Maher's hypothesis. They investigated the looseness of associations in schizophrenic speech and found that deviant verbalizations were prominent mainly in schizophrenics especially on measures of looseness of associations. However, they also note that looseness of association is present in all acute patients. This study poses a problem for the Maher position since any lack of inhibition of associations should be demonstrated with only acute schizophrenics and not other acute psychiatric groups.

Reilly et al. (1975) also suggest that the anxiety associated with hospital admission increases the amount of conceptual looseness. This observation fits Maher's position, which hypothesizes that arousal contributes to schizophrenic language. The introduction of the arousal factor based upon the Venables (1964) theory implies that Maher's position is a variant of arousal theory. However, it is clear that for Maher the causal process which affects the range of attention is that of inhibition.

The criticism against Buss and Lang is applicable to Maher since a theoretical term is used which does not have its own empirical referents. However, although evidence is not a central part of his presentation, Maher mentions work examining the editing process in schizophrenic speech that could be an empirical construct for his theory. Some recent work, notably by Cohen, Nachmani, and Rosenberg (1974), indicate that such editing deficits are mainly related to the nonparanoid. This suggests that the loose associations noted by Maher are characteristic of the nonparanoid. There is also, however, some evidence that the loose associations or a failure to edit is a function of pathology. The self-editing studies will be discussed later in the information-theory chapter. For now, we can tentatively conclude that the nonparanoid does not show the same strength of associates as the paranoid or the normal. But it is not clear whether the problem is one of editing, an I_r process, or weak associational sets as proposed by the K theorists.

The difference between the Maher theory and the S language theory of Salzinger (1971) should be clarified, since one purpose of using the Hullian model is to permit differentiating between theories even though they seem to be discussing the same process. The Salzinger theory contends that the stimulus, be it the last word in the sentence or another presented word, has the quality of appearing without context. Hence, the response reflected in language is the last direct association to that stimulus. Maher goes one step further and posits a process within the individual—inhibition—that explains why such phenomena would occur. The Salzinger position is more parsimonious, but as mentioned above, it does not seem particularly relevant to the explanation of the schizophrenic condition especially since the operations are greatly removed from the eventual theoretical construct. The advantage of the Maher position is that it permits hypotheses to be generated about the actual schizophrenic process which can generate hypotheses concerning performance in other tasks.

Other empirical constructs and recent work suggest that constructs such as inhibition or interference are too broad to provide much empirical meaning. If producing meaningful language involves a sequential process of detecting stimuli, placing them in short- and long-term memory, and of subjective conceptual organization, the stage at which the inhibition process is deficient must be determined. The inhibition theorist has not demonstrated that inhibition is a unitary process which affects all stages of information processing, nor that *V* and *K* are equally subject to its disabling effect.

Most *V* theorists use an inhibition term. They differ from Buss and Maher in that inhibition, usually in the form of a filter concept, is usually at the theoretical II level. The inhibition term used by Buss and Maher are at the Theoretical I level. At the empirical level, a large number of associations are expected by the *K* theorist such as Cameron or Bannister or attention to a wide range of stimuli is predicted by the *V* theorists. While the *I,* theorist infers from the same empirical laws the operation of a defective inhibition process, a *V* or *K* theorist does not require an inhibition term to explain the empirical findings. Hence, the burden of proof rests on the theorist postulating the inhibition process and its action in the predicted manner. For the present, there is no evidence exclusively supporting inhibition as compared to a deficit in the processes proposed by either the *V* or *K* theorist.

INTEGRATION THEORY

The theoretical framework we are developing strongly suggests the direction to be taken in explicating our position on the cause of the schizophrenic performance deficit. The multiple processes, specified by Hull as entering into a behavioral act, emphasize the complexity of psychological processes involved even in the completion of a simple task.

The integration approach to be introduced goes beyond distinguishing multiple processes. The integration construct proposes, in addition, that the deficit is exhibited in a task that requires a combination of terms and is the state produced by the simultaneous action of two processes. In a sense we are speaking of a term that states that the deficit is derived from an interaction of many parts and is greater than the sum of the parts. The schemata of the position is presented in Fig. 3.5.

The positive results with all previous theoretical approaches suggests that a study of just one process—be it perceptual, conceptual, motivational, etc.— may be too narrow a view of the elephant to provide any clear or cogent explanation of the whole animal. At this point, we reiterate our proposition that any study which has used the usual experimental procedure, supposedly manipulating one variable, perceptual or conceptual, while keeping others constant, and which has found the schizophrenic to deviate from others, has, in effect, produced an epiphenomenon. Most studies have unavoidably been observing the operation of at least two psychological processes, although assuming to examine one. Thus, the resultant deficit seems to be due to the integration process necessary to perform an action combining two processes.

Another way to examine the integrational defect is to consider task performance as a constant dialectic. Dichotomous processes, somewhat like

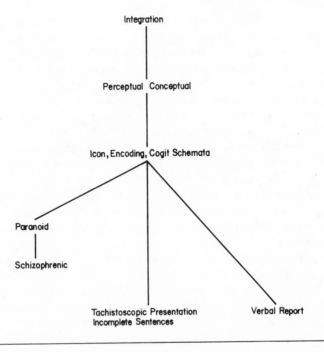

Integration

|

Perceptual Conceptual

|

Icon, Encoding, Cogit Schemata

Paranoid

|

Schizophrenic

Tachistoscopic Presentation
Incomplete Sentences

Verbal Report

V ˣ K / I   Magaro

FIG. 3.5.   Schematic representation of the theoretical structure of integration theory.

chords in music, work toward resolution. The successful resolution or synthesis, the harmony in our analogy, would be the integration of the two processes that would be productive and correct. Failure to synthesize correctly would indicate an overwhelming dominance of one process over the other and would yield an unsatisfactory synthesis that would be expressed in a deficit.

The reaction-time work of Shakow, we have just discussed, exemplifies this integrational process. Shakow (1962) has shown that as more elements are added to a task, length or variableness of PI, intensity of stimuli, etc., the schizophrenic did worse than the normal. If the task was made very simple in that the task only required an immediate response to presented stimuli, the schizophrenic deficit disappeared. The deficit increased as more demands were made in the task. The explanation was that a major set, or ability to maintain an overall perspective in the face of the demand of presented stimuli, was lacking. The interpretation of these same results using integration theory is that the schizophrenic could not integrate the perceptual and conceptual demands of the task, and as the number of task demands increased so did the deficit. It was not that the set could not be maintained but that the reciprocal activity of two processes could not be maintained. The process necessary to sustain a synchronized operation of two separate processes was lacking. The integration of the multitude of human systems is not performed as adequately by the schizophrenic as by the normal. It should be noted, however, that Shakow (1962) toys with an integration concept when he recognizes that the schizophrenic does not maintain the integration of the normal, although specific localized patterns of behavior may be intact. In fact, he suggests the need of the schizophrenic to function in separate subsystems that form basic minor sets, which are perceptual and conceptual. The schizophrenic is unable to integrate the perceptual and conceptual sets.

The characteristics of the task are crucial in understanding what processes are being elicited and what degree of integrational demand is required in a specific task. It becomes all the more important to understand the specified task response, R, in terms of the multiple processes that are merged in a particular operationalized empirical construct. Although the importance of R in its bearing on the degree of the deficit has been recognized, especially in terms of the feedback quality of R utilized by schizophrenics, we are suggesting that the requisite for a deficit is that R includes more than one process. The experimental conditions that evoke more than one process create a greater deficit, be those additional processes, feedback, conceptual, motivational, or habit dispositional demands.

An integration theory validation would require a description of how existing work could be interpreted within such a framework—that is, how the existing empirical laws could be explained by the new theoretical construct. To illustrate, the operation of an integration theory, as it applies to the schizophrenic performance deficit, requires a consideration of the processes involved in a task. The sequential components that are combined and result in a specific response have to be examined. One way of testing the integration theory itself would .be to compare similar groups on tasks that exemplify discrete segments of the task. Ideally, it would be best to present in one experimental situation variations of task components in all their permutations and to assess the relative deficits during the integration of specific combinations. We elaborate on this strategy when we present the information-processing model.

Figure 3.5 presents the level of analysis of the integration term and demonstrates the similarity of the theory to other perceptual and conceptual theories. Findings from the theorists previously discussed can be explained by an integration term at a theoretical construct II level. What is more important is that the task performance of specific schizophrenic subgroups would be expected to differ according to the type of dialectical resolution made to the integration dilemma. It would be expected that most previous work would be confirmatory mainly because most tasks are omnibus process measures requiring at least two different processes. The present organization of theories hopefully illustrates the different but related sequence in human functioning that is emphasized by each theorist. The vertical or deductive method of hypothesis testing requires an adherence to one term in the initial testing of a theory. The failure to progress beyond the exploration of one term may have created a blindness to the most important process—that of integration.

4

D, $_sH_r$, and Their Interactions as Theories of Schizophrenia

The preceding chapter focused on theories about processes that are directly stimulus related. The present chapter discusses those theories that are more structural in that they focus on processes more characteristic of the organism. The previous V and K processes may be seen as more dynamic in that they ask how the schizophrenic processes information during a constant interaction with the environment. The theories in this chapter hypothesize a process that is more of an action upon the environment and less of a reaction to environmental conditions. For example, we examine the field-dependency literature and find that the schizophrenic is depicted as field-independent or field-dependent. The point is that he exists in a predisposed state determined either by early learning or genetics. In that sense, the theorists to be discussed emphasize structural rather than dynamic states in hypothesizing about processes that usually are not subject to change.

The two major constructs examined in this chapter are those of habit and drive. The tasks relevant to those constructs are the Embedded Figures Test (EFT), size estimation, and those involving galvanic skin responses (GSR). The EFT and size estimation tasks are presented as habit constructs to emphasize their structural characteristics. Analysis of studies using these tasks demonstrates that they do not measure any one trait because they confound multiple processes. We argue that the findings can be best understood in tems of the more dynamic V or K process. Our discussion of the drive theorists questions whether or not the construct measures anything unique to schizophrenia. At best, we can infer the operation of perceptual processing. Consistent with the aim of the previous chapter, we intend to provide a historical perspective by critically examining previous operational definitions of psychological processes considered unique to paranoia and schizophrenia.

Dd THEORISTS

The theories which present a *Dd* view of the schizophrenic performance deficit usually postulate a schizophrenic deficiency in a specific drive system that differentiates the schizophrenic from other psychopathological groups and normals. The *Dd* deficiency could be seen as biological with a hereditary base although certain early experiences may be proposed to have this same effect. For example, the schizophrenic may need stimulation or social approval or human contact, and this need is the dominant motivation in an experimental situation. For example, Meehl (1962) uses this concept in a diathesis–stress model. He postulates an integrated neural deficit which produces the basic schizophrenic characteristics of cognitive slippage, anhedonia, interpersonal aversiveness, and ambivalence. The use of the anhedonia concept, which views the schizophrenic as unable to perceive pleasure because of a deficiency in the pleasure centers, is the clearest drive explanation. If anhedonia is viewed as fundamental and "a direct consequence of the genetic defect in wiring" (Meehl, 1962, p. 832), ambivalence, interpersonal aversiveness, and cognitive slippage would all be consequences of this basic disorder. Meehl's position exemplifies the use of a deprivation drive construct to explain the performance deficit. The schizophrenic is observed to be deficient in positive emotions and excessive in his avoidance motivation. The imbalance in the appetitive control system therefore predisposes him to develop the other characteristics which would explain most laboratory results.

Mednick (1958) speaks in terms of a general drive concept, *D,* but equates drive with other deprivation states such as thirst and hunger, and hence, also employs the present usage of *Dd:*

> All of the above may be taken to suggest that acute schizophrenics are organisms in a state of heightened drive. Hull's theory and extensions of this theory make specific predictions of the effect of this heightened drive state of behavior. In general, the effect of heightened drive is to increase the response strength of any habit tendencies that may be aroused in a given situation. Thus, in general, the hungrier, or more anxious, or more fearful the organism, the greater his drive and the greater the speed and amplitude of his responses [p. 317].

Although other drive constructs are sometimes used to explain the schizophrenic thought disorder, *Dd* is the primary elementary factor which creates the performance deficit.

$\bar{D}$ THEORISTS

One $\bar{D}$ theorist is *Venables* (1964), who considers the deficit to be caused by arousal disturbing the operation of a filter mechanism so that it does not function to screen out irrelevant stimuli. At one level, the theory seems to parallel a V theory, since the main behavioral problem is that of a perceptual dysfunction, which is labeled the span of attention. However, Venables is not a V theorist nor a $V \times \bar{D}$ theorist because V and $\bar{D}$ are not viewed as acting independently to influence task behavior. Rather, V is present as a direct function of $\bar{D}$. There are further theoretical constructs inferred which deal with the neurophysiological processes responsible for the abnormal arousal states of the schizophrenic, but they are not specifically stated and are not an integral part of the theory. Arousal is the main term. In perceptual or attentional performance, arousal creates a restriction or expansion of the attentional field, an effect similarly explained by Easterbrook's (1959) range of cue utilization construct. To support his own position Venables (1964) uses most of the V theorists' work. Schizophrenic subgroup differences are an integral part of the theory. For example, an overly broad or narrow attention exhibited by schizophrenics is related to the chronicity dimension.

Figure 4.1 presents a schemata of the empirical and theoretical constructs in the Venables input dysfunction theory. In the simplest form, the observables are those employed in previous work to operationalize the empirical constructs of size constancy, distance constancy, perception of relevant and irrelevant stimuli, overinclusion, stimulus generalization, and others relevant to the theoretical construct I, span of attention. A great deal of divergent data is organized clearly through the use of this theoretical construct. The actual span of attention, narrow or broad, however, is presented as a direct function of the theoretical construct II, arousal. What is most important, however, is that arousal has its own empirical laws which are explained by the theoretical construct of cortical activation. While there is some minor evidence causally relating arousal to the span of attention construct (Callaway, 1959), most evidence presented is correlational, relating the level of arousal to the span of attention. Since there is a strong emphasis on arousal determining the span of attention, stronger evidence is required.

What is especially relevant to our interest is that Venables may be one of the first theorists to operationalize the paranoid–nonparanoid dimension through a behavioral scale. The scale basically breaks groups into delusional and hallucinatory subgroups corresponding to paranoids and nonparanoids. Results on laboratory tasks, even in terms of right or left ear auditory thresholds, indicate differences between groups (Venables, 1964). Hence although most theorists discussed the problem of schizophrenic heterogeneity, Venables operationalized the dimension and presented empirical performance differences.

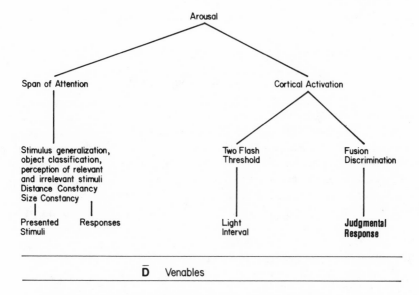

FIG. 4.1. Schematic representation of the theoretical structure of drive theories.

Thus, through a review of a great deal of data, considered by some to be rather selective (Epstein & Coleman, 1970), Venables (1964) develops a theoretical position with a specific set of operations closely tied to theoretical constructs. Although the interpretation of some arousal data is questionable (Magaro, 1972a; 1973), the theory is rather sophisticated and explains not only the different functions of specific schizophrenic subgroups and normals but also the relationship between theoretical constructs which have an empirical base. The weakness of this theory is the lack of strong support for the causal influences of $\bar{D}$ on V. Also there is a possibility that the psychophysiological measures cited are measuring a perceptual process rather than an arousal process. This problem is discussed later since it is a basic issue in drive theories.

In a recent update of his theory, Venables (1977) defends his use of the arousal term especially for the chronic patient. The theory employs neuropsychological terms (Venables, 1972) with a focus on the inhibition of the limbic system based mainly on the work of Gruzelier (Gruzelier & Venables, 1972, 1973, 1974). A new grouping of schizophrenics has emerged from this latter work, those who orient and do not orient on GSR measures. The groups do not correspond to the acute–chronic dimension since they are all mainly chronic. Speculations about the neurological base of this orienting response are made but there is only meager empirical support available. In time the importance of the neurological state should be clarified but the neglect of relating such measures to the acute condition is another weakness of this position.

(*Ds* + *Dd*) × *K* THEORIST

Mednick (1958) proposed a theory that is totally based on drive to explain the performance deficit by using two drive constructs interacting with a cognitive process. Drive produces a disorganization in behavior by primarily affecting thinking or the process of forming mediational associations. Although the Mednick position is never clearly stated, the basic paradigm describes the schizophrenic as being in high drive, which flattens the response hierarchy so that all responses, including thoughts, have an equal probability of occurrence. In addition, the schizophrenic is also fearful of specific situations, probably due to some painful event which occurred in the past. The initial stimulus eliciting fear is described as a precipitating event or a life crisis. It is assumed that such conditions exist and augment the initial drive level, *Dd*. Mednick (1958) states:

> In summary, we find that this precipitating incident has a number of uncomfortable consequences. The consequences above will tend to increase the individual's anxiety level. Unfortunately, this will, in turn serve to again raise the level and breadth of generalization responsiveness. Again, the effect of this will be to increase the probability of his encountering a fear arousing stimulus by increasing the number of such stimuli. Also, the amount of fear that a previously adequate stimulus could arouse will be increased. Again, the individual's total anxiety level is likely to continue to rise....
>
> Assuming continued stimulation from the world and/or continued thinking, this reciprocal augmentation of anxiety and generalization could theoretically continue unabated until some upper physiological limit of anxiety and/or generalization is reached [pp. 321–322].

Ds, anxiety, therefore, augments the initial high drive, *Dd*, creating an extremely high anxious, high drive (*Ds* + *Dd*) individual. The high drive also causes a great deal of stimulus generalization so that almost all stimuli including thoughts take on fear-producing qualities. Since thoughts similar to the original stimulus increase overall drive, only thoughts which are extremely remote from the initial stimulus are maintained. To the normal observer, these remotely associated thoughts appear bizarre and constitute the bizarre associations of the chronic patient.

In placing the Mednick theory into the present model we will attempt to clarify the assumptions and postulates which are implicit in what seems at first glance to be a relatively simple position. Mednick uses sets of observables from conditioning, serial learning, and stimulus generalization studies to test

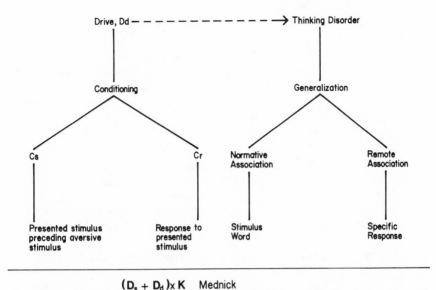

$$(D_s + D_d) \times K \quad \text{Mednick}$$

FIG. 4.2.   Schematic representation of the theoretical structure of drive by conceptual theories.

the hypothesis that schizophrenics are at a high drive. As illustrated in Fig. 4.2, Mednick uses the usual observables in a conditioning situation to derive the empirical laws relating to rate of conditioning. The differences in the speed of conditioning of schizophrenics and normals (schizophrenics being faster) would be explained by the theoretical construct of drive (schizophrenics are at a higher drive than normals). Results in generalization studies and complex learning studies all followed the same procedure, each empirical law being explained by a deprivation drive construct, Dd. Although Mednick is not specific on this point, he may have just as well proposed a $\bar{D}$, arousal, drive construct since only the general concept of drive, D, is specified. However, we will consider Dd to be the drive construct since it is the term specified by Mednick.

The theoretical development of Ds sharply contrast with the development of Dd. The latter begins with the functional relationship between variables which operationalize the empirical constructs. The empirical laws are then explained by a closely related theoretical construct. Ds, however, is only posited at the theoretical construct level without any evidence that it occurs or that it augments the initial high drive. Yet Ds is fundamental to the theory.

The theoretical construct K, number of associations, interacts with the drive terms to explain the disorganization of the schizophrenic. The experimental work of Cameron (previously discussed) provides much of the experimental support for the operation of the K construct proposed by

Mednick (1958). Most of the work indicates that when drive is varied there are changes in the number of remote associations. The differential functioning of schizophrenics and normals is explained by an empirical law that states that the thinking of high drive individuals is disrupted by the intrusion of remote and usually irrelevant thoughts which occur through the process of excessive generalization, the theoretical I construct. Such a disruption in thinking is hypothesized (Mednick, 1958) to explain the schizophrenic thought disorder, the explanatory theoretical construct II.

> Predictions from an extension of Hullian theory would suggest that the thinking of individuals with high drive would be disrupted by the intrusion of the remote and irrelevant thought units pushed above the threshold of awareness. The writer suggests that this action of high drive upon remote response tendencies is a major root of the disordered thinking of schizophrenics [p. 320].

As discussed by Lang and Buss (1965), this theory (especially the conditions specified for the interaction of Dd, Ds, and K) does not seem unique to schizophrenia. Though the theory has generated a great deal of research, no empirical support has been found for it. One difficulty which may explain the lack of supportive findings is the imprecision in relating constructs to operations or in demonstrating the logical relationship between constructs. As noted by Broen (1968), the theory is also deficient in the correct usage of Hullian terms and prediction.

While some similarities exist between the positions of Mednick and Venables, especially in their common usage of drive terms, there is one distinct and important difference. Mednick states that D increases all response probabilities, both dominant and alternate, to equal levels. Venables (1964), in an excellent critique of the Mednick position, presents evidence that D does not flatten the response hierarchy but rather increases the probability of all responses in the same order. That is, the dominant responses become more dominant and have an even higher probability of occurring.

Mednick (Mednick & Schulsinger, 1968) has revised the theory and moved away from an arousal (D) position to use a Ds term, conditioned avoidance, similar to that employed by Rodnick and Garmezy. According to this revision, the schizophrenic avoids anxiety by thinking remote thoughts. When such action becomes rewarding because of the reduction in drive, the avoidance response of disordered thought is learned. Since the schizophrenic has a greater autonomic responsivity and a faster return to basal after an emotional response (faster recovery rate) he tends to learn avoidance responses more quickly than normals. This revision does not eliminate the problems with the use of theoretical terms and with the lack of supporting data (Chapman & Chapman, 1973). The theory is still in a stage of development using a strategy of studying high risk populations which cannot be assessed at this point in time.

Arousal or drive operations used by Venables and Mednick will be examined in detail. They both have made predictions about drive using anxiety or arousal as their terms and employing data from GSR measurement. We will examine the validity of such operations.

BASAL LEVEL—GSR

Although there are many operational definitions of D, we will only examine one of the D measures—that of the galvanic skin response—and only in terms of tonic level and GRS amplitude. In using the terms—basal level and reactivity—we refer only to skin conductance since it is that measure which has mainly been used by the D theorists. Other psychophysiological measures may not be comparable and may be measuring quite different processes (Mandler, Mandler, Kreman, & Shelitan, 1961). We will now examine the specific results found with schizophrenics on a skin conductance measure focusing on the validity of the arousal term as applied to schizophrenics.

Studies have reported conflicting results when comparing schizophrenics to normals on the galvanic skin response. Reviews of the literature (Lang & Buss, 1965) have indicated that schizophrenics exhibit higher, lower, and the same basal skin conductance (basal level) as normals, as well as exhibiting smaller or the same changes in skin conductance to specific stimuli (reactivity). One source of the inconsistent results is the methodological problems found in early work studying the relative position of schizophrenics and normals on the two psychophysiological measures. First, some of the between-group differences reported in some early studies are difficult to evaluate since they were determined by inspection of sample records without any statistical treatment being applied to group comparisons (Hock, Kubis, & Rourke, 1944; Solomon, Darrow, & Blaurock, 1939; Syz & Kinder, 1928). Second, methodological problems were noted in the procedure for obtaining the skin resistance measures (Malmo & Shagass, 1949) for which standardization procedures have been suggested (Lykken & Venables, 1971). Third, the conflicting findings are mainly the result of previous studies sampling different segments of the hospitalized population, and generalizing their findings to all schizophrenics. The manner in which schizophrenia has been operationalized has varied immensely, and in some cases there has been no attempt to operationalize the term. Some studies purportedly comparing schizophrenics with normals have actually compared psychotics and normals, wth the psychotic sample composed of schizophrenics and such diverse groups as mental deficients, organics, and manic depressives (Hock et al., 1944; Paintal, 1951). Other studies have used very specific schizophrenic subtypes as representative of the schizophrenic category. These subtypes are acute-paranoid schizophrenics (Jurko, Jost, & Hall, 1952), chronic-nonparanoid schizophrenics (Howe, 1958; Pishkin & Hershiser, 1963), acute-process schizophrenics (Williams, 1953), chronic schizophrenics (Pugh, 1965; Ray, 1963), or chronic-process and reactive schizophrenics (DeVault, 1957). In view of current work which has found schizophrenic subgroup differences on most performance and psychophysiological measures, it is not surprising that studies utilizing different schizophrenic subgroups and generalizing to the entire schizophrenic category should produce conflicting findings.

Much of the current work views the basal level and reactivity of schizophrenics as an interacting function of the three subject dimensions of chronicity (in terms of length of hospitalization), diagnosis (in terms of paranoid vs. nonparanoid), and a measure of the severity of the disorder (which we have discussed as level of pathology) (Goldstein & Acker, 1967; Silverman, 1964a; Venables, 1964). The severity measure has varied the most across studies. Some severity measures recently used are the degree of thought disturbance (Goldstein & Acker, 1967), the degree of responsiveness to the environment (Bernstein, 1964, 1967), the amount of withdrawal (Venables & Wing, 1962), and the level of premorbid functioning as found in the process–reactive or premorbid adjustment (Phillips, 1953) measures. The process–reactive and poor–good premorbid adjustment dimensions will be used synonymously because of the high degree of relationship that has consistently been found between the two measures (Garmezy, 1965).

Subject Variables and GSR

The effect of pathology or level of severity will be discussed first. Magaro (1972a) presented data on basal skin conductance and GSR for normals and schizophrenics who were divided in terms of chronicity and premorbid adjustment. The main result was that the poor-premorbid schizophrenic was at a higher basal level than the good-premorbid schizophrenic, and this difference was essentially due to the high basal level of the acute–poor premorbid group. The finding that the more severely disturbed schizophrenic, in terms of a premorbid adjustment measure, was at a higher basal level than the less severely disturbed schizophrenic conflicted with previous work using other severity measures. Bernstein (1967), using an environmental responsivity measure, and Goldstein and Acker (1967), using a degree of thought disturbance measure, found the least severely disturbed groups to exhibit a higher basal level than the more severely disturbed groups and normals. Venables and Wing (1962), using degree of withdrawal as a measure of severity found results comparable to the results of Magaro (1972a). Though the paranoid–nonparanoid dimension was used by Magaro (1972a), this effect was not fully explored due to a small number of paranoids available in each premorbid adjustment × chronicity subgroup.

Not only pathology, but chronicity and diagnosis have been found to affect GSR. A later study (Magaro, 1973) with a sufficient sample of paranoids examined the differential effects of chronicity and premorbid adjustment upon basal level and GSR of other hospitalized patient groups. A higher resting basal level (RBL)—a resting condition prior to any stimulus presentations—was found in the chronic good group when compared with other schizophrenic subgroups. The main effect of chronicity was due to the chronic paranoids who were significantly higher than the acute paranoids. When basal level was examined during the presentation of the experimental stimuli on fourteen trials (TBL), the premorbid adjustment dimension was most relevant. The chronic-good nonparanoid schizophrenics increased their basal level into the high range of the chronic-good paranoids. Consequently, the chronic goods were mainly responsible for the main effect of chronicity in the TBL situation.

The most obvious factor in the GSR results was that of medication. This was especially striking in view of the basal level results where medication exhibited no significance. Medication seemed to have a differential effect by decreasing the GSR for poors and paranoids. Group differences between poors and goods or between paranoids and schizophrenics consequently only occurred in the medicated groupings. This suggests that reported GSR reactivity differences between different schizophrenic subgroups resulted from medication suppressing the GSR of specific groups such as the poors and the paranoids.

Resting Basal Level

The overall interpretation of the BL results (Magaro, 1973) was that there were no differences in basal level or reactivity between schizophrenics and other groups. Any differences found were due to the effects of the experimental situation, S, upon specific patient groups, not limited to schizophrenics, who have undergone specific "treatments." To support this interpretation, we first analyzed the resting basal level situation. Usually, resting is defined in terms of the absence of any specific task or stimulus presentations for a long enough time period to establish a constant nonincreasing skin resistance. For most subjects, this condition is not an unrealistic expectation since the experimental situation soon becomes boring. Habituation occurs early allowing a determination of the basal level. However, for some subjects, the laboratory may be an extremely novel and possibly frightening situation to which one does not readily adapt. Whereas a V theorist would assume that S is common to normals and schizophrenics, with differences in performance due to differences in V, the same data could be interpreted to support an S view that recognizes that a difference in stimulus conditions produces group differences which could occur with groups of normals given the two *S* conditions.

This interpretation of the effects of the experimental situation is supported by a number of studies. Bernstein (1967) observed that the usual RBL condition does not necessarily reflect an absence of stimulation especially for hospitalized patients. The assumption that a laboratory RBL reflects an "habitual" level of activity has also been questioned by the finding that RBL at the place of domicile and in the laboratory differ. The laboratory basal level is at a higher level than an on-ward measure at least for heart rate (Zahn, 1964). Previous work has consistently reported the chronic schizophrenic to be a higher RBL than acutes or normals (Zahn, 1964; Bernstein, 1967). The same results could also be inferred from some TBL work (Ax, Banford, Beckett, Fretz, & Gottlieb, 1970). Also, a study which grouped schizophrenics into high and low basal level groups presented length of hospitalization data indicating that the high RBL group was more chronic than the low RBL group, who were more acute (Thayer & Silber, 1971). These results suggest that any schizophrenic subgroup differences in RBL are essentially an artifact of the experimental situation. That is, the results are due to the novelty of the experimental situation for individuals who differ in the length of time spent in a stimulus deprivation condition. The patient who has adapted to a stimulus deprived environment for a long period of time would find the laboratory a novel situation and would tend to exhibit a high RBL. Due to the large contrast between the laboratory and the usual domicile, little habituation to the experimental situation would be expected. In a sense, the high RBL is a TBL since the patient would be responding to the environmental stimuli with the same degree of attention as task stimuli during an experiment. Considering the laboratory as the independent variable leads to the prediction that the long-term hospitalized, stimulus-deprived patient would exhibit a higher basal level than all other groups who would be comparable. This is what occurred in the present study. The only significant RBL finding was that chronics were higher than acutes. Theorists who use the RBL or TBL findings in support of differences in internal states such as *D* or *V* ignore the possibility that the results are not due to schizophrenia but rather to long-term institutionalization.

To reduce the intensity or novelty of the independent variable, the laboratory, one could compare normals to acutes who have not experienced long-term stimulus deprivation. The experimental situation in this case would be relatively constant and affect normals and schizophrenics equally. Studies which have used acutes report few differences between acute subgroups or between acute schizophrenics and normals. Goldstein, Judd, Rodnick, and LaPolla (1969) found no differences between acute-good paranoids and nonparanoids. Zahn (1964) reported a higher basal level for nonmedicated, acute schizophrenics, but this was mainly due to normals exhibiting a greater degree of habituation. Rice (1970) essentially found no differences between acute goods and poors on a continuous RBL and TBL measure. Fowles, Watt, Maher, and Grinspoon (1970) also found no significant differences between acute goods, acute poors and normals although trends were reported. Williams (1953) on an RBL measure and Magaro (1972a), on a TBL measure, found acute poors to be at a higher basal level than normals, but these findings may reflect the effects of medication and diagnostic subtypes which were not controlled. In summary, although there is not total agreement, there are few reported differences between normals and acute schizophrenics, especially when habituation to the experimental situation is controlled. When S is comparable for all groups, group differences do not emerge on V or D.

An analysis of the nature of the experimental task, the $_sE_r \rightarrow R$ relationship, helps to resolve the conflicting results. The potency of stimuli in the experimental task could be seen in a trial effect or a comparison of RBL and TBL. When the environmental conditions are manipulated as in a TBL situation, a greater number of subject dimensions become significant. It is not clear, however, which variables in the experimental tasks increase BL for specific schizophrenic subgroups but not for others or normals. It has been reported that normals exhibit an increase in BL when the task becomes more difficult, while the schizophrenic maintains a constancy throughout such changing task requirements (Zahn, 1964). However, results could be interpreted to suggest that specific schizophrenic subgroups will increase BL on extensively stimulating tasks. Therefore, an increase in BL for a schizophrenic subgroup may depend upon the attentional demands of the task as determined by stimulus qualities. But this is speculation.

In conclusion, we argue that interpretation of RBL or TBL differences in terms of stimulus conditions is more concrete and experimenter-related than those dealing with inferences of physiological dysfunctions. The findings about chronicity imply that the basal-level difference reported in the literature may not be as relevant to the schizophrenic process as to the institutionalization process. In light of such results, we suggest that previous studies using chronics to generalize to the schizophrenic population be disregarded. There are no RBL differences between schizophrenics and other groups, including normals, which indicate any organismic differences in habitual or ongoing somatic activity and the autonomic, organic, perceptual, motivational, etc., functions inferred. Therefore, theoretical positions such as those developed by Venables (1964)—which focus on chronic-acute differences to postulate theoretical I constructs of elevated states of sympathetic and cortical activation for the chronic schizophrenic—would seem, at the least, premature at the present time.

GSR Reactivity

Reactivity (the amplitude of the GSR) results are influenced by another treatment variable—that of medication. Magaro (1973) found that medication reduced reactivity for poors and increased reactivity of goods as compared to other schizophrenic groups and normals. Goldstein et al. (1969) also found the medicated goods to exhibit a larger GSR than the nonmedicated goods. Confirming the direction of the Magaro studies, Goldstein et al. (1969) found nonmedicated poors at a higher GSR than medicated poors which is the opposite effect of medication on goods. This similarity in results is especially significant since the Goldstein studies used double-blind procedures manipulating the administration of medication, while the Magaro studies examined those who were already on or off medication.

The effects of medication on reactivity also indicate that schizophrenic–normal differences are purely artifactual. Whereas basal level differences are due to the "hospitalization treatment," reactivity differences require another type of "treatment," that of medication, to produce schizophrenic subgroup differences. Regardless of chronicity, medication reduces reactivity for paranoids and increases reactivity for schizophrenics. In terms of an attentional framework, medication could be seen as allowing the schizophrenic, especially the good, to be as responsive to task stimuli in the experimental situation as the good paranoid. As in the BL results, goods are responsive to stimulation but in this case, it is task stimuli to which the responsivity is exhibited, as reflected in the GSR. In viewing the GSR and basal level results in terms of a total experimental situation, we perceive multiple factors interacting in numerous combinations but assessed by a solitary measure. To infer that the psychophysiological measure reflects a D process is largely conjecture in view of the demonstrated effects of chronicity and medication. BL and GSR differences can well be demonstrating the effect of a V or K process.

ₛ*H*ᵣ THEORISTS

The ₛ*H*ᵣ theorists focus on the effect of a dominant habit that is not readily modified by experimental conditions. Witkin (1965) explains the level of task performance in terms of a particular dominant habit. The Embedded Figure Test presents a figure in a complex ground and requires the subject to identify the hidden figure by separating figure from ground. The identification of the figure operationalizes the empirical construct of separation while the different colored cards operationalize the hidden figure construct. The relationship between the presented cards and the response is explained by the theoretical construct I of field dependency which is further explained by the theoretical construct II of differentiation (see Fig. 4.3 under Silverman).

Degree of pathology is not a direct function of the amount of differentiation, but is related to the amount of integration at each level of differentiation. The functioning of specific schizophrenic subgroups, as opposed to other groups, is explained by the degree of field dependency, which is further explained by level of differentiation. Any prediction of test performance, therefore, would be a function of the degree of field dependency elicited by the task and the particular subtype of schizophrenia.

Field dependency is a long-term habit which is applied to most problem-solving situations and forms the basis for a particular problem-solving strategy. Hence the designation of a cognitive style. We argue that the field dependency measure is both a V and K process measure and that performance deficits on the measure is a function of the schizophrenic's attempt to integrate both processes. Thus, although field dependency is a construct which is considered to be a long-term trait or habit, the evidence suggests that a perceptual and/or a conceptual process is basic to the task. Such an analysis allows us to explain the results with schizophrenics.

Silverman

Silverman proposes a clear $_{s_1}H_r$ theory of the schizophrenic performance deficit. Through a forceful review (Silverman, 1964a) and a number of studies (Silverman, 1964b, 1967; 1968a; Silverman, Berg, & Kantor, 1965), he produces a theory which recognizes and supports individual differences in schizophrenia. By applying the Menninger work on cognitive styles (Gardner, Holzman, Klein, Linton, & Spence, 1959; Silverman, 1964a), a systematic description of schizophrenic subgroups categorized on the commonly used diagnostic dimensions of premorbid adjustment, paranoid symptomology, and chronicity is provided. Silverman (1964a) emphasizes the attentional defects in schizophrenia explained in terms of extensive and selective factors regulating the reception and utilization of stimuli:

> The extensive aspect of attention refers primarily to the degree to which stimuli are sampled from the environment. It is inferred from laboratory tasks which emphasize perceptual scanning. Selectiveness of attention involves the *articulation* of a stimulus field into salient and irrelevant cues. It is inferred from tasks which necessitate attention to certain segments of a stimulus field and simultaneous inhibition of attention to other segments of the field. This paper accounts for striking individual differences between schizophrenics on laboratory measures of perceptual scanning and field articulation and demonstrates systematic relationships between attention–response styles and schizophrenic symptom patterns and pre-illness histories. Extreme forms of scanning and field articulation, minimal or excessive, are shown to characterize the attention–response dispositions of most schizophrenics [p. 353].

The attentional–response dispositions are central to the personality as a defense mechanism and are not viewed (Silverman, 1964a) as specific stimulus-related responses. Rather, they are general response dispositions elicited as problem-solving strategies in a variety of stimulus situations.

> Attention–response dispositions emerge in the course of physical and psychological development. Like physiological and psychological needs, they are directive; they exert a selective influence on the cognitive field. Unlike needs, however, they are not necessarily linked to a class of satisfaction-giving objects. Rather they are activated by and operate upon perceptual and conceptual incongruities (e.g., comprehending an ambiguous or complex stimulus field). Although conceptualized as learned behaviors, they are not simple "attentional habits" which are correlated with certain qualities of stimuli. Rather they are conceived of as general response dispositions which may express themselves in broadly equivalent ranges of environmental situations. It should be noted that since the two attention controls are likely to occur in an individual (e.g., high scanning responsiveness–low field articulation responsiveness, etc.). . . .
>
> The concept of "defense" is extremely useful when relating attention response patterns to modes of mastering anxiety. Thus, it is suggested that early in the development of a schizophrenic disorder, as isolations, repressions, and denials become less and less effective, the individual begins to rely on the most basic forms of adient–abient adjustive mechanisms. These mechanisms include formerly "conflict free" attention–response dispositions [p. 368].

This repetitive, dominant quality of a cognitive style leads to its classification as a $_{s1}H_r$ habit in the present system. Cognitive style is a habit loading of nonmotivational components of a stimulus such that the particular response occurs with great frequency, even though alternate responses may be more appropriate to the situation. In other words, the cognitive style is the individual's customary way of organizing all stimulus situations, and through it all specific responses are formed.

The second major construct offered by Silverman (1964a) is the empirical construct of field articulation, which is the same as the field dependency term of Witkin (1965). Silverman, however, does not use the theoretical construct of differentiation as inferred by Witkin. As with size estimation, the disparity in performance of different schizophrenic subgroups is the important contribution of the theory. The distinctive curves of the schizophrenic subgroups each constitute functions of observables. Each curve is a statement of the degree of scanning or field articulation characteristic of a subgroup and makes possible an explanation of the specific cognitive style of a subgroup.

The Silverman constructs of scanning and articulation could be considered perceptual constructs because they organize stimulus input, thus suggesting a *V* theory. However, the terms used refer to internal systems that have been learned and are independent of external stimuli; hence, their designation as habits. It may be argued (Broen, 1968) that all processes, *K* and *V*, are really habits. Such an analysis, however, blurs a crucial difference between positions. Habits are the basis of *response dispositions* that are all-inclusive methods of dealing with stimuli, internal or external. On the other hand, perceptual constructs deal with specific mechanisms utilized in specific situations. For example, in a particular task where stimuli have to be discriminated, a habit or response disposition would occur automatically and make automatic differentiations. An explanation based upon a perceptual or conceptual mechanism, however, would specify those stimulus situations that elicit the operation of a particular perceptual or cognitive process.

We favor the position that the perceptual terms which have a habit connotation are really perceptual processes. We will closely analyze the size-judgment literature in order to demonstrate that the scanning construct can best be seen as a V and/or K term. From this analysis and a presentation of recent more specific measures of perceptual processes, we will argue that a habit explanation is unwarranted from available data and that it is V and K that are crucial for understanding the schizophrenic deficit. In short, Silverman is a habit theorist in his conception of response dispositions, but he also is interested in the operation of perceptual processes in the gathering of information. However, the measures used such as field dependency and size estimation do not allow a distinction between the operation of specific perceptual processes and more general response dispositions.

There are suggestions in Silverman (1964a) that "anxiety" tends to increase the response disposition. In our terms it acts multiplicatively with $_sH_r$ to increase the response potential of the cognitive style. However, this implication is never explicitly stated. In describing the response disposition as a defense. Silverman (1964a) suggests that the habit is reinforced by reducing drive. Broen (1968, pp. 136–140) also interprets scanning as a habitual defense which is learned because it reduces the discomfort from response interference. Silverman (1964a), however, is not clear about the effect of D upon $_sH_r$, except to suggest that the cognitive style develops through a reduction of anxiety.

It should also be noted that along with field articulation and scanning, Silverman postulated another attentional mechanism, sensory input processing-ideational gating to account for the performance of long-term institutionalized schizophrenics. This mechanism may be unique to schizophrenics and exhibited by all schizophrenics under extreme stress. However, the habit is more evident in the chronic patient and is clearly perceptual in nature, similar to the filter term of the other V theorists. The effect of drive on this mechanism is to increase its activity. With this concept as well, Silverman (1964a) concentrates mainly on the habit system to explain schizophrenic behavior, with drive having a secondary value at most.

In analyzing the attentional disposition theory of Silverman (1964a) presented in Fig. 4.3, it can be seen that the observables and empirical constructs have been used by other theorists. At the theoretical I level,

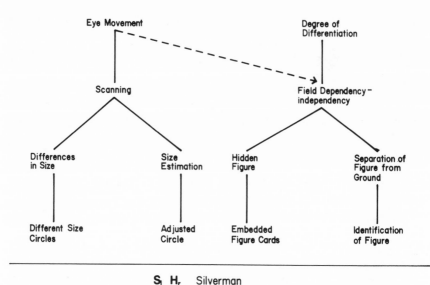

S₁ Hᵣ   Silverman

FIG. 4.3.   Schematic representation of the theoretical structure of habit theories.

however, the data are reinterpreted with the introduction of the scanning construct. The size estimation work provides the major impetus for the development of the scanning construct. The observables are the presented stimuli to which size judgments are made, usually through an adjustment method. The empirical construct of presented size differences is operationalized by the different size stimuli presented, while the empirical construct of size estimation is operationalized by the actual adjusted size estimates. The function between stimulus size presented and size estimation define the theoretical construct I of scanning. It was further assumed that the scanning construct actually was due to the theoretical construct II, degree of eye movement. However, consequent work (Neale & Cromwell, 1968) failed to find a relationship between eye movement and size estimation:

> Although the extremely deviant size estimations in schizophrenics have been attributed to eye movement, the eye-movement interpretation has not been carefully tested. The findings of Gardner and Long demonstrated only the concurrence of eye movements with particular errors of size estimation. No one has demonstrated that eye movement characteristics are a necessary condition for these errors to occur. Therefore, it is possible that eye movements are a secondary or enhancement phenomenon and that size-estimation deviations may be a function of a separate process [p. 45].

Others have articulated other problems with the scanning construct. Gardner (1970) pointed out that the best operational definition of scanning was not the function between presented stimulus size and the size estimation adjustment but rather the function between presented stimulus size and a measure of the amount of time viewing the standard. Thus, Silverman probably incorrectly defined the theoretical construct of scanning by relating size judgment to differential size presentations. Broen (1968) interprets the size estimation studies in V terms by considering the variability in attention. Scanning is related to variability of attention rather than breadth of attention as implied by the scanning terms. In view of the different interpretations of the size estimation studies, it may be questionable to use size estimation as an operation of any specific construct because of the multiple processes involved in the task. This issue will be discussed further in the review of the size judgment literature.

It should be noted, however, that the empirical laws explained by the scanning term have been partially supported. It is only the scanning term itself, with its eye movement explanation, that is most open to question. Other interpretations of the scanning construct indicate that scanning could refer to any process, perceptual, conceptual, or both.

A great deal of research has been generated from the Silverman position supporting the probable functions of specific schizophrenic subgroups, but there is no theoretical construct I that satisfactorily explains the functional relationship. Neale, Held, and Cromwell (1969) have proposed a redundancy term to replace the scanning term. But more direct tests of this term with more relevant empirical constructs are needed to create confidence in this explanation and remove it from the "semantical construct invention" category. Because the main support, the observables, has been confirmed and additional modification has been offered (Schooler & Silverman, 1969), the Silverman position is still viable. The main task is to reconstruct the empirical constructs possibly with the use of a new scanning measure, as suggested by Gardner (1970) or by the introduction of perceptual terms as suggested by Broen (1968) or even by conceptual terms as we will demonstrate. Whatever the explanation, the important step will be to develop more differentiated measures that do not have the confounding problems of the global field dependency and size estimation measures.

FIELD DEPENDENCY

The concept of field articulation or field dependence as measured by the Embedded Figures Test (EFT) is presented in the $_sH_r$ theories of Silverman (1964a, 1968b) and Witkin (1965). When the habit theorists use the field dependency measures, they are speaking of a perceptual process which has either been overlearned or is a long-term trait that may even be genetic in origin. We have classified such theorists under a habit construct by emphasizing the aspect of an enduring trait. We could have ignored this aspect of the theory and grouped them with the V theorists. We chose to make the distinction because V and $_sH_r$ theorists assign different meanings to the perceptual process. It can be seen in Fig. 2.1 that V and K are directly related to S and have to be considered as a function of S. $_sH_r$, on the other hand, is a state of the organism which is relatively independent of S and usually enters into a function with D.

The habit theorists speak of a particular "cognitive style" that refers to an internal perceptual process which is almost structurally formed and processes all stimuli in the same manner. The most serious argument against such a position is that the process, be it field-dependency or overinclusion, is situationally determined. In that case, the habit theorist who uses such measures could just as well be classified as a V or K theorist.

We are arguing that the $_sH_r$ theorists are V or K theorists, because the process studied is situationally determined. Consistent with our analysis of overinclusion, we also demonstrate that the habit measures are multiple measures reflecting several processes. We also attempt to designate which schizophrenic subgroups are most affected on the field dependency measure. We suggest that a conceptual process is a main ingredient in the field dependency measure and that the paranoid can perform this conceptual process while nonparanoids cannot.

Paranoid and Nonparanoid Differences in Field Dependency

There have been only a few studies that directly used the EFT to examine the degree of field dependence exhibited by the specific schizophrenic subgroups. Most of these studies have not been published, did not contol medication, and did not separate the schizophrenic population into enough subgroups to allow a determination of those subject variables that relate to the field dependence dimension. The available results have reported nonparanoid schizophrenics to be more field dependent than paranoid schizophrenics (Witkin, Lewis, Hertzman, Machover, Meissner, & Wagner, 1954); hallucinatory schizophrenics more than delusional schizophrenics (Taylor, 1956); poors to be more field dependent than goods (Gibeau, 1965); and chronic poors to be more field dependent than chronic goods (Bryant, 1962). The first two findings suggest that the schizophrenic group is the one who is field dependent, while the last two findings suggest that, as in overinclusion, the degree of pathology is also related to field dependency.

In order to further clarify the EFT performance level of specific schizophrenic subgroups, Magaro and Vojtisek (1971) sampled selected matched hospitalized groups at different lengths of hospitalization. Results indicated that chronics, whether they are nonparanoid schizophrenic, paranoid schizophrenic, or other types of hospitalized patients (others), exhibited a greater field dependence than acutes. An exception to this was the paranoid with a poor premorbid adjustment. That is, most patients seem to become more field dependent when institutionalized; however, the paranoid patient who has never exhibited an adequate social adjustment (poor) is not greatly affected by extensive hospitalization. This explanation is consistent with the personality descriptions of poors in general (Zimet & Fine, 1959), who never were very differentiated and, in a sense, may have been fairly pathological before entering the institution.

The overall conclusion of the study was that alcoholics and good premorbid adjustment schizophrenics are fairly similar before entering a hospital, but after the intervention of long-term hospitalization, they become more similar to other psychotic groups. As with the GSR measures, the institutionalization process, with its dearth of stimulation, makes the performance of an EFT extremely difficult. The institutionalization process aptly described by Goffman (1961) and Levinson and Gallagher (1964), has confounding effects in many areas of research in schizophrenia (Mednick & McNeil, 1968). The undifferentiated sameness of the hospital and its rigid procedures do not call for a great deal of perceptual discrimination, which explains the field-dependent performance of the chronic patient on the RFT. If there is any one group who is more field-dependent, it would be the nonparanoid (Witkin et al., 1954) who would be more hallucinatory (Taylor, 1956), poor (Gibeau, 1956), and chronic (Bryant, 1962). The paranoid is able to perform this task in the normal range.

Although the Magaro and Vojtisek (1971) study attempted to determine the performance level of schizophrenia subgroups and suggested that the stimulus deprivation conditions present in long-term hospitalization or pathology itself could be a causal factor, there was no indication of what psychological process was tapped by the EFT. We will analyze the EFT in order to determine whether it is a unitary measure or the action of multiple processes.

Processes Active in the EFT

Witkin (1950) introduced the Embedded Figures Test (EFT) to measure individual differences in analytically dealing with a field. In comparing the EFT with several measures of field dependence for both normals and hospitalized patients, Witkin et al. (1954) found that the EFT was the only measure which differentiated patients from normals, with patients exhibiting markedly higher scores. However, Witkin et al. (1954) and Witkin, Dyk, Faterson, Goodenough, and Karp (1962) concluded that the EFT was not a valid indicator of perceptual functioning for a patient group because the test proved to be uninteresting, and patients were not able to maintain the sustained attention required for successful performance. One problem with testing hospitalized patients is the lengthy administration time. Since the scoring is based on the total time required to locate simple geometric figures embedded in 24 larger configurations, each with a time limit of 5 minutes, subjects who have difficulty can take up to two hours to complete the test. This extended testing period could produce irrelevant drives such as boredom, agitation, or some other incidental motivational state. Judging from the high scores in the study by Witkin et al. (1954), patients seemed to have required a much longer administration period than other groups. If schizophrenic subjects respond more or less than other groups to the motivational demands of the task, differences in results between schizophrenics and others may be due to *D* effects rather than the intended field dependency differentiation.

There have been attempts to deal with this problem by constructing a shorter test. Jackson (1956) devised a short form of the EFT by using 12 figures instead of 24 and reducing the time limit for each item from 5 to 3 minutes. The overall adminstration time was reduced to a maximum of 45 minutes, with no apparent loss in the discriminative ability of the test. Although the shortened form offers a more efficient method of administering the EFT and reduces the motivational factors present in long-term testing, a second possible drive factor may be operating. The effect of total failure (not finding the figure within the time limit) on the early trials may affect overall performance. Since the patients in the Witkin et al. (1954) study exhibited extremely high scores, it appears that total failure was a consistent occurrence. Several studies have shown that task failure increases the deficit performance of psychiatric patients (Garmezy, 1966). Therefore, Witkin's observation that patients had problems in maintaining attention can be reconsidered in terms of the effect of early failure of items. Failing an item early in the series interferes with further attempts to complete later items. In our terms, failure on early trials may serve to condition fear or anxiety to later trials. Hence, the cards presented later in the series may contain a *Ds* quality as well as the field-dependency factor. That is, performance on the EFT may be a function of a *Ds* factor inherent in the procedure as it interacts with the field-dependency factor. In this case performance level would not reflect a field-dependency effect as much as a resultant effect on the interaction of two processes.

Another point of concern with the EFT is the validity of the individual test items. In developing the EFT, eight simple and 24 complex items were selected from Gottschaldt's original figures on the basis of two criteria: First, the figures must be of properly graded difficulty, and second, the simple geometric figures must be of sufficient variety so as to eliminate any practice effect on any one item. It was apparently assumed that all items equally measured the same type of perceptual organization (i.e., separating an item from its field). Differences in the scores of the individual items were thought to only reflect differences in terms of difficulty. However, there is some indication that such an assumption is not true. The series using the E figure could be viewed from either of two perspectives and fluctuation between the two can occur quite frequently. Although Witkin et al. (1954) noted that the E series was more difficult, he speculated that it was due to the three dimensional appearance of the simple figure. Apparently, the reversible perspective quality of the series was not considered.

There have been several studies which indicate that this additional variable in the E series is important. Relationships between the EFT and measures of reversible perspective have been reported. Haronian (1963) found a small positive correlation between reported size on the Müller–Lyer illusion and field dependence. Newbigging (1954) and Haronian and Sugerman (1966) reported a relationship between EFT performance and frequency of alternations on reversible perspective items. Small but significant correlations indicated that better EFT performance was related to increased ability to control the rate of figure reversals. The reason for the small correlation between the EFT and the geometric illusion measures is that the EFT only contains a few reversible perspective items—the E series. The reported correlation is decreased by the other series which does not contain this additional factor. Thus, the E series may be measuring an ability above and beyond the capacity to separate an item from its field (an additional complex cognitive factor), and as such may be unrelated to the remaining EFT items. The E cards, therefore, may require much more of an integration process than the other series and consequently be much more difficult for schizophrenic subgroups. In fact, it may be most responsible for any schizophrenic–other group difference.

Vojtisek and Magaro (1974) devised a procedure to modify the EFT that reduced the effect of the two motivational factors mentioned above. The administration time was reduced even further, and the possible confounding effects of early failure were minimized. The possibility that the E series of the EFT measured a type of perceptual functioning different than that measured by the remaining items was also examined. It was found that the E series did measure a different type of perceptual functioning than the rest of the items, and excluding these items produced a purer measure of field dependency. Also, the factor that best differentiated between patient subgroups was Witkin's original construct of field dependence. The E series formed a second reversible perspective factor which did not differentiate between patient subgroups mainly because hospitalized patients in general experienced a great deal of difficulty on this factor. Although the study used hospitalized patients, the findings appear to be consistent with earlier work measuring the relationship between field dependence and control of fluctuation rates. However, the Vojtisek and Magaro (1974) results demonstrate that the relationship is limited to the E series and control of fluctuation. Whether or not this relationship will be found with normals needs to be confirmed by further investigation.

What can be concluded, however, is that the EFT may not only reflect the effect of field dependency but may, in fact, be measuring the operation of other single processes such as Ds (the conditioned fear from early failures), D (irrelevant drives such as boredom from the length of the test), K (maintaining a dominant concept in a reversible perspective situation), or the interaction of these processes with field dependency. (See Silverman, 1968a, for a similar analysis of other field dependency measures such as the Rod-and-Frame.)

Wallach (1962) noted that Witkin's description of the field dependency term is similar to the analytical categorization term used by Kagan, Moss, and Sigle (1963). He suggested that the two theoretical terms may be a result of the different operational definitions that have been employed by each. Kagan et al. (1963) used measures of conceptual labeling and interpreted their results in terms of conceptual processes as contrasted with Witkin's perceptual description. Wallach's analysis implicitly questioned whether or not the two operations were measuring the same process but labeling them differently.

Messick and Fritzky (1963) attempted to discover the underlying dimension common to both tasks. In order to measure the two terms, they used a group EFT and a visual learning task. The results of a factor analysis found that the EFT had a strong memory component in addition to the field dependency factor and also loaded on an Analytic Categorization Test (ACT). Loadings on the ACT were considered to reflect on ability to highlight large figural forms against a background through an analytical process. In short, results could be interpreted to mean that the EFT has a large memory component and a conceptual component as well as the perceptual process.

Field Dependency as a Habit or Conceptual Process

Field dependency as a long-term enduring habit, an $_{s_l}H_r$, assumes that the response would be evoked in different situations. This assumption has been questioned, and the alternate position has been advanced that field dependency is a conceptual strategy that is evoked under specific stimulus conditions. As Wachtel (1972a,b) asks, is field dependency an organization of personality, basically unchangeable and applied to most situations, or is it a cognitive strategy among many which is applied when most applicable?

Witkin et al. (1962) as illustrated in Fig. 4.3, developed the theoretical structure where degree of differentiation explains the theoretical I term, field dependency, which explains the empirical laws formed by separate empirical constructs such as separateness of self, body concept, obesity, alcoholism, etc.

Wachtel (1972a) argues quite convincingly that there is a danger in considering field dependency a unitary dimension reflecting personality differences. Because Wachtel (1972b) considers the demands of the experimental situation, S, to be of prime theoretical importance in determining the use of a particular cognitive style, he argues that field dependency is a response applied in a specific situation, rather than a habit applied over many situations and reflecting a unitary process of differentiation. The field dependency process is dependent upon S just as we have considered K to be a function of S. When the experimental situation calls for a field-dependent approach, that is the strategy that will be emitted. The laboratory test is not as much a reflection of the individual but of an individual in a specific situation. The individual is not field independent or dependent but is using that strategy at that particular time.

This interpretation is supported by a study by Zuckerman (1968). He found that responses to sensory isolation were correlated with EFT scores only on the first day of testing. On the second day of testing, the correlations disappeared indicating that the field dependency style was more related to the novelty of the experimental situation. The cognitive style was a form of adaptation to the laboratory. Due to the limitations in the range of responses or styles which were available, a field dependency response was emitted. When the effect of the laboratory changed through familiarity, including familiarity with the experimenter, the cognitive style changed.

This analysis suggests that D affects EFT performance. Earlier, the length of the test and early failures were discussed as two motivational components of the test. In addition, various measures of drive have been examined in relation to their effect on field dependency. Drive has been operationalized by noise (Oltman, 1964), drugs (Callaway, 1959) or brief sensory deprivations (Jacobson, 1966; Zuckerman, 1968) and has been found to decrease and increase field independence. Apparently D in one form or another affects EFT but not in any predictable manner. Procedural steps that introduce the drive factor can only expect to demonstrate the operation of D on H, or S_dH_r. However, the precise nature of the relationship between drive and field dependency has not been demonstrated.

When the EFT is shown to correlate with another measure, it is not clear whether it is the K, V, or even habit aspect of field dependency which is responsible for the correlation. Wachtel (1972a) reports that field dependency measures correlate in the high 60s. Since two-thirds of the variance is elsewhere, it is very difficult to infer which process in the EFT is responsible for the correlation with another measure.

The argument made by Wachtel (1972a) that field dependency is a K process applied to specific situations, rather than a pervasive personality trait, is relevant to our description of paranoids and schizophrenics. Paranoids perform well on the EFT task because they can perform conceptual tasks that do not require the creation of multiple categories. The poorer performance of the nonschizophrenic reflects the inability to operate in a conceptual mode to integrate the multiple processes required by the task. The integrational demand of the EFT tasks is also greater for the chronic because there has been less experience with cognitive strategies due to his greater isolation through long-term hospitalization. The similarity of the acute schizophrenic groups to normals is possibly due to a greater adequacy in dealing with multiple processes because of their recent experiences with the demands of the outside world, however, this *ad hoc* reasoning is rather speculative.

The field-dependency studies suggest that conceptual elements are present in the task, and the nonparanoid (especially the chronic) is not as able to utilize this process as well as the paranoid or the acute patient. In contrast to the overinclusion task where the paranoid was deficient, we find that with field dependency, it is the nonparanoid who has the greatest problem. This suggests that the nature of the task is one where the conceptual demands are specified or structured, which allows the paranoid who has a large number of conceptual categories to analyze the figure and respond appropriately. The nonparanoid with few conceptual categories is dependent upon the stimulus properties of the task and hence is in a constant state of distraction.

$D_s \times {}_{s_d}H_r$ THEORISTS

Rodnick and Garmezy

Rodnick and Garmezy (1957), as presented in Fig. 4.4, provide a social censure hypothesis to explain the performance deficit using ${}_{s_d}H_r$ and D_s terms. Essentially, this position views the schizophrenic as having had censorious child-rearing experiences which evoke a withdrawal response to the parent. Through stimulus generalization, the withdrawal response is extended to most people. Interpersonal situations provoke anxiety and ultimately cause withdrawal. The withdrawal, however, does not extend in the same degree to all humans, but is mainly related to the specific parent who expressed the greatest amount of censure. Premorbid adjustment distinguishes between those schizophrenics most sensitized to the mother (poors) and those most sensitized to the father (goods). The schizophrenic, therefore, is not characterized by a state of deprivation or generalized arousal, but rather by conditioned fear. Hence, the Rodnick and Garmezy (1957) position is categorized as a D_s theory. The emphasis on the withdrawal response as the characteristic and most dominant behavior of the schizophrenic to a specific drive is the ${}_{s_d}H_r$ aspect of the theory. The interaction of both processes produces the level of the performance.

Studies that confirm the social censure hypothesis usually utilize a form discrimination or a size estimation task. The antecedent event of the

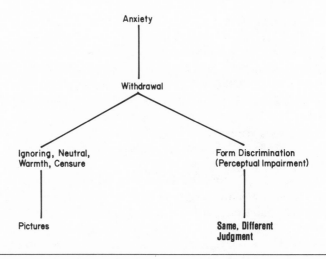

D_s x S_dH_r   Rodnick & Garmezy

FIG. 4.4.   Schematic representation of the theoretical structure of drive by habit theories.

observables are pictures with different thematic content such as a mother or father pointing a finger, offering some milk, raising an arm to strike, pushing a child away, as well as a house and tree. The consequent event is either a response indicating a size judgment in a size estimation task or a same or different judgment in a form discrimination task. The "same" judgment indicates a perceptual impairment since the comparison usually differs from the standard. Each antecedent event operationalizes a parent–child interaction such as the empirical constructs of censure, feeding, hitting, ignoring, or neutral. The task response operationalizes the empirical constructs of size estimation or form discrimination. Later work (Cicchetti, 1969; Magaro, 1972b) has questioned if the operational definition is correct; if the antecedent event may actually operationalize degrees of complexity instead of emotional content. The empirical law stating that censure creates a performance deficit is inferred from the differing performance functions for specific schizophrenics and normals. The theoretical construct I explaining the law is that of withdrawal. The schizophrenic does not perform as well as normals because he withdraws from the situation and consequently is not able to perform the task. Unfortunately, there is no measure of the explanatory withdrawal response nor a measure of the next and probably higher theoretical II construct, anxiety. It is to the authors' credit that they consider their position only a hypothesis and not a theory, and present most of their evidence at the empirical law level. They nonetheless use the anxiety and withdrawal constructs to explain the function between specific thematic content and performance.

Rodnick and Garmezy (1957) are possibly the only motivational theorists to use *Ds*. Other drive theorists mainly rely on *Dd* or *D̄*. Also the specification of the habit *ₛₐHₚ* is relatively rare. The predictions from the theory are relatively vague due mainly to the use of theoretical constructs which lack an empirical base. In fact, what at first appears as a rather straightforward empirical position becomes, in effect, a relatively speculative theory. There is little empirical support for the major theoretical constructs explaining the empirical laws since the functional relationships have not been confirmed (Magaro, 1969, 1972b). However, this position has generated a great deal of research, especially because of its potential to operationalize a number of psychoanalytic constructs. The theory's failure at the empirical construct level relegates it to the historical niche reserved for heuristic value.

The next habit measure which we discuss is that of size estimation. Once again we argue that multiple processes operate in the task, and we demonstrate that varying specific task elements changes the task demand for greater perceptual or conceptual processing, and hence performance changes. We also suggest that paranoid–unparanoid differences emerge on the task because of each subgroup's ability to meet different task demands. The social censure theory has utilized the size estimation procedure extensively to test its hypothesis. Thus, the following review will also provide the reason for its lack of empirical support.

SIZE JUDGMENTS

Our analysis of the performance deficit theories presented the variety of tasks which are employed to operationalize the theoretical constructs explaining the psychological deficit. Obviously, a task that reflects more of the concepts used by many different theorists would be popular and tend to endure. The size judgment task fits that criterion. Consequently, a great many size-judgment studies have been generated within the past twenty years, and many provocative findings have been produced. But as yet, no clear picture of the nature of the schizophrenic performance deficit has emerged. From insight gained in our preceding analysis, we expect that the morass of conflicting studies results from a lack of control of the specific experimental conditions *within* the size judgment task that determine performance level and the consequent performance deficit.

In their review of the schizophrenic size estimation literature, Neale et al. (1969) have called attention to several procedural inadequacies and methodological differences which may be responsible for the lack of clarity in size estimation research. While we also recognized the confounding effects of intratask variables, we have added to that criticism by proposing that such variables are responsible for producing a body of literature on an epiphenomenon. The effects observed on a size judgment task result from integrating separate psychological processes instead of the motivational and cognitive terms supposedly studied. The size judgment task has been assumed to reflect one psychological process such as high or low scanning, eye movement, redundancy, arousal, valuing, etc. The relationship between the theoretical explanation and the empirical events is seldom documented or clearly explicated. One reason for this is that one does not observe a pure size estimation response. One observes categorization interacting with visual acuity, perceptual judgment, memory and other responses all under various levels of motivation.

The goal in this section is to specify those experimental conditions within the size estimation task which produce the contrasting demands. We first systematically review the size estimation and size constancy work and then evaluate the size judgment results in terms of the differential effects of subject and task variables. The following review of the literature is necessarily extensive in order to specify the task and subject variables operating within each study and to indicate their relationship to the theoretical constructs used by the different theorists. The concern with the minutiae of the experimental situation should also allow a more concise evaluation of the work. The review is divided into two main sections. The first deals with size estimation and the second with size constancy research. Within the size estimation segment, the work is divided into studies derived from D and K theories. Such a division provides an historical perspective and chronological order as well as demonstrating the preferences for specific psychological methods employed within each theoretical area.

Size Estimation

Motivational Studies Employing the Method of Average Error. Size estimation research exploring the motivational causes of the performance deficit grew out of the early work of Bruner and Postman (1948) and Klein (1954). Using nonpsychiatric subjects, both studies indicated that motivational factors influenced size judgments. Stimuli including affective cues or objects with greater value were perceived as being larger than neutral stimuli (Bruner & Postman, 1948). Harris (1957) was the first to use this method to examine the effects of motivational factors on the perceptual performance of schizophrenics. Based upon the social censure hypothesis (Rodnick & Garmezy, 1957), Harris postulated that schizophrenics would be less accurate than normals in judging the size of stimuli depicting the deviant parent–child relationship because of its high negative value. Adult male schizophrenics hospitalized for less than six years performed a size estimation task adapted from the psychophysical method of average error. The scenes presented included mother–son interactions connoting maternal overprotection, dominance, ignoring or rejection, and acceptance, as well as a neutral tree–bush scene and a square. Each scene was exposed for five seconds, removed, and the subjects were then required to adjust a variable replica. Half the adjustment trials were made from a closed position (ascending trials) and half from an open position (descending trials). The results yielded no difference between the schizophrenic and normal groups on any scene. When the schizophrenic patients were categorized on the basis of the Phillips Scale of Premorbid Adjustment (Phillips, 1953), however, it was found that good premorbid schizophrenics (goods) underestimated all scenes and poor premorbid schizophrenic (poors) overestimated all but the square. These results were interpreted to support the social censure hypothesis. However, performance differences between goods and poors were also explained on the basis of a cognitive theory of different perceptual styles as defined by Klein (1954).

Zahn (1959) replicated the Harris (1957) procedure but added a condition of building affective value into the content scenes by administering verbal positive (rewarded) and negative (punished) feedback to the discrimination made to specific-content stimuli. Results indicated that all groups underestimated on all scenes except for good premorbids who overestimated on the punished pictures. In attempting to resolve the differences between his results and the opposite results reported by Harris, Zahn emphasized that his patient groups were more chronic than those of Harris. However, the discrepancy in the two studies between the performance of the normal subject was unexplained. Harris found normals to overestimate the neutral scene, whereas Zahn found normals to underestimate the unrewarded–unpunished neutral scenes. However, the addition of the noncontingent reward–punishment condition may have had a generalized negative effect on size estimation performance in all conditions.

Culver (1961) attempted to manipulate affect in a size estimation task. Good and poor premorbid schizophrenics and normals judged the size of a square and a mother picture after viewing short movies of a "neutral" or hostile mother. The change in the censure cue from an intra-task to extra-task variable apparently removed the motivational effect because no difference was found between his schizophrenic subgroups. Since patient chronicity was not reported it is difficult to interpret these results in terms of the subject variable effects considered by Zahn (1959).

In summary, the Harris and Zahn results were interpreted to suggest different subgroup performances on thematic scenes. Acute poors and chronic goods tended to overestimate while acute goods and chronic poors tended to underestimate on censorious scenes. Yet, although such findings were confounded by methodological difficulties and are easily open to alternate explanations (Cicchetti, 1969) they provided a means to test the motivational censure hypothesis which generated a great deal of interest at the time.

Motivational Studies Using a Modified Constant Stimulus Task. The next type of study to focus on the effects of motivation on size judgments employed a different psychophysical method—a variation of the constant stimulus method. In addition to chronicity and premorbid adjustment, patients were also subgrouped on the basis of the presence or absence of paranoid symptoms. Davis, Cromwell, and Held (1967) used a varied constant stimulus psychophysical method. After each 10-second presentation of the same scenes used by Harris (1957), the standard was removed, and an array containing six replicas of the standard scene was exposed. The subjects were required to select the comparison that matched most closely the remembered size of the standard. Comparison stimuli equaled 87, 90, 95, 105, 110, and 113% of the area of the standard, making an accurate match impossible, and subjects were forced to over- or underestimate on any given trial. Although Davis et al. (1967) alluded to a pilot study indicating the new method yields results similar to the average error method, no formal comparison between the two methods was reported. Results indicated that premorbid adjustment and diagnosis were related to size judgments. Decreasing degrees of overestimation were shown by poor nonparanoids, good nonparanoids and poor paranoids, respectively. Good paranoids underestimated the standard. The performance of the same acute patient groups on thematic scenes was further analyzed by Webb, Davis, and Cromwell (1966), who found that goods and poors exhibited the greatest differences on the dominance and rejection scenes. Paranoids were found to differ significantly from nonparanoids on all but the dominance and over-protection scenes.

Neale and Cromwell (1968) examined the effects of stimulus presentation time on size estimation with normal controls, acute-good paranoids, and acute-poor-nonparanoid schizophrenics. Following the constant stimulus procedure developed by Davis et al. (1967), stimulus presentation times of 10 sec., 100 msec., and a 10 msec. blank flash were employed. The blank flash was included to examine the possibility of response bias in the absence of any stimulus. The results for the patient groups were consistent with those of Davis et al. (1967). Good paranoids underestimated the standard while poor nonparanoids overestimated, and this occurred primarily on the dominance, acceptance, and overprotection scenes. Furthermore, all groups exhibited a significantly lower size estimation on the shorter presentation time than on the longer. No between-group differences were found on the blank flash condition, thus casting doubt on the operation of a response bias. The very interesting result was that at the 100 msec. condition in which the subject had to compare an image of the stimulus to the standard, paranoids as compared to normals reduced their size estimations. This result suggests that the paranoid does not necessarily direct his attention to the stimulus, but tends to make judgments in a categorical manner. He is not affected by longer presentations because he applies a judgment from a fixed category system. We discuss this process in a later chapter in which we review the information-processing literature and suggest that the paranoid processes the icon mainly from a categorical set. What is of most relevance here is that the larger size estimations in the long exposure time argue against an eye-movement interpretation of size estimation which we will discuss.

Other studies employing the same constant stimulus method found no differences in the performance of schizophrenic subgroups. Mehl (1969) recorded size estimation performance before and after brief sensory deprivation and stimulation conditions. Results showed no difference between good and poor long-term hospitalized nonparanoids and no effect due to the sensory conditions. When the results were analyzed on optimal performance trials, thematic differences were found for all groups on the overprotection, dominance, and acceptance scenes thus suggesting that specific schizophrenic subgroups are not unique in their response to motivational stimuli.

Kopfstein and Neale (1971) further investigated size estimation performance in terms of premorbid adjustment, chronicity, and paranoid diagnosis. The effects of institutionalization were assessed by including a group of chronic non-schizophrenic patients. The results indicated no differences among all patient groups. They speculated that the lack of a significant difference between schizophrenics and nonschizophrenics may indicate that previous performance differences attributed to schizophrenics in particular is characteristic of long-term hospitalized patients in general.

Neale, Davis, and Cromwell (1971) were concerned with the effects of pupil size and visual accommodation on size estimation performance. Accommodation effects were minimized, and pupil size was controlled by randomly employing an artificial pupil on one of two sets of trials. Results showed that performance differences on thematic scenes were unrelated to schizophrenic subgroup dimensions. No differences occurred among the subgroups in the level of size judgments, nor was there any effect attributable to the artificial pupil. Neale et al. (1971) related their failure to replicate previously found subgroup differences to the distance between subjects and stimuli. In short, the early work examining motivational hypothesis found significant but conflicting results. Replications of this work which used other procedures sometimes found positive results but other modifications in procedure led to negative results.

The final motivational study to be reported differs from previous studies in its focus on an important task variable. Strauss (1970) noted that earlier studies had employed the same stimulus sequence for all subjects. Varying six orders of thematic scenes with normal subjects, Strauss found a significant thematic content by trials effect and suggested that the results of previous studies had been confounded by order of stimulus presentation. Strauss, Foureman, and Parwatikar (1974) tested this hypothesis with a schizophrenic population and found a sequence effect as well as a significant paranoid-by-premorbid adjustment effect for chronic patients, independent of thematic content. Decreasing degrees of overestimation across all stimuli were exhibited by poor paranoids, good nonparanoids, and good paranoids, and poor nonparanoids respectively, with the last group underestimating the standard.

In summary, the motivational work produced positive and negative results in terms of subgroup differences on specific stimuli. However, the constant stimulus studies found the effect of stimulus content to be relatively minimal in comparison to the finding of consistent subgroup differences across stimulus conditions. This latter finding suggested the operation of specific cognitive styles and led to a shift in emphasis from a motivational to a cognitive view of the performance deficit, which is apparent in the redundance theory proposed by Neale and Cromwell (1968).

Progressing from early research primarily concerned with thematic content, Neale and Cromwell proposed a cognitive theory of the performance deficit. The redundancy theory of size estimation postulated that increased stimulus redundancy—either spatial or temporal—leads to increased size judgments. Generally, redundancy can be thought to vary directly with conditions that allow longer exposure of the standard. Greater spatial redundancy can be achieved through conditions that minimize competing perceptual cues or distracting stimuli. In varying stimulus exposure time, Neale and Cromwell found increases in size estimates on the longer exposure times as compared to the shorter exposure times. They interpreted this result in terms of temporal redundancy. They also inferred that the different size judgments of schizophrenic subgroups reflect differences in redundancy levels. Good paranoids, who underestimate the standard, were hypothesized to operate at a low redundancy level, and the poor nonparanoids, who overestimated, were hypothesized to operate at a high redundancy level. The redundancy theory, therefore, attempted to explain the consistent subgroup differences found in the early motivational studies with an individual difference construct.

Magaro (1969) performed a study which clearly demonstrated the need to shift from a motivational to a cognitive interpretation of size estimation results. In a study specifically designed to examine thematic content effects, the subject was required to draw a line to match a line directly in front of him and a line ten feet away from him. Results indicated that order of stimulus presentation was the main effect rather than thematic content. Furthermore, acute poors and chronic goods tended to overestimate, while the chronic poors and acute goods tended to underestimate relative to control groups.

There was also a suggestion that paranoids tended to overestimate while nonparanoids underestimated. The consistent performance of schizophrenic subgroups across stimulus conditions provided a possible demonstration of the cognitive style of each schizophrenic subgroup. The cognitive explanation as an alternative to a motivational explanation achieved a dominance in the Sixties directing most subsequent size estimation work.

Cognitive Studies That Use the Method of Average Error. Cognitive theorists in general (Piaget, 1950; Gardner, Holtzman, Klein, Linton, & Spence, 1959) postulated that over- or underconstancy reflects a particular cognitive approach in organizing external events. The adoption of the method of average error led the performance deficit theorist to specify the cognitive styles of schizophrenic subgroups. It was hypothesized that the performance deficit is the exhibition of the attention-response style of particular schizophrenic subgroups. Hence, the schizophrenic was viewed as exhibiting an extreme response tendency such as extensive scanning, extreme field dependency, minimal perceptual sets, etc., which produced the performance deficit.

Silverman (1964a, 1964b) formulated the most comprehensive and heuristic cognitive theory of schizophrenic size estimation performance. Building upon the work of Gardner and Long (1962) who elaborated upon the Piaget centration hypothesis (the longer the fixation time on a stimulus, the greater the size estimates), Silverman found a low but significant relationship between increased eye movements and size underestimation. Increased eye movement was thought to reflect greater sampling of the elements in the visual field, while decreased eye movement was related to a longer fixation on target. Silverman (1964b) related these findings to the size estimation performance of schizophrenics. Paranoid schizophrenics were considered to exhibit extensive eye movement (high scanning) and were predicted to show smaller size judgments. On the other hand, nonparanoids were considered low scanners (longer fixation time) and were predicted to produce larger size estimates.

To test these hypotheses, Silverman (1964b) employed an average error size estimation procedure in which subjects adjusted a circular patch of light to match the size of a hand-held disc. Results supported his predictions in that nonparanoids overestimated and paranoids underestimated the size of the disc. Silverman also examined the performance of acute and chronic paranoids in his sample but no differences were found. On the basis of his results, Silverman (1964a) extended his scanning theory to include the results of the Harris (1957) study: Acute goods were hypothesized to be overscanners (underestimators) and acute poors underscanners (overestimators). In a later study, Silverman and Goarder (1967) related saccadic eye movements to acute and chronic schizophrenic and nonschizophrenic patients. Saccadic eye movements were measured during a one-minute presentation of a target image. Afterward, size estimations were made employing the same procedure used in the previous study (Silverman, 1964b). The results supported the scanning hypothesis for nonschizophrenic patients only. Contrary to predictions, increases in eye movement for both schizophrenic groups were associated with increases in the magnitude of size estimations. This latter finding caused Silverman and Goarder to modify the scanning construct and introduce constructs dealing with information-search behavior and arousal.

McKinnon and Singer (1969) argued that Silverman's (1964a, 1967) studies were not a direct test of the visual scanning hypothesis because eye movements were not measured while judgments were being made. To provide a direct test, size estimates were made while the standard stimulus was present. Eye movements were recorded during free search and size judgment tasks for acute-schizophrenic subgroups, psychotic depressives, and normals. The results failed to support the scanning hypothesis. No relationship was found between eye movements and size estimation for any subject group. Also, unmedicated nonparanoids performed in an opposite direction from that predicted by Silverman, although medicated subjects did perform as expected.

The relationship between eye movement and size estimation was also examined by Stenn (1969). Thematic scenes were viewed for ten-second periods and correlated with size matches. Thus, unlike McKinnon and Singer, eye movements were not measured while actual size judgments were being made. A positive and significant eye-movement-size match correlation was found on the square scene, and a negative correlation was found on the scene connotating maternal censure over all subjects groups. No relationship was found on the remaining scenes. Such results were also considered to be inconsistent with the eye movement hypothesis.

In conclusion, the main contribution of these cognitive studies was the demonstration of different size estimation performance levels of specific subgroups. Interest in finding the specific mechanism responsible for the performance deficit was replaced by a focus on the cognitive styles of particular schizophrenic subgroups. This shift in emphasis occurred because the heterogeneity in the schizophrenic population was not interpreted as error variance which has to be minimized but rather as a heterogeneity reflecting individual differences. Questions of the difference between schizophrenics and normals, so prevalent in the performance deficit motivational studies, were replaced by questions of how different subclasses of normals or schizophrenics organize and approach their world. Although it was not clear who over- or underestimated, it was clear that some subgroups consistently differed in their size-estimation performance and that thematic content was a minor influence in creating this condition. It was also clear that the eye movement explanation of the degree of under- or overestimation was not satisfactory. The absence of any support for the relationship of eye movement to size estimation leaves the scanning and redundancy constructs without any clear theoretical construct II explanation. It may be that before any explanatory hypothesis can prove fruitful, an assessment of the actual determinants in the size estimation task must be accomplished. If a multitude of processes besides eye movement are required to complete the task, there is no single mechanism or measure that will account for size estimation performance.

Evaluation of the Size Estimation Operation

Task Variables Influencing Performance

Psychophysical Methods.   As noted earlier, size estimation studies have employed different psychophysical methods: the method of average error (*AE*) and a variation of the constant stimulus (*CS*) method. Siegel (1962), Neale et al. (1969), and Tate and Springer (1971) have noted that the results from the two methods may not be comparable. In the present review, the results from studies using a *CS* approach are compared with those employing an *AE* procedure for both normals and patient subgroups on the neutral and, where present, thematic scenes. Table 4.1 presents a listing of studies categorized by type of psychophysical method employed, the presence or absence of a memory component, and the use of thematic or neutral stimuli. Four *AE* studies (Harris, 1957; McKinnon & Singer, 1969; Zahn, 1959) showed that normals underestimated the neutral figure. When patients and normals were combined and their performance compared on all scenes, size underestimation was clearly the dominant response.

Using the *CS* method, four studies reported the results for normals and patient subgroups on each of the separate scenes. Davis et al. (1967), Mehl (1969), and Strauss (1970) found patients or normals overestimated on the geometric figure. Neale et al. (1971) reported normals to underestimate on the simple square, although this latter procedure may have been atypical since subjects were at optical infinity. Combining patients and normals on the *CS* studies regardless of stimulus content indicated size overestimation to be the most frequently occurring response. Thus, it appears that the two psychophysical methods lead to different response tendencies—overestimation on the *CS* method and underestimation on the *AE* approach.

Time on Interpolated Stimulus.   Postman (1947) compared the *CS* and *AE* methods on a sound intensity matching task involving a memory condition and found results opposite to those reported above. Negative time errors (size underestimation due to the apparent fading of the standard in memory) occurred on a *CS* task, and positive time errors (size overestimation

TABLE 4.1
Classification of Size Estimation Studies by
Psychophysical Method, Memory, and Content of Stimuli

Study	Method		Memory		Stimuli	
	C–S	A–E	Yes	No	Thematic	Neutral
Burner & Postman (1947)		*		*	*	
Klein (1954)		*	*		*	
Harris (1957)		*	*		*	
Zahn (1959)		*	*		*	
Ehrenworth (1960)		*	*		*	
Culver (1961)		*	*		*	
Silverman (1964b)		*		*		*
Mehl (1966)	*		*		*	
Webb et al. (1966)	*		*		*	
Davis et al. (1967)	*		*		*	
Neale & Cromwell (1968)	*		*		*	
McKinnon & Singer (1969)		*		*		*
Stenn (1969)	*		*		*	
Magaro (1969)		*	*	*	*	
Strauss (1970)	*				*	
Kopfstein & Neale (1971)	*		*		*	
Neale et al. (1971)	*		*		*	
Experiment II		*	*			*
Experiment III		*		*		*

due to apparent stimulus intensification in memory) occurred on the *AE* approach. He attributed the difference to length of match or adjustment time and suggested that the comparison acted as an interpolated stimulus. Positive time errors found on the *AE* method were thus due to the comparison stimulus which was under adjustment throughout the "match" interval, having the effect of a long duration interpolated stimulus. Negative time errors occurred on the *CS* method which involved no interpolated stimulus and generally shorter match times, although negative errors were maintained for longer time intervals. Others (Crannell, 1941; Guilford & Park, 1931; Karlin, 1953) have shown that for either method a stimulus presented between the standard and comparison will influence judgments in the direction of the magnitude of the interpolated stimulus.

As noted earlier, the *CS* method used in size estimation research differs from the traditional approach in that an array of six comparison scenes are presented at one time. Since some of the comparison scenes are thought to be sampled before selecting a match, each scene in the array can be considered to act as an interpolated stimulus. Thus, it appears that each of the two psychophysical methods employed in size estimation research contain interpolated stimuli. But since they contain a different number of stimuli, it is not surprising that differences in match times have also been found between the two methods. Zahn (1959) reported a mean adjustment time of 8.3 sec. on an *AE* task while Kopfstein and Neale (1971) found an average match time of 14.4 sec. on a *CS* task. The differences in the results between methods of the present studies may reflect differences in time on an interpolated comparison stimulus (i.e., shorter adjustment time on the interpolated stimuli in the *AE* method and longer match time on a series of interpolated stimuli in the *CS* approach). The longer time on the larger of the interpolated stimuli in the *CS* method would produce the overestimation reported in the *CS* work. The shorter time on the interpolated stimuli in the *AE* task may explain the consistent underestimation found in this work. To summarize, conflicting results in the size estimation area may be due to the size and length of time on the interpolated stimuli inadvertently employed in the size estimation procedure.

Time on Standard.   A second difference between the two psychophysical methods used in size estimation research is the duration of standard exposure time. In all *CS* studies, the standard stimulus was exposed for 10 sec., whereas in the *AE* memory studies the standard presentation time was 5 sec., Neale and Cromwell (1968) found longer presentation time to be related to increased size estimations. Thus, the predominance of size overestimation found in the *CS* approach may simply be related to longer viewing time on the standard and not at all related to the interpolated stimulus. Most scanning work has theorized that different time on standard has been responsible for subgroup differences. Hence, it is important to control or at least consider such a variable in comparing work in the area.

Stimulus Sequence.   Several of the studies (Kopfstein & Neale, 1971; Magaro, 1969; McKinnon & Singer, 1969; Strauss, 1970; Zahn, 1959) have found that size estimates increase as the number of trials increase. No one reported a negative relationship. Furthermore, Zahn (1959) and Magaro (1969) reported the greatest increase to occur between the first and second presented standard, regardless of the stimulus content. These findings suggest a general pattern of size estimation performance. Smaller size judgments may appear in the first standard presented and larger judgments on the second, with further trials leading to a gradual increase in size estimates.

Stimulus Complexity.   Harris (1957) suggested that stimulus complexity rather than thematic content could account for the differences in size judgments. To test whether or not complexity was a relevant factor, Ehrenworth (1960) compared the size estimation performance between a simple geometric figure and a complex neutral figure in the *CS* method. There was no difference between the degree of size estimation on the simple figure and the neutral complex scenes. However, for the *AE* approach, three studies (Bruner & Postman, 1948; Culver, 1961; Harris, 1957) showed increased size judgments on the complex figures as compared to the simple figures.

Stimulus Size.   Pratt (1933) and Koester and Schoenfield (1946) found that, in a memory condition, standard size was negatively related to perceived size. Bruner and Postman (1948) reported a positive relationship using a nonmemory procedure. It appears that larger standards in a memory task lead to size underestimation, but in a nonmemory condition larger standards lead to greater size judgments. Although the size of the standard may be the confounding factor in size estimation research, this point could not be fully explored since many studies did not report the size of the stimuli to be judged.

Memory.   Klein (1954) reported that when size judgments were made from memory, overestimation occurred. To test the effects of memory alone, the results on the simple geometric figure for studies using an *AE* memory task were compared with those using a nonmemory procedure (see Table 4.1). Such a comparison indicated no support for a pure memory effect, in that the level of size estimations found in the nonmemory condition were maintained in the memory condition. No comparisons could be made for the *CS* method, because all studies employed a memory task. Thus, a memory task by itself does not appear to lead to increased size estimates. However, as noted above, there is some evidence to indicate that memory appears to interact with time on an interpolated stimulus and with standard size. Therefore, Klein may have been only partially correct in attributing size increases to memory.

Thematic Stimulus Content.   Although motivational approaches hypothesized differential effects of specific thematic content on different subgroups, the most inconsistent results in size estimation studies are those dealing with the effects of stimulus content. For every study reporting a difference on specific thematic scenes, there is another reporting no difference. One possibility is that the differences in results relating to performance on affective scenes may be confounded by stimulus sequence. As noted earlier, there appears to be an increase in size judgments with increased trials. Strauss (1970) reported that size performance on thematic scenes was confounded by order of presentation. Asarnow and Mann (1978) found a similar result. Furthermore, Kopfstein and Neale (1971) showed that when sequence was randomized thematic differences disappeared. McCormick and Broekema (1978), in a repeat of the Davis procedure using the Harris slides, also did not find a thematic effect that was related to diagnostic groups. However, Strauss et al. (1974) and Neale et al. (1971) randomized presentation order and did find significant thematic differences. Thus, it appears that although stimulus sequence may act to confound size judgments, it is not a sufficient explanation of the inconsistent thematic stimuli results. Since most of the recent studies employing thematic scenes used the *CS* procedure, it may be that the task itself leads to inconsistent results, especially when it is considered that the thematic stimuli differ from the control stimuli in terms of complexity as well as thematic content (Neale et al., 1969). As noted earlier, the array of comparison scenes may also act as a series of interpolated stimuli. Subjective size judgments may then be influenced by the particular comparison scenes sampled prior to selecting a match. Such a process would allow greater variability in size performance and can mask thematic differences. The apparent confounding effects of stimulus sequence and interpolated stimuli need to be eliminated before the effect of thematic content on schizophrenic size performance can be determined.

Starting Position.   Silverman (1964b) found that nonparanoids showed a tendency towards smaller overestimations on the ascending trials, but this tendency was not shown by his paranoid group. No other *AE* studies examined this variable, but the work reported in a later section suggests it is of prime importance in predicting size estimation level and may serve as an interpolation effect.

Subject Variables Influencing Performance

In recent years, researchers have sought to reduce schizophrenic heterogeneity by classifying patients according to diagnosis, premorbid adjustment, and chronicity. Table 4.2 shows 13 full-scale studies and lists the presence or absence of control of these variables. Diagnosis refers to the paranoid–nonparanoid distinction. Prior to Silverman (1964b) no study included diagnosis, hence no motivational study employing the method of average error yields information on this important diagnostic dimension. In contrast, premorbid adjustment measured by the Phillips Scale (Phillips, 1953) is frequently considered in both cognitive and motivational studies using both psychophysical methods. To determine chronicity, it has become fairly standard to designate as acute patients with less than three years of hospitalization and to designate as chronic those with more than 6 years (Neale et al., 1969). Table 4.2 does not include the medication factor as a subject variable, but it should be noted that there is great ambiguity and imprecision about the meaning of the terms "medicated" and "non-medicated." Medication runs the gamut of psychotropic drugs, whose effects sometimes vary from individual to individual and whose dosages cannot be equated with any precision. "Nonmedicated" may mean never on medication, not on medication for 10 days prior to testing (Culver, 1961), or withdrawn from medication 30 hours prior to testing (McKinnon & Singer, 1969).

TABLE 4.2
Studies of Size Estimation Performance of Schizophrenics
Testing for Diagnosis, Premorbid Adjustment, and Chronicity Effects

Study	Diagnosis	Premobid Adjustment	Chronicity
Harris (1957)		*	
Zahn (1959)		*	
Zahn, Pilot 1 (1959)		*	
Zahn, Pilot 2 (1959)		*	
Ehrenworth (1960)			
Culver (1961)		*	
Silverman (1964b)	*		
Mehl (1966)		*	
Webb et al. (1966)	*	*	
Davis et al. (1967)	*	*	
Neale & Cromwell (1968)	*		
McKinnon & Singer (1969)	*		
Magaro (1969)		*	*
Kopfstein & Neale (1971)		*	*
Neale et al. (1971)	*	*	*

Average error studies yield consistent results only when memory is not a factor. McKinnon and Singer (1969) found acute nonmedicated paranoids to overestimate and nonparanoid patients to underestimate the standard. Silverman (1964b) found chronic nonparanoids to significantly overestimate and chronic paranoids to underestimate. All studies reported normals to underestimate the standard. Thus, the results of the AE nonmemory studies are fairly consistent: Nonparanoids and normals underestimate as do chronic paranoids, while chronic nonparanoids and acute paranoids overestimate. In AE memory studies, the results are much less consistent due in part to methodological differences: Culver (1961) did not specify chronicity, and Zahn's (1959) results appeared to be influenced by the reward–punishment condition. Harris (1957) did not categorize patients by paranoid diagnosis but found premorbid adjustment differences in his acute sample.

In the CS studies results have also been inconsistent. Three studies (Davis et al., 1967; Neale & Cromwell, 1968; Stenn, 1969) found acute nonparanoids to overestimate when compared to acute good paranoids. McCormick and Broekema (1978) found paranoids to underestimate relative to nonparanoids. Two studies (Kopfstein & Neale, 1971; Neale et al., 1971) found no significant differences between comparable subgroups. However, in comparing these significant and nonsignificant results, paranoids were found to exhibit the most consistent performance, showing only slight errors of over- and underestimation. Nonparanoids were much more inconsistent in their size matches, exhibiting the greatest degree of overestimation (Davis et al., 1967) and the greatest level of underestimation (Kopfstein & Neale, 1971). When chronic patients were considered, the picture was similar. Strauss, Foureman, and Parwatikar (1974) found a significant premorbid-by-diagnosis interaction with the greatest difference occurring between the poor paranoids and poor nonparanoids. Two studies (Mehl, 1969; Kopfstein & Neale, 1971) found no significant differences for chronic patients. As with the acutes, chronic paranoids were more consistent in their settings of slight overestimation,and nonparanoids more variable, exhibiting overestimation matches in four instances and underestimation in three cases. Normals were similar to paranoids showing a slight overestimation. Thus, at first glance the *CS* results seem much less consistent than the *AE* results, suggesting that the *CS* method leads to more variable size responses. However, further analysis of the results reveals the consistent tendency of each subgroup. Variability in performance is mainly found with nonparanoid schizophrenics due to their reliance upon the fluctuating operation of the perceptual process. Paranoids have been usually found to differ from schizophrenics performing more like normals and less influenced by task conditions; however, there are enough exceptions even to question this generalization.

In summary, then, work in the size estimation area began within a motivational framework examining a D_s term and employing the method of average error, and subsequently, the method of constant stimuli. Conflicting results within this framework led to a focus on task variables and an increased use of subject variables. This was paralleled by the development of cognitive theories emphasizing $_sH_r$ terms and mainly using the method of average error. They found the scanning hypothesis wanting but produced evidence that task variables are combined in a study, over- or underestimation will occur. In of task and subject variables suggests that when one or more of the task variables are combined in a study, over or underestimation will occur. In short, it does not seem possible to speak of a size estimation task because the operational dynamism principle has operated so extensively that the task involves a multitude of variables. Our description of nine task variables may be a conservative estimate because it was limited by those variables that have been investigated. The most ignored and possibly the most potent task variable in the size judgment task is the type of procedure—constant stimulus or average error. Other variables are the number of trials, stimulus complexity, memory, thematic content, subject variables, and starting position. A multitude of empirical events are operating which could operationalize multiple empirical constructs, produce many empirical laws (especially if subject variables are one of the events), and support all theoretical constructs. With such power to confirm theories, it is no wonder the task has been popular in research on the schizophrenic performance deficit.

Size Constancy

The size constancy work can be divided into two groups of studies. The first group provides very little information or combines diverse subgroups into the schizophrenic sample (MacDorman, Rivoire, Gallagher, & MacDorman, 1962; Perez, 1961; Pishkin, Smith, & Leibowitz, 1962; Sanders & Pacht, 1952; Weckowicz, 1957). The second group attempts some degree of differentiation among schizophrenic subgroups (Hamilton, 1972; Jannucci, 1964; Leibowitz & Pishkin, 1961; Lovinger, 1956; Raush, 1952). The following review focuses upon task variables, especially those identified as important in the size estimation research. Table 4.3 presents a summary of these findings.

Memory. A memory factor was a possible variable in only one study. Pishkin et al. (1962) presented the standard and variable stimuli in a darkened room. The subject controlled the source of light by pushing a button that triggered a 10 microsec flash of light to illuminate the scene. Chronic withdrawn schizophrenics triggered more illuminations than the normals before making a judgment. This could be interpreted as compensation for difficulty in remembering the size of the standard in order to complete the matching of variable to standard. This compensation was fairly effective because no significant difference resulted between schizophrenics and normal controls. However, the increased number of illuminations for the chronic schizophrenics also increased the time on standard. Therefore, this factor could have produced larger size judgments.

Stimulus Size. Standard size has been systematically examined in one study. Weckowicz (1957) in a nonmemory procedure presented a standard which varied in height from 1 to 20 centimeters. Results showed chronic schizophrenics deviated toward underconstancy when the standard size was larger than 6 centimeters, and this effect occurred most clearly when the standard was located at the farthest distance. Therefore, as compared to the nonmemory size estimation results which found that size estimation increased with larger stimulus size, size judgments may decrease with an increase in stimulus size in a size constancy procedure.

Ascending and Descending Order of Trials. Most of the studies required an adjustment of the variable stimulus in ascending or descending directions. MacDorman et al. (1962) reported more errors of anticipation and habituation in descending trials, but such errors decreased with practice. Harway and Salzman (1964) found normals to be least influenced by the starting position, while schizophrenics made significantly larger size judgments on descending trials. However, this effect only occurred on the first few trials. Therefore, the effect of this variable seems temporary.

TABLE 4.3
Task and Subject Variable Results in Size Constancy Studies
That Varied Standard Stimulus Size/Memory Condition/Order of Trials

	Standard Stimulus Size	Memory	Order of Presentation of Variable Stimulus	Subject Groups	Task Variable Results	Subject Variable Results
Weckowicz (1957)	A rod, 1–20 cm in length (1 cm increments) .5 cm in diameter.	X	Not adjusted from extreme positions. Alternate large and small standard.	Chronic (hebephrenics) Schizophrenic Non-Schiz patients Normals	Plots of est. of schiz deviate to underconstancy as standard increases in size. markedly so past 15m Memory — none Order — none	Chronic schizophrenics have lower size constancy than normals and non-schizophrenics.
Hamilton (1963)	diamonds 10cm 15cm rod 15 cm high, 1.2 cm diameter Bottle 13.4 penny 3.1 pack cig. 10.4 cm card 3.1 cm	X	Alternating maximum or minimum.	Chronic nonparanoids Paranoids Manic-dep Neurotics Normals	Memory — none Order — none Size — none	Chronic nonparanoids equal to paranoids & other psychotics. All psychotic normals significantly underconstant compared to schizophrenics
Pishkin, Smith, & Leibowicz (1962)	X	10 micro-sec. light flash?	X	Chronic, withdrawn schiz. Aides.	Schiz needed more illuminations than normals before judging. Order — none Size — none	No significant difference in size judgments.
MacDorman et al. (1962)	X	X	15 variables ranging from 6 to 14 in alternating ascending and descending order.	Teenage schizophrenics Normals	Memory — none Size — none Overconstancy in both groups on descending trials	Schizophrenics had more errors of anticipation & habituation which diminished with practice Schizophrenics overconstant when variables in front of standard.

Study		Stimuli	Subjects	Measures	Results
Harway & Salzman (1964)	X	Slides ranging from 3.5 to 10.5 in. A, D, A, A, D, order of presentation.	Schizophrenics Normals	Schiz. larger overestimation on descending trials.	Higher size constancy for schizophrenics, more accurate, in low-cue condition. No difference in high-cue conditions
Perez (1961)	X	Squares increasing in diameter by .25 cm from 3 to 10.5 cm. Always ascending order.	Schizophrenics Nonschizophrenics	Memory — none Order — none Size — none	Schizophrenics had higher size constancy than nonschizophrenics.
Janucci (1964)	X	Same as Perez	Paranoids Catatonics Chronic undiffern. Normals	Memory — none Order — none Size — none	No significant differences
Raush (1952)	X	Alternately descending and ascending.	Paranoids Nonparanoids Normals	Memory — none Order — none Size — none	All groups overconstant. In the dark paranoids were more overconstant than nonparanoids & controls.
Lovinger (1956)	X	Alternately descending and ascending.	Paranoids & Nonparanoids in good & poor contact. Normals	Memory — none Order — none Size — none	No significant differences between paranoids & nonparanoids. Poor contacts significantly more order constant than good contacts or controls.

Other Variables Found Throughout Size Constancy Research. In addition to the above variables, many other variables have been manipulated in the size constancy work. All of the following six variables have been shown to affect performance: location of standard, distance of standard from the subject, direction, thematic content, cues or lighting, and angle size between standard and variable. In considering *location of the standard* relative to the variable, MacDorman et al. (1962) analyzed the effect of placing the standard in front of the variable and behind it. With the standard in back, there was greater overconstancy. With the standard in front, there was greater underconstancy. *Distance of the standard* from the subject was manipulated in two studies. MacDorman et al. (1962) found no difference between judgments while Weckowicz (1957) found schizophrenics tended to be more underconstant when the standard was at the far location. Normals tended to overestimate the standard at the far location. Size constancy *directions* have generally taken two forms. Perez (1961) found higher size constancies following instructions which asked for the judgment to "look like" the standard. When the instructions asked for the match to be "physically the same" as the standard, there were no differences between schizophrenics and normals except when the standard contained thematic content. *Thematic content* of the standard was varied by Perez (1961) who found that a skull drawing elicited significantly smaller size comparisons than did a drawing of a nonsense figure or a lettered block. *Illumination and cue conditions* remain constant in most studies, but a few vary the amount of light available for viewing the standard and variable. Raush (1952) found that in a dark condition, paranoids had higher constancy values than controls and nonparanoids. Lovinger (1956) found no difference between paranoids and nonparanoids under various cue conditions. However, in a minimal cue condition schizophrenics in poor contact performed worse than paranoids or normals. Harway and Salzman (1964) found that, in three conditions of illumination, schizophrenics had signficantly higher constancy than normals. The effect of an extreme *angle* between standard and variable may increase overestimation of the standard. Raush (1952) attributes the overconstancy of his subjects partially to the effect of the 90° angle between standard and variable.

The size constancy task is more complex than the size estimation task because there are an even larger number of task variables in the former. Therefore, slight differences in experimental procedure such as differences in the angle between standard and comparison, could produce conflicting results. The inclusion of more task variables introduces more or at least different psychological processes which may explain the differential performance of specific schizophrenic groups from study to study, as well as greater confusion in the results themselves.

Besides the variation in *S,* there may be many perceptual and conceptual processes required by the task. For example, starting position and stimulus size are empirical events which could operationalize the empirical constructs utilized by V theorists. Shakow, Payne, and McGhie all vary the properties of the stimulus to produce the experimental situation which can demonstrate the V-type theoretical construct. In contrast, distance, location, memory, and angle of the standard all involve a conceptual process in emitting a size judgment. Both Cameron and Chapman hypothesize different processes which would inhibit the operation of the process. In short, almost all theorists would expect a deficit on a size constancy task. However, the reasons would differ depending upon the theorist's analysis of the empirical events in the procedure.

The preceding review and analysis of past literature provide only speculations concerning the effect of specific within-task variables. A recent study of Vojtisek (1975) illustrates a manipulation of size estimation variables. He was not as interested in the global size estimation responses as the variables in the task which produced subgroup differences. Hence, he varied size estimation memory, stimulus size, and comparison stimuli with and without the presentation of an interpolated stimulus. The measures were the traditional Point of Subjective Equality (PSE), number of correct matches with the comparison stimuli, and signal detection scores. Groups were acute paranoid and nonparanoid schizophrenics with less than one year of hospitalization. Results indicated that response bias was not an important factor, but different measures produced different results. The Percent Correct approach resulted in the finding that an interpolated stimulus affected the accuracy of the paranoids the greatest. The acute nonparanoids made the most errors when the size of the interpolated stimulus was similar to the comparison. The PSE approach led to the finding that the size of the interpolated studies produced different effects. The small interpolated stimulus produced the greatest underestimation for the paranoid. With the large stimuli, the paranoids followed normals and overestimated while nonparanoids again exhibited the least degree of overestimation. In short, the nonparanoid did not allow the interpolated stimulus to determine performance, except when the two stimuli were similar in size. Normals and paranoids followed the direction of the interpolated stimulus by increasing or decreasing their size judgments in terms of the size of the interpolated stimulus. It was also found on the PSE measure that size estimation decreased on extended memory trials. The signal detection results were similar to the other analysis and indicated that all groups had difficulty with the task containing an interpolated stimulus. Memory was important for subgroup differences, in that paranoids and normals tended to exhibit greater accuracy than nonparanoids in the brief memory condition where all groups were equal.

In general, the interpolated stimulus did not interfere with the judgments of paranoids. But the nonparanoid was most affected in the condition where stimuli were small and most physically similar. The paranoid was able to establish a conceptual framework that is not affected by changes in stimulus conditions. These results reveal the power of the task conditions. If one finds differential group effects by varying task elements, hypotheses derived from overall size judgment scores, such as those made by Silverman or other habit theorists about differential mechanisms within the organism, require an explanation of the specific task variable producing group differences. The hypothesized mechanism would have to directly relate to the effect of a specific task variable such as an interpolated stimulus, memory, stimulus size, measurement used, etc. All of these would presumably relate to different psychological states. Though the Vojtisek study examined only a few of the task variables in a size estimation task the findings of a differential effect on measures and groups indicate that these variables cannot be neglected.

Asarnow and Mann (1978) reached the same conclusion. They presented a standard stimulus alone or surrounded by smaller or larger stimuli. The standard was presented at 33 or 400 millisec, and the procedure was performed twice. They found that nonparanoids overestimated relative to paranoids while normals were intermediate, but this effect occurred only on the first administration. They cautioned that the effects of sequence could explain previous conflicting results.

In a recent review of size judgment work, Leibowitz (1974) concludes that size judgments involve multiple processes. The multiple factors are conceptual size, perceptual learning, oculomotor adjustments, and the instructions which call for the use of specific mechanisms. The assumption that size estimation or size constancy reflects the operation of one process which could be used to clarify the schizophrenic process has been abandoned.

Now the introduction of a K process as an explanation of a previously considered V process is becoming rather frequent. For example, Hamilton (1972) views size constancy as a cognitive task. He concluded that the degree of the size constancy for poor nonparanoid chronics was a function of the interaction of cognitive conserving operations and centration strategies ($K \times V$). Performance on a task, which is usually seen as perceptual, was found to relate directly to conceptual skills, and the task demand for integration of the two processes was found to be related to the type of size constancy performance. The Asarnow and Mann (1978) study, reported above, found that paranoids were not affected by background stimuli, whereas nonparanoids were affected by both background stimuli and exposure time. They explain their results in terms of Integration Theory in that:

> The somewhat greater responsiveness of the nonparanoid schizophrenics to the differences in background stimuli may be regarded as evidence of the greater reliance of nonparanoid schizophrenics on perceptual data than is the case with paranoid schizophrenics. Conversely, the consistency across the manipulations of stimulus exposure and stimulus duration on the part of the paranoids may be taken as evidence of the relative unresponsiveness of the paranoid schizophrenics to subtle variations in perceptual input [p. 103].

They further suggest that future research would be best served by an experimental situation in which conceptual or perceptual demands are added to a task and the performance of paranoid and nonparanoid schizophrenics is observed. As conceptual demands are added, the nonparanoid should exhibit a deficit reflecting an inability to produce a conceptual compensation. As the perceptual demands are added, the paranoid should exhibit a deficit indicating an adherence to a concept and neglect of the perceptual stimulus dimension. However, the operation of either process can be seen best in those experimental situations where both processes are varied. What is required is a return to very simple experimental procedures which clearly reflect the manner in which individual schizophrenic subgroups are required to integrate specific definable conditions. We believe an information-processing model meets such conditions, and we explore this possibility in a following chapter.

$$D \times {}_{s_d}H_r/M_r = {}_sE_r$$

Broen and Storms

The most theoretically consistent and clearly documented theory of the schizophrenic performance deficit is that presented by Broen and Storms (Broen, 1966, 1968; Broen & Storms, 1966, 1967). In a precise application of Hullian theory, especially the Hullian analysis of the discrimination task, Broen makes extensive use of the response and habit hierarchy constructs as they interact with drive to predict schizophrenic performance deficit. It is tempting to consider Broen as simply a response theorist because he considers the main problem to reside in the response system. However, this would be an oversimplification because the observable response system deficiency is, in effect, the result of interacting effects of drive and a novel construct—the response ceiling. Whereas previous theorists have specified the perceptual–attentional or conceptual processes as interacting with drive, Broen subsumes such processes under the category of one response which follows the same principle as other observable responses.

Broen and Storms (1966) describe the schizophrenic process as lawful disorganization. The response hierarchy of the schizophrenic is the same as the response hierarchy of the normal, except that the relative strength of the responses differ. Differences in strength between the dominant and competing responses are greater for normals than for schizophrenics. For the schizophrenic, strength of appropriate and inappropriate responses are equivalent, while for the normal, responses are ordered in degree of appropriateness. The authors therefore, view:

> schizophrenic behavior as due to greater equivalence of appropriate and competing responses resulting in disorganized response patterns. Equivalence is, of course, an ambiguous term. In our theory, equivalence of alternate responses means that response tendencies have equal strength, and when this

occurs, the probability of the alternate responses are equal. . . . The meaning of "normal behavior" is that response tendencies that are simultaneously evoked are hierarchically ordered in accordance with appropriateness, and with considerable increments between the strengths of appropriate and inappropriate response tendencies. Becoming schizophrenic is not seen as changing the content of response hierarchies in individuals, or the hierarchical order of response tendencies, but in schizophrenics the hierarchies tend to be partially collaspsed. The strengths of dominant and competing responses are more nearly equal. Near equivalence in strength leads to response occurrence being more random [Broen, 1968, p. 76].

As with many of the perceptual theorists, Broen focuses upon situations which require a discrimination between two stimuli or meanings. The schizophrenic has difficulty emitting the appropriate response—a successful task response. Rather, a related response is given. Such a response is also possible for normals but this reaction occurs at a much lower level of probability. Only when competing responses are elicited by the stimulus situation, will the schizophrenic show a deficit. In the following passage the authors describe the determination of $_sE_r$ in a discrimination situation where D is also a factor. Note the strict translation of Hull used by the authors:

In Hull–Spence theory, if two or more response tendencies (reaction potentials or Es) are presented at the same time, the likelihood that the dominant response (R_D) will occur is a function of the difference in strength between dominant and competing response tendencies $\%R = F(E_D - E_C)$. Two of the variables that affect strength of response tendencies are: (1) habit strength (H), which is a function of variables such as the number of trials where the stimulus has been followed by the response; and (2) drive (D), a general response-energizing factor which is increased by a number of conditions (e.g., stress conditions, emotional excitation). Specifically, the strength of a response tendency is a function of habit strength multiplied by drive $E = f(D \times H)$. Thus, when dominant and competing associations are evoked at the same time, the difference between their strengths, which is positively related to the probability of the dominant response, is given by the following formula: $E_D - E_C = fD(H_D - H_C)$. In sum, drive variables such as high anxiety multiply differences in habit strengths between alternate responses in response hierarchies, and are therefore predicted to increase the probability of dominant responses [Broen, 1968, p. 77].

In this explanation Broen has faithfully applied computing practices and terms from the Hull–Spence theory. However, he defects from this strictness in introducing the response ceiling construct. This construct is a substitute for the response threshold construct in the Hull–Spence system which explained why a stimulus elicited some responses and not others. The response threshold indicated the level in the response hierarchy defining the habit strength of those responses elicited by the stimulus. The ceiling construct specifies a limit also, but only of the dominant responses under specific drive conditions. In support of the ceiling construct, Broen (1968) presents evidence that indicates essentially that a high habit strength response may decrease in response strength with increased drive. A threshold position predicts that the dominant response increases in response strength with increased drive. Broen and Storms:

> attempted to account for these results by postulating a response-strength ceiling lower than maximum drive times maximum habit strength. This means that when the habit strength of the dominant response (H_D) is low, the multiplicative effect of drive favors the dominant response, but when H_D is high, the response strength ceiling may limit the multiplicative effect of drive on the dominant response. When the strength of the dominant response is at ceiling, the only effect of increased drive will be to increase the strength of responses lower in the response hierarchy, thus tending to collapse the response hierarchy and increase the probability of incorrect responses [Broen, 1968, pp. 78–79].

The effect of a ceiling on response strength rather than on habit strength postulated in this theory explains the use of M_r in the present system and its replacement in the model as affecting ${}_sE_r$ rather than H. Broen (1968) states: "The implication in the use of the term 'response strength' as being inhibited instead of habit strength is that inhibitory effects should be subtracted after the multiplicative effects of arousal have been allowed for [p. 92]."

There are, therefore, three main constructs which are used to explain the difference between normal and schizophrenic performance. One is the previously described response ceiling. Another is the habit construct which is developed from reinforced practice to a specific stimulus, ${}_{s_d}H_r$. The last is an arousal term. Broen and Storms (1966) state:

> The term arousal is used to indicate a dimension of relatively diffuse cortical and physiological activation which may be measured by changes in peripheral physiological indicants such as increases in heart rate, blood pressure, and respiration rate. The studies we will cite as having varied arousal experimentally use independent variables which are similar to variables which have been shown to lead to the general physiological changes indicative of arousal. A particular good example of such a variable is induced muscular tension [p. 267].

The Broen response disorganization theory is presented in schematic form in Fig. 4.5 and indicates the careful development of theoretical terms from specific operations. It should be noted that the terms of previous theories had to be fitted into a logical theoretical framework. Broen is most explicit in the use of intervening variables for hypothetical constructs. Even more accurate is his precise operationalizing of terms. The observables for the three constructs are clearly stated. Pressure on a dynamometer operationalizes the empirical construct of drive. Habit has its observables in the training sequence in which a particular response such as a lever push or card sort is reinforced a fewer number of times. Any stimulus can be designated as a reinforcer—a light, verbal praise, etc. The empirical constructs defined by

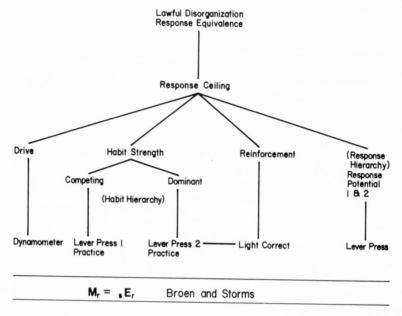

FIG. 4.5.   Schematic representation of the theoretical structure of response theories.

these reinforcement operations are the habit strengths of the dominant and competing responses that define as a group the response and habit hierarchy.

The function between changes in arousal and habit strength permits the inference of the theoretical construct, the response ceiling. This construct specifically relates to the one empirical law that states that an increase in arousal is associated with a decrease in strength of a high habit strength response and an increase in strength of a competing lower habit strength response until it equals the strength of the dominant response. Response potential is a direct function of *H* and *D* and is operationalized by performance during the task trials. It should be stressed that the habit and drive terms follow the Hullian usage in that they are operationalized by specific operations. They are no more than the rational explanation of the functional relationship (Bergmann & Spence, 1941). However, the ceiling term is defined by a specific function of the empirical constructs of drive and habit. The theoretical II level terms used by Broen are lawful disorganization or response equivalance. They explain why all task responses are at equal probability and explain the conditions necessary to induce the performance deficit.

It may be helpful to compare the Broen and Storms position to other theorists in order to specify its uniqueness. Other theorists deal with the response system as a dependent variable which is affected by the operation of another process such as a particular perceptual construct. Differences in the functional relationship between variables of schizophrenics and normals are explained by the postulated perceptual construct. Broen observes this same difference in functions, but, in addition to postulating theoretical constructs that affect the response system, he also focuses on the response system itself. Task performance, the operation of the response system, has its own governing properties and is not just an extension of the effects of stimulus condition, as would be found in a simple S–R model. Nor is it an extension of the effects of a mediational or perceptual theoretical construct, as found in the perceptual and conceptual theories. Another difference is the precision in specifying the nature of competing responses and the conditions most detrimental to schizophrenic performance.

In comparing Broen to Mednick, there is a difference in their use of drive terms. Mednick (1958) speaks of a conditioned drive augmenting a general drive level, while Broen (1968) speaks of a general drive whose level varies in different groups. The Broen position more clearly defines D by using one drive process with specific operations. Mednick postulates two drive processes, Dd and Ds, with Ds having little empirical support. Their habit constructs are also different. Mednick speaks of associational responses in the same manner as other conceptual theorists, hence the K labeling. Broen, on the other hand, specifies a habit hierarchy which is the basis of any type of response having the same predictable consequences. Mednick defines the H construct developed from a vague conceptual process, whereas Broen clearly states an H definition and accurately uses the Hullian model to predict the effects of dominant and alternate responses. Their explanation of the collapse of the response hierarchy also differs. Some have questioned whether or not Mednick accurately interpreted Hull on the consequences of increased drive on the habit hierarchy (Broen, 1968; Venables, 1964).

The last point to be stressed concerns the novel M_r term. A means of directly measuring its effect has not been suggested, but its viability would be increased if it were directly tested through a specific set of operations. Therefore, the ceiling term is not as satisfactory as other terms. It lacks direct supporting evidence and hence moves beyond the safety of the Hullian theory that has a demonstrable relationship between terms. For instance, although it is at the same theoretical level as the threshold concept, the original Hullian evocation threshold lends itself to a clearer operational definition than the ceiling construct. If the response occurs, it is above threshold. The ceiling term states that if a response does not occur it is at ceiling. Definition by an absence of response seems as hazardous as proving the null hypothesis. In short, the response ceiling construct as shown in Fig. 4.1 is a theoretical construct which is inferred from the relationship between two empirical constructs. Since this term is not based on the original Hullian theory, direct empirical support is needed to confirm its properties and its relationship to other variables. Direct empirical support for a term not included in the initial theory should be provided by the theorist who introduces the theoretical modification. This is not to say that Broen has failed to demonstrate the decreased probability of the dominant response with increased drive, but only to point out that a response ceiling has not been shown to cause this function.

Both Broen and Venables use the same arousal construct, $\bar{D}$. However, Venables uses $\bar{D}$ in a causal sense, while Broen uses $\bar{D}$ and H interacting as determinants of the resultant R. Venables (1964) also makes use of V terms for which Broen substitutes R terms. Broen interprets the V studies in terms of the strength of the competing response tendencies elicited by the irrelevant stimuli. That is, in a careful analysis of studies of the V theorists, Broen explains the results by arguing that the stimulus situations created are likely to increase the number of competing responses that produce the deficit. The stimulus situations which do not elicit strong competing responses, such as clearly discriminated irrelevant stimuli, will not produce a deficit. To reconcile the opposing theory of Chapman and to explain performance differences between chronics and acutes, Broen describes the long-term effects of response disorganization. He hypothesizes that these effects involve a defense—a secondary learned reaction to the basic aversive response disorganization—that is a reliance upon a few dominant responses to most stimulus situations. Some direct tests of the two positions in regard to the strength of a nondominant response have tended to support the Chapman position (Boland & Chapman, 1971), although Hamsher and Arnold (1976) argue against it.

Broen (1968) essentially incorporates most theories into a broad response-interference theory reinterpreting perceptual and conceptual work as response processes. In our view, Broen is speaking of both V and K processes and how both interfere with one another. We will differ from Broen by specifying the two processes which determine the deficit. Broen subsumes both processes under a more generalized explanatory term of response and as such is able to explain a V, K, D, or sHr theory simply through the effect of the nonobservable ceiling construct upon the response system. Since all processes enter or determine the response, the one which does so to a greater or lesser degree should be specified. If, on the other hand, it is just the response system that is deficient, then the exact response system such as motor or conceptual in response selection, or perceptual in terms of selecting relevant stimuli, has to be specified and its role must be demonstrated in comparison to other systems. The response system may be too general a construct to provide exact tests of the theory.

However, that is not totally fair since Broen (1973) has been focusing more upon the effect of the response ceiling on perceptual factors, especially the range of attention. Findings from this approach suggest that the theory only applies to nonparanoids in that paranoids do not show the narrowing of attention and in fact attend to more stimuli than nonparanoids. This was confirmed in a study by Broen and Nakamura (1972). They found that, in a visual tracking task performed simultaneously with an auditory signal detection task, paranoids were not distracted by the stimulus conditions while nonparanoids were distracted.

Another positive aspect of Broen's work is his use of acute subjects. Broen has mainly used acute groups and as such is not subject to the problem of confounding schizophrenia with institutionalization. Bible and Magaro (1971) present some evidence that the Broen ceiling position is applicable to acutes and not chronics. Storms and Acosta (1974) used acute schizophrenics and found the ceiling effect for the schizophrenics but not for the nonschizophrenic psychiatric controls as expected. Broen (1968) was quite aware of different deficits for acute and chronic schizophrenic subgroups, and in later work (Broen, 1973; Broen & Storms, 1977) stated a different mechanism for chronics.

The current update of the Broen theory indicates that the theory is moving toward an analysis of the chronic patients in terms of their narrowed attention (Broen, 1973; Broen & Storms, 1977). In explaining other work with chronics Broen & Storms (1977) describe chronics as those who have narrowed attention and would scan through memory until the first associate is found and this would be the response. Since this associate would sometimes be incorrect due to sentence context, the schizophrenic would produce a greater deficit. By using the explanation of the scanning of memory, Broen moves toward an information theory model to explain attention. In this position, many assumptions are made about other cognitive processes. For example, it assumes that the schizophrenic actually has an image to scan. Davies-Osterkamp, Rist, and Bangert (1977) tested the Broen model with chronics. They measured reaction time with simultaneous presentation of the stimuli in one or two different modalities. They found that rather than a tendency toward narrow attention, there was a problem in cross-modal shifts. Chronics did not increase their deficit under those experimental conditions relevant to the breadth of attention. Rather the chronic could not switch modalities or could not switch attention from the irrelevant to relevant signal. The attention deficit suggested by Broen could therefore be a matter of utilizing or integrating different sensory modalities rather than narrowing attention. However, the later constructs especially that of scanning memory relate only to chronics, and hence may not be very relevant in a discussion of schizophrenia. What is clear is that the Broen discussion of schizophrenia has been one of the main springboards to current attempts to apply information theory procedure to this area. Before becoming more explicit about the results of such efforts, we must now discuss the subject arm of our function between schizophrenia and performance. We now make the case for the separation of schizophrenia and paranoia. The results we have just reviewed suggest that this is the main dimension in terms of a separation of two different cognitive processes, once confounding dimensions such as chronicity and pathology are controlled.

5
Schizophrenia and Paranoia

In Chapter 2 we discussed how psychology modeled itself after the physical sciences, especially in constructing hypothetical terms to meaningfully organize the bewildering mass of empirical data about human behavior. In the impulse to explain, the awesome task of adequate description may have been too quickly abandoned. Theorizing and predicting without adequate descriptive categories may have generated potentially misleading explanations for phenomena whose empirical relations are vague. We argue in this chapter that the reliance upon the theoretical construct, schizophrenia, without adequate operationalizing or even attempts at operationalization, has generated a paradigm for research in schizophrenia which has obscured the empirical differences between paranoids and nonparanoids, and hence, the empirical laws derived from laboratory tasks. Previous chapters focused upon the measures defining those causal terms which explained the psychological mechanisms within the schizophrenic. Results consistently indicated that, on most laboratory tasks, the paranoid—nonparanoid dimension is especially important for specifying the subject group who exhibits a deficit, especially when patients are acute. The present discussion focuses upon the major distinction within schizophrenia, paranoids vs. nonparanoids.

In this chapter, we first briefly review the empirical and conceptual history of the paranoid construct in terms of the dominant paradigm that considers it a variant of schizophrenia. Next, recent studies that compare schizophrenics and paranoids are reviewed to demonstrate an identifiable paranoid process independent of the schizophrenic process. We expect to show that paranoids are not schizophrenic and that schizophrenics are not paranoid, although some behaviors may be common to both groups. Through a review and analysis of the current operational definitions of the two groups, we then attempt an accurate definition of these two categories on the basis of clinical, behavioral, and empirical observations. This will be followed by a discussion in general terms of the process unique to each group. However, it should be noted that although we attempt to distinguish the paranoid from the schizophrenic in the present chapter, a later chapter will suggest a higher-order theoretical term related to both disorders. Finally, we present some evidence suggesting that the two conditions exist in childhood and could be so recognized if the current method of clasifying paranoids with schizophrenics were not so pervasive and blinding.

THE EMERGENCE OF A PARADIGM

Despite consistent theoretical and empirical recognition of separate categories, mainstream clinical and research traditions have, until quite recently, tended to regard the paranoid as a type of schizophrenic. This appears to be a legacy from the "Age of Classification" when the systems of Kraepelin and Bleuler brought some order to the mass of clinical observations (Zilboorg & Henry, 1941). Kraepelin (1919) included paranoids, catatonics, and hebephrenics under the single term *dementia praecox* on the basis of the hypothetical common organic etiology and the expected deteriorated outcome. However, he also was explicit about distinguishing the paranoid from the schizophrenic. Kraepelin noted that paranoia was a primary disease of the intellect which had the secondary phenomena of delusions that could produce emotional stress (Kraepelin, 1976). He also warned that the true paranoid had a fixed delusional system which should not be confused with the schizophrenic who may have a few meager, disconnected, or confused delusions. The main characteristic of the paranoid (Kraepelin, 1976) was "the insidious development of a permanent and unshakable delusional system resulting from internal causes accompanied by a perfect presentation of clear and orderly thinking, willing, and acting [pp. 212–213]." The occurrence of hallucinations was considered rare although there may be warning or assuring voices. Kraepelin thought that pure paranoia was relatively rare,and identified an intermediate and more populous condition between paranoia and schizophrenia, which he called paraphrenia. The schizophrenia-paraphrenia-paranoia dimension was defined by the degree of formal thought disorganization, with delusional but well-organized cognition occupying the paranoia end of the continuum.

Bleuler (1950) coined the term schizophrenia to replace *dementia praecox* and added a fourth subtype (simple). He grouped paranoids with catatonics and hebephrenics because all exhibited a disordered associative process.

Bleuler argued that pure paranoia was so rare that it should be disregarded as a formal diagnostic category. He classified paraphrenics as paranoid schizophrenics by identifying the cardinal paranoid symptoms—delusions and ideas of reference—as special instances of the associative disturbance common to all schizophrenics. However, he also noted the clear clinical difference between paranoid and nonparanoid types and, thus, expended a great deal of effort to justify the inclusion of paranoids as schizophrenics.

Thus, while Kraepelin and Bleuler both accepted the possibility of a separate condition called paranoia, neither considered it a separate category from the nonparanoid types. This is the conclusion that has prevailed until the present although, interestingly, Bleuler (1950) clearly recognized the tentative nature of this nosology:

> Under the term dementia praecox or schizophrenia we thus subsume a group of diseases which can be clearly distinguished from all other types of diseases in Kraepelin's system. They have many common symptoms and similar prognoses. Nevertheless, their clinical pictures may be extremely varied. This concept may be of temporary value only inasmuch as it may later have had to be reduced (in the same sense as the discoveries of bacteriology necessitated the subdivision of the pneumonias in terms of the various etiological agents) [p. 4].

Opposing the tradition of descriptive psychiatry, the dynamic schools searched for the etiological dynamic unique to each diagnostic group. Dynamic theorists consistently distinguished between the paranoid and the nonparanoid on basic personality dimensions such as source of anxiety and major defense (Freud, 1894), level of development (Klein, 1948), and characteristic reactions to therapy and transference (Fromm-Reichman, 1946; Searles, 1959). In each of these formulations, the paranoid was seen as reaching a more advanced developmental level, emotionally and cognitively, than the nonparanoid. Freud saw the schizophrenic's major defense as repression, while the the paranoid's was projection. Klein (1948) differentiated the paranoid and schiziophrenic according to their personality structures, which formed at different developmental periods. The schizophrenic is unable to discriminate interpersonal reality on any consistent basis, while the paranoid achieves and maintains a rudimentary discrimination based on the early personifications of "good me" and "bad not-me." Searles (1959) reported that the paranoid maintains a consistent though unrealistic notion of the therapeutic relationship, while the nonparanoid is unable to develop any consistent notion of therapy. The dynamic distinction between paranoid and nonparanoid has been emphasized by Henderson and Gillespie (1956), who developed a separate diagnostic category for paranoid states because they exhibited a distinct underlying type of personality (Foulds & Owen, 1963). There is thus considerable suport from dynamic theorists for the notion that schizophrenia and paranoia are separate entities with different prognosis, onset, history, and dynamics.

One reason for classifying paranoia as a separate psychosis is that although paranoids distort reality as does the schizophrenic, there is little disturbance in rational thought. Kant (1798) differentiated paranoia from other psychotic processes by its lack of formally disordered thought processes. For Kant, paranoia is:

> ... that disturbance of the mind in which everything that the madman says is indeed consistent with the formal laws of thinking ... but in which the subjective impressions of a falsely inventive imagination are taken for actual perceptions. Of this class are those who believe they have enemies everywhere; who regard all expressions, remarks, or other indifferent actions of other persons, as intended for them as traps set for them. Often, they are, in their unfortunate madness, so ingenuous in analyzing that which others unwittingly do, in order to explain it to their own satisfaction, that, if their data were only accurate, one would have to pay every tribute to their intelligence [p. 15].

Kant's emphasis on the phenomenology of paranoid cognition has been frequently repeated by clinicians and theoreticians, with the result that there has been considerably more agreement on the description of paranoid than nonparanoid schizophrenia. Sullivan (1953) speaks of the "spread of meaning," Cameron (1947) of the "sudden clarification," Bowers (1974) of the "press for meaning," Abrams, Taintor, and Lhamon (1966) of the paranoid's "metahypothesis," and Young and Jerome (1972) of "rigidity of internal representaion." Most well known, perhaps, is Cameron's (1951, 1959) formulation of the paranoid's trait of overinclusion culminating in the pseudocommunity discussed in Chapter 3. These explanatory constructs from divergent theoretical backgrounds and approaches owe their essential similarity to an agreement on defining paranoid symptoms and an awareness of the notably different phenomenology of paranoia and schizophrenia. However, even with such agreement on processes unique to paranoia at a theoretical level, the traditional conception of a common disease with possibly an organic basis has remained dominant, both clinically and experimentally, resulting in the inclusion of paranoid and nonparanoid psychotics in the category of schizophrenia.

Empirical results revealing group differences were frequently explained as different manifestations of a common psychological, physiological, or biochemical defect. Prior to 1950, researchers typically reported results for schizophrenics, uncategorized with respect to subtype. Research results were variable and unstable; hence, more homogeneous groups of schizophrenics were sought to reduce intersubject variability and permit a comparison of results across studies. Recently, the nonparanoid–paranoid distinction has been considered to reflect separate processes requiring separate theoretical constructs. This change is mainly due to the consistent differences between paranoids and nonparanoids which are reported on laboratory tasks, usually with paranoids performing like controls (Buss & Lang, 1965; Chapman, 1974; Johansen, Friedman, Leitschuh, & Ammons, 1963; Lang & Buss, 1965; Payne, Caird, & Laverty, 1964; Shakow, 1962, 1963).

A subtle change in the use of schizophrenic and paranoid diagnostic labels is also evident in hospital diagnoses, which probably occurred without an awareness of the empirical results supporting the distinction. Most hospital diagnoses of schizophrenia include labels of paranoid or undifferentiated, rather than the previous labels of catatonic, hebephrenic, or simple. Katz, Cole, and Lowery (1964) reported that 76% of all schizophrenics admitted to state hospitals in New York were diagnosed either as paranoid, undifferentiated, or unascertained. A Maryland state hospital reported 71% of schizophrenic patients were paranoid or undifferentiated. Outpatient clinics in the United States in the early 1960s diagnosed 74% of their patients as paranoid or undifferentiated (Weiner, 1966). Hence, both in clinical research and practice, there is a gradual movement toward a dichotomy within the general class of schizophrenia. We believe the evidence goes even further to support a distinction, not only between types of schizophrenia, but of two separate conditions—the paranoid and schizophrenic. Such a trend encourages a more accurate and replicable means of distinguishing between the two groups.

The current neo-Kraepelinian clinical classification of the various schizophrenias, which has used the traditional diagnostic process to arrive at the empirical constructs has been criticized for poor reliability (Schmidt & Fonda, 1956), poor validity (Chapman, 1974), and empirical and conceptual disorganization (Blashfield, 1973). More recent operational definitions which have improved both inter-judge agreement and prognostic power include distinctions between good and poor premorbid history (Phillips, 1953), acute and chronic status (Strauss, 1973), and paranoid and nonparanoid symptoms (Goldstein, Held, & Cromwell, 1968). Evidence has accumulated, however, which suggests that these empirical constructs are not independent. Paranoids are more likely to be good premorbids, while schizophrenics are more likely to be poor premorbids (Goldstein, 1970), good premorbids become chronic less often than poors (Farina, Garnezy, Zalusky, & Becker, 1962); and paranoids tend to be under-represented in chronic cohorts (Strauss, 1973). However, while premorbidity and chronicity may reflect one dimension, the paranoid dimension has been found to be independent of the two (Johansen et al., 1963).

In examining the paranoid–schizophrenic distinction, the level of pathology as represented by the process–reactive dimension must be given special attention. The degree of pathology reflected by premorbid adjustment or process–reactive dimension should not be confounded with a measure of paranoia or schizophrenia. For example, if a diagnostic scale measured a degree of thought disorder, it would classify according to the level of pathology, with the schizophrenic exhibiting the greater degree of pathology. It is important to isolate differences between the two groups while controlling for pathology. A recent study by Heilbrun and Heilbrun (1977) clearly demonstrates how differences in the paranoid condition coincides with levels of pathology. Using a content analysis of delusions, they compared reactive and process paranoids. The delusions of reactives were more integrated, varied in content, actively oriented toward the environment and less autistic. In short, the reactive paranoid showed better organization, greater articulation, and more modulation. The greater the pathology, the more the paranoid resembled the disorganized thought process of the schizophrenic. Hence, not controlling for level of pathology in selecting a sample of paranoids and schizophrenics may tend to produce samples of integrated and nonintegrated patients which would obscure the differences between the two subgroups. Since our purpose is to specify distinct processes in groups and not differences in level of disorganization, ideally we should only review work using the good premorbid schizophrenic and consider the poor or process type to reflect the effects of extensive or long-term pathology. Hopefully, the next decade will produce the research to allow such a review; at present, it is only an ideal.

OPERATIONAL DEFINITIONS
OF PARANOIA AND SCHIZOPHRENIA

Two recent reviews discuss operational definitions of paranoia and schizophrenia. In his review, Calhoun (1971) notes that research has used three different methods to make the distinction between paranoid and nonparanoid schizophrenics: (1) official hospital psychiatric diagnosis; (2) behavior ratings based on specific characteristics of the two groups; and (3) self-report using scales such as the Minnesota Multiphasic Personality Inventory. Calhoun examined the possibility that these various means of differentiation may not lead to the same groups. Relatively low correlations were found among the three methods of differentiating paranoid and nonparanoid schizophrenics. Calhoun suggested that behavioral ratings with adequate specification of behaviors to be rated may provide more consistency across studies than that provided by the usual hospital diagnosis.

In their review, Ritzler and Smith (1976) also noted that research in the past has not clearly defined paranoid and nonparanoid schizophrenia. In a recent five-year survey of the literature, they found that the diagnostic specification for the paranoid subclassification could be grouped into five categories: (1)

diagnostic criteria unspecified; (2) staff or hospital diagnosis, no further specification; (3) diagnosis confirmed by two clinicians; (4) diagnosis specified by standard scales or checklists; and (5) diagnostic signs and symptoms fully specified.

The major problem with the paranoid subclassification determined by staff diagnosis alone is that of reliability. With diagnostic styles and preferences varying from institution to institution, staff diagnosis is little better than no specification at all, especially in a research effort where operational definitions are necessary.

The method of distinguishing paranoid schizophrenics from other subclassifications on the basis of confirmation by two clinicians working independently also presents problems. The reliability suggested by an agreement by two clinicians is limited by the fact that the diagnosticians are from the same institution that produces the same problem found using staff diagnosis. There is no explicit specification of the operational definition that allows precise replication.

In contrast, studies that specify the diagnostic criteria give the paranoid diagnosis an explicit operational definition. Unfortunately, as review of the studies using this method reveals, nearly every study used different criteria. Thus one cannot generalize from study to study without first comparing the definitions used in each case, which are usually different.

Studies which use standard diagnostic inventories and explicit checklists to determine paranoid subclassification have advantages in that each subject receives a score or rating on a paranoid or nonparanoid scale. The problems of subjective judgment and cross-institutional diagnostic preferences are minimized. However, Ritzler and Smith (1976) suggest that one problem involved with this method of differentiation is that the scales differ in their measurement of the paranoid subtype. They therefore suggest that caution should be taken in equating subjects diagnosed by different standard scales. However, a recent study (Cantrell & Magaro, 1978) found that most of the usual scales show a high degreee of agreement with correlations at least in the 60s.

Behavioral scales that have been used to separate schizophrenics from other groups, or paranoids from schizophrenics within the schizophrenic group, are the New Haven Schizophrenic Index, the Symptom-Sign Inventory, the Symptom Rating Scale, and the Maine Paranoid–Schizophrenic Rating Scale. The New Haven Schizophrenic Index (NHSI) is a symptom checklist which differentiates schizophrenic from nonschizophrenic populations in a number of different types of treatment settings (Astrachan, Harrow, Adler, Brauer, Schwartz, Schwartz, & Tucker, 1972). In testing for the reliability and validity of the scale, first, three nonclinicians reviewed material from 25 randomly selected cases resulting in an interrater agreement of 84%. Next, charts of 422 patients diagnosed as schizophrenics from six different treatment settings serving the same geographic area were reviewed as well as 100 charts that might be expected to confuse the diagnosis of schizophrenia. The percentage of patient's charts with a diagnosis of schizophrenia that were categorized on the NHSI as schizophrenic was 87.4%. The percentage of nonschizophrenics selected to confuse the diagnosis of schizophrenia, yet categorized as schizophrenic on the NHSF, was 13%. Even though the NHSI reliably and validly distinguishes schizophrenic and nonschizophrenic populations, the scale does not distinguish between paranoid and nonparanoid schizophrenics.

The Symptom-Sign Inventory (SSI) was constructed by Foulds (1965) to measure signs of mental illness while excluding personality traits. Administered individually, it uses a self-report procedure in which 10 items for each subscale are questions posed directly to the patient in a structured interview. Subscales for paranoid and nonparanoid schizophrenia are included in the SSI. Gordon and Gregson (1970) found that the paranoid and nonparanoid groups were not significantly separated on these subtests of the SSI. In order to minimize misclassification errors, they differentially weighted a subset of items that were found to discriminate the paranoid from the nonparanoid. The resultant instrument was a weighted SSI consisting of 11 items with a cut-off score of 5. All subjects scoring less than five were considered nonparanoid schizophrenic, and all scoring above five were considered paranoid schizophrenic. The misclassification rate on this scale is about 16%. Since the weighted subtest is considerably quicker to administer and demands a reassessment in relatively few cases, it seems to be a powerful alternative to the full SSI if it can be cross-validated. Current research, however, has found this weighted measure to be the least similar to other paranoid measures (Cantrell & Magaro, 1978).

Some difficulties arise when using the full SSI or the weighted SSI in determining paranoid and nonparanoid schizophrenics. First, since the SSI is a self-report measure where the patients are queried directly, it is obvious to the patient that the purpose of the interview is to elicit information concerning his illness. The work on impression management suggests that patients may manipulate the scales in order to create a desired impression of themselves rather than present themselves in terms of their symptoms. Second, since the questions in the SSI are stated in the present tense, they elicit information concerning the patient's present condition, which may be due to influencing factors such as stress or medication. In assigning patients to groups, one is usually interested in long-term states. As we noted in the beginning of the chapter, Kraepelin (1976) states that "a permanent and unshakable delulsional system" is a defining characteristic of paranoia and must not be confused with the schizophrenic who may have a few meager, disconnected, or confused delusions. If a paranoid response is obtained from the patient, it is not possible to determine whether the person has a permanent delusional system or is experiencing an uncommon temporary delusion. If a negative response is obtained to a paranoid item, it could indicate that medication or some other factor such as a desire to impress staff is temporarily suppressing the delusional system.

The Symptom Rating Scale (SRS), a behavior rating scale, was developed by Jenkins, Stauffacher, and Hester (1959) as a means of translating the symptoms observed in the course of a conventional psychiatric interview into quantitative data. Cohen, Gruel, and Stumpf (1966) provided evidence that the 20 SRS items can be reduced to a smaller number of stable factors. The five factors are: (1) Uncooperativeness; (2) Depression-Anxiety; (3) Paranoid Hostility; (4) Deteriorated Thinking; and (5) Unmotivation. Paranoid Hostility is related to paranoid schizophrenia, while Deteriorated Thinking is related to nonparanoid schizophrenia.

Even though the SRS reliably distinguishes paranoid and nonparanoid schizophrenics, there is a disadvantage in using this scale. The factors used in the SRS to differentiate the paranoid and nonparanoid subclasses do not adhere to the usual definition of these two groups. Kraepelin defined paranoia as including a "perfect preservation of clear and orderly thinking, willing, and acting." Kraepelin also states that the occurrence of hallucinations are rare in paranoid schizophrenics, although they may have visions or hear voices which warn or assure. The inclusion of the items of "Thinking Disorganization" and "Hallucinatory Voices" in the Paranoid factor of the SRS reduces the face validity of this factor. Others (e.g., Overall & Gorham, 1962) have found that the occurrence of thought disorganization and hallucinations is more descriptive of nonparanoid rather than paranoid schizophrenics.

In view of the difficulties cited concerning the use of the NHSI, the SSI, and the SRS, the Maine Paranoid–Schizophrenic Rating Scale was developed to overcome these problems. The Maine Scale was initially developed by Vojtisek (1976), who adapted the scales of Venables and O'Conner (1959) and Overall and Gorham (1962). It consists of a five-item scale for paranoia and another five-item scale for schizophrenia. Each item requires rating a single symptom on a five-point labelled, Likert-type scale. The ratings on the five items of each scale are summed to yield total scores for paranoia and schizophrenia. The information for the scale is obtained from the patients in an interview and also from the patients' charts. A cut-off score of 12 for paranoids and 10 for nonparanoids with a gap of four points between the two categories has been used in order to clearly obtain distinct subclasses for research purposes. However, other users of the scale have taken just the highest scale and have found comparable results.

Abrams (1978) and Cantrell and Magaro (1978) have shown that in three experiments the scale has good test–retest and interrater reliability for both the paranoid and nonparanoid subscales. A factor analysis indicated that four of the five items in each scale carry the most weight. The fifth item is not related to the factor and accounts for most of the error in the scale. The scale is presented in Appendix A. The scale was also shown to have good criterion validity, provided by the pattern of relationships found between the scale and tests of psychological functioning. The tests of construct validity were mainly found to relate to the schizophrenic subscale, although ratings of pathology did not correlate with either scale, indicating that they are more measures of the condition than temporary states. The concurrent validity measures indicate that the scale is comparable to the SRS and the SSI.

The Maine Scale is not subject to the criticisms made against the other scales. Since the Rating Scale requires information both from the patient and from the patient's chart, it eliminates the possibility that the interviewer will obtain only the patient's desired impression of himself. Also, using information from the patient's records ensures that the rating will be based upon the patient's long-term state rather than the temporary condition at the time of the interview. In addition, an important advantage of using the Maine Scale is that it distinguishes paranoid and nonparanoid schizophrenics according to clear and traditional operational definitions.

We should briefly address the question of the relationship between delusions and paranoia, especially since the delusion is probably the major sign used by most clinicians and included in most research instruments. The developing DSM-III still maintains that to diagnose paranoid schizophrenia, delusions must be present, and as such continues the trend of considering the delusion the prime diagnostic sign. A problem with using such an operational definition is that in many cases the delusion may be no more than a clear organized body of thought that is considered incorrect. Maher (1974) questions the diagnostic significance of the delusion in itself and considers the delusion as an appropriate means to explain the unusual sensory experiences that are experienced in acute schizophrenia. The delusion, therefore, becomes no more than a rational way of explaining sensations which are not shared by others. In this sense the delusion in itself is not pathological but an appropriate means to explain sensations which do not have a consensual explanation. People sending down radioactive waves to destroy is the only way the paranoid can explain the sudden feelings of fear and other somatic signs which no one else seems to experience. In this sense, the delusion per se is not pathological but rather a logical way to explain experiences which do not have a more commonplace explanation in the culture. The fact that the delusion also has elements of suspicion, persecution, or grandiosity also can be seen as pathological in itself as there are many systems of religious or political thought that can be seen as quite grandiose or filled with themes of persecution.

In summary, if one accepts the logical process active in a delusion, then one can only consider it pathological in terms of its improbability. However, here one is left with the problem that the delusion is only a matter of who is right. In situations such as Watergate, what could have been considered delusions became social and political insight when the improbable became known as probable. Also, if one considers the emotional component of the delusion as pathological—jealousy, suspiciousness, grandiosity, or persecution—then one has to consider political and religious systems which evoke the same themes and are seen as quite appropriate. (See Hoffstadter, 1965, for a discussion of these themes in politics or Cohn, 1961, for an analysis of a religious movement. Also see Eiduson, 1962, for a discussion of the physical scientist as deriving the benefits of paranoia.)

Our contention is that the delusion is no more than a sign of a syndrome which includes not only certain belief systems but also a particular cognitive style that can be clearly differentiated from other schizophrenics. In effect, we would follow most clinicians and researchers in the area and consider that the delusion is the most accurate predictor of a certain personality, which with increasing stress will exhibit greater degrees of pathology until the point where all actions in the world are included in the explanation provided by the delusion. The delusion, therefore, reflects the basic raw material of the thought process that is particular to the paranoid and is exhibited in states of pathology. We would accept an adjusted paranoid in the sense that he would not exhibit delusions but would organize the world with the same form of cognition. An excellent discussion of this paranoid process is a recent book by Meissner (1978) who presents the range of expression of the paranoid process in all levels of adaptation. Hence, although we study the paranoid at his extreme so to speak, when he has become hospitalized and is exhibiting the most blatant symptoms, we do not imply that this is the natural or even customary state of the process. It is the point, however, when he is most recognizable and, hence, the delusion becomes the identifying mark which allows the categorization to occur and the investigation of the process to begin.

RESEARCH FINDINGS

Research findings are now presented that have consistently pointed to a separation of the paranoid from the schizophrenic on empirical grounds. The point of this section is not to review extensively but to demonstrate the pervasiveness of the empirical work and theory that has found this separation but which has fallen short of the next logical step of completely separating the paranoid from the group of schizophrenics. The dominant explanatory system, which considered all subtypes to be variations of the basic schizophrenic deficit, has biased the interpretation of empirical results for the past 20 years. The early V theory work of Shakow (1962) on reaction time was the first extended body of research that suggested significant differences between paranoid and nonparanoid schizophrenics. Although the V theory results were mainly confirmed with chronic nonparanoids, the dominant paradigm of seeking a unified explanation for all forms of the schizophrenic deficit did not permit the difference between paranoids and nonparanoids to be fully explored; hence, it was only noted. Thus Shakow (1962) speculated that the paranoid pattern of rigid conceptualization seems "to represent an over-reaction to the underlying trend towards disorganization which exists in the psychosis." Here a potentially important empirical finding, which distinguished the paranoid from the nonparanoid especially in terms of not exhibiting the dominant perceptual problem, received only post-hoc explanation rather than verification and careful study to preserve the unifying explanation that schizophrenics of all kinds suffer from "segmental set." McGhie (1970) also applied his perceptual theory and operations to all schizophrenics, including paranoids, but concluded that his results may apply primarily to nonparanoids. However, the direct comparison of schizophrenics and paranoids has not been undertaken.

A somewhat similar development occurred with the K theorists such as Cameron. A contemporary of Shakow, he recognized the unique dynamics (Cameron, 1938) of the paranoid subtype, but persisted until the 1960s in using overinclusion as an explanatory construct for all types of schizophrenic thought disorder. As we have seen, Payne also moved toward a clearer separation of groups when he hypothesized that overinclusion was more a paranoid than a nonparanoid problem.

In summary, research in schizophrenia by some V and K theorists has tended to follow the theoretical bias of the dominant paradigm, which has called for a single unifying theoretical explanation of at least two reliably differentiated behavior patterns. Nonetheless, theoreticians and researchers have recognized the differences between paranoids and nonparanoids. Investigators who separate these groups usually find significant differences between them. We will now review some experimental findings in order to reconceptualize the relation between paranoid and nonparanoid psychoses.

Symptoms

Two major approaches to paranoid vs. nonparanoid symptomatology have been factor-analytic studies of these groups and investigations of them with psychodiagnostic tests. Guertin (1952), in a factor analysis of 52 symptoms in 100 hospitalized psychotics, found two general factors, one of which described the paranoid and the other the nonparanoid. The paranoid factor included concern over issues of right and wrong, sexual concerns, and feelings of persecution and suspiciousness. The nonparanoid factor included motor retardation, loose associations, social confusion, and lowered affect. These distinctions are supported by the work of Lorr and his associates (Lorr, 1953,

1955, 1964, 1966; Lorr, Jenkins, & O'Connor, 1955; Lorr, Klett, & Cave, 1967; Lorr, Klett, & McNair, 1963a; Lorr, Klett, McNair, & Lasky, 1963b; Lorr, McNair, Klett, & Lasky, 1962; Lorr, O'Connor, & Stafford, 1960), who generated first 10, then 5 factors of psychoses using the Inpatient Multidimensional Psychiatric Scale (Lorr, 1953). Of the 10 factors, some seem clearly related to the paranoid, some to the nonparanoid, and some to affective psychoses. The three which relate to paranoid states are Hostile Belligerence, Paranoid Projection, and Grandiose Expansiveness. Nonparanoid factors included Conceptual Disorientation, Motor Disturbances, Disorientation, and Perceptual Distortion. Three other factors, Retardation and Apathy, Anxious Intropunitiveness, and Excitement, were related to the depressive or manic-depressive psychoses, although all factors clearly cut across traditional diagnoses. A later investigation reduced the number of psychotic factors to five (Lorr et al., 1967). Two factors were associated with paranoid symptoms, two with nonparanoid symptoms, and one with depressive symptoms. The Paranoid Process factor included delusions of reference, persecution, conspiracy, control, and body destruction, ideas of personal superiority, and perceptual distortions including auditory, olfactory, and kinesthetic hallucinations. The Hostile Paranoia factor contained perceptual distortions and verbal belligerence. Nonparanoid factors were Disorganized Hyperactivity (excitement, conceptual disorganization, and motor disturbances) and Schizophrenic Disorganization (retardation, disorientation, and conceptual disorganization). A factor called Intropunitiveness was associated with depressive symptoms. Also, as mentioned previously, factor analyses by Payne (1961) and his co-workers found that paranoids are primarily overinclusive while nonparanoids show a slowness in response.

These three series of factor analyses suggest that paranoids differ from schizophrenics in being less confused and withdrawn, more hostile, and more likely to organize their experience through delusions, which may also distort their perception. The nonparanoid symptoms include disorganized motor, motivational and thought components. In general, the essence of the cognitive aberration seems to be disorganization in the nonparanoid and hyperorganization in the paranoid.

Psychological Tests

Two psychodiagnostic tests have been shown to reliably differentiate between paranoids and nonparanoids; the Rorschach (Weiner, 1966) and the Wechsler Adult Intelligence Scale (Schafer, 1948, 1954; Weiner, 1966). On the WAIS, paranoids score higher on Comprehension, Arithmetic, and Picture Completion (Schafer, 1948; Weiner, 1966), and better on WAIS-type analogies. On the Rorschach, paranoids less frequently employ color naming, and have better form level, organization, and field articulation than nonparanoids. Payne (1961) concluded that IQ and other intellectual functioning in paranoids is markedly less distorted than in other nonparanoid schizophrenics. Lothrop (1961), summarizing research on conceptual performance, also notes that paranoids have consistently been found to display less conceptual impairment than nonparanoids. In summary, the pattern of paranoid–nonparanoid differences on these tests indicates again that the paranoids' conceptual capacity is relatively intact. Nonparanoids do not organize stimuli and react to them.

Weiner (1966) presents an extensive analysis of paranoid–nonparanoid differences on psychodiagnostic tests. We only cite the differences on what are considered cognitive dispositions, although Weiner (1966) also discusses test signs relating to impulses and defenses: "A number of significant contributions indicate that paranoid and nonparanoid schizophrenic persons exhibit personality differences that are in part determined by their disparate cognitive dispositions [p. 306]." The test signs that differentiate the paranoid are those structural variables that reflect the more intact personality. They exhibit a higher $F + \%$s and a higher $D\%$s than nonparanoids, indicating a greater personality integration. $W\%$s indicate that paranoids produce fewer Ws than normals, and nonparanoids produce more. The reverse is true for $Dd\%$. Paranoids are above normals and nonparanoids below (Weiner, 1966). As on a field-dependency measure, the nonparanoid makes a more global response to the total stimulus field as a unit of meaning, while the paranoid finds meaning in every tiny demarcation.

Weiner (1966) describes the paranoid as seeking the "true" or "hidden" meaning in the perceptual field. However, one could also infer that he disregards the perceptual field and applies his concepts whether they fit the percept or not. His "doing violence to the blots" is more than insisting that his concepts will be heard. There is no assimilation of the blot as percept just as there is little assimilation of most sensory data. The paranoid's preference for M over C is another sign reflecting the ideational style of the paranoid, which suggests that he is searching for the significance of environmental events (Weiner, 1966). However, Rapaport, Gill, and Schafer (1968) argue that the rigidity of the paranoid works against the production of M responses.

Laboratory Tasks

Since most of the studies that highlight the paranoid–schizophrenic distinction are reviewed in other chapters, they are not presented in detail. First, studies investigating the perceptual functioning of paranoid and nonparanoid psychotics are sampled from the work on sensory threshold, psychophysiological measures of perceptual processes, and complex acuity determination. The literature on sensory thresholds indicates that paranoids' thresholds are the same as normals, but nonparanoids may have lower thresholds than the other two groups. Maher (1966) notes that nonparanoids have a lower threshold for apparent movement (Saucer, 1958, 1959; Saucer & Deabler, 1956), which disappears with phenothiazine medication. Rappaport, Hopkins, Silverman, and Hall (1972) report that "studies employing visual threshold and gustatory acuity measures indicate that acute nonparanoid patients not on medication may actually be hypersensitive to low intensity stimuli [p. 20]." The Rappaport group has also found, in an auditory signal detection task comparing paranoid and nonparanoid schizophrenics on and off phenothiazines, that "paranoid schizophrenics are relatively hyposensitive to auditory stimuli; nonparanoid schizophrenics on the other hand are relatively hypersensitive, but this is demonstrable primarily under conditions where sensory sensitivity is more important than the ability to focus attention, that is, under conditions where signals are difficult to detect [p. 25]." Phenothiazine medication acted in opposite ways depending on paranoid–nonparanoid diagnosis; the sensitivity of paranoids was increased but the sensitivity of nonparanoids was decreased.

It may be that paranoids perform differently than nonparanoids under medication because they maintain different sensitivities. Singh and Kay (1978) extensively examined a number of schizophrenic subtypes on 33 measures of psychopathology while off and then on medication. Besides psychological measures such as the Color Form Preference Test, they were examined on psychophysiological measures and the effects of neuroleptics. Their conclusion was that:

> The paranoid schizophrenics are probably a class by themselves and should be considered as clinicopathologically, and perhaps etiologically, distinct from the nonparanoid schizophrenics. In almost every area we studied, they stood apart from the nonparanoids. This was true in terms of cognitive-developmental tests, indices of arousal and attention, anticholinergic-neuroleptic antagonism and its relation to prognosis and outcome and the relationship between autonomic arousal [p. 6].

Silverman's (1972) review of work on the psychophysiology of perception separated paranoids from nonparanoids and concluded that paranoids are augmenters [i.e., they increase the intensity of stimulation on the kinesthetic figural aftereffect (Silverman, Buchsbaum, & Henkin, 1972), pain tolerance measures (Ryan & Foster, 1967; Silverman, 1967), the visual figural aftereffect (Kelm, 1962; Landauer, Singer, & Day, 1966) and the cortical average-evoked response]. Nonparanoids are reducers on these procedures (i.e., they diminish incoming stimulation). Paranoid–nonparanoid differences are so consistent with paranoids hyposensitive and nonparanoids hypersensitive that the augmenting–reducing dimension was suggested to be a predictor of *type* of schizophrenia if psychosis develops.

In terms of complex acuity, Silverman (1964b) also reviews evidence on scanning or extensiveness of visual range from studies on size constancy and size estimation in which paranoids are found to be extensive scanners and nonparanoids minimal scanners. A recent and interesting study by Cegalis, Leen, and Solomon (1977) may clarify this finding. They report that chronic schizophrenics (mostly nonparanoids) had greater visual detection in the visual periphery than normals. This suggests that nonparanoids derive greater information from the areas of the field that would require extensive scanning. The results supports Magaro's (1969) finding that the nonparanoid scans the visual field more extensively. However, these findings could also be interpreted to mean that nonparanoids do not need to scan extensively because they are more sensitive to peripheral stimuli. Thus, they have a wider range of input, whereas the paranoids lacking such a range without scanning must scan to make up for their "reduced" sensitivity.

The review of findings in Chapter 4 on field dependency also indicates that paranoids differ from nonparanoids by being more field independent and, hence, possibly more developed conceptually than schizophrenics. What is relevant to the present discussion is the theorizing of Silverman (1964a). He has argued that both measures of scanning and field articulation vary with degree of systematization of delusions; the more systematized the delusions, the more extreme the scanning and field articulation. Experiments comparing paranoid and nonparanoid conceptual performance have either studied problem solving on a variety of tasks, or manipulated set or expectancy in recognition tasks. Paranoids tend to overinclude in their conceptualization (Payne et al., 1964) and tend to reach erroneous conclusions quickly rather than waiting for more information (Abrams et al., 1966). "The paranoid operates with the metahypothesis that, to process his experience, it is preferable to form an incorrect hypothesis than none at all. Furthermore, the greater the degree of paranoid severity, the stronger this metahypothesis [p. 495]." Also, Binder (1958), who used subjects with high Pa scores on the MMPI, found that those with high Pa scores had the same intolerance for ambiguity as found in clinical paranoids. McReynolds, Collins, and Acker (1964) found that delusional schizophrenics attempted to identify more pictures and identified more pictures correctly than nondelusional schizophrenics, supporting their hypothesis that the former group has "a stronger tendency to organize ambiguous stimuli in a meaningful way [pp. 211–212]."

Recent studies reviewed by McDowell, Reynolds, and Magaro (1975) and Young and Jerome (1972) also supported the hypothesis that the paranoid differs from the schizophrenic by attributing meaning according to rigid conceptual expectations. This strategy functions adaptively in situations where the expectation is justified, but maladaptively where the expectation is not justified. This is the same phenomenon that alerted Shakow to the paranoid–nonparanoid difference in reaction time experiments, which he termed the difficulty in forming a segmental set. When the preparatory interval length is changed, paranoid performance decreases for the next few trials, whereas nonparanoid performance changes less. What is called both rigidity of set and difficulty in forming a set are two aspects of the same process. For the paranoid, new sets are difficult to acquire because established sets become rigid. Generally, these rigid sets generate expectations for probable events. In this sense delusions, which may be seen as pathologically exreme examples of sets, anticipate improbable and therefore deviant events. Their lack of validation marks them as deviant.

Bassos (1973) presents an effect of rigid sets when he found that paranoids are much more likely than normals or nonparanoids to distort remembered, affect-laden material in ways that reflected delusional themes, even when considerable constraint was present in the form of definite meaning. Forgus and DeWolfe (1974) found that paranoids, but not nonparanoids, respond to the Logical Consequences Test with dominant concepts predicted from their delusions. In short, paranoids, as distinct from schizophrenics, tend to assign specific meaning to all stimuli in a stereotyped manner. At times their rigidity may be beneficial in that they are also less suggestible than nonparanoids. Ham, Spanos, and Barber (1976) found that paranoid symptoms were negatively related to subjective measures of suggestibility as used in hypnosis research. This suggests a greater independence of thought and possibly a lesser need for a dependency relationship that could only be met by extensive institutionalization, the solution most often found by the nonparanoid.

In a discussion which is similar to our explanation of the paranoid and the schizophrenic, McConaghy (1960) states that there are two types of deviations in associational patterns, a strengthened capacity to assign logical meaning to events or a weakened capacity to exclude irrelevant associations. In the former case, established meanings resist conflicting associations, and in the latter case, the thought process becomes vague and characterized by intuition rather than reasoning where meaning is elusive. McConaghy considers the first a characteristic of paranoid and the second characteristic of nonparanoid thought. We will come to this same conclusion in our review of the information-processing literature, but for now we can anticipate our discussion of Integration Theory, in which we will postulate that paranoids rely on conceptual processes without adequate constraint being imposed by perceptual data. Schizophrenics rely primarily on perceptual data without adequate categorization and classification from conceptual processes. The demands of the situation determine if the schizophrenic or paranoid cognitive process is adaptive or maladaptive. The "set" effects observed are due to the ability or, in fact, necessity of the paranoid to construct conceptual categories that could override stimulus information. On the one hand, the schizophrenic lacks a conceptual schema which permits the stimulus field to "transmit" with the "noise" of constant varied stimulus activity. Intuition is no more than not imposing consensually validated meaning upon events, which would occur with the weakened capacity to exclude irrelevant associations as spoken of by McConaghy (1960). Looking on the positive side of this coin, however, would be the schizophrenic's ability to receive a wide range of perceptual information.

The theoretical constructs of conceptualization and perception are related in our system to the diagnostic terms of schizophrenia and paranoia. These functions form the empirical laws relating to performance on a variety of tasks. Both psychological processes are common to all individuals. However, one is dominant in the diagnostic groups as operationally defined by a paranoid-schizophrenic scale. It is this dominance that creates the expected empirical functions and justifies the creation of a specific category of paranoid as distinct from schizophrenia.

The separation of paranoids and schizophrenics has therapeutic implications. Paranoids are underrepresented in chronic cohorts (Strauss, 1973), which suggests that paranoids possess more of the skills required for hospital discharge and community tenure. Kowalski, Daley, and Gripp (1975) found that paranoids performed better than schizophrenics even in a behavior modification program. Depue and Woodburn (1975) report paranoid cohort's diagnoses are changed to some form of nonparanoid schizophrenia as the sample remains institutionalized. The mechanism behind the unusual chronic paranoid may be actual symptom change to a nonparanoid picture. Given the adequate reliability of this diagnostic distinction (Blashfield, 1973), it seems unlikely that so high a percentage of paranoid diagnoses were mistaken; rather, it seems more parsimonious to suggest that paranoids do become nonparanoid in the traditional hospital environment. As we have seen in the discussion of field dependency, the monotony of the hospital ward decreases any resident's ability to form simple perceptual discriminations, and this includes nonpsychotic patients such as alcoholics (Magaro & Vojtisek, 1971). A patient who relies extensively on organizing the perceptual field with a rigid conceptual set is left with nothing to organize; hence, the conceptual (delusional) world becomes looser, and eventually the patient displays the loose associations of the schizophrenic. Such an analysis suggests that the relevant dimension for the paranoid is his level of conceptual organization, and those patients heretofore classified as "paranoid-schizophrenic" should henceforth be classified "paranoid-integrated" or "paranoid-nonintegrated" as suggested by Foulds and Owen (1963). On the other hand, the nonparanoid is not as affected by sensory isolation of long-term institutionalization, nor is he as adaptable to the social environment. Hence, he more likely fits the social definition of the poor premorbid adjustment patient and remains in the hospital longer, falling into the chronic category.

The idea that the paranoid who is "integrated," in the Fould's sense, would not be requiring hospitalization and would, in effect, have a good prognosis implies that the paranoid could function in the society and not be grouped into the clinical population if he was not exhibiting conceptual disorganization. Such reasoning suggests that the paranoid adaptation may be quite beneficial in some cultural institutions. We will briefly pursue this thought.

If, as our interpretation of the literature suggests, the paranoid cognitive style is a particular manner of coping with the environment, the paranoid should be found outside clinical settings. He should share the essential mechanisms and descriptions of the clinical paranoid, but lack the most exaggerated delusional characteristics. This paranoid should be studied both to assess the cognitive style without potentially confounding hospitalization effects, and also to investigate the mechanism of pathogenesis. This suggested extension of the study of psychopathology is necessarily speculative because there is little sound research focusing on the successful adaptation of paranoids and schizophrenics. The initial tasks would be to discover the identifying signs of the nonclinical paranoid, and the current roles available that would be expected to support a paranoid adaptation.

The nonclinical paranoid should share attributes of the clinical paranoid without the social conditions which make obvious this deviance. Thus, the non-clinical paranoid should also have rigid, simplified basic concepts which may be used to organize a wide array of unrelated data. London (1931) suggests that one such basic cognitive structure for the paranoid is a clear view of the kind of relationship that is threatening to him. As soon as a small element of that picture appears, he generalizes that similarity to the entire relationship in which it appears. Thus the paranoid needs clear-cut relational structures, ideally permitting a minimum of unstructured human relations. The role must not make perceptual demands for accurate recognition of novel stimuli; rather, it must encourage elaboration and enrichment of a few themes. The role must permit the expression of suspicion and hostility, and permit, or better yet, require a rigid belief system without much chance for change.

The idea of the paranoid as a cognitive style without pathological symptoms is not foreign to personality theorists (Shapiro, 1965), but it is to the area of psychopathology. It would seem that a merger of the two fields of interest may provide us with a more meaningful conceptualization of a condition without the confounding effects of institutionalization or, possibly more important, the behaviors produced when labeled as psychotic or mad (Magaro, Gripp, & McDowell, 1978). We just do not have the data to intelligently draw conclusions about the paranoid or the schizophrenic who is functioning in society without the stigma of illness. Certainly there is a call for research to move in that direction.

CHILDHOOD PARANOIA
AND SCHIZOPHRENIA

The separation of paranoids and schizophrenics is not only relevant to psychopathology in adults but also to childhood schizophrenia. The problem is more serious in this area because the distinction has not been applied even though the diagnostic category of childhood schizophrenia is no longer defensible. The stringent guidelines initially used for the diagnosis of childhood schizophrenia are no longer applied (Bennett & Klein, 1966). The category now includes such a heterogeneous group of children that it has become meaningless. Numerous authorities in the field have expressed concern over the magnitude of variability among children included within the single diagnostic category of childhood schizophrenia. Goldfarb (1964) concluded after a ten-year investigation on childhood schizophrenia that one key finding was the awareness of "the heterogeneity of schizophrenic children and their individual differences in genetic background, congenital disposition, psychosocial experience, capacity, defense characteristics and response to treatment [p. 621]."

The theme is reiterated in a recent study (Goldfarb, Goldfarb, Braunstein, & School, 1972) of the speech and language of 25 schizophrenic children which were compared to those of normals in 82 different speech and language areas. The results showed that the schizophrenic children exceeded the normals in 50 of the 82 areas in the amount of the disorder. However, no single pattern of disorders was isolated within the sample of schizophrenic children. In fact, opposite trends were sometimes observed. One such instance was the voice volume results. The voices of some of the schizophrenic children were found to be too strong while others were too weak. The lack of consistency within group patterns can also be seen on physiological measures. Piggott and Gottlieb (1973) concluded that "the lack of consistent patterns in childhood schizophrenia was due to the heterogeneity of the children included within the diagnosis of childhood schizophrenia [p. 102]."

Psychiatry has not attempted to make distinctions within the childhood schizophrenia category. The prevalent attitude is summed up by Kanner (1960): "The general pattern cannot be subdivided in the same manner in which adult schizophrenia has been subdivided. None of the adult 'types' stand out sufficiently in children to warrant any kind of analogous grouping [p. 731]." In many ways childhood schizophrenia has been a wastebasket category containing the leftovers from other identifiable disorders. For instance, elaborate systems were developed to describe infantile autism (i.e., Rimland, 1964; Tustin, 1972) and those not fitting the syndrome were given the diagnosis of childhood schizophrenia, a relegation to an "undifferentiated whole." Such gross categorizations mistakenly suggest that the diagnostic category is unified by a single theoretical explanation.

Historically, in the field of child psychiatry, the generalization has prevailed that paranoid symptomatology in children does not exist. Bradley (1945) in a review of psychosis in children stated that "some psychosis of adults, such as paranoia . . . do not occur at all in children [p. 135]." He cited in support of this statement the complete lack of delusions in childhood schizophrenics. Bender (1947) also argued that important paranoid tendencies such as projection and a belief in external control were absent in children. Projection, considered by many as the paranoid's chief defense mechanism, was purportedly not found in young children. Instead the main defense is that of introjection (i.e., good mother/bad mother). The other missing symptom involves the paranoid belief that someone or something outside of himself is responsible for his experience and/or actions. A review of selected clinical observations illustrates the need for a reappraisal of this situation.

Clinical Reports

In an early study, Despert (1938) identified ideas of persecutions in nine of 29 diagnosed childhood schizophrenics. The lack of detailed description of the children precludes an unreserved conclusion that these nine children could be differentiated from the population of childhood schizophrenics as paranoids. It does, however, represent an initial step in identifying essential characteristics of a paranoid diagnosis. Despert (1938) also reported another interesting characteristic of these nine children. Eight of the nine experienced a late onset of symptoms, after age ten. This information will become useful in comparing childhood symptoms in relation to adult paranoids.

Mosse (1958) also described a late onset case in an article that discussed 60 cases of childhood schizophrenia. Mosse's primary objective in this report was to illustrate how many of the 60 children were misdiagnosed. The importance of Mosse's work is the availability of his in-depth description of subjects, especially in his description of Robert, age 9. Robert is particularly interesting because of a triad of symptoms: delusions, hostility, and control. The delusions displayed by Robert involved his belief that he was being followed by various people. Mosse pointed out that while he did not consider Robert's delusions to be genuinely paranoid, there was an important element that linked them to paranoid symptomatology, Robert's hostility. Mosse hypothesized this to be a forerunner to genuine paranoid delusions. The last important symptom observed in Robert involved control by an external force. He believed that some "introjected body" was controlling his habit of stealing, and that this outside control should be blamed for such actions and not himself.

O'Neil and Robins (1958) also supplied evidence for the existence of paranoid children. They conducted a 30-year follow-up of 526 children who were previous clients of a child guidance clinic. The age of the children at the time of inital clinic intake was between 7 and 17. The authors noted that one-third of the subjects in the group labeled "pre-schizophrenic" manifested odd ideas and paranoid trends. These ideas and trends were not elaborated but were simply noted as being "vaguely paranoid ideas [p. 387]." Examples of such ideas involved an overconcern for personal harm (i.e. inflicted by germs) and a high level of suspicion towards other people.

The case of Marvin, age 10, presented by Esman (1960), supplies additional support for the existence of paranoid symptomatology in children. Marvin's symptoms suggest a paranoid behavior pattern. They include a late onset of symptoms, delusions, feelings of persecution, outside controlling forces, a negativistic-hostile attitude and suspicion towards others. Esman reported that the most frequent delusional themes involved other children picking on Marvin, and creatures from outer space "attacking" him. Esman (1960) concluded that to his satisfaction these represented clear-cut paranoid delusions.

Bender (1947, 1953, 1954, 1956) provides both general and specific descriptions of a subgroup of childhood schizophrenics who display paranoid behavior patterns. In differentiating among childhood schizophrenics, using an age of onset criterion, she describes the "pseudopsychopathic," whose behavior is very similar to what would be expected for a paranoid child. Though her description of this pseudopsychopathic group of children varies somewhat depending on the stage of development of her work, some of the characteristics remain constant. They are good premorbid adjustment, an onset of symptoms which is later than any other group (between the ages of 10 and 11½), and a symptomatology which commonly includes paranoid persecutory ideation, delusions, and aggressive-hostile-negativistic tendencies. A detailed description of such a pseudopsychopathic case, Tom, is provided (Bender, 1959). The earliest complaints of Tom's behavior involved hostile and aggressive behaviors (i.e., disobedience, fighting and verbal abuse). Through the course of six admissions, Tom's behavior became increasingly antagonistic and defensive. By the age of eleven clear-cut paranoid symptoms were observed, including suspicion of others and outside control (i.e., voices). Although Bender (1959) did not report the existence of a clear-cut delusional system, paranoid tendencies in Tom's thinking was reported by a staff psychiatrist.

Jordan and Prugh (1971) report on 22 children with a diagnosis of schizophreniform psychosis. The authors hypothesized that an inability to cope with the usual developmental issues of the early school age period kindles the schizophreniform's initial psychotic experience. Thus by definition, a good premorbid adjustment period—up to approximately 6 years of age—is essential for this diagnosis. In response to the stress situation of this period (i.e., leaving mother for school) these children utilize the defense mechanisms of denial and projection. They also experience a deterioration of reality testing, which is replaced by fantasies and delusions, characterized (Jordan & Prugh, 1971) as "poorly organized paranoid delusions [p. 325]." Ideas of reference and persecution are the most common themes of the delusions. A typical example consists of tales of dangerous enemies out "to get" the child, often accompanied by a protecting "ally."

One of Jordan and Prugh's subjects, an 8-year-old boy, provides an illustration of the type of delusional system utilized by many of these children. This child believed that he was in personal danger from German soldiers who were disguised as civilians watching him from the street. Due to his imagined danger, the boy kept a "magic" gun under his bed for protection. The boy feared most being attacked from behind. He expanded his delusional system by including the interviewing psychiatrist in this fear. During the session he became increasingly suspicious of the psychiatrist and when it came time to leave the room the boy insisted that he walk out last. This presumably was done to avoid an attack from the rear. The psychological testing on this child revealed projection to be his major defense mechanism.

To summarize, a good premorbid adjustment period, a negativistic-aggressive attitude, hostility, suspicion of others, delusional systems, and a projection defense mechanism is found in case history reports of children diagnosed as schizophrenic. Such a syndrome resembles the adult syndrome of paranoia as reported in factor analytic work. As previously discussed, the primary syndrome in the Lorr et al. (1963a) study is labeled "Paranoid Projection." This syndrome is defined as beliefs or convictions that attribute to others a hostile, persecutory or controlling intent. The fundamental variables loading on this factor include delusional beliefs, beliefs that others are talking about you, feelings of persecution, beliefs that others are conspiring against you, and beliefs of outside control of your actions. An additional syndrome related to paranoid projection was hostile belligerence. The major variables related to hostile belligerence are verbal expressions of hostility, an attitude of disdain, a sullen attitude, irritability, grouchiness, feelings of resentment, and suspicion toward others. These are the same behaviors noted in the clinical reports of some schizophrenic children.

A prominent feature of both the clinical reports and the factor-analytic studies is the relationship between hostility and paranoid symptomatology. Hostility has served as a theoretical explanation for adult paranoid phenomena (i.e., Colby, 1977) and has been suggested as a forerunner to genuine paranoid delusion (Mosse, 1958). This speculation may be useful in terms of identifying childhood paranoia. A theoretical explanation of how hostility could be precursor to genuine paranoid symptomatology is supplied by Lorr (1964). In the developmental sequence, the young child quickly learns that open displays of hostility toward power figures are dangerous. In response a safer course is adopted, inner resentment. Gradually the child may begin to attribute these withheld feelings to other persons or objects. If this action goes uncorrected, a fertile ground for a general malevolent attitude toward others is laid. The proposed sequence continues with this malevolent attitude developing into paranoid symptomatology (i.e., ideas of persecution). Since harboring these feelings is potentially very anxiety arousing, the last step is to remove them from the child's responsibility (i.e., outside control). The sequence proposed by Lorr (1964) includes the eight major symptoms that constitute Lorr's simplex model. The list of symptoms, in increasing order of severity, includes: a hostile attitude, verbalized hostility, resentment, a tendency to blame others, a feeling of being persecuted and conspired against, a belief in being controlled by other people or forces.

This simplex was empirically tested by Reiss and Elstein (1971) who classified subjects as either paranoid or nonparanoid schizophrenic using Lorr's model as their criterion. The subjects for this study consisted of a family unit including the hospitalized child, his mother, and his father. Twenty-four such units were divided into one of three conditions: paranoid, nonpnaranoid, and control. Each family unit was given a battery of perceptual and cognitive tests. A multiple discriminant analysis indicated the highest degree of differentiation occurred between the paranoid and nonparanoid, and control. Each family unit was given a battery of perceptual and cognitive tests. A multiple discriminant analysis indicated the variety and patterning of stimulation they were attempting to process. Conversely, the paranoid subjects were viewed as being hypervigilant of the stimuli they encountered. This resulted in the formation of elaborate conclusions being based on a minimal amount of evidence.

Heilbrun (1972, 1973) has considered the social-perceptual adaptive styles of male children in response to maternal aversive control. Two primary styles have been identified—open and closed. The closed style is a relatively passive style where the child utilizes an avoidance-withdrawal response to his mother's control. The open style is a much more active response in which the child attempts to change his mother's evaluation of himself. In order for this change to occur, the open-style child is highly vigilant to external cues since he must become keenly sensitive to his current status. Furthermore, it is hypothesized that certain qualities of the open-style child predispose him to be a high risk for paranoia. Heilbrun identified seven behavioral properties of the open style, which, when acting together, serve as the etiological predisposition for paranoid symptomatology. These properties are a low self-esteem, sensitivity to social evaluation, broad external scanning, low interpersonal trust, defensive projection, intolerance of ambiguity, and an inflexible social ideation. These qualities are meant to reflect a cognitive style that is independent of any pathology. Moreover, according to Heilbrun, this particular style provides a strong basis for potential paranoid development, which can be observed, even in the developmentally immature subject, before the onset of genuine paranoid symptomatology.

Heilbrun's theory attempts to describe a condition that occurs in childhood. The actual empirical work is too meager to allow any conclusions to be drawn. That is one of our points. The descriptive system used in psychiatry may have obscured differences that have existed and blunted the thrust of any investigation that would have discovered paranoia in children. The clinical data is rich with description if not with actual differential labeling. In the Reiss and Elstein (1971) study suggesting that there are two distinct family trends, one paranoid and one nonparanoid, we may see the beginning of a conception of children as paranoid and nonparanoid. The evidence reviewed strongly suggests that the cognitive style of the adult schizophrenic and the adult paranoid can be seen in childhood.

In conclusion, there is some support for applying Kraepelin's conclusion about the paranoid to childhood schizophrenics. Even in childhood, the paranoid may be distinguished by his conceptual adaptation that differentiates him from the schizophrenic and possibly other groups, including normals. Recent work is moving toward making this distinction clearer and is beginning to offer separate etiologies. At present there is insufficient evidence to confirm any specific etiologies. We offer a developmental analysis of the two processes in the Integration Theory chapter.

Now, we must move back to a consideration of the data that bears upon the psychological functioning of the adult paranoid and schizophrenic. We believe we have demonstrated the existence of two separate conditions. It is our next task to attempt to specify their cognitive styles. For the effort, we turn to the empirical observations as they have been produced in an information-processing research strategy.

6 Information Processing in Schizophrenia and Paranoia

INTRODUCTION

Our analysis of laboratory tasks and their results, presented in the first three chapters, strongly suggests the direction to be taken in explicating the cognitive processes in schizophrenia. The multiple processes, specified by Hull as entering into a behavioral act, emphasize the complexity of psychological processes involved in the completion of even a simple task. Yates (1966), in a critique of studies in the performance deficit area, makes the same point and alludes to the information processing path we will follow:

> It is, in this author's view, even more a function of a consistent failure to separate out different levels of analysis. Thus, where failure occurs, as in reproducing visual designs by drawing, it is obviously impossible to determine whether the failure is sensory (peripheral), perceptual (data-processing level), central, or motor—or some combination of these. As we shall see, these distinctions are of crucial importance [p. 125].

In addition to the problem of measurement with a multiple demand task, another problem concerns the complexity of the higher-order processes themselves. Can any form of cognitive activity, such as those measured by overinclusion or field dependency, be considered by itself without assessing the interacting effect of other conceptual processes? Does the study of one conceptual process in itself present an artificial picture of conceptual activity analogous to employing one psychological construct to describe the total schizophrenic process? Because perceptual and conceptual functioning involves complex systems, any single task cannot provide data sufficient for a clear understanding of perception and conceptualization. In short, the individual's cognitive map (to use an old learning term) is a multitude of dimensions, with a set of interactions being the clearest description of the cognition of the paranoid, the schizophrenic, or any other group. The conceptual system of Scott presented in the *K* chapter reflects these concerns as well as the investigations of developmental theorists such as Piaget and Bruner. This problem leads us to seek a methodology which distinguishes between the stages in cognition. Up until this point, our purpose has been mainly to question the use of tests supposedly measuring a unitary process and to suggest the specific processes operating in schizophrenics and paranoids. We now examine recent work, which has more finely operationalized the cognitive processes, to see if their interactions can be described and related to the paranoid and the schizophrenic.

We must acknowledge our debt to Neale and Cromwell (1977), who present a similar analysis in a recent review of their early work. Their criticisms of the concept of attention parallels our discussion of other terms currently used:

> Our previous review found many faults with both theory and research on attention in schizophrenics. Perhaps the most salient deficiency lay in the definition of the attention construct itself. From this initial problem, a number of other, equally serious difficulties arose. First, the relationships between the construct and various operationalizations of it were weak—the notable example here was size estimation, whose relationship to scanning by eye was shown to be negligible (Neale & Cromwell, 1968; Mackinnon & Singer, 1969). In later work, it was also shown that the many tasks that supposedly reflected attention shared little common variance (Kopfstein & Neale, 1972). Second, the breadth and vagueness of the then fashionable attentional constructs and their isolation from modern cognitive psychology created a situation that did not seem to require a sophisticated measurement of information processing. Thus, performance on the tasks used to measure attention most likely reflected the operation of many processes. The interpretation of performance differences between schizophrenics and controls became in itself a difficult, indeed hazardous, enterprise.
>
> Research on attention and schizophrenia has, of course, continued. As we saw in our earlier review, the definitions of attention that (either explicitly or implicitly) guide this research have remained very broad. Thus, we still find a wide diversity of tasks, from discrimination learning (Nolan, 1974) to vigilance (Kornetsky, 1972), all interpreted as reflecting attention. We think that this broad use of the term attention does not clarify or increase our understanding of schizophrenic performance. Instead, perhaps it is time to adopt more modest, but potentially more fruitful, goals. One of these is the understanding of specific aspects of information processing in schizophrenia [p. 127].

Having assessed the futility of tasks involving multiple processes, they began to work with an information theory strategy. We also follow this direction and review the evidence that has been produced since the early work of Yates (1966). We show that an information theory procedure answers the objection of global tasks and begins to clarify the differences between schizophrenics and paranoids. A previous chapter discussed the distinction between paranoia and schizophrenia and offered a means to operationalize the type 4 arm of our function. In the following section, we define our main terms—perception and conceptualization—and focus on specific operations that are involved in these processes. In discussing the stages of information processing, it is beyond the scope of the book (and certainly beyond the author's understanding) to explain the many points of disagreement or the mathematical quantification used in the area. We will be content with the use of an overall model as used by Neisser (1967, 1976), Shriffrin and Schneider (Schneider & Shiffrin, 1977; Shiffrin & Schneider, 1977), and Hayes-Roth (1977). We use the classic work in the area to illustrate the operation of the processes of interest, so that the reader with even a passing acquaintance with the area should be able to evaluate our progress in devising tasks that separate processes for individual study. The review of research in schizophrenia, which uses information theory methods, will bring up-to-date the understanding of schizophrenia that has developed using such a framework.

AN INFORMATION-PROCESSING MODEL

The Icon

Figure 6.1 shows a flow chart of an information-processing model constructed to organize the research in schizophrenia. The process begins with the external stimulus, which creates its internal representation in the organism through an optical transformation. The resulting image or icon is a short-term process, lasting approximately a second in most experimental conditions.

The iconic image is nothing more than a configuration of lines and colors varying in length, width, or contrast. Hence, much research and theory centers upon the question of how this mass of basic elements is translated into a meaningful representation of an object. In other words, how is an icon matched with a category to produce pattern recognition? The reader is referred to Gibson (1950, 1966) for a discussion of the complexity involved in this process, especially in terms of the effect of optical patterns and perception. It will suffice for the present discussion to focus upon two

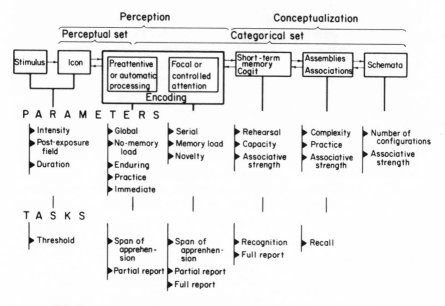

FIG. 6.1.   An information-processing model defining terms and processes. Parameters of each stage in the process and the tasks used to measure each process are so indicated.

encoding processes that could operate sequentially (Neisser, 1967) or in a parallel either–or relationship (Shiffrin & Schneider, 1977).

Preattentive Processing and Focal Attention

Neisser (1967) describes two processes involved in the encoding of the icon—preattentive processing and focal attention. Preattentive processing produces an initial discrimination of the iconic pattern into holistic parts, a process of segmentation which creates figural units. For example, in looking out the window, without moving my eye I receive a mass of stimuli which could be discriminated into trees, grass, leaves, branches, signs, students, and animals. To "see" the tree, its characteristics first have to be discriminated from this field. The preattentive process only separates the tree from the field. In fact, the process does not involve recognizing the segment as a tree. The preattentive process only discriminates a form which is separated from the field for further analysis.

The sequential, focal-attention process acts upon this segment of the field, the tree, to begin the process of analysis of attributes in order to construct a percept from a segment of the icon. The focal-attention and preattentive processes are types of attention which isolate information by the selection of specific elements in the icon. These two encoding processes result in our forming an initial recognition of a pattern, which becomes meaningful as the two processes sequentially transform the image into attributes that can then be categorized as an object. As phrased by Neisser (1967): "Here it is determined that an object is round and nubby in texture, or a triangle, or a long lost friend [pp. 89–90]."

We must remember that the two processes, as shown in Fig. 6.1, are sequential in the normal course of pattern recognition. In the usual situation by the usual individual, a sequential process proceeds and results in a recognition of an object. We will be speaking of the unusual situation or the unusual individual who does not necessarily sequentially process and, hence, may rely upon one process more than the other. Before proceeding to a discussion of the use of either process in a nonsequential fashion, we briefly describe some of the parameters of the encoding process and the icon.

Sperling (1960) was the first to demonstrate the duration of the icon by requiring a partial and full report of a stimulus field presented tachistoscopically. The partial report condition required a report of one row of a letter matrix. A full report required the repeating of the total matrix. With the partial report technique, the crucial condition was signaling the subject which row to report after the total matrix was presented. There was almost total accuracy if the row signal appeared immediately after the termination of the stimulus field. However, as the signal was delayed, accuracy diminished to about 50% after a 1-sec. delay. This is the same level of accuracy of the full reports. In short, after a second the subject could not "read-off" the image but had to rely on verbal memory as one would in a full report situation. Each letter would have to be searched in memory which requires 40 msec. per item. It was concluded that icon duration was a fading process that lasts about a second depending upon conditions such as stimulus intensity, preexposure field, and stimulus exposure time. However, in order to examine icon processing, a stimulus cannot be exposed for longer than 200 msec. to avoid the effects of eye movement.

One factor influencing iconic processing is perceptual set. The operation of this set is demonstrated in a study by Haber (1966), in which he trained subjects who were presented with figures varying in shape, color, and number to report in terms of dimensions rather than objects. Those subjects receiving specific coding instructions reported the dimension specified first; that is, they read-off the elements in the dimension before reading others. This could be considered the operation of a perceptual set, in that the dimension instructions influenced the initial discrimination of information. Neisser (1967) states: "The perceptual set operates by affecting what the subject does during the brief period of iconic storage [pp. 40–41]."

Another construct of relevance here is the span of apprehension or the amount of material that can be read-off the image into short-term memory. Sperling (1960), supported by numerous replications, estimates the number to be between 3.8 and 5.2. When the task is simply to count and not identify the number of objects the span increases to 6. Another factor of limitation for the span of apprehension is the capacity of verbal memory to accept the encoded material.

Short-Term Memory

As seen in Fig. 6.1, the next structural unit after the icon is short-term memory. The icon has been transmitted, and the preattentive and focal processes have operated upon the icon resulting in a set of attributes. Immediate memory is a short-term associational linkage, which provides the conceptual categories for translating attributes into recognizable forms (i.e., providing the name of the pattern). The debate about whether the translation is through verbal or visual processes is not important for our present purposes. We will only note that it is short-term and subject to conditions in the immediate present.

The category in short-term memory can probably determine the percept especially during focal attention. Just as a bias could operate at the preattentive process stage by influencing what is segmented from the field (e.g., the perceptual set mentioned earlier), a bias also could occur in terms of what attributes are grouped to define the object. Some rather well known studies demonstrate the operation of such a bias. Bugelski and Alampay (1961) presented subjects with a figure that could be seen either as a rat or the face of a man. Those subjects first receiving pictures of animals saw it as a rat while those subject not previously primed saw it as a man. Bruner and Minturn (1955) presented the number 13. When subjects were pretrained on letters, they saw a B but when they were trained on numbers they reported a 13. The subject, in effect, is set to search for attributes which fit the primed category.

A perceptual set influences the course of the preattentive process, and a categorical set influences the course of focal attention. The question of interest to us is if some individuals are more subject to a perceptual set while others are more subject to a conceptual or category set. If there are individual differences in the use of preattentive processing or focal attention, we would suspect that these are greater perceptual set effects for schizophrenics and greater category set effects for paranoids.

We see in Fig. 6.1 that the information in short-term memory is categorized. Short-term memory is a series of what are usually called nodes, which, through associational linkage, form simple conceptual categories. The red, round, shiny figure becomes an apple through being categorized in short-term memory. The capacity of short-term memory is approximately seven words or as stated by Miller (1956) in his classic paper, 7 ± 2 units of material or what he labeled as "chunks." Numbers or letters are transformed into message units, 3 and 2 become 32, and B, U, and Y become BUY. The elements encoded are rehearsed or grouped into an initial labeling concept such as a simple word. Material enters verbal memory at the rate of about 170 msec. per digit or 100 msec. per word in a phrase (Neisser, 1967). The chunks can be considered memory slots, which can be symbolic units or numerals. Obviously, cognitive efficiency increases as these slots are more and more symbolic (Bruner, 1966). However, if these slots are somewhat inflexible and prescriptive, that is, there are only so many symbols which all material has to fit, we would suspect that any encoding would be highly stereotyped.

Assemblies and Schemata

Hayes-Roth (1977) presents a current view describing an associational network model in which simple lower-order representations are organized into larger, more inclusive units of meaning. At this stage, we are involved in the process of conceptualization or how information is processed so that it is usable. Hayes-Roth phrases the question in terms of knowledge acquisition or the enlarging of memory units very similar to the process proposed by Hebb (1949).

The theoretical assumptions begin with the definition of a *cogit*, the basic information unit which is a discrete memory representative. This structural unit is in short-term memory, and, as shown in Fig. 6.1, develops into the category-set or schema. The cogit is activated in an all-or-none fashion by the recognition of the cogit in some external stimulus. The greater the experience with a cogit, the greater the strength of the cogit, and the greater the probability of its activation. The learning of elementary memory representations begins with their activation by the stimulus that contains the appropriate components. With more trials, the specific memory representations are established in a relational configuration, which is strengthened by greater usage. For example, the letters are formed into a word, and after extensive usage a simple word is formed. The configuration is unitized, at which time it becomes a discrete memory representation activated in an all-or-none fashion. In effect, there is a two-stage process where elements are first learned and stored in memory, and then followed by the elements being formed into a whole concept which is again learned as a conceptual unit. Hayes-Roth (1977) states: "Thus, over the course of an individual's experience with a knowledge strucutre, the memory representation of the structure is assumed to progress hierarchically from a collection of independent but related parts to a single, integrated representation of the structure as a whole [p. 261]."

A configuration of cogits reflects all relationships simultaneously and is assembled by associations. Associations follow the same laws as a cogit in that strength is determined by prior experience. A cogit in a configuration is associatively activated in an all-or-none fashion by stimulating any element of the association. An assembly is formed by a group of associates and could build higher-order assemblies whose strength is again determined by the strength of the lower-order elements as associates and by a decreasing function of its complexity. The greater the complexity, the less the strength of the configurations. Lastly, an assembly can become a unit in itself that has all the properties of a cogit, the basic elementary unit. This functionally independent conceptual system, which we labeled a schemata in Fig. 6.1, is also strengthened or weakened by experience and is activated in an all-or-none fashion by a stimulus that includes only a subset of the information represented in the assembly.

The Hayes-Roth (1977) theory asserts that information processing changes through learning when the elementary cogit is influenced by higher-order assemblies and when higher order assemblies are modified by the introduction of new cogits. The information subsumed in a single cogit changes through experience and strengthens or weakens the assembly. As the strength of the cogit influences the strength of the assembly, so can the assembly modify the strength of the cogit. Thus, normal information processing is a two-way system with reciprocal effects among the schemata, the category, and the percept. In other terms: "A schema is that portion of the entire perceptual cycle which is internal to the perceiver, modifiable by experience, and somehow specific to what is being perceived. The schema accepts information as it becomes available at sensory surfaces and is changed by that information; it directs movements and exploratory activities that make more information available, by which it is further modified"(Neisser, 1976a, p. 54). This constant interaction of percept and concept in deriving meaning is crucial to our understanding of information being derived from a constant dialectic, which cannot be accurately described if only one term is considered in isolation.

Neisser (1976) introduced the concept of figural synthesis to describe perception. Figural synthesis is the higher-order term that includes the action of all processes that occur during the duration of the icon, including the feedback effect of the category. However, in order to understand this very abstract but crucial process, we must first discuss two terms that are similar to the Neisser terms of preattentive processing and focal attention.

Automatic and Controlled Processing

Schneider and Shiffrin (1977) empirically and quantitatively demonstrated the operation of what are labeled automatic and controlled processing. In their admirably thorough review, they demonstrate the action of an automatic processing strategy. Through repeated practice, a sequence of memory nodes are formed that become active in response to a particular stimulus input without the necessity of active control by the individual. In this stage, the processing of material is automatic, because an element in the stimulus activates the cognit—the basic unit of further conceptualization. Once activated and practiced, automatic processing is difficult to modify or ignore. It is not limited by memory load or number of distractors but only requires an initial discrimination of stimulus elements into sets that are practiced.

Controlled processing, on the other hand, is a sequential search operation that processes each element in the set and is a function of set size and memory load. Controlled processing can be seen in a task that requires a serial comparison of a list of words in order to find a match. The process is under the control and attention of the subject and makes extensive use of short-term memory storage to consider all matching possibilities, which also provides greater accuracy in novel situations. The two processes operate in different types of situations, depending upon past experience and the degree of categorization of the items in search. Automatic processing is much faster than controlled processing because the latter is serial in nature and dependent upon memory load.

Automatic and controlled processing parallel the Neisser terms of preattentive processing and focal attention respectively. The Neisser (1963) work, where subjects were able to recognize target letters in a field of letters by a global, rapid, relatively inaccurate manner, demonstrates the preattentive process. But it also demonstrated automatic processing if one assumes extended previous practice with letters throughout life, which allows the controlled processing stage to be bypassed in the particular task.

A more global processing strategy is involved in preattentive or automatic processing and a more detailed serial-order processing in the focal attention or controlled processing. The difference, then, is if one has to assume a segmenting and *then* a scrutiny of the segment, or if the two can be parallel or situation specific.

The terms used by Neisser and those used by Schneider and Shiffrin differ, therefore, in terms of sequence. Preattentive processing is always the initial process that segments the field, after which focal attention operates. Automatic processing, which we consider comparable to preattentive processing, cannot occur without an initial categorization of objects through controlled processing, the term comparable to focal attention. However, this sequencing difference of the two theories may be illusory if one recognizes that preattentive processing also is determined by past experience, as shown in the perceptual set work where, even at the early process of segmenting the field with specific categories, prior controlled search had to occur. For example, the tree is separated from the field in the initial preattentive process because of one's experience with trees, the prior learning involved in controlled search. In that sense, the object has already gone through the controlled processing stage. Though preattentive processing may seem to be always the primary stage, its initial holistic segmentation is actually developed from prior examination. Stimulus elements consequently have already been determined to be appropriate for further detailed focal attention.

We will accept the Shiffrin and Schneider results indicating that the two processes are situation-specific and dependent upon practice and attempt to demonstrate that the paranoid consistently engages in a controlled processing strategy, while the schizophrenic prefers automatic processing. We will accept that for most individuals in most situations, it is a rapid progression from preattentive or automatic to controlled processing. However, this may not always be the approach of choice at all times, such as when one is attempting to get a "feel" for a situation or attempt other global perceptions of reality. For example, some drug use is aimed at experiencing reality or seeing objects without substance or constancies. Our point is that it is only in some experimental situation that all subjects go from automatic to controlled processing. We argue that they only do so when the task demands it. If the task is to combine elements in an unusual manner one may profitably move from controlled to automatic processing and remain at the preattentive stage. When there is a choice, the cognitive strategy of different individuals may be reflected. Our task is to specify those individuals and their strategy. An issue of great relevance to psychopathology is the dualistic nature of the two processes, which can operate in a sequential relationship but can also operate differentially in individuals. That is, one individual may use one more than the other.

Once the processing of specific material begins, however, automatic processing can be seen as forming the discriminations hypothesized by Neisser (1967). Preattentive or automatic processing could also influence attention. Schneider and Shiffrin (1977) state:

> A type of automatic sequence... is one that modifies ongoing controlled processing by attracting attention to a specified locus or node. In particular, when subjects in search tasks are consistently trained to recognize certain inputs as targets, these inputs acquire the ability to initiate automatic attention responses. These attention responses then direct attention (i.e., will direct controlled processing) automatically to the target, regardless of concurrent inputs or memory load, and enables a correct detection to occur [p. 2].

In other words, once preattentive attention has separated specific elements from the field, subsequent trials or tasks with the same stimulus will produce the same segmentation of the field. Focal attention would consistently operate upon the same segment or be bypassed directly into short-term memory. Figure 6.1 presents a curved line going from short-term memory to automatic processing to show this by-pass function. However, automatic processing may also interfere with controlled processing, especially if automatic processing has been practiced and the stimulus field is common to both.

One other point has to be stressed. The memory nodes which are automatically processed are derived from long-term memory. According to Schneider and Shiffrin (1977): "Since an automatic process operates through a relatively permanent set of associative connections in long-term store, any new automatic process requires an appreciable amount of constant practice to develop fully [p. 2]." This implies that the conceptual schema will influence the type of processing since the greater the experience with the assembly, the more likely for automatic processing to occur with that stimulus set. Moreover, if an individual consistently relies upon schemata to deal with the stimulus world, especially novel aspects, he could more likely engage in a serial search and exhibit detection functions resembling controlled processing in order to find the elements which fit the schema.

The Schneider and Shiffin work adds an important quality to the Neisser constructs. One is that preattentive processing is a matter of practice with conceptual set. Once the categories are set, such as letters in a field of numerals, specific letters in a set of letters, or signs of anger in a face, and the practice is extensive, it is extremely difficult to modify what you perceive. We discuss later the possibility of one process operating inappropriately, that is, in situations where the other is more efficient. For now, we note that the Schneider and Shiffrin work suggests that the two processes are independent and not necessarily sequential, although they usually develop sequentially with practice.

Figural Synthesis

This detailed discussion of the two modes of processing is helpful for an explanation of Neisser's figural synthesis term. Figural synthesis is the process which combines the forward and backward flow of processes that occurs even during the brief duration of the icon. According to Neisser (1967), any resulting percept is a constructive act where the memory category, the preattentive process, the focal analyzers and other individual processes construct a percept that does not exist. He states that "the mechanisms of visual imagination are continuous with those of visual perception—a fact which strongly implies that all perceiving is a constructive process [p. 95]." To explain that which is added beyond the input of the icon involves an active constructive process of creating rather than transmitting information.

The similarity of the figural synthesis term to our integration term is obvious. We consider the integration of conceptual and perceptual information as crucial to creating knowledge. For Neisser, figural synthesis is a metaphor, a term that is beyond the direct observables and yet relating them. It emphasizes that the perceiving of an object is more than preattentive processing or focal attention. Investigators disagree about the relative importance of the two processes. For Bruner (1951, 1966; Bruner, Goodnow, & Austin, 1956), the conceptual category is the crucial element in determining the percept. Possibly for some individuals in some situations that is the case. However, Gibson (1966) and others stress elementary visual processing in the initial processing of a stimulus, since it is shown that much perceptual activity can be explained solely by the physical structure of the environment. We view it as a constant dialectic where individual differences with an emphasis on one process over the other are possible. Our integration term stresses the need to balance the category against the icon, the preattentive process against focal attention, automatic processing against controlled processing. We follow Neisser (1976) in conceiving of information flow as a circular flow of activity where concept and percept interact in an exploratory manner over the world of stimulation. An object appears, has qualities which we sample and modify through the assembly which modifies the percept, and is fitted into another concept. Continuously we repeat the cycle, "making sense" of our observations, and, in the process, "changing our minds" in regard to what exists. It is not only the categorization of the stimulus but the different manner in which an object is "seen" that is the constructive perceptual act. Even at the most elementary level of perceiving, the balancing begins and must be accounted for if the complex phenomena observed in psychopatholgy are to be explained.

Neisser (1976) recognizes that information theory cannot adequately explain perception if it does not explain the effect of long-term memory organized into conceptual schemata. He consequently presents an information theory model which is, in effect, circular rather than linear. We followed his direction and, hence, must present a word of caution in interpreting our linear processing model. We do not interpret the model literally because information does not simply flow from the percept to the concept. Our thesis is that information processing is a strategy with individual difference components emphasizing expectancies at different points in the series.

Individual differences may emerge in the proportional use of automatic or controlled processing. Automatic processing automatically assigns the objects into categories without further analysis. The categories are established, as in a letter set or signs of anger, and the percept is constructed.

The point is made by Gestalt psychology with the various illusions in which the actual character of the object changes under different directions. An example of this is the "wife and mother-in-law" picture used by Leeper (1935) or the Salvador Dali painting used in the text by Lindsey and Norman (1972). In each case, after having specific information, the object appears to be a different character. Long-term memory or schemata enter in and influence the perception (e.g., the encoding of the stimulus). The priority of elements of the icon is established as in a perceptual set situations, and the icon is read accordingly. The individual who relies upon controlled processing provides meaning by analysis of iconic elements. However, if the same category guides the search for the elements in the field, he will come up with the same conclusion (i.e., anger from the lines in the face). The validity of a category is immediately accepted, and he immediately enters into automatic processing. This individual is processing as any subject in the laboratory except for the quickness of using the controlled process to arrive at automatic processing. The category here is eminently powerful so that the world is consistently perceived through categorical sets.

Attention

The reader has probably noticed that we have not mentioned the concept of atttention in our discussion. The perceptual theories, discussed in Chapter 3, had evolved to the point of postulating that selective attention was the main problem in schizophrenia. The main difficulty seemed to be that the schizophrenic could not select the appropriate stimuli, and, in effect, had too broad a range of attention. The interest, therefore, had centered upon the selection of stimuli, maintenance of focus, and the shift of the focus to stimulus components (Zubin, 1975). The V theorists such as McGhie, D theorists such as Venables, H theorists such as Silverman, and R theorists such as Broen have all focused upon some aspect of attention. They differed in regard to their definition of attention such as range or selectivity. They also differed in regard to the attention problem being secondary to a drive state or the primary causal factor. In each case, however, an aspect of the schizophrenic problem is seen as residing in some attentional mechanism.

There has been no consensus on the problem of attention in schrizophrenia because there is no single construct of attention. There are a multiple set of operations that share the same name of attention with a wide variety of operations. Boring (1970) has listed 10 definitions of attention that range from the reaction to one stimulus to the unconscious as a framework that directs events. In effect, attention could define the whole linear processing model we have presented in Fig. 6.1. In that case, we are not surprised that there is confusion about the attentional characteristics of the schizophrenic since the operations measure the total span of information processing. The quotation at the beginning of this chapter by Neale and Cromwell (1977) articulates the same message in more detail. Shakow emphasized set, Broen emphasized breadth, and McGhie concentrated upon selection. In each of these cases, the schizophrenic shows a deficit. To clarify the nature of this deficit, it is more important to ask whether the particular strategy used by the schizophrenic is inappropriate or whether the schemata necessary for such a seemingly "perceptual" process is not available. We would only be asking a confusing question if we asked about the attention of the schizophrenic. We would be asking an irrelevant question if we asked about the filtering of the schizophrenic.

Schneider (1978) concisely comments on the use of attention terms in the research in schizophrenia. He first notes that theorists using attention models have not kept pace with the models of attention developed in the experimental literature. He briefly traces the attentional mechanisms that have gathered empirical support in the past 20 years. Most of the V theorists such as McGhie followed the Broadbent (1958) model, which offered a filter mechanism that completely blocks out competing messages. The schizophrenic, therefore, was considered to have a "leaky filter." He could not completely block out competing stimuli; hence, he was constantly distracted.

Later, it was discovered that alternate messages were not completely filtered out in processing information. This led to a modification of the filter mechanism as a quick-switch, all-or-nothing filter to the attenuator proposed by Treisman (1969). Deutsch and Deutsch (1963) moved further away from a filter of incoming stimuli and located the filter in the entry into memory, which shifts the interest to the importance of particular memory organizations. Broadbent (1971) moved the concept even further into the conceptual processes by proposing a response set, called *pigeonholing*, which focuses upon the meaning of stimuli. The meaning of a stimulus is determined, and that fits a particular pigeonhole which has a priority. Some meanings have higher priorities than others, and those are more likely to be processed than others. All information is first processed for meaning, and then further filtering or processing occurs for those high meaning messages.

For Schneider (1978), the importance of such a shift in the meaning or location of the mechanism of attention is that it raises the question that the schizophrenic has different preferences for content rather than some deficit in attention: "It may be that the nature of the material considered important— not the actual ability to attend to it—is where the problem lies in schizophrenic attention. . . . The ability to mobilize attention may not be as impaired in schizophrenia as is the ability to choose which stimuli are appropriate for attention [p. 485]." Schneider (1978) goes even further and questions the validity of a cognitive experiment in that the material presented in the experimental situation may just not have a high priority meaning, and hence performance appears to be deficient. The nonschizophrenic may be able to, or understand that he has to, accept the experimenter's definition of relevant stimuli. The schizophrenic may not engage in such collusion and appear deficient.

It may be, however, that it is not a simple matter of shared definition of meaning hierarchies but rather that the schizophrenic does not have an ordered set of pigeonholes and hence cannot develop a set of priorities. A study by Hemsley (1976) compared the effects of distraction, which would reflect problems in filtering, as redefined by Broadbent (1971) in terms of selectivity of clear physical stimuli, to that of pigeonholing, which was operationalized by the degree of response uncertainty. (In this case, it was a card-sorting task in which response uncertainty was varied by the number of elements to be sorted in a deck). The results indicated that stimulus distraction was not as important for schizophrenics as response uncertainty, which supported an interpretation of the deficit being more of pigeonholing rather than filtering. For us, the movement of the concept of attention from the selection of physical elements to the force of meaning implies that the term could be equivalent to information processing. Neisser (1976a) puts this point quite concisely: "When perception is treated as something we do rather than as something thrust upon us, no initial mechanisms of selection are required at all [p. 84]." All the stages involved in determining meaning from the initial icon to the large assemblies would all be subsumed under the concept of attention. "The listener follows a message by picking up the information that specifies it as a separate event, and the information that specifies its content and meaning. The more information he finds available (contextual, spatial, etc.) the easier this task becomes" (Neisser, 1976a, p. 84). The question becomes: Why use such a global term when the interest is in specific processes?

The concept of attention as a conceptual process rather than a perceptual filtering is a drastic shift in the meaning of the construct. The shift is recognized as a selection at the response rather than the input side of the information flow process. However, the shift in the specification of the attentional mechanism does call for a consideration of the type of attention that is rooted in such dissimilar cognitive processes. In effect, it is only clear which attention is being spoken of when the operations are specified. It seems to us that an information-processing model specifies the processes that are spoken to by the attention theorists and in a more clear, differentiated manner. That is the reason we do not use the term. We will speak of the same phenomena, but we, hopefully, will have isolated the components, at least theoretically.

Our historical review of theories focused upon the filtering of physical stimuli just as the prevalent concepts of attention were enthralled with the process. Current theories of attention have moved to consider the forces of the concept. This idea is of most interest to us especially when considered as part of an information-processing system. Considering this more recent use of the term is especially important when attempting to specify differences in attention to different schizophrenic subgroups.

The early Deutsch and Deutsch (1963) formulation of attention emphasized the selection of material through the operation of assemblies in the memory processes. All material is processed, but only the relevant material is remembered and processed into memory, depending on personal interest or the demands of the tasks. Attention, therefore, is a matter of how the assembly influences the incorporation of material. The assembly produces the distinction between relevant and irrelevant material, and in this manner the stimulus field is discriminated.

The operation of this selection mechanism is demonstrated in a task used by Neisser and Becklen (1975). They presented dual visual messages imposed upon one another and found that subjects easily followed one message or the other with the same ease as if one message was presented. As in an auditory shadowing task, the unwanted message is ignored even though the stimulus events are not physically separated. The distinguishing characteristic in the situation is the intrinsic structure of the task that is formed by anticipations. "Only the attended episode is involved in the cycle of anticipations, explanations, and information pickups; therefore, only it is seen. Attention is nothing but perception. We choose what we will see and anticipating the structural information it will provide" (Neisser, 1976a, p. 87).

Attention as involving the action of our assemblies is the crucial point in our characterization of the paranoid and the schizophrenic. If there is no schemata by which to process information, stimulus attributes are not processed into meaningful information, or knowledge. That is the main problem we attribute to the schizophrenic. On the other hand, the paranoid has the schema to process and will process most information into knowledge. However, the schemas here have such strength that almost all physical cues are converted into one message. As the skilled subject in a shadowing task is able to pick up secondary or embedded messages while the naive subject completely misses such information, the paranoid is able to process in terms of the "hidden agenda" as well as the primary message. That is, a skilled subject or a determined subject is able to utilize two schemata at the same time. Spelke, Hirst, and Neisser (1977) showed that students could read a story while copying words that were spoken, even to the point of writing the category of the words while not showing a decrement in reading speed or comprehension. Viewing the paranoid as being in constant search of the hidden meaning in everyday events, it is not surprising that he received dual messages although it would be expected that processing time would be slower and more deliberate. We find evidence of this in our analysis of the data. In short, we can infer that the more skilled the perceiver, the more he can perceive because of his organization of information. The amount of organization and hence the amount of material processed constitute the difference between the schizophrenic and paranoid. Explanation of this difference does not require an attention term or a filter mechanism to explain such results. We refer to Neisser's *Cognition and Reality* for a more detailed and convincing discussion of the reasons against positing a filter construct to explain perception.

Definition of Terms

The definition of our terms followed from our model. *Perception* consists of the processes acting upon the icon. Neisser (1967) states: "The only way to use the term 'perception' sensibly is in relation to the extended processes that go on as long as the icon continues [p. 41]." *Conceptualization* consists of the associational processes that operate after the formation of the cogit. It is clear that in some situations, and with some people, the percept comes more from the force of the icon than the force of the category, while in other situations, or with other people, the reverse is true. There can be no absolute separation of the two processes except in an artificial abstract flow chart. Figure 6.1 shows that the arrows linking perceptual and conceptual processes flow both ways. The initial icon is going to influence the resulting cogit just as the cogit influenced by larger schemata is going to influence the initial encoding of the icon. It is clear that there are two structural units—the icon and short-term memory—but it is the forces emanating from each (almost as opposite magnetic poles that create the magnetic field) that are the figural synthesis of Neisser or our intergration. *Integration* is a theoretical II construct, a metaphor in Neisser's terms, which occurs when two separate and opposing processes create a state solely from their action upon one another. Hence, our definition of terms emphasizes the direction of information flow.

PARANOID AND SCHIZOPHRENIC INFORMATION PROCESSING

We are postulating that the paranoid consistently works backwards from the schemata to the icon while the schizophrenic works forward. The paranoid reports what is mainly influenced by the schemata while the schizophrenic reports what is mainly received on the icon. However, there are two ways to process the icon. The preattentive process, which becomes automatic with practice and results in a global unanalyzed percept, analogous to an undifferential whole response in the Rorschach. The subsequent focal attention or controlled processing uses the attributes of this form and begins the subsequent search and matching to the concept. Novel situations require this longer matching operation because there is no set that is learned to form the consistent mapping of the stimulus field. Using our Rorschach analogy, this would be comparable to defining all the parts of the blot in detail to construct a larger concept.

Either process can be used in the service of gathering information. The schizophrenic engages the preattentive process in most situations although certainly not in that situation where a serial processing is required to determine the nature of the stimulus. He will prefer to use the preattentive process and report global percepts or elementary concepts. He will however employ the nonpreferred controlled processing, although poorly, to produce a more detailed and accurate (at least in terms of consensually validated concepts or categories) picture of the world if he is so required. However, the schizophrenic will be less adept at controlled processing, and even less so at automatic processing, if the situation is novel and he, thus, has to create the automatic processing categories. Hence, on most laboratory tasks, he will appear slower or inaccurate, because the task requires both processes performed in a limited time period. Specifically, we will predict that the schizophrenic will perform as well as normals in an experiment that demands automatic processing and be deficient in those experiments that require controlled processing. While the schizophrenic may sometimes use controlled processing, he will do so in a slower manner because it is not a preferred strategy.

We would also predict that in those studies which examine the effect of the cogit assemblies, the schizophrenics will show the greatest deficit. It is here where the greatest difference will emerge between schizophrenics and normals or paranoids. The schizophrenic does not engage in the conceptual process, the forming of strong assemblies and schemata. Hence, any task which relies upon such associated processes will demonstrate the greatest schizophrenic deficit. The schizophrenic's difficulty is not at the initial organization of cogit configurations, where each cogit is identified with a discrete memory representation activated by an external stimulus, but at the stage where the initial associations are formed. Hence, consequent assemblies would be of minimal strength. In effect there would be little "practice" of associating two cogits, the cogit configurations would never gain strength, and there would not be consistent conceptual categories or schemata.

Controlled processing is most characteristic of the paranoid. Information is processed in an active serial search with a reliance upon the category. This statement does not mean that the paranoid never uses automatic processing. In fact, we propose that in well practiced situations, automatic processing would occur at the level of normals, because controlled processing has removed the novelty from the situation and created the discriminative set where automatic processing can operate. We are predicting that the paranoid will prefer controlled processing when confronted with a novel situation and will maintain that process for a longer period of the time. The emergence of each preferred information-processing strategy will be dependent upon the novelty of the task. The greatest deficit will occur when automatic processing is required, and the cogit should have the least influence on the percept. That is, when straight recognition in terms of figural characteristics are required without a categorical set, the paranoid should exhibit the greatest deficit. The paranoid will show the least deficit when using common assemblies or schemata. Schemata strength should be greater than normals, unless the requirement is to utilize many categories or contrasting schemata.

The paranoid moves from the concept, category in immediate memory, toward the percept. His categorical set operates so that the controlled processing is a biased search for specific attributes. Once again, the paranoid can also utilize automatic processing. Once he is satisfied that the categories are established, he can automatically assign stimuli to those categories without much attention to the stimulus field. Hence, he responds almost totally with the cogit which could cause many errors in detection if the experiment was so designed that the percept is not expected from the context of the situation. The initial cogit will determine what is perceived long after the conditions may have changed.

An example of the long-lasting effect of automatic processing is provided by Shiffrin and Schneider (1977). They discuss a study in which the subject had to search for a group of letters in another set of distractor letters. After leaving the laboratory, subjects reported a difficulty in reading other material as the practiced set "jumped out" from the page. Analogously, we hypothesize that the paranoid functions by consistently mapping the world with some words or faces as parts of a definite set. Automatic processing could thus result in an unusual perspective or a delusion.

The strength of the configural assemblies that provides the categorical set causes the paranoid uniqueness. In the paranoid's acquisition of knowledge, there are a limited number of higher-order assemblies composed of an associated group of cogit representations, which are consistently activated by a portion of many stimuli. The cogits and the cogit assemblies are similar to normals, especially when the stimuli are neutral. However, when stimuli produce information about the object's goodness or badness, the cogit assemblies of the paranoids are different. One configuration is related to another configuration in a rigid predictable fashion. That is, the strength of specific configurations are high, so that a configuration is strengthened to the point of unitization. This unit then can unite with other units in a personal schemata, which is the paranoid delusion or rigid conceptual framework.

An analogy of the paranoid conceptual process is found in the work demonstrating that unitary, higher-order memory representations are acquired through construction of lower-order representations. Chase and Simon (1973) observed that chess masters "chunked" a greater number of pieces in their reconstruction of positions than did nonmasters. The chess master could reconstruct common chess games almost perfectly, while he was no better than a nonmaster with random configurations of pieces (De Groot, 1965, 1966). As the elements become organized into unitary conceptual configurations by a process of experience, there is an integration of parts into a sequence in which the parts lose their separate identity. The paranoid, like the chess master at his game, continually operates upon the world in this fashion. His "game" is the relation of the world to himself which is organized totally with higher-order representations.

The paranoid only moves one way. The assembly determines the cogit and there is little effect of the cogit upon the assembly, except if the material is in a neutral system. In an area of information where there are no assemblies developed and the controlled processing occurs, such as in the use of nonsense syllables, the paranoid may perform like normals. The paranoid has extensive assemblies, wide conceptual categories, created by heavily practiced, extensive associative configurations. It would be expected that without a limit being placed upon the activation of the total assembly by the nature of the task, the paranoid would emit the total assembly, thus, possibly, appearing to be overinclusive. However, when the task is defined, as in the Bannister procedure where the associative assemblies such as good, bad, mean, etc., are specified, there would not be deficit. Also in the field dependency measure, where the object is neutral and hence not related to any assembly , there is no deficit. The deficit occurs when information, which has an assembly, is pitted against information with another assembly such that only one has to be incorporated. The prose passages in the distraction study of Payne are examples of this. When the distractors were presentations of tones, they had little effect on the overinclusive patient. When increasingly meaningful words and then prose passages were used, there was a greater deficit. The less meaning or information in the message, the less the eliciting of competing conceptual configurations or assemblies and, hence, the less the performance deficit. The nonparanoid would not be affected by the conflict between two assemblies because he does not maintain extensive assemblies and responds at the cogit or cogit configuration level. It is a matter of emphasis. Everyone uses both processes, especially in the novel situation of the laboratory. The schizophrenic prefers the automatic, and the paranoid prefers the controlled. The laboratory sometimes does not allow that choice, and, when one or the other is required, the relevant group's specific deficit occurs.

Since the novelty of the stimulus field and practice in a set are the crucial variables in the use of controlled processing, it is important that we exclude from consideration those studies using chronic patients. The long-term institutionalized individual is by definition restricted to a constant stimulus field with no practice with novel stimuli. They do not experience the varying stimulus fields as would occur while driving a car or walking in a crowded street. While such a conclusion may be premature because the effects of long-term instutitonalization have not been clearly determined, for some degree of experimental control, it seems to be better to err on the conservative side rather than continue to possibly confound schizophrenia with institutionalization. A recent study by Goldstein and Halperin (1977) certainly supports this approach. They administered a large number of psychological and neurological tests to chronic and active patients. The major finding was that length of institutionalization was the best predictor of performance, especially with complex tests. In fact, when comparing schizophrenic patients to neurological patients, the neurological tests differentiated the long-term from the short-term patient better than organics and nonorganics.

To demonstrate the distinction between groups and between stages of information processing, we now examine the work focusing on discrete stages in information processing in paranoids and nonparanoids. The rest of this chapter discusses the research that has examined the stages of initial detection, short-term memory, and conceptual organization of acute schizophrenics and paranoids. Unfortunately, few of the studies have made a clear diagnostic distinction. Since our goal is inclusiveness, we review the greatest number of studies that have used schizophrenic patients. We will infer patient groupings from partial descriptions whenever possible.

Iconic Storage

The first stage in Fig. 6.1 is the icon itself. In reviewing the three studies that actually measure the icon, the central question is whether or not the schizophrenic or paranoid has the same iconic display as other groups. Obviously if there is a faster icon decay, there is less time to "read" the icon, and further processing would be impaired. Three factors which affect the icon are post-exposure field, intensity, and exposure duration of the stimulus. The first studies examined the icon by varying stimulus duration.

In the first part of a study by Saccuzzo, Hirt, and Spencer (1974), stimulus exposure time of one letter was varied to determine the exposure needed for a criterion of 80% accuracy. The only significant difference was between chronics and other groups. They also tested the threshold for one letter among seven others and again found no significant differences with nonchronic groups. After practice the means of the nonschizoprhenic psychotic controls was 3.00 and 11.06, while the delusional schizophrenics were 6.36 and 43.00 in a one- and eight-letter condition respectively. In short, by varying one iconic parameter—exposure time—there was no difference in the icon for delusional patients.

The study also varied the post-exposure field by masking so that the duration of the icon was manipulated from 50 to 300 msec. Trend analysis revealed that, while all groups improved with the increases in interstimulus interval, the schizophrenic groups increased at a different rate than the nonschizophrenic groups. Delusional patients required almost twice as long as normals, 300 msec., to reach a level found in the no-masking condition.

Unfortunately, the total hospitalization of these schizophrenic patients was not included, so the chronicity status of what probably are paranoids cannot be accurately determined.

A later study by Saccuzzo and Miller (1977) compared acute delusional schizophrenics with college students on a backward-masking task to determine the critical interstimulus interval for the two groups. The procedure required the detection of *T* or *A,* with increasing interstimulus intervals between the presentation of the letter and a mask until the subject could identify the target letter. Results indicated that acute delusional schizophrenics were less resistant to the effects of the mask, requiring a mean critical interstimulus interval of 11.05 msec. as compared with 4.15 msec. for the normals. The schizophrenic group also showed a significant improvement over trials, whereas the normals reached asymptote in the second session.

In the first study, delusional patients did not differ from other groups, whereas in the second, they did. This seeming discrepancy may be explained by the differing threshold procedures used: exposure time and masking. There is an assumption that in the masking procedure the mask "erases" the image. However, the Erickson and Collins (1964) work, as well as others, indicate that the mask could summate with the prior image.

A recent study using the same masking procedure makes this same point. Steronko and Woods (1978) also varied the critical interstimulus interval and presented several letters masked by two side-by-side *M*s. Using a group of college students who showed schizophrenic type profiles on the MMPI, they found that, although the schizophrenic profile group did not constantly differ from another inflated profile group, they did differ from a noninflated profile group by requiring a longer delay of mask. Steronko and Woods (1978) offer an interpretation of their results in terms of both iconic storage and encoding:

> However, the possibility remains that a significant effect of the pattern mask under the masking conditions of the present study was to degrade the icon of the target by concatenation, resulting in one unintelligible icon rather than two distinct icons. If this is true, it suggests that the deficit in processing found in the 2-7-8 group may be due to a deficit at, and/or before, iconic storage. The longer mask delay required to attain recognition of the target may be due to the need for more time for the icon to develop, either because of impairment in the system prior to iconic storage or in the storage system iteself. If iconic storage takes more time to develop, the mask is able to combine with the former icon at a later point in time than with a quickly developing icon. Another possibility is that icon formation occurs normally but that the icon persists for an abnormally long time period. This would also explain a summation effect at a longer mask delay than the control group. The effect in either case would be confounding pairs of icons, leading to perception which is less than adequate [p. 488].

Hence, the deficit found in the Saccuzzo masking work may be due to either iconic storage or slowness in iconic processing. This encoding process could be also affected by different encoding strategies. In the Saccuzzo work, where a mask of *W*'s followed the exposure of *T* or *A*, there is the possibility that the finding of differences in icon strengths between the groups with masking may have been due to the paranoid waiting for greater certainty with the summated figures. The improvement over trials exhibited by the paranoids, and not by the college students, could have been due to developing a greater confidence in their performance. Furthermore, the appropriateness of the control group of college students is questionable. The college students were probably superior to the general population, especially to the social group from which the paranoids were drawn and differed solely on the basis of a general familiarity with the testing situation.

Even if the results were not affected by a response certainty bias, the actual interstimulus interval of 11.05 msec. is so short that it is difficult to conceive of how this creates any form of deficit in processing information. Neisser (1976) clearly states that such time periods are not encountered in everyday life, in which eye movements require at least 200 msec. with no masking conditions.

The conclusion from the meager data on the strength of the icon is that there is possibly some difference between paranoids and others. Although we predicted that paranoids as compared to schizophrenics would have the greater difficulty with the initial encoding stages, especially in terms of processing off the icon, the significance of the finding is questionable. Since none of these studies included nonparanoids, the nature of the schizophrenic icon strength is not known.

Encoding

The span of apprehension is considered to be the amount of information that can be processed off the icon into short-term memory. The duration of the icon is measured by the amount of information that is processed without the use of short-term memory involving rehearsal. However, the two encoding processes demonstrated by Schneider and Shiffrin (1977) (automatic and controlled processing), or the similar two processes described by Neisser (1967) (preattentive processing and focal attention), occur at this stage. Hence, the span of apprehension is not a simple measure of the duration of the icon, but also includes the encoding process.

The distinction between the two processes in the span of apprehension task becomes important when we consider the different methods used. Sperling's (1960) technique, described earlier, involves a partial report of a presented matrix. At varying times after stimulus termination, the cue denoting the segment to be reported is presented. Another technique is a forced-choice recognition procedure developed by Estes (1965). A letter is presented in a matrix of letters, and the subject must detect the target letter. The task requires a search of the matrix which allows different search strategies to emerge. Hence, differences in the relevant span could be due either to the time taken to search the display or the duration of the icon itself. If one can assume schizophrenics, paranoids, and others have equal iconic images, we can then assume the span measures reflect differences in encoding. There is no direct test of this assumption for nonparanoids. However, considering the results found with paranoids, the assumption is certainly tenable.

Using a forced-choice letter recognition task, Neale, McIntyre, Fox, and Cromwell (1969) found that good premorbid paranoids differed from normal controls when required to report the detection of a target letter, which was presented with several noise letters. They did not differ when the target letter was presented alone. The exposure duration was 90 msec. According to the mean detection scores obtained on a large matrix (8 letters), normals processed 4.48 letters, good premorbid paranoids processed 2.52 letters, and poor nonparanoids processed 2.4. Both schizophrenic groups were somewhat acute (less than three years of total hospitalization). While span of apprehension for normals is equivalent to what is found for normal samples, the good paranoids produced a longer encoding time. If the poor nonparanoids are not just more pathological (being poors) and represent the nonparanoid, we conclude from these results that the nonparanoid also has difficulty in the initial encoding of the icon.

A later study (Neale, 1971) reduced exposure time from 90 to 70 msec., added displays of 4 and 12 to the 1 and 8 display matrices used in the previous study, and added appropriate control groups of hospitalized nonschizophrenics and prisoners. Again, there were no detection differences when the simple target letter was presented alone. However, the schizophrenics were not able to detect the target at a display size of 4, indicating that the processing limit was below that point and probably similar to the limit found in the previous Neale et al. (1969) study. Controls were able to process at the display size of 8. What is most revealing is that acute paranoid and nonparanoids were directly compared and were not found to be different. This finding, since it also compares the schizophrenic group to appropriate controls, strongly suggests that both schizophrenics and paranoids exhibit a problem in encoding.

In order to further examine the schizophrenic's detection of stimuli, Neale (1971) suggested varying the distinctness of the target. McIntyre, Fox, and Neale (1970) used this method with college students and found that accuracy increased with a greater dissimilarity between target and distractors. They explained that the increase in accuracy was due to a process similar to Neisser's preattentive processing in that, with greater dissimilarity, the elements do not have to be fully processed, which would permit a more rapid and efficient search. Davidson and Neale (1974) manipulated the signal–noise similarity to determine whether or not such manipulation had a differential effect on acute schizophrenics and controls. They found that the signal–noise similarity affected acute schizophrenics in the same manner as controls. Performance improved for all groups as noise letters became more dissimilar from the target letter. However, at all display sizes, the processing limit for the schizophrenic group was again found at display size 4. Although paranoids were not differentiated from schizophrenics, it probably can be assumed from their previous work that the two schizophrenic subgroups did not differ. In effect, it is strongly indicated that paranoids and nonparanoids have a smaller span of apprehension than others.

The studies by Neale and others used letter detection in a forced-choice technique and consistently found processing difficulties in the iconic memory of acute schizophrenics, paranoid and nonparanoid. Both groups process approximately 2 to 3 letters, while controls process between 7 and 8. The question is whether or not both groups used the same strategy in this situation. In other words, did normals use automatic processing throughout the task when the signal–noise ratio increased, and did the paranoid and schizophrenic do the same with controlled processing? The study does not allow a discrimination between processing strategies. It does not indicate how normals processed information nor whether or not the schizophrenics engaged in controlled search, even though an automatic search was more appropriate.

By varying letter similarity, the crucial dimension—type of processing—may not have varied. In performing the task, the subject must decide which process to use, assuming that levels of novelty and practice are equal. It may be that controls tend to engage automatic processing more readily and, hence, read the icon quicker and achieve more detections. As pointed out by Schneider and Shiffrin (1977), individual differences emerge in the use of each strategy in even the most highly controlled, well-practiced experiments with highly motivated subjects. One way the results of the Neale work could be explained is if the schizophrenic used an inappropriate search strategy during the span of apprehension. Instead of using the automatic processing of the normal with a clear recognition of categories (letters that are targets and letters that are distractors), he uses the time-consuming serial controlled processing. Consequently, his search rate is consistently below normals but follows other conditions, such as the signal-to-noise ratio. Contrary to our hypothesis, however, paranoids and schizophrenics did not differ, which suggests that both used a controlled search strategy. It is not clear why this occurred nor whether it occurred for different reasons. Paranoids would be expected to engage in controlled search as part of their usual strategy. The schizophrenic, however, is expected to utilize the preattentive process and not engage as much in focal attention. Hence, automatic processing should be a more comfortable strategy. But the demands of the experimental situation to report accurately may have encouraged the schizophrenic to adopt a controlled search, which is not the preferred mode of processing. Thus, he performed at a lower level than normals.

In summary, we have argued that the Estes method allows two search strategies to be used and that both schizophrenic groups probably attempted that which was least adaptive in terms of rate of detection. Hence, we conclude that the rate of processing the icon in these studies is more related to processing strategies than actual iconic strength. We now discuss three studies that demonstrate the difference in processing strategies of schizophrenics and paranoids, when involved in an information processing situation.

Russell and Knight (1977) report a series of three studies, which we would not usually consider because of their use of chronics. Whereas it is usually found that chronics are deficient, they found that chronics were equal to prisoner controls. More important, they systematically varied the stages in information processing, which allows us to discuss stages of information processing for paranoids and schizophrenics. The sequence of studies followed the Neisser model. They began with a search task, which could engage either automatic or controlled processing. Subjects examined a list of letters for one target letter. There were two sets of distractors, one set sharing figural characteristics with the target and the other not. The question was whether or not the schizophrenics engage in automatic processing as normals do or whether they analyze the non-target letters to a greater depth in a controlled processing strategy. (See Schneider & Shiffrin, 1977, pp. 16–17, for a discussion of the procedure used to examine automatic processing.) If both groups engaged in an automatic processing strategy, they would be equally affected by the degree of similarity of the nontarget letters. There were no significant differences found between groups, with all groups exhibiting the same search rate. However, normals required much more time for the similar element distraction. Schizophrenics exhibited more errors, indicating a tendency to underanalyze context letters. Paranoids exhibited the same response time, both when the distractions shared elements and when they did not, which suggests the use of controlled processing.

The next experiment focused upon recognizing sets. The subjects reported "same" if the display set contained replicates of one letter, and "different" if another member of the alphabet was present. In short, the task was to detect an odd letter in a set. Since the subject was not searching for a particular letter held in memory, there would be few effects of a category as we have used the term. While both processes can be used, if controlled processing is used, there should be an increase in reaction time with an increase in the number of elements processed. We also would expect that a "same" judgment takes longer than a "different" judgment because, with the latter, the detection of an odd letter would terminate the search before completing the series (Schneider & Shiffrin, 1977). In short, if one used a serial search strategy, the greater the number of elements in a trial, the longer should be the increase in reaction times, and trials allowing a termination response of "different" should be shorter than trials requiring an exhaustive search indicated by a "same" response.

The results suggest that a controlled processing strategy was used. Collapsing over groups, the greater the display load, the longer the reaction time. Also, the "different" condition with three odd elements was faster than the "different" condition with one odd element. A most interesting result is in the significant groups × display load interaction. Although subgroup differences did not reach significance, paranoids in the "same" and "different" condition show the same search activity. They increased their reaction time as the size of display increased. Controls and schizophrenics exhibited approximately the same times at all display sizes in the "same" conditions. Also, whereas controls made more than three times the errors in the similar element condition than in the different element condition, paranoids only made twice as many errors. Taken together, these results suggest that normals were using automatic processing, which would produce faster response times and more errors in the condition where the distractors were similar to the target. We infer that paranoids used controlled processing because their time for sets with similar and dissimilar distractions were the same, and their rate of errors in each was equivalent, but their overall time relative to normals was longer.

Also, when there was only one odd letter in the displays, similar functions were found for all groups. There was a greater increase in time at the larger display size. When three odd letters were presented, the tendency was for the paranoids to decrease their reaction times on the larger display sizes. Since they only had to detect one odd letter, it would be expected that, on some trials, the different letter was close to the beginning of the series and search was terminated quickly. Controls and, to some extent, schizophrenics seemed to have taken as long with the large set as small set because the times were the same. This suggests that the use of an automatic search through the total set was still quicker overall than the serial search that is terminated.

In the third experiment, two sets of letters were presented, with letter clusters varying from three to six letters. The subject had to view one set and then check the next set to match the letters. The letter sets consisted of nonsense sets and words. The response required a judgment of "same" or "different." This task relies much more on short-term memory than the previous study, especially for the nonsense set. There were more errors in the "different" condition than in the "same" condition. There were no significant differences in error rates by groups. When response time was measured, response to words were faster than nonwords and the difference increased

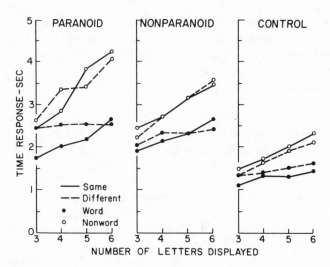

FIG. 6.2. Group mean response times as a function of display load, Experiment 3. (From Russell & Knight, 1977.)

with the number of letters in the set. Trends with group differences are presented in Fig. 6.2. Paranoids exhibited longer reaction times, the greater the size of the letter set, except if the set was a single letter. Controls performed in a similar way across display sizes and word and nonword conditions. From the nonsignificant differences, the authors (Russell & Knight, 1977) inferred that the overall differences in processing time between schizophrenics and controls reflected differences in processing strategy: "In the present context, the slower responses could reflect the greater time consumed by schizophrenics in performing operations involved in setting up a search and/or in organizing and processing the vocal response [p. 24]."

The results of these experiments support our hypothesis about the different search strategies of paranoids and schizophrenics. The paranoids were affected by set size and the conditions of same or different—results reflecting a process of serial search. Schizophrenics and normals seemed to engage in an automatic processing, which would not produce such effects. Unfortunately, in this study, there is too much within-group variance to produce the significance on the relevant interactions. Also, paranoid performance was correlated with age, suggesting that the age of the patient and not only diagnosis produce such functions.

A study in our lab (Pic'l, Magaro, & Wade, 1979) directly examined the use of controlled and automatic processing by acute schizophrenics and paranoids. We analyzed the number of errors by each group in a task that required the enumeration of dots presented at 17 msec. The rising function of paranoids with the increasing number of dots presented indicates that more errors occur when there are more dots to count. In the controlled processing function presented by Schneider and Shriffin (1977), a function of frame size, number of figures in the field, produces the same function. When one counts, accuracy is dependent upon the number one can count before the icon fades. Schizophrenics, on the other hand, exhibit the same number of errors across five display sizes, indicating automatic processing. Normals and nonschizophrenic controls performed like the paranoids. Although we discuss this study further when we talk about hemispheric specialization, it will suffice for now to note its support of our hypothesis that paranoids engage in controlled processing, while schizophrenics use automatic processing. Another recent study (Clooney & Murray, 1977) used a similar methodology. They presented a task that required the detection of the odd letter in series of two, three, and four letters. The major finding was that paranoids processed serially when making both "same" and "different" judgments, whereas schizophrenics did not exhibit this strategy.

In summarizing up to this point, the results of the iconic imagery work do not clearly indicate whether there is a deficit in encoding or in the strength of the icon. It does not seem that the strength of the icon itself is less in paranoids at least in any significant manner. The threshold results by Saccuzzo et al. (1974) indicated no differences between paranoids and normals. According to both exposure time and masking methods, there is little or no deficit displayed by paranoids, especially when the type of control group is considered. The masking condition revealed that paranoids require a longer interstimulus interval to perform as well as controls. However, it may have been the mask itself, rather than the icon, that produced differences.

In summarizing the span of apprehension studies, a slower rate of processing is reported for both schizophrenics and paranoids. We attributed these findings to both schizophrenic groups using a controlled processing strategy in the Estes forced-choice procedure, rather than the automatic strategy employed by controls. The work we have been able to find suggests that the two processes could be differentially employed by the different schizophrenic subgroups. Paranoids employ controlled processing, while normals and schizophrenics employ an automatic form of processing.

We next discuss the end of the encoding process and whether or not there are any paranoid–schizophrenic differences in short-term memory. At this point, the process of conceptualization begins with the initial cogit. Just as the initial icon is not assessed to be deficient for schizophrenia subgroups, it is not expected that short-term memory by itself is deficient. The stage of information processing which distinguishes between schizophrenics and paranoids is in the encoding stage.

Encoding into Short-Term Memory

There are many ways to study short-term memory. One method involves the full report technique. Whereas the partial report only requires the reporting of a segment of the field and does not demand a large memory load, the full report involves the reporting of the full matrix and, hence, involves rehearsal in short-term memory. In short, the individual must read the total display off the icon and rehearse it until it can be reported. It should be clear that the short-term memory procedures using full report also involve encoding because the report is made from the processing of the icon after a brief tachistoscopic presentation. Hence, the full-report technique measures both short-term memory and encoding, with the latter being less of a factor than in the partial-report technique. There are two reporting techniques—a verbal and a written report—with the latter requiring a greater memory storage because it takes longer to write than verbally report material.

Full Report. Sperling (1960) maintained that the full-report technique involves what is initially available to the subject and his ability to remember and report that information. If paranoids differ in the manner in which they encode the icon, we would expect that they would also perform more poorly in the full report, unless extended exposure times allow enough time to overcome the initially slower processing. The three studies that employed the technique with schizophrenic groups report conflicting results.

Spohn, Thetford, and Woodham (1970) reported the results of tachistoscopic presentation of six consonants, which all had to be reported under a constant exposure condition (50 msec.) and a varying exposure condition (50, 250, 750, 1100 msec.). The schizophrenic group was distinguished in terms of chronicity, paranoid status, and premorbidity. The control group was normals. They found that, with a constant exposure of 50 msec., the overall difference between schizophrenics and normals was significant. Furthermore, a significant triple interaction revealed that the acute nonparanoids were similar to normals and superior to acute paranoids on most trials. Under varying exposures, similar results were found, with the paranoids performing more poorly, while the nonparanoids were similar to normals. Results also revealed that as exposure duration increased, the difference between normals and the schizophrenics (nonparanoids) increased. Although all groups improved their performance with longer exposure times, the schizophrenics did not make use of the increased exposure time to process material as much as normals, thus exhibiting their greatest deficit at the longest exposure time. Hence, congruent with previous results on iconic imagery and encoding, as well as with the theoretical expectation, paranoids continue to exhibit a deficit while schizophrenics perform like normals. This study controlled for level of memory and intellectual functioning, which gives greater credibility to differences being due to the processing involved in moving into short-term memory.

Since some aspects of the procedure differ from those of other studies, they will be discussed. The subjects were presented with a 2 × 3 matrix filled with consonants, and rather than verbally report the letters, they were asked to write down the letters in a six box grid. The task requires that the displayed letters be quickly encoded and then stored in memory. It also allows much more time to be spent in rehearsal of items because the task demanded a recall in written form. The finding that the greater deficit for paranoid was at the longest exposure durations suggests that normals used the longer exposure time to rehearse, while paranoids spent a greater time encoding the letters. This finding suggests that the encoding difficulty or strategy of the paranoid could be exhibited as a memory problem.

This finding, however, has not been replicated in later work. Cash, Neale, and Cromwell (1972) used a full-report technique but did not require the writing of the response. The verbal report was of a 4 × 4 matrix containing 4 or 8 letters. Results showed no difference between schizophrenics and normals at either display size. Whereas the same laboratory produced differences between normals and schizophrenic groups on the partial report, no differences emerged on the full report. To understand the differences in their results and their partial report work, Cash et al. (1972) suggest a closer examination of the Estes forced-choice procedure:

> In the partial-report technique, the features of an irrelevant element must be processed to the point where S is assured it is not the target letter. Then S must shift to another element without the necessity of processing each element completely and registering it for later recall. By contrast, the full-report technique requires S to process the features of each element to the extent it can be named and registered for later recall. Therefore, the difference in results which may occur for the two techniques cannot be attributed solely to short-term memory factors. Differences in specific central processing operations may also be involved [p. 326].

In our terms, the forced-choice technique used in the partial report could be biased toward automatic processing instead of short-term memory. Normals using this strategy would outperform those using controlled processing. The full-report technique, however, forces everyone into the same procedure and differences disappear. The superior performance of normals over schizophrenics in the partial-report studies can then be due to the processing strategies we have suggested. The lack of significant differences reported by Cash et al. (1972) was due to the verbal report allowing enough time to use controlled processing off the icon and still rehearse. The conflicting result reported by Spohn et al. (1970) was due to the paranoid spending so much time serially encoding that he did not have the time to rehearse before the memory was lost in the writing of the stimuli. The small difference in procedure placed just enough of an added memory load that subgroup differences emerged.

Knight, Scherer, and Shapiro (1977) also used the full-report procedure with a written response to a 3 × 3 matrix of letters. Subgroups of schizophrenics were determined by level of overinclusion, premorbid adjustment, and chronicity. Although it was found that the overinclusion score was the best predictor for performance on the partial report, premorbid adjustment and the Payne A score were the best predictors of the full report score. The Payne A measure, as we discussed in a previous chapter, is related to concreteness as originally proposed by Goldstein and is, hence, heavily weighted by intelligence. The less pathological overinclusives, as well as normals, did better in the partial than in the full report, which is expected because of the added memory stage involved in the full report. The more pathological underinclusives, and middleinclusives, the two groups who were deficient in coding the icon in the partial report condition, did not show any difference between partial and full report. When recall is required, either in terms of reading the icon or processing out of short-term memory, it is the most pathological who are deficient. The less pathological process the icon as normals, and they utilize short-term memory.

What is relevant to our discussion of differences in encoding strategies is the author's explanation of the deficit. The underinclusives are seen as not deficient in iconic image, but in transferring that information from the spatial array into the sequential verbal response. In short, Knight et al. (1977) suggest that the schizophrenic deficit is in the encoding process and not in the icon. However, the conclusion must be qualified. The group exhibiting the encoding problem were the most pathological, and what may be most accurately said is that at a high level of disorganization, a patient group may produce an encoding deficit or a deficit at any level of processing. Certainly, with the more pathological groups, one would expect less involvement with the task and less rehearsal.

A recent study by Oltmanns (1978) is very relevant in that he found that the encoding problem was also exhibited in the recall of auditory material. Also, the careful methodology allowed a direct examination of the effects of the encoding process on the necessary sequential steps required in short-term memory. As such, this study is of direct relevance to our hypothesis about how the schizophrenic processes information. Unfortunately, paranoid schizophrenics were not separated from nonparanoid schizophrenics, although paranoid states were excluded, which may suggest the study is most relevant to the thought process of the acute nonparanoid.

Oltmanns (1978) examined the operation of short-term memory while presenting distractors by the use of one digit and two word-span lists. The first word-span list varied the strategy under which segments of the memory list were to be rehearsed. The second varied the rate of stimulus presentation. In both tasks, distractor words were presented. The results were that schizophrenics were more distractable, and this was especially so for words in the beginning of the list. Also, increased presentation time did not benefit schizophrenics to the degree it did controls, and they made more intrusive errors. The explanation was that irrelevant words interfered with the schizophrenic's ability to engage in the rehearsal or recoding of words into short-term memory. The words at the beginning of the list could be rehearsed with longer presentation rates. Only controls took advantage of this time. Schizophrenics did not engage in this higher level processing and engaged in a passive strategy. Oltmanns (1978) reports: "Schizophrenics, on the other hand, must rely more heavily on sensory store, where both relevant and irrelevant items are represented. The probability of an intrusive error is thus increased [p. 224]."

The manner of Oltmanns' (1978) explanation of these results was quite similar to our interpretation of the schizophrenic deficit involving the encoding process, and it explains how this same problem can be carried over into an auditory short-term memory task:

> These considerations lead to the following picture of distractibility in schizophrenia. Information processing may be roughly divided into active (controlled) and passive (automatic) operations (Neisser, 1967; Schneider & Shiffrin, 1977) which may be seen as different levels of processing (Craik & Lockhart, 1972). Active processes, such as rote rehearsal, coding, and some forms of memory search, must be carried out in a serial fashion and are strictly limited in capacity. For many schizophrenics, the presence of salient, extraneous stimuli disrupts these controlled processes. Passive operations, on the other hand, are not so vulnerable to distraction. The deterioration in active processing of relevant material is not due to inappropriate coding or rehearsal of irrelevant stimuil. Active processing does not shift to irrelevant stimuli; it simply becomes less efficient in handling relevant stimuli [p. 224].

In our terms, the schizophrenic has a problem with distractors during controlled processing, because controlled processing is not a preferred strategy. When the memory task could be improved by a serial form of processing, the schizophrenic shows the greatest deficit by exhibiting less recall of that segment of the memory list that is most benefited by a serial approach. The schizoprhenic uses automatic processing and more intrusive errors occur during this approach.

In short, this study is very informative in that it introduces a method that allows the encoding process to be examined as it operates upon auditory short-term memory. The use of distractors, serial positions, and presentation rate allow an examination of the processes active in items entering memory.

The results indicate that the type of encoding that occurs during the presentation of a visual stimulus field is the same that occurs when memorizing an auditory field. So, as we inferred from the studies examining encoding into short-term memory of visual material, the nonparanoid schizophrenic prefers automatic processing and does not engage in serial processing. He, thus, will show a deficit when such a strategy is required in the performance of the task.

We are coming to the conclusion that there are not necessarily schizophrenic deficiencies in early stages of information processing. Only when the task demands a strategy that the schizophrenic does not engage in, due to a difference in processing style or degree of pathology, do differences emerge. When the task discounts such differences, the deficiency may disappear. The nature of task demands also explain the paranoid's difficulty. When the task permits variation in approach, the paranoid will take the longer, more definitive approach which provides clearer information, although not much encoding speed, that will affect the transmission into short-term memory.

A recent study supports this interpretation of the paranoid strategy. Neufield (1977) found, in a sentence-verification task, comparing paranoid and nonparanoid patients (less than 2½ years of total hospitalization) and normals, that time-per-constituent comparisons were similar among the groups, but the paranoid exhibited an elevated latency. The subject was required to compare a statement with a picture of the statement (in this case, a statment of color and the actual color). Neufield (1977) concluded that the elevated latency of the paranoid was only a difficulty in selecting items "due to an inclination toward seeming indecisiveness [p. 63]." According to our analysis, the paranoid searches for certainty in his approach to a task that is provided by a controlled processing strategy and produces a longer response time. The elevated latency is not in the response system but in the initial encoding, which in a sentence-verification task is reflected in the time to respond.

Short-Term Memory

The following studies use recognition tasks to measure the operation of short-term memory. At this stage, we are discussing the cogit and its possible associations in short-term memory. A cogit is a single bit of information such as a letter, a number, or a word. In the usual recognition task, cogits are learned and recognition memory is tested using a list of similar stimuli. A related method uses a paired-associate recognition task in which pairs of stimuli are learned and the subject is tested for recognition of the match to one of the pair. In the first case, there are no associational configurations required. In the second case, a configuration is utilized with specific associations. Hayes-Roth (1977) explains that the strength of the association is a function of recency and frequency. Recognition memory, therefore, measures the strength of the associated value of the cogit in terms of these factors. The icon and the encoding are not a primary part of the task because stimuli are presented for long periods of time.

Most recognition studies have not found subgroups nor schizophrenic versus control differences in recognition. Nachmani and Cohen (1969) found no difference between controls and a mixed patient group of acute nonparanoid schizophrenics. For both groups, accuracy improved over trials, in the same manner. Bauman and Murray (1969) also reported no difference between a group of normals and a mixed patient group of paranoid and nonparanoid schizophrenics (probably mostly acute), even though the alternatives in the recognition list were semantically or acoustically similar to the correct words. Koh, Kayton, and Berry (1973) presented words and high- and low-association nonsense syllables in a recognition task to young, acute, nonpsychotic nonparanoids. Again the recognition memory of schizophrenics in a signal detection analysis was found to be as good as that of normals. A frequency effect measuring recognition for high frequency words, as contrasted to low frequency words, and a trial effect were the same for all groups. The conclusion was that regardless of frequency, conceptual categories or association values, the recognition memory of schizophrenics is as good as normals.

On the other hand, Traupmann (1975) reported a deficit in a process schizophrenic group. Recognition lists included the list item, a synonym, an antonym, and a rhyme for each of the list items. While the focus was on varying word lists in terms of imagery and categorization, he found that reactive schizophrenics and students recognized more words than process schizophrenics. Interpreting the process-reactive dimension as a measure of pathology, this study demonstrates only that the less pathological perform like normals while the more pathological perform less well. Knight, Sims-Knight, and Petchers-Cassell (1977) found, in a test of picture recognition, that good premorbid schizophrenics performed as well as normals and nonpsychotic controls, but all differed from process schizophrenics. Again, only pathology related to a recognition deficit.

Reported differences in the recognition memory can be accounted for by the chronicity or pathology of the schizophrenic groups, the nature of the control groups, and the peculiarities of the tasks employed. For example, the deficit of the process schizophrenic group in Traupmann's study can be attributed not only to pathology, but also to chronicity. The effects of chronicity were demonstrated in the Klinka and Papageorgis (1976) study in which the Rattan and Chapman multiple-choice vocabulary test was used to study associative intrusions in short-term and long-term schizophrenic, nonschizophrenic, and nonpsychiatric inpatients. The variable which accounted for associative intrusions was the length of hospitalization, and not diagnosis.

It could be argued that deficits in short-term memory may not be in the storage capacity, but in the access to short-term memory. However, a recent study (Koh, Szoc, & Peterson, 1977) found no support for this hypothesis. Using acute nonparanoid schizophrenics and the Sternberg (1975) procedure, which involves recognizing a word in a set presented previously (the memory set), they found that schizophrenics did not differ from other hospitalized controls. All groups exhibited the same task functions, such as an increase in reaction time with a large memory set and a serial position effect. Although schizophrenics were slower than college students in overall reaction time, they were not slower than patient controls. Hence, in a rather precise examination of recognition memory, this study demonstrates that short-term memory scanning is intact for schizophrenics.

In the next study, the schizophrenic's poorer performance can be explained by the particular method used. Russell, Bannatyne, and Smith (1975) used acute subjects and a paired-associate task to maximize the associational value for the recognition task. Both groups improved when the associational links were high, but normals had a slight but significantly greater recognition than schizophrenics. Because this study manipulated associational links, it examined the effects of assemblies, our next stage, rather than the cogit. Their second experiment in the same study found that while normals' recognition was higher than that of schizophrenics for the high-association list, the schizophrenic recognition mean for both lists was the same. Schizophrenics recognized more items on the low association list than the normals. Clearly, the conditions of high association between list and cue words was advantageous for the normals and not for the schizophrenics. Again, the suggestion here is that a difference exists in assemblies, but not with the initial cogit of short-term memory. The next group of studies focuses more directly upon associative linkage as we analyze the recall memory tasks. Up to this point, we can conclude that the cogit, when presented, is recognized. The next question is whether or not it can be organized into units in the normal manner.

Assemblies

Recall places a greater load upon the cogit assemblies, which are either subjectively organized by the subject with some form of mneumonic device or by the experimenter by varying characteristics of the word set, such as with the use of high associational or imagery words. In either case, the process requires that the subject produce a set that is more than comparing a stimulus to a cogit, as in the recognition tests. Nachmani and Cohen (1969) explain this distinction in terms of two processes:

> In recall, S first samples an item from an underlying set that consists of list and extra list subsets. The S then goes on to the comparison stage which determines

the probability that the sampled item will be emitted as a response. In the comparison stage, S decides whether the sampled item was, or was not, in the list subset.... In recognition only the comparison stage is included, as E himself performs the sampling for A [p. 512].

Recall tasks, either in the form of paired associates or in recall of a complete stimulus list, encourages the development of cogit assemblies. Investigators manipulate the associational value of words because the associational and linguistic relationships which play an insignificant role in recognition are crucial to recall (Koh et al., 1973). Hence, recall tasks are a test of the ability to form or use cogit assemblies.

While acute schizophrenics and paranoids do not have difficulty with recognition tasks, a deficit in the recall memory in schizophrenics, but not paranoids, has been repeatedly demostrated, especially if the subject has to form his own cogit assembly. Investigation has usually centered on locating the source of the difficulty. We expect that the nonparanoid has the greatest difficulty with the strength of configurations, while the paranoid has strong idiosyncratic higher-order assemblies, which interfere with the formation of new assemblies.

There are many ways to examine the strength of the assembly. Studies have examined the strength of the association in an assembly by employing memory facilitators such as semantic structure, organization, and categorization, as well as by having the subject form their own mneumonic devices. Another method is to analyze recall protocols to examine normative and subjective organization. Another procedure focuses on editing and the operation of the assembly at the output stage of communication. We shall consider each of these areas in order.

Strength of Association.   Traupmann (1975) studied the effects of imagery and categorization on recall. Imagery facilitated retention and retarded forgetting for student controls and reactive schizophrenics. Similar results were found with categorization. These results indicate that memory facilitators of imagery and of categorization had generally the same effect on reactive schizophrenics as normals. Similarly, Calhoun (1970) studied the effects of payoff (payment for recalling words) and information cues (hints regarding the conceptual category of the words) on recall performance of reactive paranoids, reactive nonparanoids, and process nonparanoids. He found that reactive paranoids and reactive nonparanoids recalled the same number of words. Although paranoids were affected by information cues and training, whereas nonparanoids were affected by information cues and payoff, the payoff effect for nonparanoids accounted for only 8% of the variance, indicating that they took advantage of informational cues as well as paranoids. Traupmann, Berzofsky, and Kesselman (1976) studied proactive inhibition release in acute schizophrenics and paranoids and found that recall with rehearsal prohibited was the same for schizophrenics and paranoids. Organization was not possible and, hence, the groups did not differ.

From these studies it could be concluded that the schizophrenics, paranoids, and normals can form assemblies by the use of associations. However, the question remains whether they can do as well as other groups. Russell et al. (1975) found, in a cued-recall task, that schizophrenics (paranoids and schizophrenics combined) were significantly inferior on a high association list of paired associates. Both groups made use of the associates, but schizophrenics formed fewer associations between the cue and the test word. The authors argued that the greater the associational links provided, the better would be the performance of normals and the greater the deficit of schizophrenics. In a second experiment, the same authors created high- and low-association recognition lists in which the cue words were embedded in the recognition lists rather than presented separately as in the first experiment. The groups did not differ in the low-association list and in fact, acute schizophrenics recognized more words than normals. The normals, however, were superior in the high-association task. The normals were able to use the embedded word cues in the high-association list, whereas the schizophrenics made no use of the associational structure and recognized the same number of words on both lists. In this experiment, the schizophrenics were all acute nonparanoids. In short, the schizophrenic may not use associational cues unless they are an obvious part of the procedure, and even then they are not used to the extent of controls. Similar results were also found in the study by Koh and Kayton (1974). Input–output concordance, which reflect the degree to which subjects were able to utilize the order of input as a mneumonic device, was used by normals but not by young acute nonparanoid schizophrenics.

The next study provides clear evidence that while the schizophrenic has associations similar to normals, they are not as strong. Larsen and Fromholt (1976) compared the mneunomic organization in free recall of normals and schizophrenics with first-rank Schneider's symptoms. The task involved sorting until two consecutive sorts were identical. This was followed by a recall task. Normals required fewer trials to criterion. Once the schizophrenics had met criterion, their recall was the same as normals. Also, recall of words adhered to categories in both groups, and an analysis of sorting indicated no differences between the groups. However, schizophrenics were observed to sort less systematically, changing their sort systems more often. In short, schizophrenics were found to sort in a similar way as normals, but their performance was less systematic and reflected less consistent categorical or subjective organization. While the strength of the assemblies are not at the level of normals, their categories were the same as normals.

Another recall procedure employs delay conditions or interpolations of report procedures. These studies also indicate that memory capacities are limited in acute schizophrenics. Koh and Kayton (1974) compared recall performances of young, acute, nonparanoid schizophrenics and normals on lists of words with low frequency, imagery, concreteness, meaningfulness, and affectivity under delay and no-delay conditions. They found that the recall of normals was superior to that of the schizophrenic group. Analysis of serial position effects indicated that both groups followed the same function, although schizophrenics were consistently inferior. The longer the delay between learning and response, the greater the deficiency for the schizophrenics. Also, there were greater intrusion errors, either from within or external to the memory list, for schizophrenics in both delay conditions. Hence in this experimental situation, nonparanoid schizophrenics cannot use the cogit assembly to aid recall. When the schizophrenic had to impose his own schemata upon the word list to form assemblies, they exhibited a deficit. The previous studies (Calhoun, 1970; Traupmann, 1975), which provided memory facilitators or "assembly builders," found no deficit suggesting that the schizophrenic does not normally engage in forming assemblies, but can do so if directed by experimental conditions.

The next study not only demanded that the schizophrenic form his own assembly but provides a hint to why it is difficult for him to do so. Bauman and Kolisnyk (1976) studied interference effects in the short-term memory of acute schizophrenics. The task involved the recall of seven digits but the order of recall was varied. The first analysis examined just the first response of each subject in each serial position. Although normals exhibited superior recall over positions, there was no group interaction indicating that schizophrenics followed the same recall function found with normals. Greater recall was found in the beginning and the end of the list. The next analysis examined the effects of the interpolation of the subject's responses on recall (i.e., the degree of recall once the subject had to recite prior digits). Here it was found that schizophrenics had poorer recall the more they had to recall prior digits. They also made more omissions and insertions but fewer reversals than normals. The conclusion was that as the schizophrenics responded, they experienced greater difficulty with retrieval. Bauman and Kolisnyk (1976) suggest that the problem was that of response interference, which was due to the lack of processing:

Some may argue that schizophrenics fell increasingly further behind normals as the number of outputs increased because of a rehearsal problem. Search through memory, as indicated by Shiffrin (1970) and Norman (1966), may be considered as a sequential or serial activity, rather than a random one. Subjects usually begin at some point in the task and sequentially scan through memory until they locate the item to be retrieved. The digit recall task in this experiment required covert rehearsal prior to each response. If, for example, the first digit probed was the fourth in the input sequence, then the subjects would have to rehearse the first three digits in the series before he/she arrived at the response. Thus, seven memory searches were required for each presentation of a seven-digit list. Because the memory search was serial, it follows that digits in the first input positions were rehearsed more frequently than were those in the last. Since the role of rehearsal, as suggested by Bernback (1970) and Bjork (1970) is to produce replicas of a single memory trace, thus enhancing the probability of long-term storage, it may be that the last input items particularly were lost from schizophrenic memory store because of inadequate rehearsal.

The subject was required to recreate the total list in order to present the digit at the expected position. Another way of expressing this process would be that they were required to "utilize" the list (i.e., form the individual cogits into an assembly in order to form a single memory unit). We would contend that the schizophrenic was not able to do this because he does not usually engage in the serial activity that is necessary for such unitization. Possibly the results can be explained in terms of rehearsal, but from our analysis of the encoding results, we suggest that they do not serially process in any stage of information processing, but prefer the more holistic preattentive distinctions or automatic search. As the authors note in the previous quotation, the task requires a serial processing in rehearsal. We postulate that regardless of rehearsal, the task requires a strategy of serial processing, controlled processing, and that strategy in itself is not a usual schizophrenic approach to forming assemblies. Hence, there would be a deficiency in the formation of assemblies for the schizophrenic if such a process was required and not aided by experimental conditions.

Subjective Organization.   Koh et al. (1973) make the most direct attack on the question of associations and higher-order assemblies. Following Miller's (1956) unitization theory, they hypothesize that the schizophrenic cannot "chunk" input material into larger units to lessen the load of short-term memory. In our terms, he cannot develop the associational strength of cogits to create strong assemblies. Using a fixed and free recall procedure which explores the type and quality of the cogit assemblies, they were able to examine the subjective organization, degree of categorical clustering, and hierarchical clustering schemas used by young, acute, nonparanoid, nonactively psychotic schizophrenics.

They found that schizophrenics do not use normative categorical clustering schemes to the same extent as normals, nor do they use as much subjective organization to facilitate recall. Normals were superior with both uncategorized and categorized word lists. While controls increase their categorical clustering (recalling items together in the same category) and subjective organization (grouping items together through trials) over trials, schizophrenics did not. Remembering that the recognition memory was the same for schizophrenics and controls in this study, the problem for nonparanoids was in the chunking process. The schizophrenic did not chunk to any great degree, nor did he organize by any common method. That is, the organizations developed by the schizophrenics widely differed from each other and controls. This idiosyncratic subjective organization suggests that the schizophrenic has loose conceptual associations and they do not remain within common conceptual categories. Poor recall, therefore, was due to the lack of strong assemblies, which are due to a lack of strong associations. Hence, even though the cogit has the same strength as normals, as evidenced in the lack of group differences in the recognition studies, associations which form the assemblies are weak. Since the use of organizational schemes place the nonschizophrenic patient group between schizophrenics and normals, the authors conclude that the organization deficit in schizophrenics is a matter of degree and not quality.

The diminished use of categories and subjective organization may apply to other patient groups. Russell and Beekhuis (1976) used mainly chronic, paranoid schizophrenics, depressives, and normals and employed a procedure including sorting and recall. They found that patient groups did not differ in their normative recall-clustering. There was a significant difference between normals and the two patient groups, but not between the patient groups. In terms of subjective recall clustering, normals had significantly greater clustering than either patient groups who again did not differ. The patient groups were aware of the categories but were apparently unable to use them in the recall task. While this study may suggest that the same organization problem found in schizophrenics may also be found in paranoids or depressives, the sample was too confusing, in terms of diagnosis and chronicity, to derive any real conclusions.

The studies reviewed up to this point indicate that the recall memory of schizophrenics is impaired because the associations between cogits are not as strong for schizophrenics. The studies by Russell and Beekhuis (1976), Larsen and Fromholt (1976), and Traupmann et al. (1976) indicate that schizophrenics are aware of categories and associations. This is also supported by Traupmann's (1975) findings that reactive schizophrenics are aided by categorization. The problem is that the associations are not as strong nor as common as they are with other groups. Several studies have suggested that while the schizophrenic's associations are intact, although not at the strength of others, stress can create an even greater weakening of the associations in an assembly. If it is the associational strength of the assembly that is weak, it would be expected that stress would tend to weaken further the assembly and produce greater deficits.

There are several studies which report the effects of stress. DeWolfe (1971) reported that in a recall of associations that followed a word association test, subjects placed under high stress differed in terms of the disturbance of association. Reactive and process schizophrenics differed in the type of deficit recorded, with process schizophrenics giving more "loose" associations. In another study, DeWolfe and Youkillis (1974) examined word associations of process and reactive schizophrenics under high and low stress. Under high stress, both groups had the same number of loose associations; however, in low stress, the reactives showed greater improvement. Thus, these studies suggested that even for the less pathological schizophrenics, stress increases the disturbance of associations.

Koh, Kayton, and Schwarz (1974) created stress conditions by placing a time limit on a sorting task. The acute, nonparanoid schizophrenics first sorted words into piles on the basis of relatedness under no time limit. Analysis of hierarchical clustering schemes revealed that the schizophrenic scheme was the same as the other two groups. Under time pressure, however, differences between the groups could be detected in terms of measures of group consensus, topographical similarity of the hierarchical clustering schemes, and strong common clusters. Generally, the schizophrenics became more idiosyncratic, reducing overall group consensus.

When asked to revise their time-pressured sortings until they were satisfied, the schizophrenics reduced the group differences. In summary, acute, nonparanoid schizophrenics apparently have associational structures which are not completely different from normals. However, under time pressure their associational links become even more idiosyncratic and less constrictive or stereotyped.

In summary, evidence indicates that acute or reactive nonparanoids have normal but weak associational structures, which they do not utilize efficiently when stress is created. The stress of having recall stimuli presented to them may also cause disturbances in stability and influence associational structures. Thus, these studies suggest that the source of the schizophrenic deficit may be the weakness of associational structures, which are further weakened by stress. Furthermore the finding of Larsen and Fromholt (1976) suggest that the recall deficit may also be modifiable. Schizophrenics only require more time to form associational links. Once the associational links are brought up to strength by more practice, recall is as good as normals. The cogit assembly of the schizophrenic can, therefore, achieve the same strength of normals, but it takes greater frequency of activation. This finding will have important implications for the treatment we will discuss in the last chapter.

Self-Editing. Another method of assessing the strength of associates is the self-editing task. Here it is assumed that words have a hierarchy of association values such that if you present a word it would cue the listener to a correct associate. The task is similar to the familiar Pass-Word game in which the listener has to select the correct associate with only associational cues being given by the speaker. Another procedure involves presenting a pair of words and one associate for the speaker to detect which of the two words was the referent. While subjects are sometimes required to give cues so a listener can select the referent word, in other procedures the referent is an object such as a color to be selected from an array of other colors. Using this method, it is hypothesized that if the strength of the associations are weak or the associations are different for the presented stimulus, a deficit would be exhibited. A problem with all of these studies (except one) is that they have used chronic patients. The one study that uses acutes could be interpreted, not in terms of editing activity, but in terms of the strength and size of the assembly.

Cohen and Camhi (1967) compared normals to chronics and found that they didn't differ in the listener role, but normals were superior in the speaker role. In the listener role, the subject had to choose the correct word of two with the aid of a cue word. The speaker had to provide the cue, and in this study, the cues given by schizophrenics were not deciphered by either the schizophrenics or normals. The authors argued that the results do not suggest that the associations are idiosyncratic for schizophrenics. If they had idiosyncratic associations, they would not have performed well in the listener role. They concluded that the schizophrenic does not edit his associations to produce the most adequate associate, and, therefore, is deficient only in the speaker role.

Smith (1970) modified the task, attempting to separate the factors of association strength and editing. In addition to the regular procedure, the subject was required to select the better of the two cues for the referent. The cue varied in terms of requiring either just a comparison to the referent (the word to be chosen) or requiring a comparison to both the referent and the nonreferent. Results showed that the associations were not different for schizophrenics, indicating that their associations are not more deviant. However, normals did choose better cues than schizophrenics when the two cues were provided. The schizophrenic had the greatest difficulty when the cue had to be compared to both the referent and the nonreferent in order to select the best cue. As in the Cohen and Camhi (1967) study, the schizophrenics were chronics, hence, the results indicate that chronics have the same associational strengths as normals but they do not necessarily utilize these associations advantageously. They do not edit or compare one association with another to select the one having the greatest information value.

Process and reactive schizophrenics were compared by Kantowitz and Cohen (1977), who also found group differences in communication accuracy. Normals were more accurate than schizophrenics, but the reactive and process schizophrenics were not significantly different. Also it was found that if increase in response latency and utterance length can be interpreted as indication of self-editing activity, such activity is diminished or even absent in chronic schizophrenics.

Lisman and Cohen (1972) also sought to pinpoint the source of the self-editing difficulty. Using words that elicited highly dominant responses and others that elicited weaker associations, subjects were asked to respond under two conditions: first, with the first word they could think of, and second, with an unusual response. Significant group differences were found in both conditions, but only for words having high dominant associations. Normals produced significantly more dominant responses when they were told to produce the first word they could think of, and schizophrenics produced significantly more dominant responses when an unusual word was required. The authors inferred from their results that chronic schizophrenics cannot edit out common responses when idiosyncratic responses are appropriate, nor can they edit out personal idiosyncratic responses when dominant responses are appropriate. Although it is not clear why the chronic produces just the opposite of what is demanded. We have noted that it is the chronic but not necessarily the acute who will consistently produce the dominant response.

The same form of associational problem has been found with acute, nonparanoid schizophrenics. Cohen, Nachmani, and Rosenberg (1974) found differences between acute, nonparanoid schizophrenics and normals on a task in which colors were used as the referent. Normals and schizophrenics served as listeners with the novel condition that the schizophrenic is served as the listener to his own description. When the hues were more similar, both speaker groups had greater difficulty in communication. Schizophrenics were similar to normals when the differences in hue were greatest, but were significantly worse with the more similar hues. The greater the amount of discrimination demanded, the greater deficit displayed by the nonparanoids. In addition, the schizophrenics were not even able to more accurately detect their own cues than were normals. The authors concluded that the schizophrenic does not edit out a sampled response. An alternate interpretation is that the schizophrenic does not have the cognitive complexity or the necessary associates in an assembly to communicate the fine discriminations needed in the similar hue condition. The effect was found for nonparanoids, and it was suggested from other work that paranoids may perform differently.

Our criticism of the self-editing work is based on the finding that schizophrenics perform well in the listener role and mainly show a deficit in the speaker role. Also when tasks increase in complexity, as in the Cohen et al. (1974) study, schizophrenics exhibit the difference from normals on the more difficult tasks. Hence, what this work demonstrates is that the more difficult the task, the greater the deficit for chronic patients which is not surprising and may have nothing to do with an editing process. Chapman and Chapman (1973) make the same point in regard to the recall and recognition tasks as well as the word-communication tasks used by Cohen and his co-workers:

Nevertheless, the supportive experimental evidence offered by Cohen and his co-workers is flawed. The evidence from the Cohen and Camhi and the Nachmani and Cohen studies was in terms of differential deficit, that is, a greater schizophrenic deficit on one task than on another. As discussed previously in this book, a comparison of schizophrenic and normal subjects on two tasks were matched on discriminating power. In neither study was there any attempt to match the two tasks on discriminating power. The word-communication task of Cohen and Camhi is not suitable for investigating differential deficit, because scores on the speaker and listener tasks are intertwined in such a way that their relative discriminating power cannot be separately established [p. 270].

To express the problem in other terms, the experimental tasks of the inhibition theorists, as discussed in Chapter 3, is to demonstrate the added inhibition process independent of differences in cognitive organization. The editing studies do not prove that an editing deficit exists rather than a difficulty in assembly formation, which can be demonstrated in the expressive form through language or in the form of associative intrusions. Another methodology, using acute patients, is required to demonstrate equal associative strength, not common associates, and a deficit in inhibition.

SCHEMATA

The next group of studies attempt the study of the schemata. We postulate that the paranoid encounters problems when different assemblies are activated by the same stimulus or when the task requires a shifting of assemblies according to task demands. The work investigating assemblies found the nonparanoid to be deficient. Here we will find evidence that he can be superior to paranoids and normals if the schemata elicited are misleading.

The paranoid is equipped with a set of enduring assemblies or schemas, which he reaffirms by seeking data which may be assimilated by them. The paranoid does not have problems with recall but only when flexibility—the use of multiple conceptual assemblies—is required. Hence, it would be expected that the strength of such assemblies would tend to incorporate most material encoded and even interfere with processing if an assembly was activated when the action of another schemata was required.

McReynolds (1960; McReynolds, Collins, & Acker, 1964) used the McGill Closure Test with chronic delusional and nondelusional schizophrenics to measure the ability to complete an ambiguous picture. They found that the delusional patients attempted and identified more pictures than the nondelusional. They inferred that delusional or paranoid patients have a stronger tendency to organize ambiguous stimuli in a meaningful way. The partial stimulus was able to activate assemblies more readily for paranoids because of the stronger associational links. Normals were not tested, but it would be expected that they may even be less adept at this task than paranoids.

Abrams, Taintor, and Lhamon (1966) operationalized the assembly much as McReynolds et al. (1964) did using the Street Gestalt Completion figures. In this case, however, paranoids were not compared with nonparanoids. Rather, patients of several diagnoses were categorized into four groups representing increasing degrees of paranoid symptomatology. The hypotheses were that the severely paranoid patient should reject (i.e., find no meaning in) fewer cards than the mildly paranoid patient, and in a task where the judgment must be based on incomplete amounts of data, the more paranoid subjects would tend to form atypical and incorrect judgments rather than none at all. The first hypothesis was unconfirmed. All paranoids performed the same. The second hypothesis was confirmed. The assemblies of those who were more paranoid were activated more than those who were less paranoid suggesting stronger associative assemblies for the greater the paranoia expressed.

A study by McCormick and Broekema (1978) used another experimental approach that produced results that could be interpreted in a similar manner. They presented stimuli that initially were ambiguous and then increased in clarity. Nonparanoid and paranoid schizophrenics would name the stimulus at varying degrees of ambiguity and also rate their confidence of their recognition judgments. Heart rate patterns were also recorded during performance. The alcoholic controls made few responses when the stimulus was most ambiguous. As the slides become clearer more responses occurred. They rated themselves as 100% confident after making several consecutive correct responses. Nonparanoids performed similar to the controls.

Paranoids on the other hand, made more responses to the ambiguous stimuli and also rated themselves as 100% confident in their responses. The physiological data also indicated they were the most involved with these ambiguous slides. Most interesting is that this task strategy did not detract from overall performance. The paranoid, in effect, constructed a stimulus on much less information than the other groups. He was not only more interested in resolving the ambiguous stimulus situation but constructed a percept and was quite confident in what he saw. This process is similar to the conceptual set studies such as the Bruner study where a B or 13 is presented, and the subject "sees" a number or a letter depending upon what he was primed to see. The nonparanoid showed his greatest involvement with the clearer stimuli. There was a percept to encode and report. The paranoid did not find the interest in such a single perceptual act but preferred to operate upon the ambiguous stimulus with a schemata. The situation where information had to be created, so to speak, was of the most interest.

This work suggests that the paranoid has tighter assemblies then others; the associations forming the schemata are more rigidly fixed. This idea suggests the work of Bannister, which was presented in detail in the earlier chapter on conceptual or K process. Bannister (1971) expects paranoids to have tighter construct systems then nonparanoids. The evidence in prior work was relatively weak, but Gamble (1975) suggested this was due to problems in the diagnosis of paranoia. He administered the Bannister Grid test to integrated, nonintegrated paranoids, and nonparanoids using the Foulds (1965) criteria. He found that paranoids were no different than nonparanoids in terms of the degree of association between constructs, but that paranoids were more consistent in the pattern of association. In other words, the paranoids had the same number of associations as nonparanoids, but they were clearly tied into a schemata while nonparanoids did not have such a schemata. Hence, this study nicely demonstrates the difference between paranoids and schizophrenics. In Bannister's terms, the associational structure of cognition is consistent for paranoids, while for nonparanoids a looseness of association occurs, which is not formed into any consistent pattern. As we found with the subjective organization studies, the patterns of associations may be idiosyncratic but, they are consistent and, hence, form a stable schemata for the paranoid.

Another difficulty experienced by the paranoid is his inability to shift assemblies appropriately. Young and Jerome (1972) found that in a task in which subjects were required to solve a series of problems where the relevant cues changed the demands of the task, paranoids consistently performed less efficiently than nonparanoids. It appears that his task was sensitive to the predicted paranoid conceptual tendency not to utilize different schemata. When the conceptual set leads to a misinterpretation of the situation, it would be expected that nonparanoids would be most accurate. Szekely (1950) required schizophrenics to balance a scale with several common objects so that without further manipulation the scale would eventually go out of balance. Among the common objects was a candle. Schizophrenics, as predicted, discovered the correct solution significantly more often than normals: To use a lit candle on one side of the scale, so its loss of weight through burning would satisfy the conditions of the problem. Unfortunately, this report (Carini, 1973) fails to specify what is meant by "schizophrenics," and we do not know whether this refers to nonparanoids only or to a group of schizophrenics of various subdiagnoses. From the reports of most Russian research, we would expect that the subjects were chronic nonparanoids, hence their performance would be as expected. This result is similar to that of Sarbin, Juhasz, and Todd (1971), who instructed groups of schizophrenics and normals to identify an odor where there was none. Schizophrenics were less influenced by the reasonable expectations generated by the directions and were more accurate than normals in judging no odor to be present. Again, no subgroup data are presented, although we expect such results to be characteristic primarily of nonparanoids.

Similar results are reported by Polyakov (1969) who found, in both auditory and visual modalities, that an ambiguous signal is identified by normals according to the probabilistic constraints of context more so than by schizophrenics. For example, in the auditory presented sentence, "The photographer made a pretty_____," normals will most frequently identify the ambiguous (muffled by noise) term as "picture," and when "picture" is in fact present with noise, they identify more words correctly than schizophrenics. When the ambiguous term is an unlikely one, however, such as "box," schizophrenics are correct significantly more often than normals in identifying the muffled word. These results support the hypothesis that nonparanoids rely on the perceptual qualities of the signal, which enable them under such conditions to perform better than normals.

These results suggest that as tasks are varied from straight encoding to the incorporation or creation of schemata, there is an initial deficit for paranoids and a subsequent deficit for schizophrenics. There are two studies that used such an experimental strategy and confirmed this expectation. Yates and Korboot (1970) examined the performance of acute and chronic nonparanoid schizophrenics, acute and chronic paranoids, and acute and chronic neurotics on identification tasks increasing in complexity. Stimulus materials were lines, symbols, and words. On all five levels of complexity with words, there was no difference between chronic and acute nonparanoids, but they were worse than other groups. In other words, nonparanoids, regardless of chronicity, experienced difficulty with the verbal material, but such a difficulty did not occur with perceptual material, the lines and symbols. The acute paranoid did not differ from the neurotics and tended to be significantly faster than the two nonparanoid groups.

The effect of task demands operating differentially on the two schizophrenic groups was also reported by Hirt, Cuttler, and Genshaft (1977), who used paranoids and nonparanoids with medical impatients as controls. They designed a series of tasks to include increasing complexity: motor, motor plus interference, perceptual, perceptual plus interference, symbolic I, symbolic I plus interference, symbolic II, and symbolic II plus interference. Generally, nonparanoids were found to be significantly slower only on the symbolic tasks. Paranoids were significantly faster than the other two groups. Unfortunately, chronicity status cannot be determined from the data supplied, and it is probable that the nonparanoids were chronics, if 2 years of total hospitalization is used as a criterion. These paranoids, on the other hand, may have been acutes. The study demonstrated that as the conceptual demands of the task were varied, and more conceptual demands were added, the more the nonparanoids showed a deficit. Thus, while the nonparanoid has greater difficulty in tasks calling for the use of the schemata, the paranoid utilizes his schemata and, in that manner, assimilates more material.

A demonstration of the strength of these enduring schemas is found in Schneider's (1976) study, in which he compared delusional and nondelusional schizophrenics on a dichotic shadowing task that used three topics as distractor/shadowing material. While the loudness of the distractor did not differentially affect the groups, the one topic which did affect the delusional groups, as compared to other groups, was delusional material personalized for each paranoid subject. Unfortunately, Schneider did not control for the personal relevance of the delusional material for the other groups. Rather than having a message of personal relevance for each of the nonparanoids, they were given the delusional material constructed for each paranoid subject. It would be expected that anyone would be more distracted by material that personally related to him, Hence, the strength of the assemblies for each group was not measured.

With tasks of increasing complexity, the different strategy or conceptual characteristics of the paranoid emerge. Neufield (1976) studied paranoid and nonparanoid schizophrenics (with cumulative hospitalization of less than 3½ years) and normals. The task involved judging the similarity between word pairs on a 1 to 9 scale. The multidimensional scaling solution compared the judgments of the three groups in terms of the dimensions they used. Results indicated that the paranoid group used more dimensions than normals and nonparanoids. This provides evidence for the greater conceptual differentiation of the paranoid. While the paranoids used greater dimensionality, they were still much less accurate than the normals. Neufield inferred from this finding that since scaling solutions tended to fit less accurately the paranoids' judgments, there was greater unpredictability in their judgments. That is, this finding may be reflective of the paranoid's finer discrimination but more idiosyncratic conceptual ordering. Because each paranoid used his own individual categories, a greater variability occurred within this group. Grodin and Brown (1967) found a similar result. Chronic paranoids were compared to normals and required to judge faces varying in facial characteristics on a friendly–unfriendly dimension. Paranoids did not use different characteristics such as chin length, and hence, as a group, did not differ from normals. However, there was much more individual variation within the paranoid group, suggesting that there was no single dimension or dimensions used by all pararnoids. They varied between themselves more than normals in the stimulus dimensions they used to form their judgments.

In another study of the stimulus processing of multiple stimulus dimensions, Neufield (1976) again found the paranoid schizophrenic to be significantly different from normals. In the first task of judging schematic faces and visual forms, though the schizophrenic groups were less sensitive to the variation of dimensions in the stimuli, they were not handicapped by it in their judgment. Paranoids were found to differ from normals in the relative contribution of stimulus dimensions to their judgments. In the second task of judging similarity between word pairs, paranoids were again found to differ from normals in their ability to combine stimulus dimensions for accurate verbal judgments. In the case of verbal stimuli, both schizophrenic groups were apparently as sensitive to the semantic dimensions of variations, but the paranoids were significantly less able than normals to utilize these dimensions to produce interstimulus relationships. In short, in making judgments involving multiple dimensions of visual forms, schematic faces, and word pairs, the paranoids did not use these dimensions as normals did; they used them idiosyncratically.

In another task involving complex cognitive processing, differences among acute paranoids, nonparanoids, and normals were found in relative similarity judgments of color samples. Gregson and Fearnley (1974) manipulated the complexity of processing by increasing the number of colors and varying the sizes of the color samples. When group performance was analyzed in terms of the predicted performance function, the performance of the controls best fit the predicted function in most conditions. However, in the most complex condition, which involved processing attributes directly, the performance of the nonparanoid best fit the model. The perceptual judgments made by the nonparanoid more closely resembled mechanistic processing as would be recorded by a camera. In contrast, a measure of balanced attention indicated that the paranoids in each condition had the greatest imbalance of attention, whether or not the strategy was appropriate for the condition. Different "strategies" were employed by each group. The paranoid overused conceptual control to the point where it interfered with more appropriate processing. On the other hand, the nonparanoid's lack of conceptual control enabled him to process complex perceptual material more appropriately.

Summarizing the information processing results, paranoids and schizophrenics exhibit a difference in the encoding process, which we hypothesize to be due to different types of processing. They are equivalent to normals in short-term memory, as shown by the recognition memory work. However, when assemblies have to be formed, as in the recall memory work, paranoids are able to do so, but nonparanoids do not because of the low associational strength of their assemblies. The associates are present, and not necessarily deviant, but they do not have the strength of activation of normals or paranoids. The paranoid, on the other hand, has problems with the schemata. The work on complex cognitive processing indicates that when assemblies are pitted against one another, the paranoid reveals a deficit while also demonstrating that his schemata, although as well formed and discriminative as normals, may be idiosyncratic.

To conclude, this relatively exhaustive review of the literature reveals a bit of consistency. The work focusing upon the initial encoding, our perceptual process, finds that the paranoid has the greatest difficulty. However, as we progress to the work examining long-term memory involving assemblies—our conceptual process—the nonparanoid emerges as being deficient. However, strength of the assembly is not always adaptable for the paranoid, as he again exhibits a problem when flexibility of schemata is required. The nonparanoid does not exhibit such a problem.

Integration theory considers each group's dominant cognitive style, which is appropriate in some situations and not so in others. It is adaptable when the situation calls for the preferred process and maladaptive in that situation which calls for the nonpreferred process. The normal integrates the two styles. He is able to switch from one to the other and form a figural synthesis, which enables one process to operate in tandem with the other. This chapter focused upon the operationalism and a demonstration of the perceptual and conceptual processes in each group. In reviewing other evidence that demonstrates the value of the integration term, we become more speculative. In the next chapter, we offer an explanation of the etiology of each process to deepen our understanding of how they could develop as separate processes without the unifying effects of integration. After we have considered the scope of the integration term, we again return to the two cognitive styles and relate them to current theory in hemispheric specialization.[1]

---

[1]When this chapter was initially written, there was little interest in individual differences or differential strategies employed in processing information. Certainly, the idea that there were individual differences in such a seemingly structural system was not close to the mainstream. Lately, however, there seem to be some indications that a major focus within the area will be the interest in differential processing strategies. Two recent sources (*Strategies of Information Processing,* edited by Geoffrey Underwood, Academic Press, N.Y., 1978; *Modes of Perceiving and Processing Information,* edited by Herbert L. Pick, Jr., and Elliot Saltzman, Lawrence Erlbaum Associates, Hillsdale, N.J., 1978) have reviewed the growing interest in the types of strategies that can influence information processing. Hence, the idea that different groups such as paranoids and schizophrenics employ specific processing styles or strategies is not a foreign idea when one considers the numerous ideas emerging on the different styles of receiving information and the characteristics of those who employ specific preferences. I would hope that the next wave of interest will relate differential strategies to personality and psychopathology.

7

The Integration of Perceptual and Conceptual Processes

INTRODUCTION

Our interest up to this point has been to specify the cognitive process of schizophrenics and paranoids. We have attempted to answer the "What is" question (see Fig. 1.1, Chapter 1) by postulating the constructs of perception and conceptualization to explain the characteristic style of each group. Now we attempt to answer the "Why is it" question. Why does the paranoid rely upon conceptualization and the schizophrenic upon perception?

The last chapter operationalized perception and conceptualization in information-processing terms and concluded that the schizophrenic does not have strong associates to create stable assemblies. He is comparable and sometimes superior to normals in his encoding of the icon, as long as the task does not require the use of a cogit. To derive information, he will tend to use preattentive or automatic processing rather than focal or controlled attention. Following Neisser's model, we define this stage of information processing as perceptual. The paranoid, on the other hand, prefers the focal attention type of processing. This controlled processing is more accurate and slower than the automatic processing, does not permit the holistic concept, and is more affected by the cogit. The cogit assemblies are extremely strong and only create difficulties when the task requires a switching of assemblies or creating schemata from new combinations of assemblies. We have defined this stage of information processing as conceptualization.

We have localized the schizophrenic and paranoid deficit at different stages of information processing and have assumed that the two stages work simultaneously to create a "normal" information flow. Whereas the schizophrenic, due to his lack of consistent assemblies, does not utilize the perceptual process to modify his schemata. Thus, for either group, the "construction of knowledge" is not comparable to that of normals. There is no figural synthesis (to use the Neisser term), or, in our terms, an integration of perceptual and conceptual processes is absent. To answer why there is no combining of the two processes, we must move to a higher and more speculative theoretical level and discuss the integration term. Although we have defined operations and cited research supporting the theoretical construct I of perception and conceptualization, we have not presented any research supporting the theoretical construct II, integration. We now attempt that task, and in the next chapter provide the theory with a neurological basis.

The integration construct introduced here goes beyond the recognition of the multiple processes involved in a laboratory task. The integration construct postulates, in addition, that the deficit is exhibited in a task that requires a combination of terms and is the state produced by the simultaneous action of two processes. Thus, the deficit is derived from an interaction of many parts and is greater than the sum of the parts. The "construction" action of figural synthesis has this same quality and, as such, is difficult to operationalize, except as the combined action of separate processes.

Any study which has used the usual experimental procedure, supposedly manipulating one variable (perceptual, conceptual, etc.) while keeping others constant, and has found the schizophrenic to deviate from others, has, in effect, produced an epiphenomenon. Most of these studies have unavoidably been observing the operation of at least two psychological processes, although purporting to examine one. The observed deficit could be due to the failure to integrate the processes necessary to perform an action rather than a deficit in one process.

Another way to conceptualize the integrational defect is to view task performance as a constant dialectic. Dichotomous processes, somewhat like chords in music, work toward resolution. The successful resolution or synthesis, the harmony in our analogy, would be the integration of the two processes that would be productive and correct. Failure to synthesize correctly would indicate an overwhelming dominance of one process over the other and would yield an unsatisfactory synthesis or the expression of a deficit.

INTEGRATION VIEWS OF SCHIZOPHRENIA

An integration concept is not a new approach to the schizophrenic deficit. To name just a few, Rado, Buchenholz, Dunton, Karlen, and Senescu (1956) have advocated a popular view of schizophrenia, which is based on the lack of integration of pleasure and pain. Meehl (1962) further expanded this position by defining the basic deficit as an integrative neural defect, especially in terms of kinesthetic feedback. Heath (1960), on the other hand, postulated a chemical cause for the integrative defect and considered it most evident in response to stress. He hypothesized that the performance deficit could be diminished if rigid structure is provided. The schizophrenic cannot integrate feelings, especially of pleasure, and the proprioceptive diathesis, which defines who he is at that time. He is forced to use a single process, intellect, which permits him to follow orders.

But the conceptual process is not syntonic and hence dissipates under stress and he reverts to the less adaptable perceptual process. The schizophrenic can function well when the rigid structure supports the fragile conceptual organization, and he does not have to integrate emotional and cognitive processes.

Bogoch, Belval, Dussik, and Concan (1962) propose an integration-synthesis hypothesis based upon the relationship between neurochemical changes and clinical inprovement. Improvement occurs with greater organization due to a greater synthesis of function. Less integration is characteristic of the more pathological schizophrenic condition. Chapman, Hinkle, and Wolff (1960) present one of the most generalized views of integration as an ecological system. In essence, most integrative functions are viewed as relatively fragile and of four types: expression and meeting of needs, capacity to respond to symbols, defense against stress, and maintenance of organization. The integration deficit may occur through tissue damage or by destructive patterns of interaction with the environment. In any case, an integrative problem would be characteristic of schizophrenia and reflect an inability to synchronize processes into an adaptive behavior system.

Werner (1948) used the concept of hierarchic integration as the basis of his genetic psychology. Level of development is the process of achieving a higher level of integration, where many elements are fused together in a differentiated synthesis. Friedman (1952), following the Werner model, related the level of differentiation and integration to level of functioning in schizophrenia. A more recent and explicit description of an integration theory is that of Kitamura (1974), who specifies six types of regulative functions that permit performance at a particular time. The common element of all the regulative functions is that they involve the integration of differing psychological systems such as mental, motor, and automatic. McDowell (in press) elaborates upon the use of Integration Theory as it applies to the assessment of particular populations.

The Feffer Developmental Theory

An integration system much more similar to that proposed here, especially in its level of analysis, is the decentering position developed by Feffer (1967). He uses Piaget's (1950) concept of mature reasoning, which involves a subordination of the perceptual sensory impression to conceptual categorizations. The subordination takes the form of an equilibrium, whereby a wide number of stimuli are considered at once in a process of simultaneous decentering. Integration is an act of maintaining active perceptual and conceptual processes at the time, which is a normal "mature" adaptation.

If these two processes are not integrated, according to Feffer (1967) there is: "a lack of reciprocal influence between different aspects of experience or, at a more formal level, a lack of contact between systems of functioning [p. 18]." Then, the characteristic schizophrenic symptoms appear which are either associations not tied to perceptions or perceptions not grouped into conceptual categories. Feffer (1967) states:

> The decentering concept can serve as a relatively direct interpretation of certain central characteristics of the schizophrenic thought disorder, namely, an inordinate emphasis upon specific perceptual details to the exclusion of a general principle, an alternatively exaggerated overinclusion based upon a Procrustian disdain for specifics, and the abrupt discontinuous jump from one associative content to another [p. 20.]

The performance deficit, therefore, is due to a problem in decentering, in which one process is acting unaffected by the other. Although Feffer extends the concept into the realm of interpersonal relations to explain schizophrenic symptom patterns, the main construct is an associative disturbance, which is due to the inability to maintain the equilibrium of perceptual and conceptual aspects of objects. In our previous terms, K and V cannot function adequately by themselves because a union of the two processes are usually required on most tasks. A reciprocal corrective influence, a decentering, or a lack of isolation of systems is crucial to successful task performance. In the schizophrenic, either the later conceptual assemblies do not modulate the earlier iconic processing or the encoding does not affect the activation of assemblies. In either case, the terms are not acting reciprocally and, hence, a deficit is produced when both processes are required.

The Carini Self-Content Theory

Carini (1961) has provided the most insightful and relevant analysis of the relationship between perception and conceptualization. Working toward a theory of symbolic transformation, Carini also saw the advantage of using scientific models to construct a theoretical structure that would provide the postulates applicable to existing empirical observations. As we used Hullian Theory as a model to organize existing theoretical terms and propose postulates, Carini used Newton's laws of motion as a model to construct a theory with two major postulates. The first states that experience will equal our symbolic meaningful representation if no physiological stimulation is present. The second is the inverse, stating that our experience will be perceptual if no symbolization is present. These postulates correspond to the first two laws of motion, which are statements describing the empirical laws of acceleration and no acceleration. These states are then abstracted into second-order theoretical terms, laws of motion, which are able to explain the empirical events. When the theory is applied to the orbital motion of the planets, predictions are confirmed because the theory can account for the interacting processes of inertial and gravitational motion. "For any empirical motion then, some portion of both abstracted components must always be present, and this means that some acceleration and some gravitational motion is always to be found in actual motions" (Carini, 1961, p. 5).

Newtonian laws provided Carini with a model to elucidate the manner of interaction and resultant form of two psychological processes. The two postulates concerning psychological experience parallel the two Newtonian laws of motion. "Instead of acceleration as a subject matter then, the subject matter is our visual experiences, our visual perceptions" (Carini, 1961, p. 6). The first process involves symbolic representations that are idea-like in form, having many relations with other things, and representative of other things, equivalent to conceptual assemblies and schematas. The other process similar to our perceptual encoding process involves a sensory presentation that is basically a sensory impression such as a retinal image, which has little meaning in itself.

Having established the basic theoretical structure and the specifications of the crucial processes, Carini (1961) then explains the relationship between them:

> In everyday life our perceptions come to use as related rather than in the absolute fashion that occurs in isolation, and this leads investigators to the view that they not only occur more often but are more important for the purpose of investigation. It is forgotten that while percepts seldom are absolutely isolated, the opposite is true for many images and for concepts. In the higher mental processes the relativity of stimulation that occurs in perception is minimal. Though in perception the symbolized meaningful component will always be small, it will loom correspondingly large in memory and in concept formation or thinking [pp. 18-19].

The two processes are always in operation, and even though we have described the schizophrenic as being inadequate in the use of conceptual categories and the paranoid with the preattentive perceptual encoding, we are never speaking in absolutes because both processes are always present. As discussed in the chapter on theory construction, a theory developed from studying one process can only be relevant when considering the condition where only that one process occurs. In life, that is never the case. Borrowing an example from Carini, when an apple falls from a tree, the inertial component is almost negligible compared to the force of gravity. If one described the processes active in that condition, one term could be applied to explain motion. However, when other forms of movement are considered, such as the movement of bodies in outer space where gravity is minimal compared to inertia, the theory is clearly not adequate. In our case, studying the conceptualization of the schizophrenic without considering other processes would only create a theory that is most appropriate to outer space. Finally, Carini requires that his theory of symbolic transformations be tested by varying the two processes concomitantly in order to eventually attain a mathematical equation that unites the two postulates into one formulation.

Of special interest to the present discourse is Carini's (1961) extrapolation of the theory to schizophrenia. The schizophrenic differs from the normal in that the interchange between abstraction and the sensory experience is essentially an interchange between equals. Such an interchange exists because the schizophrenic does not develop adequate symbolic representatives. "As a result, the conceptual development which should be a function of the development of the symbolized meaningful representatives does not occur, and consequently there is a failure to develop a set of hierarchic ordering principles which would state the rules for the priority of the one or the other [p. 24]." This is our description of the integrational deficit of the schizophrenic.

His theory of symbolic transformations states that experience is the integrated product of "meaningful symbolic representations" and "sensory, physiological stimulation." Moreover (Carini, 1973), "because there is a symbolic component and a sensory or physiological one to each experiencing, then development, both normal and abnormal, are defined by the ratio of the symbolic to the sensory component [p. 132]." For Carini, these symbolized representations (which we call assemblies) literally transform perception. He reviews a number of Russian experiments reported by Polyakov (in Cole & Maltzman, 1969) and several American studies (Carini, 1955; Sarbin, Juhasz, & Todd, 1971; Wapner & Werner, 1957) that compare the cognitive performance of schizophrenics and normals. Each experiment involved illusions or misleading cures, and in each, schizophrenics performed better than normals. That is, the expectations of normals caused a deficit while schizophrenics seemed relatively uninfluenced by such expectations. Carini (1973) states:

> The reason why schizophrenics can attend to latent features is that they have not developed the symbolized meaningful representations that give one concept priority over another concept, just as their concept does not have sufficient priority over a percept....

Not having conceptual rules for ordering and integrating percepts and concepts, he cannot properly undertake the other person's point of view and everything must be judged in relation to his own self [p. 137].

We should clarify one difference between our theory and Carini's. He explains the performance of all schizophrenics as the result of early arrest in, or deviation from, the normal development of the relation between percept and concept. While we concur that schizophrenics in general do not have adaptive "rules for ordering and integrating percepts and concepts," we find evidence that schizophrenic subgroups solve this problem in different ways: nonparanoids, by employing perceptual processes and paranoids, by employing conceptual processes. To repeat ourselves, Integration Theory suggests that the type of nonintegrative resolution differentiates schizophrenic subgroups. The paranoid resolves the problem by relying on conceptual processes which, being poorly integrated with perceptual processes, are not modified or refined by nonvalidating data from the environment. The paranoid processes data by forcing or distorting percepts into existing conceptual schemata. Nonparanoids, on the other hand, resolve the problem by relying on encoding, which is not integrated with conceptual structures and therefore is not related to former patterns of events or to logical schemes or organization. Nonparanoid and paranoid symptoms, then, are seen as the expression of the particular resolution due to a lack of integration.

This all too brief description of the Carini position reveals the similarity in purpose, procedure, and conclusion with the thrust of the present theory. Working out a completely different content area, the study of visual perception and symbolic transformation, Carini had to walk the same steps. He first incorporated principles of theory building in order to construct his theory, found that an integration of processes is crucial to explain empirical events, concluded that an integration process was of central importance in understanding the nature of the schizophrenic deficit, and finally, described the schizophrenic resolution as a lack of integration.

The Blatt and Wild Boundary Defect Theory

Blatt and Wild (1976) also present a theory of schizophrenia that has a developmental analysis similar to the present theory. Their review of the theories and empirical findings in schizophrenia is organized in terms of developmental stages. Their analysis of the research focuses upon concepts of perceptual processes, cognitive processes, a sense of self, and interpersonal relationships. In discussing results in these areas, they distinguish between the paranoid and the nonparanoid, which is most relevant to our position.

They hypothesize that the underlying process responsible for the deficiencies found in any specific process is that of boundary. The schizophrenic impairment in perception, cognition, and interpersonal relationships is basically a boundary defect. Blatt and Wild (1976) state: "In developmental psychology, the capacity to experience, perceive, and represent a sense of separation between objects is also considered to be one of the earliest and most basic developmental steps [p. 5]." Without a boundary between self and world, there is no ego and, hence, internal and external events become confused, and everything fuses into a nondistinct mass of confusing stimuli. Without separate objects, there cannot be separate representations of them and, thus, there can be no concepts. Without concepts, thinking is impossible, which precludes a definite sense of self, or of external reality, or of separate persons. Hence, interpersonal relationships are impossible. They further propose that the nonparanoid is more primitive in development then the paranoid and, thus, suffers from greater boundary disturbances. Poorer performance on the tasks which are considered measures of perception, cognition, and interpersonal relations are symptomatic of the boundary disturbance.

They use the work done in the general area of reality testing, symbolic processing, and interpersonal relationships to support their position. Paranoids and nonparanoids are distinguished in terms of different aspects of reality testing, including contact with reality, the sense of body, sense of time, perceptual articulation and attention. These factors are used to explain the respective deficits in symbolic and interpersonal processes. We repeat their conclusions from each of these areas (because it supports our insistence upon the paranoid–schizophrenic difference) by adding further points of distinction between the two groups.

Reality testing involves the ability to distinguish internal and external events. Confusion about the boundaries which separate thoughts or fantasies and actual events is found in hallucinations and delusions. While the schizophrenic is involved in false reality production, substituting a false world for the real one, the paranoid is involved in distortion of basically accurate perceptions through a conceptual elaboration.

The other important boundary experience is the experience of the body as the self or, in other terms, the ego from the rest of the world. In normal development, the body is experienced as being definite, whole and substantive. Nonparanoids and paranoids differ in bodily experiences in terms of "barrier" and "penetration" responses. Barrier responses indicate the acknowledgment of boundaries—surface, structure and substance. Penetration responses suggest a penetrability of boundaries. Using the work of Fisher (1964, 1966), they report that paranoids differ significantly from nonparanoids in manifesting more barrier and less penetration responses.

Also, the paranoid exhibits a greater awareness of body, while the nonparanoid does not mention the concept of body.

In relation to a sense of time, if the boundaries between objects or between self and object are not experienced, it follows that there will be a distortion in the sense of time. The less the experience of boundary, the greater the distortion of time. As would be predicted from their experience of boundaries, nonparanoids would have a smaller appreciation and less understanding of the past, present and future than the paranoid.

The experience of boundary as reflected in perceptual accuracy follows our analysis. Studies on perceptual fusion, perceptual constancy, size estimation, and field dependence are used to support the distinction between the paranoid and nonparanoid. Perceptual fusion is the tendency to fuse two stimuli together, which is observed in a light separation task where the length of time to perceive lights as separate is measured. The perceptual fusion deficit is found primary in nonparanoids, while the tendency to resist perceptual fusion is found more often in paranoids. For Blatt and Wild, this finding reflects the paranoid's inability to maintain boundaries and the paranoid's tendency to rigidly maintain boundaries.

The next area reviewed, the ability to focus attention, also leads to conclusions that support our position. Flexible, mobile, or easily directed attention is necessary for accurate assessment of the external world. The nonparanoid and paranoid differ significantly in their ability to maintain focus; the nonparanoid seems to be highly distracted by the multitude of stimuli, unable to selectively attend to relevant ones, while the paranoid has an overly active attentional mechanism which tends to relate even irrelevant stimuli to a single basic scheme.

The differing cognitive styles of the two subgroups are also inferred from the work on symbolic processes found in concept formation, language, and thinking. For example, the authors note the well-established fact that the paranoid shows less of an intellectual deficit than other pathological subgroups. The paranoid's cognitive style is to maximally organize data by rigid, narrow constructs, while the nonparanoid employs broad, vague categories to organize a minimum of material. In terms of language capacity, the paranoid's greater ability for differentiation enables him to have a greater complexity in his language. In comparison, the nonparanoids uses simple forms of language. Finally, in terms of thought disorder, research indicates that the greater the impairment of body articulation, the greater the thought disorder and the more serious the disturbance. This implies that the thought disorder of the nonparanoid is more disturbed and disordered than that of the paranoid. As one would expect from such conceptual confusion, interpersonal relationships are disturbed by the fusion of boundaries, which would result in what has been considered a symbiosis, the fusion of self with others.

In summary, the Blatt and Wild (1976) analysis is based upon the concept of boundary articulation, which explains paranoid–nonparanoid differences in terms of their cognitive, perceptual, and interpersonal styles. Developmentally, the nonparanoid is judged to be more primitive, with greater fusion of self and objects. The lack of boundary in the nonparanoid is discussed in terms of hallucinations, "penetration" responses, distortion of time, a perceptual fusion deficit, field dependence, distractibility, and simpler language forms. In our terms he doesn't develop constructs to organize the percepts, which requires boundaries to be meaningful. In contrast, the paranoid overarticulates concepts, permits extensive boundaries but little use of the percept. His delusions, "barrier" responses, perceptual fusion resistance, field independence and mere complex language forms are analyzed in terms of his use of boundaries.

The similarities between the Blatt and Wild approach and our presentation are obvious. The differences are in terms of the explanations for the different styles of the paranoid and nonparanoid. Blatt and Wild (1976) consider the schizophrenic condition to be primary to both paranoids and nonparanoids. The paranoid, in effect, is defending against the schizophrenic condition by constructing a rigid conceptual world. Our analysis explains the paranoid's construction of his own world on the basis of his own defenses in terms of his higher stage of development. Our position would not consider a schizophrenic underneath every paranoid anymore than we would expect a paranoid underneath every compulsive. They are different personalities who may share a common problem—the inability to integrate conceptual and perceptual material. We prefer the explanation that the schizophrenic does not utilize conceptual material, and the paranoid does not utilize perceptual. While the Blatt and Wild (1976) position considers the nonparanoid deficit as greater, in our analysis they are solely different conditions. Even though the paranoid condition develops later because the conceptual process resides in a later developmental stage, it is not necessary to conclude that one disorder is more primitive. It is, in terms of our level of empirical understanding, just a difference in developmental stages, which permits different conditions.

By specifying that the problem is a boundary defect, Blatt and Wild, in essence, view schizophrenia as a conceptual deficit. As the authors note, a boundary is only one kind of concept, possibly more important than some others since it relates to the self, but still only a concept. Hence, the appropriate question is not why boundaries exist, but why concepts do not exist. This change in the question illustrates the difference in the two theories. We could look at why reality testing does not occur, why perceptual accuracy does not occur, why self concepts are not accurate, etc.; however, this would be a chase after the symptoms. If we knew why concepts do not occur, the symptomatic expressions of that cause would be self-explanatory. The answer must lie in a higher-order construct. Instead Blatt and Wild (1976) have introduced an empirical construct, boundary defect, and treated it as a theoretical construct to explain other correlative empirical constructs. The boundary term, as operationalized by Fisher (1964), correlates with the other empirical constructs such as poor reality testing, perceptual accuracy, field dependence, etc., but it does not answer the "why" question of the theoretical construct. Why is there a lack of conceptual categories for the nonparanoid and a lack of use of perceptual material for the paranoid?

In the Blatt and Wild use of the paranoid and nonparanoid empirical constructs, which refines the schizophrenic term and allows greater functional prediction, their theory moves in the direction of the present theory. However, the failure to recognize the need for an explanatory theoretical construct beyond the boundary term creates a tautology because an empirical construct is used to explain another equal empirical constant. Integration Theory, on the other hand, moves to the theoretical construct level, with the integration term hypothesizing a mechanism that can explain the lack of normal conceptual or perceptual processes, while at the same time predicting differences for paranoids and nonparanoids on each process at the level of the empirical law.

The Russian View of Integration

The Russian literature bearing upon the schizophrenic defect is also moving toward an integration deficit view. Theorizing from the nature of the orienting response, the concept of probabilistic prognosis was developed to explain the tendency of individuals to anticipate future events through the formation of cognitive frameworks that enabled accurate predictions of impending situations. Schizophrenics were found to exhibit a disturbed orienting reaction indicating a lack of probabilistic prognosis (Feigenberg, 1969). The schizophrenic reacts to new situations in an nonintegrative manner, i.e., not organizing past and present events to anticipate future activity. In an experiment using the Carpentier illusion, where the usual response is to judge a smaller sized object to be heavier because of prior experience with larger objects, a large number of schizophrenics did not create illusory errors but judged actual weights (Feigenberg, 1969). The proprioceptive perceptions of the schizophrenic were not influenced by the conceptual framework necessary for perceiving the illusion. While on most tasks the schizophrenic's dominant perceptual process creates a deficit, on an illusion-type task he produces fewer errors than nonschizophrenics. This was confirmed also by Polyakov (1969), who reported a series of studies that showed superior schizophrenic performance on tasks which require the use of low probability images or associations. When the task requires highly probable perceptions, the schizophrenic does worse than the normal. The accurate perception of the stimulus itself, seemingly shorn of a conceptual framework, allows the schizophrenic to produce the unusual or creative image which, in effect, is an accurate reflection of the stimulus world.

Other studies report similar results. Szekely (1950) required schizophrenics to balance a scale with several common objects such that without further manipulation the scale would eventually go out of balance. Among the common objects was a candle. Schizophrenics, as predicted, discovered the correct solution significantly more often than normals: the use of a lit candle on one side of the scale, whose loss of weight through burning would satisfy the conditions of the problem. Unfortunately, this report (Carini, 1973) fails to specify what is meant by "schizophrenics," and we do not know whether this refers to nonparanoids only or to a group of schizophrenics of various subdiagnoses. From the reports of most Russian research, we would expect that the subjects were chronic nonparanoids, hence their performance was as expected. This result is similar to that found in an American study. Sarbin et al. (1971) instructed groups of schizophrenics and normals to identify an odor when there was none. Schizophrenics were less influenced by the reasonable expectations generated by the directions, and were more accurate than normals in judging no odor to be present. Again, no subgroup data is presented, although we expect such results to be characteristic primarily of nonparanoids.

Signal detection methodology has generated several experiments (Polyakov, 1969) relevant to the integration theory. In both auditory and visual modalities, an ambiguous signal is identified according to the probabilistic constraints of content more by normals than schizophrenics. For example, in the auditorily presented sentence, "The photographer made a pretty _____," normals will most frequently identify the ambiguous term (muffled by noise) as "picture." When "picture" is in fact presented with noise, they identify the ambiguous word, thus correctly significantly more often than schizophrenics. When the ambiguous term is an unlikely one, however, such as "box," schizophrenics are correct significantly more often than normals in identifying the muffled word. These results support the hypothesis that, for nonparanoids, poor perceptual-conceptual integration and over-reliance on the perceptual qualities of the signal enables them, under certain conditions, to perform better than normals. Specifically, the perceptual compensation of nonparanoids should result in superior performance when stable or dominant conceptual categories are a hindrance to task performance.

A failure of adequate integration can explain not only the divergent data obtained in investigations of the schizophrenic performance deficit, but also the different task performances and clinical-behavioral pictures of paranoid and nonparanoid schizophrenics. Moreover, a failure of integration at different developmental levels would also explain autism and childhood schizophrenia. We attempted that explanation in a previous work (Magaro,

Miller, & McDowell, 1976), on which we now elaborate in discussing the developmental patterns that utilize a process of integration.

THE DEVELOPMENTAL RESOLUTION
OF THE INTEGRATION PROBLEM

The integration theory explains the schizophrenic performance deficit as an inability to integrate perceptual and conceptual processes in a normal manner. Developmental theories such as Piaget's (1952) and Werner's (1948) have made clear that an integration or equilibrium between perception of the world and internal conceptual structures is necessary for adequate adaptation. We use the Piaget theory of development to expand our concept of integration and to explicate the processes by which, and the stages in which, an arrest in perceptual-conceptual integration produces the syndromes of schizophrenia and paranoia in children and adults. In Chapter 5, the means of operationalizing schizophrenia and paranoia were discussed as was the possibility that paranoia exists in childhood. The following section provides a developmental analysis for this position.

Piaget and Integration

For Piaget, mental development involves the creation of increasingly complex and adaptive psychic structures, or schemas. In very early stages of life, these are sensori-motor schemas, the reflexive equipment of the neonate. Schemas of an elementary sort are present from birth, and are transformed normally during the second year into truly representative structures [i.e., the child progresses from a stage of reflexive motor schemas to internal representations (albeit illogical and partial) of objects, space, time, and causality]. Schemas are related to the environment by the adaptive processes of assimilation and accommodation. Assimilation is the process by which the environment is apprehended through existing schemas, and accommodation is the process by which existing schemas are modified to fit more closely with data gleaned from the environment. Thus, the infant's placing of objects in his mouth is a largely assimilative action, the application of the sucking schema to many elements. But each of these actions also involves accommodation, or the variegation and differentiation of the sucking schema based on the different properties of mouthed objects. Piaget stresses that these two basic adaptive functions are highly interrelated, complementary processes. Both are present simultaneously in every act. When a child grasps a toy, it is assimilated through the existing grasping schema but also accommodated insofar as a different sort of grasp facilitates its manipulation. This different sort of grasp is registered as a different action-object sequence compared to others.

The mode of these adaptive processes is always active. In the very young child, this activity is reflexive, motoric, and external; in the adult, it is willful, abstract, and internal. The adult performs operations on objects mentally without having to act in reality. For Piaget (1972):

> Knowledge is not a copy of reality. To know an object, to know an event, is not simply to look at it and make a mental copy, or image of it. To know an object is to act on it. To know is to modify, to transform the object, and to understand the process of this transformation, and as a consequence to understand the way the object is constructed [p. 38].

Assimilation and accommodation are dialectically involved in each act. They function to restore equilibrium in the face of new data. "In the act of knowing, the subject is active, and consequently, faced with an external disturbance, he will react in order to compensate and consequently he will tend toward equilibrium [p. 42]." We proposed that Piaget's theory of adaptation, in which the dialectic processes of assimilation and accommodation produce equilibrium at successively higher levels of schema-complexity, is translatable to a theory of integration of conceptual and perceptual systems.

Flavell (1963) sees assimilation rising from "the fact that every cognitive encounter with an environmental object necessarily involves some kind of cognitive structuring (or restructuring) of that object in accord with the nature of the organism's existing intellectual organization [p. 48]." That is, assimilation involves the fitting of perceptions into existing schemas (cognitive structures). This may do some violence to what we call objective reality, e.g., the thumb and breast are different objects, but when both are assimilated in the sucking schema the perceptions of each are assigned to a single conitive structure. Thus, in our terms, assimilation is a largely perceptual process, a process permitting the assignment of data to an existing cognitive structure. According to Flavell (1963), accommodation, on the other hand, is "the process of adapting oneself to the variegated requirements or demands which the world of objects imposes upon one. In even the most elementary cognition, there has to be some coming to grips with the special properties of the thing apprehended [p. 48]." Accommodation thus refers to a cognitive process in which cognitive structures are modified to better fit the data of perception. Piaget's equilibrium of these two "processes which regulate themselves by a progressive compensation of systems" is in our model the integration of perceptual and cognitive processes.

In our view, then, information processing always involves two systems of functioning, perceptual and conceptual. These systems are normally integrated (characterized by a good fit between the structures in both). Under the impact of novel or discrepant data, however, their integration is threatened (i.e., there is no conceptual schema for perception). In such conditions of disequilibrium (which for Piaget, as we shall see, normally occurs to induce cognitive growth at three transitional phases), one of three solutions may occur: (1) the schema may be modified to fit the new perception (accommodation); (2) the percept may be distorted in order to fit existing schemas (assimilation); or (3) a combination of both may occur, as is usual. Any of these solutions tends to reestablish equilibrium, although the third, an integration of perceptual and conceptual processes, leads to the most stable and efficient adaptation. We concur with Piaget that his dialectic process of adaptation exists across all stages of development, and that it is crucial to normal growth. In our theory, childhood and adult schizophrenia are behavioral expressions of a failure to integrate, to achieve a stable "fit" between conceptual and perceptual systems. The level of development at which a failure of integration occurs determines clinical symptoms. Failure at very early stages produces autism, at later stages, childhood schizophrenia. Moreover, an inadequate integration at the stage specific for childhood schizophrenia may remain subclinical due to favorable environmental conditions. But it will persist as a predisposition to manifest paranoid or nonparanoid adult schizophrenia, depending on the congruence of adolescent integration to the type of resolution adopted in childhood.

Stages of Integration and Childhood Schizophrenia

At birth, the infant is equipped with reflexive schemas (e.g., sucking, tracking, grasping), which become differentiated through repetition. For Piaget, accommodation and assimilation are inseparable at this point. The infant's schemas are purely motoric, and thus the organism cannot distinguish between an object and its activity with that object. They are a single experience. There is no difference yet between the infant's actions on an object (assimilation) and the object's actions on him (accommodation). Flavell (1963) states:

> In short, agent and object, ego and outside world are inextricably linked together in every infantile action, and the distinction between assimilation of objects to the self and accommodation of the self to objects simply does not exist [p. 59].

Piaget (1954) calls this early, assimilative phase "egocentrism"; the infant can see the world from his own view only, without knowledge that others exist:

> Through an apparently paradoxical mechanism whose parallel we have described apropos of the egocentrism of thought of the older child, it is precisely when the subject is most self-centered that he knows himself the least, and it is to the extent that he discovers himself that places himself in the universe and constructs it by virtue of that fact [p. xii].

Not only are accommodation and assimilation undifferentiated, they are also antagonistic at the same time. Since the infant cannot distinguish actions from their consequences, any accommodation to novel objects, "can only be experienced as frustrating" (Flavell, 1963, p. 60). There is an opposition between the conservative assimilation of familiar objects and the progressive accommodation to the novel. According to Piaget (1954):

> In their initial direction, assimilation and accommodation are obviously opposed to one another, since assimilation is conservative and tends to subordinate the environment to the organism as it is, whereas accommodation is the source of changes and bends the organism to the successive constraints of the environment [p. 352].

A crucial development during the first 6 or 8 months of life is, for Piaget, the articulation of and complementation between accommodation and assimilation. Knowledge of both self and nonself depends on this differentiation. For the infant, there exist only unrelated motor schemas; instead of objects, there are object-action patterns. The infant cannot distinguish between self and object. Objectification of reality occurs simultaneously, as assimilation and accommodation differentiate. The emergence of an object schema, a rudimentary cognitive structure, is the first truly accommodative process to result from the infant's early assimilatory acts. The development of the object schema, then, is in our view the first step toward a properly integrated adaptation.

During this stage of "infantile egocentrism," no real equilibrium or integration is possible. Stimuli are experienced as qualities of being. The separation of conceptual processes, and their dialectic relation to perceptual processes in the enterprise of adaptation, are the first movements toward a true systematic equilibrium at a higher level of complexity. It is with this adaptive resolution (i.e., the differentiation of perceptual and cognitive processes and the attainment of object schemas), that we believe the autistic child has grave difficulty. For the autistic, objects never "drop out" of action patterns, and thus he must continue to apprehend reality through the motor schemas of the early sensori-motor period. A child who uses language for more than simple and immediate repetition is not in our view autistic. Intentional use of language indictes the child has concepts, while we believe the autistic has not developed conceptual thought.

The schizophrenic child, on the other hand, manifests poor reality contact through fantasy, delusions, and hallucinations (Kanner & Eisenberg, 1956). He is seen as achieving only a partial "body image," and as having "blurring," "fuzzing," or "melting" percepts (Despert, 1968; Mahler, 1968). This child uses langauge that is idiosyncratic and distorted. Jeri and Sanchez's (1971) review of three cases of childhood schizophrenia, with onset between 6 and 10 years, provides further evidence of language problems. They concluded that the children were quite similar in some respects to adult schizophrenics, but also include language disturbances, learning disabilities, and body-image distortions of the face.

Other studies provide evidence of the effects of early developmental arrest in schizophrenic children. Mook (1973), in an empirical study of 20 schizophrenic children, reports that they functioned in the preoperational stage of cognitive development, with aspects of more primitve levels. In a series of excellent studies comparing infantile psychoses (onset age 2 or under) with late onset psychoses of childhood (onset age 5 and over), Kolvin, Garside, and Kidd (1971a) were able to differentiate the two groups on the basis of frequency and discriminative power of symptoms. For infantile onset, gaze-avoidance and abnormal preoccupations were both the most frequent and most discriminative symptoms. For the late onset group, hallucinations were the single most frequent and powerful discriminators. Kolvin et al. (1971b) also found that age of onset was associated with IQ; infantile psychotics demonstrated a significantly greater deficit than later onset psychotics. This is in an accord with our view that a lack of integration interferes with progressive cognitive development.

The schizophrenic child achieves an initial differentiation in a relatively normal fashion, attaining object constancy and self–object differentiation. He resolves the disequilibrium of the sensorimotor period and enters what Piaget calls the "pre-operational period" of ages 2-4, characterized by the capacity for representational thought. But this period involves its own form of disequilibrium, requiring a new integration of perceptual and conceptual processes. It is with this second period of normative disequilibrium that the schizophrenic cannot cope, and in which his psychic development is consequently arrested.

For Piaget, the resolution of "infantile egocentrism" of the sensori-motor period establishes only a temporary equilibrium. The child is now capable of directed searching, remembering, and more complex internal representation. He can consequently process more and subtler data. But the overwhelming availability of such data soon disrupts the equilibrium between assimilation and accommodation. The child's cognitive organization is not stable in the face of much new data; now he accommodates from moment to moment with schemas that are not exercised repetitively and thus do not become permanent. This lack of stable integration leads once again to a form of egocentrism. In this stage (Flavell, 1963), the child is:

> egocentric with respect to representations, just as the neonate was egocentric with respect to sensori-motor actions. . . . The child repeatedly demonstrates an inability to take on the role of the other person, to see the other's viewpoints and coordinate them with his own. This is seen clearly in language where he makes little attempt to adapt his speech to the needs of the listener [p. 156].

The child cannot yet treat his own thought processes as an object of thought. He neither justifies his reasoning nor looks for contradictions in his logic. He still lacks the stable schema of self-as-object. Flavell (1963) states:

> One of the most pronounced characteristics of pre-operational thought is its tendency to center, as Piaget says, attention on a single, striking feature of the object of its reasoning to the neglect of other important aspects and by so doing, to distort the reasoning. The child is unable to decenter, i.e. to take into account features which could balance and compensate for the distorting biasing effects of the single centration. Like the young sensori-motor infant in the field of direct action, the preoperational child is confined to the surface of the phenomena he tries to think about, assimilating only those superficial features which clamor loudest for his attention [p. 157].

Preoperational thought, then, can focus impressionistically or sporadically on this or that stimulus, but cannot integrate these separately schematized perceptions into any sort of organized conceptual totality, or what Piaget calls "secondary schemata." Concepts tend to be concrete rather than abstract, absolute rather than relational. They refer neither to individuals who possess stable identities nor to classes of similar objects. Phenomenologically, experience in this stage of development is disjunctive, holistic, and immutable. Secondary schemata are those concepts that supply perspective, but these have not yet been attained, since their acquisition represents the resolution of the disequilibrium of this period. Flavell (1963) states:

> Piaget uses the term "transductive" for the types of reasoning by which the preoperational child links various preconcepts. Neither true induction nor true deduction, this kind of reasoning proceeds from particular to particular. Centering on one salient element of an event, the child proceeds irreversibly to draw as conclusion from it some other perceptually compelling happening [p. 160].

The child in this period also tends to make associative connections, rather than truly implicative and causal ones. He "juxtaposes" elements rather than relating them logically. His reasoning is syncretic; a multitude of diverse elements are inchoately but intimately co-related in a global, noncritical schema. The child does not distinguish, for instance, between play and reality, assigning to each an equal validity. The child in the preoperational period must therefore develop a stable integration between conceptual and perceptual processes.

There are three possible resolutions to this period. The first is the normal resolution, in which concept and percept continually operate in an integrated fashion, with each modifying the other. This type of resolution is most efficient and adaptive. The second, or "perceptual," resolution occurs when the child does not progress beyond the initial disequilibrium of this period. Piaget's description of the preoperational child fits the "perceptual resolution." This child continually alters his concepts to fit immediate perceptions. The influx of perception is not ordered by the concept; rather, conceptual schemata vary with each perception. In Piaget's terms, the child has a dominance of accommodation. This resolution corresponds well with descriptions of the majority of childhood schizophrenics. The child has symbols, language, and a primitive notion of the other, but has not developed the stable, "secondary schemas" necessary to integrate these percepts with a stable representation of the world. Integration is fleeting at best, and perception dominates conceptualization, with schemas dissolving as new elements are apprehended. Thus both perceptions and concepts appear distorted and fantasized. We call this perceptual resolution "childhood schizophrenia, perceptual type."

The third resolution of the disequilibrium of the preoperational stage, is what we call a "conceptual resolution." As stated earlier, the child in the preoperational stage is "egocentric with respect to representations." The child with a conceptual resolution develops a few connections between concepts. Initially these connections are tenuous, unstable, and threatened by discrepant percepts. Therefore, to maintain these emergent cognitive structures, the child disregards or distorts perceptual influence. While he continues to differentiate and develop his concepts, their relation to perceptual reality becomes more discrepant. He disregards perceptual data in order to retain the validity and stability of his concepts. In Piaget's terms, assimilation is dominant. Thus the child with a conceptual resolution appears to have concepts and behavior that are idiosyncratic and egocentric. But the process leading to these idiosyncratic concepts is different from the process of the perceptually-bound child, whose concepts are ever changing to accommodate different stimuli. Instead, these concepts are tied to such a limited perceptual base that they appear to be delusional or without a frame of reference. We call this type of resolution "childhood schizophrenia, conceptual type."

Our terms should again be clarified because we are using a new language to describe the constructs of our theory. Our definition of assimilation as "perceptual" and accommodation as "conceptual" are meant to clarify the role of each in intellectual development, which is our focus in this section. But since these terms refer to different aspects of information processing that results in a single process—adaptation—they both have perceptual as well as conceptual referents. In assimilation, the percept is fitted into an existing schema, even if that fitting involves distorting the uniqueness or salient features of the perceived. In accommodation, a new structure is generated, permitting the identification of the percept as unique or different from others.

Piaget makes clear that these processes are always both present in any interaction with the environment, and that they are in roughly equal proportion (equilibrium) in normal adaptation. Both processes are necessary for construction of a percept or the creation of knowledge.

In describing adult schizophrenia as the result of an imbalance between these processes, we believe that the paranoid overemphasizes assimilation. That is, the paranoid's conceptual assemblies are quite rigid and unique, and thus, percepts are distorted to fit existing schemas (ideas of reference, delusion, etc.). Nonparanoids overemphasize accommodation; thus percepts generate new conceptual associations that are not repetitively exercised in future assimilations (assemblies) and are therefore too weak to organize similar percepts (depersonalization, hallucinations, etc.). We therefore refer to the paranoid's adaptation as "conceptual" and the nonparanoid's as "perceptual," stressing the maladaptive consequences of the paranoid's reliance on assimilation and the nonparanoid's reliance on accommodation.

We thus postulate two types of child schizophrenia, perceptual and conceptual, corresponding to the two types of nonintegrative resolutions at the preoperational stage. We believe that the little empirical work available supports a differentiation of subgroups in childhood schizophrenia. That is, clinical reports, in addition to describing perceptual-type symptoms, mention symptoms of the conceptual type: delusions, ideas of reference, grandiosity, etc. However, as seen in Chapter 5, children displaying either type of resolution are all grouped under the dominant category of schizophrenia.

In summary, integration theory views childhood schizophrenia as the result of an inability to resolve the disequilibrium of Piaget's preoperational stage with normal integration. Two types of nonintegrative resolution are possible; perceptual and conceptual. Each of these leads to a type of childhood schizophrenia, schizophrenia and paranoia.

Adult Paranoid and Nonparanoid Schizophrenia

We have described how a period of disequilibrium normally leads to a higher level of adaptation and integration, and how a failure to make the integrational resolution can lead to the two types of childhood schizophrenia. There is a third period of disequilibrilum described by Piaget. We hypothesize that this third period of disequilibrium, occurring in early adolescence, will exacerbate a previously inadequate integration in the preoperational stage, producing the syndromes of paranoid and nonparanoid adult schizophrenia.

A nonintegrative resolution in the preoperational stage may or may not produce symptoms severe enough to be diagnosed as "childhood schizophrenia," depending on a variety of factors (severity of disorder, intelligence, environmental demands, etc.). However, either nonintegrative resolution functioning as a predisposition may be exaggerated in the third period of disequilibrium. It will then be manifested as a form of adult schizophrenia—the perceptual resolution leading to nonparanoid schizophrenia and the conceptual resolution leading to paranoid schizophrenia. We now explore the mechanisms by which this process occurs.

In Piaget's theory, the third period of disequilibrium between accommodation and assimilation occurs when the child begins to acquire "formal operations" (age 11+). Formal operations are highly abstract, internalized actions involving hypothetico-deductive and future-oriented reasoning. In this transitional stage, the child moves from thought centered on the concrete and present to a conceptual structure including the abstract, the hypothetical, the possible (Inhelder & Piaget, 1958):

> Formal thinking is both thinking about thought (propositional logic is a second-order operational system which operates on propositions whose truth, in turn, depends on class, relational and numerical operations) and a reversal of operations between what is real and what is possible (the empirically given comes to be inserted as a particular sector of the total set of possible combinations) [pp. 341–342].

As in all transitional stages for Piaget, this new and untried mode of functioning leads to egocentrism. Here egocentrism takes the form of "the omnipotence of thought," with a disregard for any practical obstacles or reality that may face its proposals (Inhelder & Piaget, 1958):

> The indefinite extension of powers of thought made possible by the new instruments of propositional logic at first is conducive to a failure to distinguish between the ego's new and unpredictable capacities and the social or cosmic universe to which they are applied. In other words, the adolescent goes through a phase in which he attributes an unlimited power to his own thought so that the dream of a glorious future or of transforming the world through ideas (even if this idealism takes a materialistic form) seems to be not only fantasy but also an effective action which in itself modifies the empirical world. This is obviously a form of cognitive egocentrism. Although it differs sharply from the child's egocentrism (which is either sensori-motor or simply representational without introspective "reflection"), it results nonetheless from the same mechanisms, and appears as a function of the new conditions created by the structuring of formal thought [pp. 345–346].

This period has a differential effect on children who have not achieved a stable integration in the preoperational period. The child with a perceptual resolution will not progress through the transition to the stage of formal operations. This adolescent will find himself progressively further behind, and isolated from, his peers. He will not evince the "omnipotence of thought" of this period. His school performance is likely to become increasingly atypical for his age level. His behavior will appear more and more unusual, until he is ultimately called "schizophrenic."

On the other hand, the adolescent who made a conceptual resolution in the preoperational period will meet the transition to formal operations with some eagerness. His type of resolution, which will have alienated him from peers during latency, will now appear as a facility for abstract, conceptual thought. He may for a time even attract peers seeking to emulate his capacity for abstraction. But he can only incompletely adopt "formal operations," because the few conceptual categories on which he has relied since early childhood do not admit of perceptual correction or modification. Thus he will not achieve the integration of formal operations as will his peers. He will expand and abstract his concepts, but, without a perceptual base, these concepts will become progressively more isolated from reality. Eventually his concepts may become so discrepant that he will be diagnosed as "paranoid schizophrenic" or he will find a cultural niche that finds such thought admirable as we mentioned in a prior chapter.

We here reviewed the evidence in Chapter 5 that a predisposition for adult schizophrenia exists at an early age. Examples are that adult schizophrenics are poor achievers and socializers as children (Barthell & Holmes, 1968), and use language characterized as "unclear" and by "driven overproductivity of talk" (Namache & Ricks, 1966). Moreover, this predisposition may not be seen as pathological in childhood. Although a noticeable disturbance prior to age 5 is a good predictor of adult schizophrenia, more schizophrenics show disturbances in early adolescence than in childhood (Watt, 1972). We would also predict that a majority of children facing difficulty in integration will opt for the "perceptual" solution because it is favored by the normative dominance of perception over cognition at early ages. Supporting this hypothesis, Robins (1966) reports that only 1/3 of preschizophrenic children showed "odd ideas or paranoid trends."

Other evidence suggests that paranoid schizophrenics at least partially achieve a higher developmental level than nonparanoids. Zigler and Levine (1973) report a positive relationship between paranoid status and premorbid competence, which they cautiously interpret as an indication that paranoids have "obtained a higher developmental level in their premorbid period" than nonparanoid schizophrenics. They report further evidence by Sommer and Whitney (1961) and Zigler and Phillips (1961) that supports the view that paranoids have achieved higher premorbid levels of development. Zigler and Levine (1973) cite Johannsen's (1961) reading of Sullivan "that paranoid schizophrenics' communication impairment is less severe and genetically later in origin than that of the other schizophrenic subgroups [p. 58]."

Siegel (1953) compared the Rorschach performances of paranoid and nonparanoid schizophrenics with those of children 3–10 years old, concluding that:

1)...the perception of the paranoid schizophrenic corresponds to the more differentiated but little integrated perception of children between six and ten years of age, whereas hebephrenic and catatonic perception resembles the global, amorphous, perceptual activity of three to five year old children.
2) The perception of the paranoid schizophrenic is more intact and closer to that of the normal adult than is the...perception of the hebephrenic and catatonic patient.
3) ...paranoid perception is a combination of both genetically early and genetically late characteristics [p. 161].

Interpretation of Research in Terms of Piaget and Integration Theory

The Integration Theory states that paranoids will perform more like normals than nonparanoids when conceptual processes (e.g., memory, maintaining sets) are more important than perceptual ones in task performance. Hence, it predicts that, on most tasks, paranoids would show less deficit (i.e., perform more like normals) than nonparanoids. We have shown this distinction of groups by task in prior chapters. We now present selected studies that we have previously reviewed, interpreting them by using the assimilation and accommodation terms to demonstrate the relationship to Integration Theory terms. We hope that such a review will clearly indicate the areas where Integration Theory terms could be investigated.

Generally, most tasks, like successful living in a highly interdependent world, depend more on conceptual skills than perceptual ones. Thus the paranoid usually fares better by "normal" standards than the nonparanoid. On the other hand, the theory also implies that a task requiring accurate perception with conceptual processes being relatively less important (or opposed to task success) should yield opposite results, with schizophrenics performing better than paranoids. The Young and Jerome (1972) study reported earlier found such results in a task requiring subjects to solve a series of problems in which the relevant cues changed, a task characteristic that was carefully explained in the directions. Paranoids consistently performed less efficiently than nonparanoids. In interpreting the results, Young and Jerome (1972) suggest that:

There was something wrong with the paranoid subjects' conceptualization of the task.... Rigidity of internal representation is.... suggested by the paranoid subjects' loss of efficiency when the problem class was changed.... it appears that their conceptualization of the task was too detail-bound to permit adjustment to a change in a quite arbitrary aspect of the problem context.... Tasks that emphasize a need for adjusting internal representation would be more effective than this one-change task in revealing possible differences in the ability to make effective adjustment in conceptualization [p. 444].

It appears that this task was sensitive to the predicted paranoid conceptual emphasis on assimilation of data to existing schemas. Binder (1958) used varied levels of cue specificity and found that higher paranoid scale MMPI scores are associated with a tendency to withhold perceptual responses until a relatively low amount of uncertainty is present: "The pattern seems to indicate that Ss who answer MMPI items in the direction of maximum disturbance are least likely to make inductive inferences on a recognition situation on the basis of inadequate information [p. 141]." Such results also suggest a new interpretation of paranoid scanning. Instead of viewing high scanning as a perceptual style, we see it as a consequence of paranoid reliance of assimilation (i.e., the fitting of data to already existing categories). It may be a mistake, then, to assume that the paranoid scans because he "needs" more data than other groups (Silverman, 1964) or is "motivated" to reduce anxiety by fitting percepts to structures (McReynolds, 1960). Rather, the paranoid is equipped with a few enduring categories or schemas (more than the nonparanoid schizophrenics, fewer than the normal) that he reaffirms by seeking data which may be assimilated to them. Remember the results with subjective organization in schemata in the previous chapter: The paranoid had problems with recall *only* when a flexibility—the use of multiple conceptual assemblies—was required.

Two studies have approached this question of the relation between percept assimilation and paranoid conceptualization fairly directly. McReynolds, Collins, and Acker (1964), employed the McGill Closure Test with delusional and nondelusional schizophrenics and found that "delusional schizophrenics have a stronger tendency to organize ambiguous stimuli in a meaningful way than do non-delusional schizophrenics [pp. 211–212]." The test consisted of "44 incomplete pictures of common objects. . . . In each picture certain lines and shapes have been left out, and others inserted so that typically it is not immediately apparent what the picture is. When one gains an insight into the content, however, the object stands out clearly [p. 211]."

Delusional subjects both attempted significantly more pictures and identified significantly more correctly than nondelusional subjects. The schizophrenics had fewer and weaker associate structures (schemas) with which to make sense of sensory data. Paranoids differed from nonparanoids in that they could supply missing information better. This is expected from our theory. We would, however, expect the results to reverse in a task where, for instance, the incomplete pictures were surrounded by a misleading context (which might be supplied by directions or actual alteration of the cards). In such a case, we would expect the nondelusional's recognition to be better than delusional's recognition, the latter being more influenced by notions about the thing, rather than the thing itself. McReynolds' (1960) theory is that "unassimilated percepts" cause anxiety for the paranoid, who is therefore motivated to account for much data through the "sudden clarification" (Cameron's phrase) of the delusion. But this theory cannot explain why paranoid and nonparanoid schizophrenics differ so dramatically with respect to assimilation, and why assimilation reduces anxiety in the first place. In terms of the present speculations on the development of the integration, these different cognitive styles can be traced to the point in development where the integration failure first occurred.

A study by Abrams, Taintor, and Lhamon (1966), previously described, builds on McReynolds' theory. These authors offer a similar description of paranoid conceptual strategy:

> In the face of new experiences, a perceiver has the option of formulating new hypotheses to assimilate them or of leaving them unexplained pending the collection of more data, i.e. suspending judgment. The tendency to take the latter option, when circumstances permit, is commonly called open-mindedness or tolerance of ambiguity....
>
> It is a thesis of this study, following McReynolds, that paranoid individuals find it difficult to be open-minded or tolerant of ambiguity. Confronted with a large quantity of anxiety-provoking percepts, the products of his hypervigilance, the paranoid has developed a strategy of urgently forming assimilatory hypotheses [pp. 419–420].

This experiment operationalized assimilation much as McReynolds did, using the Street Gestalt Completion figures. In this case, however, paranoids were not compared with nonparanoids. Rather, patients of several diagnoses were categorized into four groups representing increasing degrees of paranoid symptomatology. Abrams et al. (1966) found that the "assimilation tendency" increases with severity of paranoid symptoms, and that "in a task in which the judgment process must be based on incomplete amounts of data, paranoid subjects tend to form atypical and incorrect judgments rather than none at all. In other words they tend not to suspend judgment, but to assimilate even at the price of accuracy [p. 492]." The authors conclude that "the paranoid operates with the metahypothesis that, to process his experience, it is preferable to form an incorrect hypothesis than none at all. Furthermore, the greater the degree of paranoid severity, the stronger this metahypothesis [p. 495]." This "metahypothesis," in integration terms, is the conceptual compensation for difficulty in integration.

An interesting study that could be reinterpreted in terms of the cognitive styles of paranoids and schizophrenics involves an experiment in which the two groups were compared on the Oppel–Kundt and Müller–Lyer illusions. The Oppel–Kundt illusion is considered a secondary illusion which is less obvious with smaller children and mental deficients, and, hence, is considered to become more prominent with increasing cognitive growth. The Müller–Lyer illusion is considered a primary illusion, hence, it is found to diminish with age. Letourneau (1974) found that paranoids exhibited a greater Oppel–Kundt illusion than schizophrenics, but the Müller–Lyer illusion produced no significant differences between schizophrenics and paranoids. The results were interpreted in terms of a scanning hypothesis, which was not able to explain the lack of group differences on the Müller–Lyer illusion. A scanning hypothesis would have predicted that the illusion should have been smaller with paranoids due to their extensive scanning (Letourneau, 1974). Integration Theory can explain all the results more completely. It proposes that the paranoid would only be distinguished from the schizophrenic on tasks which demand a conceptual cognitive style. The secondary illusion includes such a demand, and the paranoid exhibited a greater illusory effect on this task. In contrast, the Müller–Lyer illusion is not found to be related to age or to differentiate between those with differing intellectual abilities. Hence, it is not a conceptual task. In this case, the paranoid–schizophrenic difference did not appear because the task did not demand the cognitive style of either group. Unfortunately, a control group was not used, which would be a necessity in determining the comparative difference in the performance level of the schizophrenic group. It would be expected that, relative to normals, the schizophrenic would do better on a primary illusion since its demand is perceptual.

Since previous work did not usually directly compare schizophrenics and paranoids, McDowell, Reynolds, and Magaro (1975) designed an experiment, using the Russian ambiguous stimuli methodology described above, to directly test the cognitive styles of paranoids and schizophrenics as predicted by Integration Theory. A signal detection task was employed to demonstrate the interaction between task requirements and paranoid-nonparanoid adaptation. It was predicted that where optimum performance should be improved by conceptual processes (expectation of a high-probability message), paranoids would perform better than nonparanoids, but that in the same task altered so that such expectations hinder performance (low-probability message), nonparanoids would perform better. It was also predicted that normal performance would be intermediate between schizophrenic groups in both high- and low-probability stimulus conditions, because normal adaptation represents an integrated mean between these two schizophrenic deviations.

Ten nonparanoids, ten paranoids, and ten hospital aides listened to sentences ending in high- or low-probability words masked by one of five levels of white noise. As predicted, paranoids and normals identified the masked word significantly more accurately than nonparanoids when task performance was facilitated by conceptual processes (expectation of the probable ending as in a conceptual set). When expectations operated to decrease performance (improbable endings), subgroup performances tended to reverse, although differences were not statistically significant. Had there been more subjects per group, the trend may have reached significance in this condition also. In general, predictions from Integration Theory regarding schizophrenic subgroups' relative performance on the two task conditions were supported. Generally, the effects of the paranoid's conceptual emphasis and the nonparanoids' perceptual emphasis were most clearly demonstrated in the medium-difficulty ranges. The paranoids' performance curve flattened in the high-probability condition, and the nonparanoids' curve flattened in the low-probability condition. Paranoid performance was maximized where expectation of the probable ending should improve performance. Nonparanoid performance was maximized where *lack* of such expectations permitted more accurate recognition of the ambiguous signal. Normals performed significantly better than either schizophrenic group in the low-probability condition. The prediction that normals would function in an intermediate level in both conditions was not supported leading to the new hypothesis that normals switch their processing strategies depending upon the situation.

A signal detection analysis in the same study suggested a different formulation of the integration process of normals. Normals were only slightly biased toward high probability responses. They were not as biased as either schizophrenic group, and performed better over all conditions than either subgroup. Their performance may be the result of an ability to shift processes with task demands. Hence, they perform like paranoids on probable end-words and like schizophrenics on improbable end-words. Another possible explanation is that the schizophrenics' poor integration lowers overall performance, and that the specific style adopted in lieu of adequate integration cannot fully compensate for the basic defect except under unusual conditions.

In summary, the results for the pathological groups tended to support Integration Theory predictions, and provided some clarification of its account of normal integration. Normals have the ability to modulate between perceptual and cognitive strategies as task requirements change.

In conclusion, we claim that inability to integrate perceptual and conceptual processes is the etiologically significant dysfunction. Failure to achieve an integrative resolution in a normal period of disequilibrium prevents or distorts further development. The differing clinical syndromes are distinguished etiologically by the period of disequilibrium at which integration fails and by the type of nonintegrative resolution adopted. Childhood schizophrenia is the result of a failure to make an integrative resolution in the second period of disequilibrium, age 2–4 years. Two subgroups of childhood schizophrenia are described, corresponding to the two possible types of nonintegrative resolution—perceptual and conceptual. The third period of disequilirium, occurring in early adolescence, is seen as exacerbating an inadequate integration made in an earlier period, leading to the syndromes of paranoid and nonparanoid schizophrenia. The common element at any stage of disequilibrium is the lack of integration between psychological processes. Whether it just applies to schizophrenics and paranoids or to all pathological groups is open to question.

We replace the developmental terminology with a neurological conception in a following chapter. At that point, the constructs of perceptual and conceptual processes are replaced with constructs relating to the functions of the hemispheres. Integration is replaced by constructs dealing with interhemispheric transmission. The present chapter attempts to explain the development of pathology in terms of dynamically related processes, which are rooted in developmental theory applied to normals. The Information Theory chapter discussed the exact nature of the psychological processes. The last chapter looks at treatment directions suggested by the present conception. Before this, however, we will speculate upon some other etiological factors that might give rise to deviant developmental patterns.

Speculations on Initial Predispositions

Our discussion has centered on the mechanisms of pathology. We have described the development of psychological processes that are manifested in schizophrenia and paranoia. However, we have not yet explained why the developmental problem occurs in the first place. Why is it that some children emphasize one developmental process over the other? We have described how the observables (empirical data and clinical observations) can be explained by the theoretical terms of perception and conceptualization. We have also offered another, higher-order term of integration to indicate the relationship between two processes. We would now like to offer a speculative explanation of the factors responsible for a lack of integration in development, adding closure to our discussion.

Assuming that the proper amount of stimulation is necessary for the formation of appropriate cognitive structures, and that integration is the process of incorporating sensory stimulation into developing cognitive structures, we will focus on the amount of stimulus input to explain why the posited psychological mechanisms are deviant in the pathological groups under consideration. We speculate that the initial causal factors reside in the match between receptor thresholds and parental stimulation in early childrearing stages. Stimulus input is a function of two main variables: the threshold of the receptor and the amount of stimulation by the mothering figure during early infancy.

It seems clear that during infancy there are wide individual differences in the sensitivity of the child to incoming stimulation (Escalona, 1973). For example, there is evidence that infants exhibit different thresholds with tactile stimulation (Bell, 1960), pain (Lipsitt & Levy, 1959), responsivity of psychological systems to stress (Grossman & Greenberg, 1957), and habituation (Bridger, 1961). We suggest that there is an optimum amount of stimulus input that is required for normal cognitive growth. Too little input can result from either extremely high thresholds or low parental stimulation. Too much stimulation would result from the inverse. The direction of the stimulus input deficiency, over- or understimulation, would determine the particular syndrome or type of integrational resolution. An optimal amount of stimulus input can be obtained even if one of the input variables is abnormal because the source can compensate for the threshold, and vice-versa. That is, even if the child had extremely high thresholds and required intensive levels of stimulation to respond, a highly stimulative mother extensively and intensively interacting with the child would produce an optimal level of stimulus input. Similarly with the child with very low thresholds, the minimally interacting or even the ignoring mother could produce an optimal level of stimulation. Therefore, the child with a genetically determined deviant receptor threshold would not necessarily exhibit the pathological phenotype. The degree of parental stimulation deviating in the same direction would result in an optimal but unfortunate match.

We have previously hypothesized (Magaro et al., 1976) that autism could be due to understimulation, and schizophrenia due to overstimulation. Childhood schizophrenia, on the other hand, could be due to high sensitivity coupled with a normal or a highly stimulating environment. The hypersensitive child develops object schemas easily, but this hypersensitivity becomes troublesome during the preoperational stage. Such a child fails to develop secondary schemas because the onslaught of perception is too immediate and overwhelming to allow connections to form between remembered events (perceptual resolution). Or, if concepts are connected, these connections are so tenuous and precarious that the child defends them against all further input of perception (conceptual resolution). Thus, the hypersensitive child never establishes an integration between conceptual and perceptual processes. In effect, we are reformulating the genetic-environmental argument in terms of innate receptor sensitivity and amount of parental stimulation. The sensory threshold factor would conform to estimates of heritability, while the degree of parental stimulation would estimate the degree of conditionability.

The main thrust of the present discourse is not to determine ultimate causes. Our purpose has been to elucidate, with a developmental framework, the psychological mechanisms responsible for behavior considered pathological. Once this task is accomplished with some degree of certainty, clinical behavior may be more understandable. If the processes which differentiate pathological groups can be described, we should know what to investigate when looking for ultimate causes, whether they are located in the central nervous sytem, the peripheral receptor system, childrearing patterns, or the pineal gland. The next chapter explores more specifically the neurological substrate, which most clearly demonstrates the differential processes of schizophrenics and paranoids as well as the possible mechanism of integration.

8

Hemispheric Specialization in Schizophrenia and Paranoia

INTRODUCTION

We began our discussion of schizophrenia by noting that the results of much experimental work could be explained by task demands for perceptual and conceptual processes. We argued that schizophrenics and paranoids were differentially affected by such task demands. The central role of the perceptual and conceptual processes in the explanation of behavior led us to refine our terms through an information-processing model. We also defined the higher order Integration term and offered a developmental explanation of perception and conceptualization, stressing their formation through stages of development. We now offer a neurological explanation of the two processes in order to describe a current research direction, as well as to provide Integration Theory with a neurological substrate.

Describing certain psychological functions by means of the operations of specific hemispheres has now become a means to explain phenomena from the evolution of man to specific psychological processes such as mirror-image discrimination (Corballis & Beale, 1976). This rapidly evolving area is relevant to our discussion because the processes assigned to each hemisphere are the same as those we have been discussing in the explanation of schizophrenia and paranoia. Although it is admittedly dangerous to assign meaning by correspondence, the similarity is too great to ignore or to wait for more conclusive evidence to unit the two areas of study. Besides, there is some evidence which does make feasible the possibility that differential hemisphere functions are the neurological substrate of the constructs proposed by Integration Theory.

As we discussed in the first chapter, there is a need to develop a complete postulate set in the area of schizophrenia, while at the same time trying terms closer to observables. The Information Theory operations presented a means to clearly tie constructs to observables. The hemispheric constructs offer a means to relate behavioral constructs to neurological terms. The ability of the present theory to so readily make the translation encourages a greater interdisciplinary view of schizophrenia.

We have defined perception as the process of encoding during the presentation of the icon, which could involve automatic or controlled processing. Automatic processing creates distinctions in a preattentive formation of elements which is global and holistic. Controlled processing is a serial search, which sorts stimulus elements in a systematic focal fashion. Conceptualization has been defined as the forming of cogits into assemblies. The cogit can operate as the category that determines the set for automatic processing or can be validated by controlled processing. In either case, the cogit is part of an assembly, which is united with other assemblies to form a schematic. Such hierarchical construction extends down to the encoding process and may determine the type of encoding employed. In most instances, when encoding is performed in a normal situation, the schemata requires controlled processing to form the percept that matches an acceptable category. When the situation is practiced, automatic processing suffices to create the same end. On the other hand, if the assembly and hence the cogit is not as powerful, controlled processing may not be employed to any great degree and automatic processing may suffice even in the novel situation. Here the attributes of the stimulus are processed without the necessity of establishing the logical conceptual order of the assembly.

The correspondence with hemispheric specialization involves the description of the role of each hemisphere in processing information. The right hemisphere is the locus of visuospatial, nonlinguistic activity which corresponds to automatic processing. The left hemisphere is described as containing the verbal-linguistic processing, which corresponds to the operation of the assemblies. Integration is the stimulus operation of perception and conceptualization or the figural synthesis of encoding and assembly construction that produces a meaningful concept of knowledge. This interdependent interfacing process corresponds to transcollasal transmission, whereby the hemispheres constantly exchange information to provide a complete processing of events. We have hypothesized that the schizophrenic and the paranoid prefer or are limited to specific modes of processing. We find in the hemispheric dominance literature that, although hemisphere functioning is dependent upon the specific material processed, some groups prefer one hemisphere over the other. There is also some evidence that the schizophrenic exhibits right hemisphere dominance, with both groups having a major difficulty with transcallosal transfer.

Most of the early hemisphere work indicates that the nature of the stimulus material determines which hemisphere controls processing and responding. Early studies focused on the verbal–spatial distinction. Later studies have suggested that a distinction based on the requirement for analytic or gestalt processing more adequately explains the results. In either case, the hypothesis is that when stimuli are presented, both hemispheres will begin to process the material, but some types of material will be processed more competently and more quickly by one hemisphere. Hence, the hemisphere more competent relative to the task will dominate.

In contrast to the clear influence of processing demands is the additional factor of individual differences in hemispheric functioning. The individual either through past experiences or present dispositions will have a preference for the use of a hemisphere. Thus, though it may be detrimental to task performance, the less competent hemisphere may be used. This is not to say that the individual switches hemispheres at will, but that individual preferences may supersede task demands.

We first review the literature which specifies the nature of hemispheric functioning in terms of stimulus material. We then qualify the conclusions of such linear effects by examining the role of individual differences. Since we expect the schizophrenic designation to define a subset of individuals who will deviate from the usual processing of stimulus material, we then review the meager evidence on hemispheric function in schizophrenia with special attention to schizophrenic–paranoid differences. From Integration Theory, we would expect schizophrenics and paranoids to deviate from the usual hemispheric processing of stimulus materials. The schizophrenic would show a preference for right hemisphere activity, while the paranoid would show a preference for left hemisphere activity. In either group such preferences could be due to deficiencies in transcallosal transfer.

TASK DEMANDS AND
HEMISPHERIC FUNCTIONING

Sperry (1973) presented the first work with commissurotomized patients, indicating that hemispheric competence seemed to determine hemispheric dominance. The hemisphere specialized for the kind of processing required seemed to assume control of the response systems. For example, Levy, Trevarthen, and Sperry (1972) found that when two different facial stimuli were presented, one to each hemisphere, commissurotomized patients recognized the stimulus presented to the right hemisphere. This suggests that hemispheric dominance—the hemisphere that controls processing and behavior—is determined by hemispheric competence. Investigators have described hemispheric competence in terms of the verbal/spatial dichotomy and the gestalt/analytic dichotomy.

Within the framework of the verbal/spatial distinction, Kimura (1966) suggested that each hemisphere contains a particular processing center, the verbal center occurring in the left hemisphere (LH) for the most part, and the spatial processing center in the right. Levy (1974) came to the same conclusion in the examination of the performance of commissurotomy patients on a cross-model spatial relations test. Each hemishpere used a specific strategy to match stimuli. The LH preferred the use of a language description approach while the right hemisphere (RH) used a perceptual-spatial differentiation. Thus, it could be expected that spatial material that arrives in the RH can be more quickly processed than verbal material, which must be transferred to the LH for processing. The location of the different centers would explain the differential abilities displayed by the left and right hemispheres, and why the RH is more competent and speedier for visuospatial material and the left for verbal material. Furthermore, the necessity of transferring material transcallosally to the appropriate center would explain the longer latencies and greater inaccuracies found in the presentation of material "inappropriate" to each hemisphere.

The alternate explanation of the processes inherent in each hemisphere uses the analytic versus gestalt processing distinction. To test directly whether or not the view of the dichotomous functioning in terms of analytic/gestalt processing might be more accurate, Patterson and Bradshaw (1975) designed a study that involved the presentation of schematic faces, which could be varied in analytic and gestalt features. Subjects were asked to judge whether or not members of a stimulus pair were different or the same. The pairs were presented in various ways: both to the right hemisphere, both to the left hemisphere, the first of each pair presented to the left, and the first of each presented to the right. The tasks also varied in terms of requiring short-term and long-term memory. The interpretation of their results support the view that gestalt processing is characteristic of the right hemisphere, and analytic processing characteristic of the left.

Similarly, Levy et al. (1972), in bilateral presentation of chimeric stimuli, found that hemispheric dominance was primarily determined by the processing requirement of the task rather than the nature of the stimuli. Analysis of subjects' comments revealed that the left hemishpere was inclined to pick out distinctive features of the stimuli instead of treating it as a unit. Bever and Chiarello (1974), in studying cerebral dominance for recognition of melodies in musically experienced listeners versus naive listeners, offer further support for this view. It was found that experienced listeners used the left hemisphere, suggesting analytic processing, and naive listeners used the right for holistic processing.

Semmes (1968), in her analysis of the sensory and motor capacities of brain-injured patients, suggests a mechanism to explain the analytic/gestalt processing found in the different hemispheres:

It is proposed that focal representation of elementary functions in the left hemisphere favors integration of *similar* units and consequently specialization for behaviors which demand fine sensorimotor control, such as manual skills and speech. Conversely, diffuse representation of elementary functions in the right hemisphere may lead to integration of *dissimilar* units and hence specialization for behaviors requiring multimodal coordination, such as the various spatial abilities [p. 11].

This point of view explains how the dichotomy of analytic/gestalt processing can subsume the dichotomy of verbal/spatial. Moreover, it can explain the findings that the right hemisphere is capable of some verbal processing, the left hemisphere is capable of some verbal processing, and the left hemisphere of spatial processing. This evidence suggests that competence can be most accurately defined in terms of gestalt-analytical functioning and that verbal-spatial is one of the examples of that form of processing because the verbal requires the analytical process and spatial tasks the necessity for a gestalt. The right hemisphere would treat a stimulus as a unit and not segment the field. Since the left hemisphere prefers to analyze segments of a stimulus, the recognition of faces would be expected to be a right hemisphere function especially if face recognition was a global process in which specific features were not analyzed. The interesting work by Harmon (1973) shows that faces could be recognized even when they are nothing but gross blurrs. Harmon used a computer to gradually distort the features of faces, ranging from quite distinctive to severe blurring. At the most extreme blurring, where facial features are completely obliterated, recognition was still 60 percent. The recognition could not depend upon feature identification as only the most gross characteristics remain. The overall gestalt, however, had meaning which could not be obtained from an analysis of stimulus components. This would be the means used by the right hemisphere to process information which should also occur in the auditory channel.

To anticipate our direction, the two different types of processing could be characteristic of paranoids and schizophrenics. Serial controlled processing is analytic, while automatic processing uses gestalts. The correspondence is very clear. Since we expect the schizophrenic to be the automatic processor who uses gestalt processing, we would expect him to prefer the right hemisphere. Since we found the paranoid to prefer serial processing or analytic type functioning, we would expect him to prefer the left hemisphere.

However the processing of each hemisphere is described, studies with commissurotomized patients, using tachistoscopic hemi-field presentation, lateral eye movements, and EEG measures, generally imply that hemisphere functioning is specialized. Nebes (1974), in a review of studies with commissurotomized subjects, reported the following findings relating to perceptual and linguistic functioning. The left hemisphere is proficient in all language skills as well as arithmetic calculation. The language capacities of the right hemisphere are not as completely understood, but apparently it is capable of simple association of objects to their names and of tactually retrieving an object when an abstract description or a definition of the object's use is given. It is also more competent in performing two general types of mental operation: generating a whole from fragmentary information and visual recognition, even for verbal material. The functions are not as clear when the right hemisphere is required to comprehend verbs, or sentences which require distinguishing between active and passive voices, singular from plural and present from future tense.

There is apparently competition between the hemispheres for control of motor or expressive output. When the response required is a verbal one, the left hemisphere can apparently override the right and control the action. In situations where the right hemisphere is more competent, it can exercise control of the motor system even over the right hand. Levy and Trevarthen (1976) extended their earlier conclusions about hemispheric specialization to determine which hemisphere took control of processing and responding. They presented tachistoscopic black line drawings of common objects, with different stimuli simultaneously presented to both hemispheres. Instructions, presented in an ambiguous, structural, or functional mode, called for matching the tachistoscopically presented material with pictures in free vision. With ambiguous instructions, each hemisphere performed according to its superiority, appearance matches being performed by the right; function matches by the left. When the instructions required appearance matches, they tended to be made by the right hemisphere; similarly when function matches were required, left hemisphere control was observed. The left hemisphere showed competence for verbal/linguistic skills and the right hemisphere demonstrated competence for holistic operations and visual recognition. Trevarthen (1974) summarizes such results by concluding that the perception of the shape, organization, and whole structure is best formed in the RH which can store a whole image adapted to a matching task, while the LH is better at recognizing familiar features in the object and employing verbal symbols to communicate the nature of the object.

When the methodology involves tachistoscopic presentation of stimuli to the right or left visual half-field, the results are similar. Words and letters are recognized faster when they are presented to the right visual field, and hence processed by the left hemisphere (Berlucchi, 1972, 1974; Davis & Schmit, 1973; Hellige, 1975; Kimura & Dunford, 1974; McKeever & Huling, 1970; Mishkin & Forgays, 1952; Rizzolatti, Unilta, & Berlucchi, 1971; Young,

1974). Stimuli with visuospatial factors such as depth perception (Dunford & Kimura, 1971), facial recognition (Rizzolatti et al., 1971), complex shapes, and line orientations (Berlucchi, 1974; Fontenot, 1973) are better recalled when presented to the left visual field, hence to the right hemisphere. Moreover, the superiority of the right hemisphere for memory of complex shapes has been demonstrated by Dee and Fontenot (1973) and Egeth (1971).

However, studies directing attention to the specific nature of the verbal material presented to the visual fields indicate that earlier findings concluding that only the left hemisphere is specialized for verbal functioning is an oversimplification. Familiar concrete nouns are also recognized by the right hemisphere. Ellis and Shepherd (1974) report that both abstract and concrete words are reocgnized better when they are presented to the right visual field. However, Hines (1976) found that, while the right visual field is superior for familiar abstract nouns, there was a decreased asymmetry for familiar concrete nouns. While this suggests that the right hemisphere has some capacity for verbal processing, Leiber's (1976) results are explained by transfer of verbal material received in the right hemisphere to the left. Leiber's study involved high- and low-frequency words and pronounceable and nonpronounceable nonwords. While reaction time and error rate measures revealed a right visual field advantage for both classes of words, there was no difference between hemispheres in the recognition of nonwords. She concludes that meaning is a more salient factor for wordness than pronounceability, and the lack of hemisphere differences in recognizing nonwords may be due to transcallosal transmission of letter-strings from the right to the left hemisphere. This implies that the right hemisphere has no capacity for verbal processing. Findings by Caplan, Homes, and Marshall (1974) adds to the complexity of hemispheric specialization. They used three classes of words: simple nouns (e.g., danger, river, chapter), agentive nouns (e.g., worker, writer, leader) and category-ambiguous noun/verbs (order, murder, offer, father) which were presented unilaterally and randomly to either visual field. Agentive nouns were more easily recognized with right visual field presentation than words from the other two classes, and both agentive and category-ambiguous nouns were more easily recognized than simple nouns with left field presentation. Such findings indicate that the linguistic capacities of both hemispheres cannot be easily explained by either the verbal/spatial or analytic/gestalt dichotomy.

To determine whether or not tachistoscopic procedures themselves biased processing toward material in the right visual field, Mackavey, Curcio, and Rosen (1975) conducted a series of experiments. To clarify the nature of the RVF superiority for verbal stimuli, they presented material horizontally and vertically, with and without the requirement to report stimuli at central fixation, to determine the effect of the normal scanning tendency. Results support the RVF superiority for recognition of verbal material. The authors suggest that bilateral presentation that results in larger hemispheric differences may better reflect hemispheric functioning. When material is presented simultaneously to both hemispheres, inhibitory influences may operate to create greater asymmetry. Therefore, the implication for visual split-field research in hemispheric functioning is that unilateral presentation may reflect the "pure" ability of a hemisphere, but only with bilateral presentation will the normal functioning of the hemispheres be observed.

To summarize, the findings of hemispheric dominance with commissurotomized patients are confirmed by studies employing visual half-field presentations. That is, verbal material is processed more efficiently by the left hemisphere, and visuospatial material by the right hemisphere, although the right hemisphere, does also possess some verbal capacities.

Studies using EEG measures of asymmetry report similar results. Galin and Ellis (1975), using measures of EEG activity and evoked potential, found that asymmetry reflected hemispheric specialization; for example, there was greater activity in the left hemisphere for verbal tasks (writing from memory a low-imagery article read in a newspaper) and greater activity in the right hemisphere for the performance of perceptual tasks (a block design task). Similarly, Doyle, Ornstein, and Galin (1974), using a frequency analysis of hemispheric EEG, found that left hemisphere tasks (verbal and arithmetic tasks) had higher ratios (right/left) than right hemisphere tasks (spatial tasks, e.g., modified Kohs block design and magic etch-a-sketch). Dumas and Morgan (1973), using the asymmetry of occipital alpha as their EEG measure, found that linguistic (pressing a button every time a designated word was read) and mathematical tasks (counting by twos; silently adding a series of numbers; counting by 8½s) activated the left hemisphere, and spatial tasks (face recall and modified Nebes' ring test) activated the right hemisphere. Similar results were found by Robbins and McAdam (1974) and Morgan, McDonald, and MacDonald (1971), with left hemisphere tasks involving verbalization and arithmetic calculation, and right hemisphere tasks involving imaging without thinking. Furthermore, Furst (1976) reports that subjects who perform with greater activation in the right hemisphere perform right hemisphere tasks more efficiently than subjects with less activation.

Another means to study lateralization has been that of eye movements. Day (1964) first noticed that, when asked a reflective question, subjects consistently looked either to the right or left, depending on the nature of the questions. Subsequent studies focusing on this gaze tendency confirmed the hypothesis that for verbal questions, the subjects looked right and for spatial questions, they looked left. This effect can be weakened or destroyed by several factors that were present in several studies, which did not confirm the general findings. These factors summarized by Kinsbourne (1974a) are confrontation by the experimenter, confrontation by the sound of experimenter's voice, and the subjects' set to respond other than straight ahead. Thus, if subjects are made self-conscious of their eye movement or are asked to fixate on a point (e.g., on video apparatus), the effect of the particular kind of question is lost; that is, direction of eye gaze will not be related to the nature of the reflective question. The Schwartz, Davidson, and Maer study (1975) did not conform to Kinsbourne's stipulations (subjects faced the experimenter), but nevertheless found the differential effects of certain types of questions. They report that emotional questions elicited greater left eye movement (indicating the activation of the right hemisphere) than nonemotional questions. Furthermore, when questions requiring both spatial and emotional processing were given, there was greater right hemisphere activation. With verbal, nonemotional questions, the left hemisphere was activated.

In summary, studies employing lateral eye movements suggest that the nature of the material to be processed—verbal versus spatial—determines hemispheric activation. (Galin and Ornstein, 1974, discuss the need for further refinement in experiments using lateral eye movements.) Eye movements to the right are interpreted to indicate left hemisphere activation, which are observed with verbal questions. Left lateral eye movements indicate right hemisphere processing, stimulated by spatial questions. These results are obtained generally with the experimenter behind the subject. With the experimenter confronting the subject, we will see that individual personality differences emerge.

Research employing EEG measures, visual half-field presentation, and lateral eye movement with normal and commissural patients consistently confirm hemisphere specialization. Whether the left hemisphere's specialization is more aptly described in terms of verbal/linguistic processing or analytic processing, it is clear that in general the left hemisphere is more competent for such tasks. Similarly the right hemisphere is more proficient for visuospatial or gestalt processing tasks. There is some evidence that, in a limited way, the right hemisphere is capable of verbal processing, and the left hemisphere of spatial processing. However, before we begin the analysis of the differential effect of tasks with schizophrenics, we should first establish that individual differences affect hemispheric activity.

INDIVIDUAL DIFFERENCES AND HEMISPHERIC FUNCTIONING

There are two major explanations of the mechanisms of hemispheric specialization that qualify the earlier competence hypothesis and offer room for individual differences to emerge. The first to be discussed deals with the capacity of the hemisphere, which can modify which hemisphere is used. The second deals with the orientation of a hemisphere as determined by past experiences. Both explanations suggest that the individual can influence the dominance of a hemisphere.

Geffen, Bradshaw, and Nettleton (1973), in their studies involving interference tasks, suggest dominance will be determined by the degree of processing load and that the limited capacity of a hemisphere can be overloaded, in which case the other hemisphere may then assume control. They studied the effects on reaction time of secondary musical and verbal tasks. Subjects were required to respond vocally to digits presented randomly in the left and right visual fields. Without a competing task, digits were more quickly processed by the left hemisphere. This result was also found when subjects were required to perform a secondary musical task. However, when a secondary verbal task was simultaneously performed, faster responses were given to digits in the left visual field. These results reveal that laterality can be reversed by overloading the capacity of a particular hemisphere.

This finding suggests that some individuals may be constantly engaged in one hemisphere so that any additional demands such as an experimental task produce an overload, and they are forced to function in the least preferred hemisphere. An alternate explanation, which does not involve the complicated overloading process, simply states that individuals may "prime" one hemisphere rather than the other. Such priming determines hemisphere dominance.

Kinsbourne (1970) has proposed the notion of "perceptual orientation" to explain which hemisphere is activated in a given task. Perceptual orientation is a form of set or priming that is determined by previous tasks, so that the primed hemisphere will assume control of processing. The perceptual orientation view proposed by Kinsbourne postulates that dominance is dependent upon the balance of activation of the hemispheres. Thus, if the left hemisphere is more active, material presented to the right visual field will be processed more accurately and faster. Bowers and Heilman (1976), within the context of Kinsbourne's view, designed a study to differentially activate the hemispheres with two kinds of warning signals—verbal and nonverbal sounds. In partial support of Kinsbourne's hypothesis, it was found that reaction times by the right hand were significantly faster when verbal warning signals were given. Presumably, the verbal warning signals activated the left hemisphere, causing a reduction in reaction time.

Bruce and Kinsbourne (1974) also tested this model by activating the left hemisphere with a secondary task of holding a list of words in memory. The primary task involved the recognition of complex visual forms. Without a memory load, subjects recognized slightly more forms in the left visual field. However, recognition accuracy was significantly better in left hemisphere trials than in right hemisphere trials when subjects had to hold a verbal memory load. Presumably, the activity of holding verbal material in memory activated the left hemisphere to produce better recognition accuracy for left hemisphere trials.

Hellige and Cox (1976) studied the effects of verbal memory loads on the recognition of complex visuospatial stimuli by left and right hemispheres. The memory loads consisted of two, four, and six nouns; the complex forms were 12-point and 16-point polygons. They conclude from their study that factors of "cerebral hemisphere specialization, stimulus codability, selective perceptual orientation and selective cerebral hemisphere interference interact in systematic ways to produce overall laterality effects [p. 216]." Klein, Moscovitch, and Vigna (1976) summarized their findings in a similar way. Specifically, Hellige and Cox found that a relatively easy verbal memory load of two or four nouns improved recognition accuracy on right visual field trials. This lends support to Kinsbourne's perceptual orientation theory which implies that the storing of verbal material activates the left hemisphere which biases attention toward the right visual field. However, when the verbal memory task was more difficult (involving six nouns) the recognition accuracy dropped below the levels found with storing two or four nouns. The authors speculate that more difficult experimental tasks overload the capacity of the left hemisphere and interfere with the processing of the visual stimuli from the right visual field. They point out that the effect of the verbal memory loads is similar to the effect of the subjects' spontaneous activity in experimental conditions. Without careful experimental control of the conditions, spontaneous activities may load verbal memory and thus confound experimental results.

Kinsbourne's model and the evidence purportedly supporting it requires further analysis. The position states that hemispheric activation is a factor which determines laterality effects. Therefore, when stimuli are presented in the visual field contralateral to the more activated hemisphere, performance will be more accurate and faster. The model seems to suggest that if one hemisphere is activated, that hemisphere will dominate processing and responding. To test this hypothesis, different stimulus material should be presented to both hemispheres under conditions of balanced activation and unbalanced activation (one hemisphere has been primed). According to this model, activation of a hemisphere will cause it to dominate, regardless of the nature of the stimulus material. For example, when verbal material is presented and the right hemisphere activated, it will dominate processing and responding. However, the studies conducted within the context of this model have studied only the effects of activation on only one hemisphere's performance on given tasks. The empirical data suggests only that responses are more accurate and faster in the activated hemisphere as compared with performance when it isn't activated, not that the hemisphere will dominate processing. One could argue that by increasing the proficiency of a hemisphere's functioning through selective activation, its competency is increased, hence increasing the probability of its assuming control of processing and responding. The question then to be resolved is whether or not that increased proficiency will be sufficient to overcome the distinct advantage of hemispheric specialization (i.e., whether or not a primed right hemisphere will ever be more proficient in the analytic or verbal processing than the left hemisphere so it can assume control of processing).

In summary, Kinsbourne's model could be interpreted to suggest that activation will determine dominance by either causing the activated hemisphere to assume processing and responding regardless of specialization, or resulting in increased proficiency of the activated hemisphere, which will allow it to assume control. In either case, the possibility is raised that response dispositions produced by prior hemispheric activity can determine hemispheric functioning.

Other explanations of hemisphere dominance are based on response dispositions developed through past experiences. Gazzaniga (1971) suggests that whatever hemisphere is more successful at reinforcement will be dominant. Evidence for the hypothesis that the hemisphere that is most successful at obtaining reinforcements will dominate comes from experiments with split-brain monkeys (Gazzaniga, 1971). Each hemisphere of the split-brain monkeys was taught a different visual discrimination task and was differentially rewarded. The dominance proved to be flexible and dependent on the effects of reinforcement: The hemisphere that had proven itself successful in earning reinforcement became dominant. Galin (1974) suggests that this may be a factor determining dominance in intact human beings as well. The left hemisphere's general dominance is reflective of the success of its verbal capacities in successful manipulation of the environment, whereas a spatial gestalt sort of processing, although necessary in early life, is of secondary importance in the social interpersonal actions that dominate later life. Galin (1974) goes further in suggesting that, since the hemispheres process sensory input in differing ways, they may lead to divergent interpretations of reality, which he describes as the development of two separate systems of consciousness. Each system's tendency toward action may be oppositional. An approach tendency may be favored by one and an avoidance tendency favored by the other. The LH, possibly due to its past success in attaining reinforcements, may win control most of the time. While it may not effectively turn off processing in the RH, it may "settle for disconnecting the transfer of the conflicting information from the other side [p. 576]." As a result, the dominant hemisphere would be acting as if it were disconnected from the other. The point of interest to our discussion is that not only may a specific "consciousness" arise, which may characterize one subject group as compared with another, but the reason for the separation of one information processing approach from another is that of a problem in interhemispheric transfer. We shall suggest a similar conclusion when we analyze literature on hemispheric specialization in schizophrenia.

Possibly the clearest presentation of individual dispositions and hemispheric functioning is that of Levy and Trevarthan (1976), who have proposed the notion of meta-control. They suggest that an expectation of processing requirements determines which hemisphere will be dominant for a particular task. Levy and Trevarthen studied four commissurot-omized patients on a task that required the matching of pictures tachisto-scopically presented. The pictures were halves of black line drawings of common objects, which, when presented in a particular way, are perceived as whole. Patients were given varying instructions to determine whether the stimuli presented to right and left hemispheres were matched in terms of structural appearance or functional/conceptual category. The study was designed to observe how the hemispheres might compete for control under various conditions. Earlier studies (Levy et al., 1972) had indicated the possibility that rather than dominance being determined by speed and competence, dominance may be determined by dispositional lateralization; that is, according to Levy and Trevarthen (1976): "a hemisphere assumes control of processing as a result of set or expectation as to the nature of processing requirements *prior* to actual information processing [p. 300]." Earlier studies revealed that, in free response situations in which either hemisphere may take control, the less competent hemisphere often took control.

In this particular study it was observed that meta-control systems generally tended to activate the hemisphere appropriate to the task. However, it was also observed that meta-control systems sometimes aroused the hemisphere that was not specialized for the task. The activated hemisphere would then operate in a mode inappropriate to the task. Thus, the authors concluded that hemispheric activation depends on expectations about the nature of the problem to be solved, and not upon hemispheric specialization.

It would be expected that if expectations affect hemispheric activity, the particular instructions in an experiment could influence the hemisphere used. Warren, Peltz, and Haueter (1976) presented words differing in arousal, imagery, concreteness and meaningfulness. Subjects were instructed to either "silently construct a sentence using the word" or "to construct a visual image of the object or idea represented by the word." Marked reduction in left hemisphere alpha activity relative to the right hemisphere activity was found under verbal encoding instructions, while under visual image encoding instructions, alpha activity in the two hemispheres was almost symmetrical. One possible inference from this finding is that expectations generated by instructions can affect hemisphere dominance.

In summary, these studies show that response dispositions may be affected by reinforcement history, expectations of processing required, and possibly instructions. Further evidence for individual differences is found in lateral eye movement studies.

Gur, Gur, and Harris (1975) studied the result of having the experimenter behind the subjects. They found that with the experimenter behind the subject, the differential effect of question-type was found with verbal and spatial questions. Solution of arithmetic problems did not elicit consistent responses. However, with experimenter facing the subject, they found that individuals consistently moved their eyes in one direction, regardless of question-type. They speculated that individuals have preferred modes of processing, which come to the fore when the focus shifts from problem solution (experimenter behind the subject) to an anxiety-provoking situation (experimenter facing the subject). Hence, there certainly seem to be situational events that affect hemispheric activity. It is only the next step to the idea that the individual can exert some control over such events and elicit a preferred hemisphere. Certainly the mass market interest in biofeedback devices, which permit hemispheric stimulation, suggest that at least some people believe in such a possibility.

The above explanations of possible hemispheric control do not directly answer the question of pre-existing individual differences in hemispheric preference. The individual difference areas studied most extensively have been those of sex and handedness. The overall result has been that handedness and sex affect hemispheric lateralization [i.e., gender (male) and handedness (right-handed) tend to contribute to greater lateralization].

Three studies using EEG measures have found differences between males and females. Ray, Morell, Frediani, and Tucker (1975), using measures of EEG power, found that males demonstrated desynchrony in certain tasks and females did not. They reported that males showed relatively greater right hemisphere desynchrony during visualization and musical tasks, and greater left hemisphere desynchrony during verbal and mathematical tasks. In contrast, Davidson, Schwartz, Pugash, and Bromfield (1976) reported from their study of bilateral alpha activity that women showed greater significant task-dependent changes in EEG asymmetry and men did not. Women showed greater right-hemisphere activity during emotional versus nonemotional trials. Within the group of right-handed subjects, females exhibited significant asymmetry between whistle and talk conditions. Males showed no such task dependent shifts. In view of the conflicting reports of gender differences, Tucker (1976) designed a study to resolve the question of laterality differences in males and females. He used three different kinds of tasks: a synthetic visuospatial task, an analytic visuospatial task, and vocabulary tests. EEG power measurements were taken over the left and right temporal, parietal and occipital regions. The analysis of results in terms of peak alpha power revealed significantly different performances for females and males on these tasks. Males produced a right-hemisphere specialization for the synthetic visuospatial task. Females, produced a greater desynchrony in EEG readings over the occipital regions for the other two types of tasks. Males also appeared to have greater specialization (left hemisphere) for some verbal processing than females. It was also observed that both hemispheres were used for perceptual analysis in females and in males. In summary, the results of these studies indicate that the nature of the task, gender differences, and site of EEG recordings all affect laterality findings.

Evidence for the effect of handedness is found in two studies using EEG measures. In a recent study, Shaw, O'Connor, and Ongley (1977) used an EEG measure of interhemispheric coherence or synchronicity and power to compare right and left preferent individuals in baseline periods and while performing arithmetic and spatial imagery tasks. A high degree of interhemispheric coherence in EEG activity was found during the baseline rest period. When subjects engaged in spatial imagery, coherence increased for 8 of the 11 right preferent individuals and decreased for 8 of the 11 left preferent individuals. This synchronicity difference was statistically significant, whereas power difference scores did not discriminate between the two groups. Similar results were found with the arithmetic task. Additional effects of handedness are reported in another study which revealed the influence of familial handedness. Davidson et al. (1976) not only found the effect of gender but also of handedness. When EEG asymmetry of right-handed males and females was investigated during self-generated cognitive and affective tasks, significant asymmetries were found only with the subjects with no familial left-handedness.

The effect of gender and handedness has also been found in a study using tachistoscopic hemifield presentations. Kimura (1969), using unilateral hemifield presentation, found right-hemisphere superiority in a task of spatial localization only for males. This finding of a differing lateralization in females was supported by the findings of McGlone and Davidson (1973). They reported that females were superior on a spatial localization task with right visual hemifield presentation. Hannay and Malone (1976a, b) found that both sex and familial handedness affected cerebral asymmetry of functions. In recognition tasks of nonsense words presented unilaterally and vertically, familial right-handed males exhibited greater right visual field superiority than familial right-handed females. In addition, no visual field effects were found for the nonfamilial, right-handed females, indicating an even lesser degree of lateralization. Bryden (1965), using both a dichotic listening test and a tachistoscopic recognition test, found right-handers significantly more accurate with material presented to the right side, in contrast to left-handers, who failed to exhibit right–left differences. Sherman, Kalhavy, and Burns (1976) reported similar results on the effect of handedness. In tasks of recall of abstract and concrete nouns using right- and left-handed subjects, only right-handed subjects showed a significant superiority in the recall of highly concrete words.

The evidence from EEG and tachistoscopic hemifield studies indicate that handedness and gender affect laterality. Left-handed and female subjects appear to display a different pattern of lateralization, and perhaps, less lateralization than right-handed males. This is further supported by the finding that, while dextrals and sinistrals have nearly identical verbal IQs, the performance IQ for dextrals is higher than for sinistrals (Levy, 1969). According to the Levy-Sperry hypothesis of hemispheric specialization (Marshall, 1973), left-handedness may indicate bilateral representation of language skills. The lower performance IQ of sinistrals suggests that the development of language capacity in the right hemisphere is accomplished to the detriment of visuospatial processing. In summary, these studies indicate that hemisphere research, which neglects handedness and sex, ignores variables that affect laterality.

Hemisphere studies using lateral eye movements have not focused on the effect of these two variables. However, Gur et al. (1975) report that left-handers' eye movements are more haphazard when the experimenter is behind the subject, and this tendency is uncorrelated with problem type. They infer from this finding that left-handers are probably less lateralized.

In summary, studies using tachistoscopic hemifield presentations, EEG measures, and lateral eye movements report the effect of individual difference variables on hemispheric processing. Evidence suggests that females and left-handers are less lateralized than males and right-handers. Hence, task demands have smaller laterality effects for such individuals. Furthermore, results which reflect sex differences in functioning need to be carefully analyzed in terms of the specific nature of the tasks required. The general distinction of spatial versus verbal stimuli may obscure the subtle differences which can be found. Tucker's study also reveals the need for specific regional EEG readings, which, if neglected, will result in a crucial loss of information about regional processing.

Finally there has been some work which has examined personality differences in relation to hemispheric activity, mainly measured by preferred eye movement. For example, left movers purportedly are more emotional (Day, 1968); are more "inner directed" (Bakan, 1971; Day, 1967; Gur & Reyher, 1973); have higher hypnotic susceptibility (Bakan, 1969; Gur & Gur, 1974); and have more right EEG alpha. Gur and Gur (1975) reported that left movers score higher on the use of the defense mechanisms of repression and denial, whereas right movers report more psychosomatic symptoms, and score higher on use of projection and "turning against others."

In conclusion, evidence suggests that sex, handedness, or personality affect laterality findings. The last dimension is of special interest as we attempt to designate paranoid and schizophrenic preferences.

SCHIZOPHRENIA AND
HEMISPHERIC FUNCTIONING

Research on the hemispheric functioning in schizophrenia is meager. Applying the methodology of hemispheric work to the area of schizophrenia has just begun. The research question is whether or not the schizophrenic and the paranoid maintain a preferred hemisphere, which is not appropriate to some tasks but is appropriate to others, hence, explaining the differential performance of both groups relative to each other and normals. Empirical findings suggest that rather than a preferred hemisphere or a structural deficiency in one hemisphere, a problem with the interconnections between hemispheres best explains the research to date.

This distinction is crucial for our position, since we postulated that dominance is a function of lack of integration of the two hemispheres. Hemispheric research methodology may provide one of the only possible means to test for interhemispheric relationships. Hence, we closely examine such work as we review the literature in hemispheric dominance in schizophrenics.

Translating the specific deficits of the paranoid and nonparanoid into terms used in this area, we would predict that the paranoid is deficient in the right-hemisphere gestalt/visuospatial processing and the nonparanoid in the left-hemisphere analytic/verbal processing. The paranoid's conceptual ability (LH) and the nonparanoid's perceptual ability (RH) results in LH dominance for paranoids and RH dominance for nonparanoids. Furthermore, an integrative deficit is hypothesized to result from either interhemispheric disconnection, which prevents integration, or the respective deficits create a weakening of the integrative process. The studies discussed in the following pages are the only studies we have been able to uncover which focus on hemispheric functioning in schizophrenia. While analysis of these studies reveals some support for the hypothesized deficits in the schizophrenic subgroups, the failure to distinguish between the subgroups obscures the observation of specific deficits. In discussing these studies we focus on whether or not there is a particular hemispheric dysfunction, and, if there is, whether or not it is due to a problem in interhemispheric transfer. We predict that certain groups utilize one hemisphere more than the other. The question remains, however, if the hemisphere is dominant in certain groups because of some characteristics of itself, or because the group cannot transfer material to the more appropriate hemisphere. We first consider the evidence for hemispheric dysfunction.

Specific Hemisphere Dysfunction

Research in schizophrenia lends support to the view that hemispheric dysfunction occurs. Flor-Henry (1973) has conducted extensive reviews of studies that support his conclusion that schizophrenia involves a temporal-limbic dysfunction in the dominant hemisphere. The evidence cited to support his conclusion include findings that schizophrenic-like psychoses are associated with organic disorders, that schizophrenic psychoses are associated with temporal lobe epilepsy, and findings from studies of erceptual abilities and laterality in schizophrenics. Flor-Henry (1976) also finds support for his conclusion in studies of laterality, where he concluded that similar laws govern LH speech specialization, dextrality, mixed laterality and dysphasia, on the one hand, and lateral preference, dextrality–sinistrality, concordance for, and severity of schizophrenia, on the other. Similarly, other studies have revealed a higher percentage of cross-dominance in schizophrenics. Gur (1977) compared the frequency of handedness, eye dominance and visual acuity in normals and schizophrenics and found that schizophrenics exhibited more left-sidedness than normals. Such laterality differences, as well as the organic pathologies found in the left-hemisphere areas of psychotic patients, and temporal lobe epilepsy found in the left hemisphere, suggest that patients exhibiting schizophrenic symtomatology suffer from neural disorganization and increased deficiency (Flor-Henry, 1976).

Gruzelier and Hammond (1976) also infer from their studies of chronic schizophrenics that schizophrenia is a dominant hemisphere temporal-limbic disorder. To support their hypothesis, they cite evidence from their studies of bilateral asymmetries in absolute auditory thresholds and electrodermal orienting responses. Whereas normals do not display bilateral asymmetries in thresholds, schizophrenics exhibit a propensity toward weaker left- than right-hemisphere function. Similarly, skin-conductance orienting responses indicate an asymmetry with reduced sensitivity in the left hemisphere. Other evidence of left temporal lobe pathology is provided by Bazhin, Wasserman, and Tonkonogii (1975). In their study of tone thresholds, the right ear exhibited higher thresholds, and this was greater for patients with a greater severity of verbal hallucinations. Beaumont and Dimond (1973) also found impaired performances in the left hemisphere of schizophrenics in that they were worse at matching letters than normal controls.

However, one recent split-field study focusing on processing in each hemisphere has not confirmed the hypothesized left-hemisphere dysfunction. Clooney and Murray (1977) required paranoid and nonparanoid schizophrenics to make same–different judgments to tachistoscopically presented clusters of letters. Analyses of reaction times provided no evidence that patient groups performed differently when stimuli were presented to the right or left hemisphere. This study was marred by procedural problems. Exposure time was too long for single hemisphere examination, and using solely letters would tend to bias functioning toward the left hemisphere. Hence, this procedure would have made it difficult for hemispheric asymmetries to emerge even if they were present.

A recent study by Gur (1978) used the split-field technique in a task that required the recognition of syllables and the location of dots. Schizophrenics showed the same visual field effect as controls, but performed worse than controls when the dot location task was presented to either hemisphere. The syllable test found that schizophrenics were superior in the right hemisphere as compared to the left, while the normals exhibited the exact opposite effect, being more accurate in the left hemisphere than the right. Gur (1978) interpreted these results to indicate a left-hemisphere dysfuntion for schizophrenics. Considering that schizophrenics did much worse than controls over both right and left hemisphere on the dot location tests, and that, on the syllable task, the schizophrenics not only did better on right-hemisphere processing than left and almost better than normals, it could be interpreted that the schizophrenic shows a right-hemisphere superiority rather than a left-hemisphere deficit. This result would certainly support a hypothesis of right-hemisphere superiority for schizophrenics, except that paranoids and schizophrenics were combined because they did not differ from one another. Another problem with the subject population was that the schizophrenics were mainly chronic.

The study in our laboratory (Pic'l, Magaro, & Wade, 1979), discussed in the information-processing chapter, also tested for hemisphere dysfunction with tachistoscopically presented stimuli. It was found that letter identification was performed significantly better in the left hemisphere than the right, but this occurred for all groups including schizophrenics. Dot enumeration also produced a hemisphere effect for normals, psychiatric controls, and paranoids, who performed better with right-field presentation than left, as expected. However, schizophrenics performed equally poorly in both hemispheres and significantly worse than all other groups. However, while Gur (1978) found the same hemisphere effect in both groups, the present study found all groups but schizophrenics to exhibit the hemisphere effect.

Only a focus on the task demands themselves, the Sa we spoke about in the first chapter, can clarify the apparent disagreement of the Gur (1978) results and ours. On the verbal task, Gur scored as a correct response the report of the whole syllable rather than a report of individual letters, which was different from tasks used in our and other studies. According to Gur's explanation, the schizophrenic subjects used both the right and left hemispheres to process the syllables when stimuli were presented to the right hemisphere. Since only the left hemisphere is capable of phonetic analysis and the syllable task was best performed by the schizophrenics when stimuli were presented to the right hemisphere, Gur inferred a left-hemisphere dysfunction in schizophrenics. She concluded that the left-hemisphere dysfunction is at the initial stages of phonetic analysis. Unexplained is how the left hemisphere can process the syllables at all when receiving the stimuli from the right hemisphere, if there is a left hemisphere deficit in the initial stages of phonetic analysis. As Gur states, no phonetic analysis is possible in the right hemisphere, so whatever occurs in the left hemisphere after transfer from the right hemisphere must include "initial stages" of phonetic analysis. Yet Gur states that the left hemisphere is deficient in these stages of phonetic analysis. Hence, the same group difference that was found with left-hemisphere presentation should also have been found with right-hemisphere presentation, or even more so, because only the left hemisphere can process this task, according to Gur, even when presented to the right hemisphere. She did not find the right hemisphere deficient. Therefore, either her interpretation of the processing demands of the task is incorrect, or schizophrenics can process syllables in the right hemisphere.

Hemisphere Functioning and Information Processing

To further explain the split-field results, we should consider the information processing demands required by the task. We have suggested that with right-hemisphere presentation, the initial holistic processing of the right hemisphere (e.g., Nebes, 1974; Patterson & Bradshaw, 1975) allows the complete retention of the icon. The right hemisphere "maintains" the icon, while the left hemisphere performs the phonetic analysis. In contrast with right-hemisphere presentation, the left hemisphere's typical approach would result in detail-by-detail processing (e.g., Levy et al., 1972; Patterson & Bradshaw, 1975), i.e., processing single letters.

The discussion of controlled and automatic processing presented above is relevant to this issue. Controlled serial processing as compared with automatic processing is capacity-limited; hence with an increase of information load, there is an increase in errors or reaction time. In contrast, automatic processing does not stress the capacity limits of the system, and there is no increase in errors or reaction time with an increase in load. In regard to hemispheric function, past work reviewed suggests that each hemisphere is dominant in specific stages of information processing. The functions of the right and left hemispheres in terms of automatic/gestalt/preattentive processing and controlled/analytic/focal processing respectively are supported by hemisphere studies (e.g., Levy et al., 1972; Nebes, 1974; Patterson & Bradshaw, 1975). For example, studies of brain-damaged patients (Hecaen & Angelergues, 1962) indicate that patients with right posterior cerebral lesions behave as though preattentive structuring had not occurred. Thus, preattentive processing may be a function of the right hemisphere. Similarly, patients with intact right hemispheres and lesions in the left hemispheres drew pictures without detail, having a good gestalt (Warrington, James, & Kinsbourne, 1966), indicating that focal or controlled processing may be a function of the left hemisphere.

The increasing errors with increases in dot-display size for all but the nonparanoid group suggests that controlled or left-hemisphere processing was used by all but the nonparanoid group, who used automatic or right-hemisphere processing. The proficiency of left-hemisphere processing was most apparent at the smaller frame sizes, where serial processing is most accurate and where differences between groups (nonparanoid versus the other three) are most evident.

The results produced by the dot enumeration task also allow an interpretation of the schizophrenic deficit in terms of bilateral processing. All but the nonparanoid group tended to do better with right-hemisphere presentation. This suggests that on the dot task, selected for its right hemisphere bias, all but the nonparanoid group used serial processing by the left hemisphere, which was most proficient when supplemented and enhanced by an initial gestalt processing by the right hemisphere. Nonparanoids did not utilize the more proficient serial pocessing. With right-hemisphere presentation, nonparanoids used their preferred mode (automatic processing), did not utilize the appropriate serial processing of the left hemisphere, and hence performed poorly. Thus, the significantly poorer dot performance by the nonparanoids with left-hemisphere presentation reflects either an inappropriate processing strategy (Levy & Trevarthen, 1976) or transfer difficulties which resulted in a lack of integration of processes.

A similar analysis could be applied in explaining the results of the syllable test used by Gur (1978). The syllable test is comparable to the dot enumeration task in requiring bilateral processing. When the stimuli were presented to the right hemisphere, schizophrenics did not differ from normals because the holistic processing of the right hemisphere retained the full icon. However, with left-hemisphere presentation, controlled processing used by the schizophrenics may have been too slow, not allowing completion of the processing before the icon faded. Since phonetic analysis, according to Gur, could only be accomplished in the left hemisphere, with right-hemisphere presentation, schizophrenics apparently transferred the information to the left hemisphere to produce performance comparable to those of normals. However, in dot-enumeration, left-hemisphere processing, while preferable, was not necessary. Hence, the schizophrenics did not tranfer and process bilaterally, and consequently performed more poorly than groups that used bilateral processing.

We have explained these hemisphere results in terms of the type of information processing used by schizophrenics as compared to paranoids. A serial processing strategy is used by normals, paranoids, and psychiatric controls, and this process is mainly confined to the left hemisphere. Schizophrenics used automatic processing and performed poorly in both hemispheres, possibly indicating that all material is performed in the right hemisphere. Hence, even though paranoids, psychiatric controls, and normals use a serial approach to count the briefly presented dots and do this best with left visual field presentation, the schizophrenics make estimates of the total iconic image, and this occurs in both hemispheres. Since it may be that such a visual approach is more common to the right hemisphere, the results may be interpreted as indicating that the schizophrenic transfers all material to the right because the left is not preferred or is not as functional.

Another study also did not find a hemispheric dysfunction, but did find evidence of differential processing strategies with schizophrenics and paranoids, which could indicate the use of a preferred hemisphere. In this case it is the paranoids who again show the preference for processing in the left hemisphere. Young (1974) presented matching tasks for two possible types of consonant pairs; physically similar letters or letters without a physical similarity but with the same name. Letters were presented both unilaterally and bilaterally to three groups consisting of schizophrenics, paranoids, and nonpsychotic controls. The two dependent measures were the number of correct responses and the latency of a manual classificatory response. There were no differences between groups on either measure. In all groups, the letters with the same name but not physically similar were processed significantly more rapidly when presented to the left hemisphere than when presented to the right hemisphere. There were no hemispheric differences for matches that were physically similar. However, paranoids were more accurate on physical matches than other groups, which was due to a strategy to treat physical matches as though they were name matches. That is (Young, 1974), they took longer to process the physical stimuli by assigning them names and then processing them:

> The superior accuracy of paranoids on physical matches might therefore represent suspicion of the "tricky" physical trials, and the adoption of a verbal-conceptual processing strategy which minimizes the possibility of spatial-configural confusion. Such a strategy is, of course, consistent with the notion that acute paranoids are attempting to reassert left hemisphere control in an effort to bring the "unruly" right hemisphere under its dominance [p. 59].

This would have been expected to be the processing strategy employed by paranoids. However, the results were mainly trends. A problem with this study was that the visual stimuli was exposed for 220 msec., which is of sufficient duration to permit enough eye movement to sample material presented in the opposite visual half-field. Also, the paranoid–schizophrenic distinction was not extended beyond the level of the patient's incoming diagnosis, which we have noted to be notably lacking in reliability. The results suggest, however, that hemispheric preference exists in paranoia as well as schizophrenia.

The next study provides data that requires detailed analysis. Alpert, Rubinstein, and Kesselman (1976) used a shadowing task to observe differential hemispheric functioning in hallucinating schizophrenics. Verbal stimuli consisting of semantically well-integrated sentences and poorly integrated sentences were presented monaurally to the right and left ear, while a masking noise was presented binaurally. As expected from other findings on the competence of each hemisphere, normals better recalled the more semantically well-integrated sentences than the poorly integrated sentences and only in the left hemisphere. The right hemisphere did not show this distinction. Both sentences were recalled equally poorly as would be expected if linguistic properties are not a function of that hemisphere. In contrast to normals, the nonhallucinators distinguished between sentences in the right hemisphere and not in the left. This suggests that the nonhallucinatory schizophrenic is utilizing the right hemisphere to recall events and is facilitated by the semantic properties in the normally nonpreferred hemisphere.

The other significant finding involved the interesting group × ear × sentence type interaction. The nonhallucinators were mainly responsible for the differential effect. They did more poorly than both other groups on well-integrated sentences, poorly integrated sentences, right ear presentation, and left ear presentation. They did not recall material when well-integrated material was presented to the left hemisphere nor when poorly integrated material was presented to the right hemispere. They only did as well as normals when the poorly integrated material was presented to the left hemisphere, and the well-integrated material was presented to the right hemisphere. That is, they do the same as normals in the condition in which the hemisphere is required to process information that is not suited for that hemisphere. When the material matches the appropriate competent hemisphere, normals do well and the nonhallucinators do poorly. Since they differentiated sentences in the right rather than the left hemisphere, they apparently use the right hemisphere as the normals use the left. Also, while normals process well- and poorly integrated material equally poorly in the right hemisphere, nonhallucinators perform in a similar manner in the left. The most parsimonious conclusion is that left and right hemisphere processes are reversed in nonhallucinators.

An important aspect of the measurement procedure must be noted. The significant results only emerged when recall of the complete five element sentence was measured. Differences began to emerge at the end of sentences when the object or verb-object phrase was examined, and significance was only found when all such elements were combined to produce the larger number of observations. The recall of the end of the sentences differentiated groups. Also, Alpert et al. (1976) noted that "the nonhallucinators perform the recall task at a phonetic or single word level rather than utilizing retrieval strategies involving sentence-level meaning units [pp. 262–263]."

Our previous discussion of information processing tendencies for paranoids and schizophrenics indicated paranoids engage in a controlled processing strategy and, hence, create errors at the end of a message that is serially processed rather than "chunked" into a whole sentence. According to this analysis, the nonhallucinators seem to be the paranoids. This inference is supported by the previous work by Alpert (Mintz & Alpert, 1972), which used a similar task and found that nonhallucinators differed from hallucinators in an unwillingness to guess in a shadowing tasks. This response characteristic was found with paranoids in other studies. From the definition of the two groups, it is also likely that the hallucinators would be schizophrenics because they exhibit a schizophrenic item (the hallucination) on a schizophrenic–paranoid scale. Therefore, it appears tenable that the nonhallucinators were paranoids who engaged in serially processing information, hence, making more errors at the end of a series.

Although they use serial processing to be certain of the data, such careful encoding creates difficulties at the end of a series when time limits the length of the ichoic trace. The other groups attempted the automatic global process and derived the meaning from the total sentence, hence, not making the end of series errors as did the paranoids. In this study, the paranoid's quest for certainty led to a deficit while the schizophrenic's grasp of the whole led to a normal performance level.

This interpretation does not explain why the paranoid was more discriminative in the right hemisphere, for it is there that he distinguished between sentence structures. However, both sentence types required left hemisphere processing. As noted by the author, even the poorly integrated sentences were rich in organizational cues. A conclusion that might be drawn is that material presented to the right hemisphere was quickly transferred to the left, and this was done in a holistic fashion that did not permit serial processing. The paranoids, in effect, would be forced into chunking, at which time their recall level is comparable to normals. In effect transferring from the right hemisphere required the switching of a recall strategy away from the controlled processing of a more holistic automatic processing, which permitted more recall of the end of the sentences and hence a more normal performance.

In other words, words encoded in the right hemisphere have to be transferred to the left to create a sentence. Normals do this quite readily as the two processes are well integrated. Hence, their performance with poor- or well-integrated sentences do not differentially affect the transfer, and the meaning in each is derived to the same degree after transfer to the left hemisphere. The nonhallucinator—the paranoid—when transferring from the right to the left, cannot serially process and must transfer in total. Hence, like the normal, he finds benefits in the well-integrated or chunked message. Such an interpretation is quite speculative, and there is too little work comparing schizophrenics and paranoids to support any interpretation of such results.

In general, the results reported in the literature are conflicting. Some work suggests a left-hemisphere preference but the split-field studies are conflicting. There does seem to be differences in processing strategies between schizophrenics and paranoids, and this may be more relevant than structural deficiencies. A processing strategy may be located in a particular hemisphere and, hence, there may be more of a preference to function more in one hemisphere than the other. The schizophrenic may appear to be more oriented toward the right hemisphere and the paranoid toward the left, but this may not imply a structural deficiency in the nonpreferred hemisphere. There is no work we have been able to find that distinguishes between preference and dysfunction in the hemispheric functioning of schizophrenics and paranoids.

Some evidence for hemispheric preferences in schizophrenics and paranoids is provided by a study using lateral eye movements. A recent study in our lab (DeSisto, Rice, & Magaro, 1977) examined eye movements under the conditions of experimenter in front and in back and using both verbal and spatial questions. The groups were schizophrenics, paranoids, and psychiatric controls. The paranoid would be hypothesized to be a right-mover, and the nonparanoid, a left-mover. It was found that question type was not important and that the experimenter-behind condition increased eye movements. Most important, paranoids exhibited significantly more right eye movements and schizophrenics more left eye movements regardless of question type. That is, schizophrenics showed a preference for the right hemisphere and paranoids for the left. The greater the opportunity to exhibit eye movement (i.e., with the experimenter behind), the greater the preference effect. Hence, in a study comparing schizophrenics and paranoids using lateral eye movements, there is a clear differential effect.

A recent study studied eye movements using mainly schizophrenics. Schweitzer, Becker, and Welsh (1978) examined eye movements to the presentation of verbal nonemotional, verbal emotional, spatial nonemotional, and spatial emotional questions. They found that schizophrenics produced more right lateral eye movements on the spatial emotional, verbal emotional, and verbal nonemotional questions than normal controls. The spatial emotional questions were in the same direction but did not reach significance in the comparison of groups. As in the DeSisto et al. (1977) study, question type did not demonstrate a significant effect. What was different, however, was that schizophrenics in this study made more right eye movements, suggesting left-hemisphere activation, rather than left eye movements as found by DeSisto et al. (1977). Curiously, there is no analysis in the Schweitzer et al. (1978) study of the number of left eye movements nor the number of stare responses. The authors interpret their findings in terms of the schizophrenic activating the left hemisphere more than a normal control group. It should be noted that, prior to the questions elicited by the experimenter in front, subjects were asked to think about the questions and answers that may have primed the use of the left hemisphere. However, this does not necessarily explain why the schizophrenic activated the left hemisphere more than the right.

Gur (1978) also reported on a lateral eye movement study using chronic schizophrenics and paranoids. She found that schizophrenics and paranoids both made more right lateral eye movements than normal controls.

Interestingly, even though the effect did not reach significance, the greatest amount of right eye movements were made by paranoids, followed by schizophrenics and lastly by normals. Gur (1978) concludes that the disposition to produce right eye movements activates the left hemisphere, which is most dysfunctional. It is recommended that therapy follow a course of encouraging a shift toward use of the right hemisphere.

What can be concluded from these three studies on lateral eye movement? Both Gur (1978) and DeSisto et al. (1977) would agree that the paranoid activates the left hemisphere. The Gur (1978) results show that the schizophrenic also follows the same pattern, while DeSisto et al. (1977) finds that schizophrenics are more left movers. Schweitzer et al. (1978) supports Gur (1978) by also finding that schizophrenics are right movers. Both Gur (1978) and Schweitzer et al. (1978) used chronic patients and no psychiatric controls. DeSisto et al. (1977) used psychiatric controls and acute patients to produce their results. It will probably be only with the greater specification of subject groups that lateral eye movement tendencies in schizophrenics and paranoids will be clarified.

In summary, the work focusing on the functioning of each hemisphere suggests that schizophrenics and paranoids do have a preference, and this preference may be determined by the type of processing inherent in each hemisphere. The question of structural deficiencies is open, and it is expected that much of the coming work will focus upon this issue. However, besides the question of a structural deficiency or preference for a hemisphere function, there is also the more difficult question of the relationship between the hemispheres. We have proposed that the underlying cause of the dominance of a hemisphere or a particular type of processing is due to a lack of integration between the two processes conceptualized in terms of hemisphere functions or stages of information processing.

Interhemisphere Transfer

We now discuss more directly the possibility that the less competent hemisphere is used because transcallosal transfer is not adequate. At this point, the neurological analogue is the corpus callosum, which creates the relationship between the hemispheres. The two functions of the corpus callosum are to integrate bisymmetric control systems to produce an adaptive orientation of the whole organism and behavioral unity, which synchronizes the timing of motor behavior and balances opposing tendencies. Callosal section therefore would release alternate responses to a particular situation from the superordinate decision processes that creates behavioral unity (Kinsbourne, 1974a). To create such unity, the corpus callosum must transmit excitatory and inhibitory messages across the hemispheres in order to combine information from the two hemispheres, which creates the synthesis of function. Thus, in studies of perception, the corpus callosum is part of the mechanism by which perceptual capacity is distributed in the whole perceptual field so that the creating of a percept depends upon integrative processes of subcortical and cortical activity (Trevarthen, 1974). In effect, the association cortex is expressed as a symmetry, a bilateral "whole" organism, which is assured by the commissures, the neurological substate of integrated behavior.

To bring the function of the corpus callosum into the information processing model, we again rely upon Kinsbourne (1974b) who clearly relates RH function to preattentive processing and LH function to focal attention, as discussed in Chapter 6. Just as both information processes are required to form a percept, so both hemispheres require integration. He notes that patients with right hemisphere lesions do not perform preattentive structuring. Their focal attention seems to wander across the stimulus field or focus on a dominant stimulus element (Kinsbourne, 1974b, c). The two hemispheres are required to control attention by establishing an appropriate balance and by guiding the focus of preattentive structuring and the consequent focusing of elements. The point is that it is the function of the corpus callosum to establish the balance between the two information processing functions to create the required synthesis. We would, therefore, predict that the dominance of a hemisphere for paranoids and schizophrenics is due to an inability to transmit information across hemispheres adequately. Hence, they are both left with a reliance upon one hemisphere to the detriment of their performance.

Some studies provide support for the hypothesis of transcallosal difficulties in schizophrenia. Flor-Henry (1973) revealed that right/left energy shifts in different cognitive tasks, and the abnormal time course deviations of these ratios suggested a sluggishness in the psychotic. This finding led him to hypothesize that psychosis was a defect of interhemispheric integration. Rosenthal and Bigelow (1972) report that the only significant differences found in comparing the brains of schizophrenics and those of a matched group was the thickness of the corpus callosum. That of the schizophrenic group was an average of 18% thicker. If increased interhemispheric communication is interpreted as leading to inadequate integration because of an overload of the system, then the increased size of the corpus callosum is taken as a defect of interhemispheric integration.

Beaumont and Dimond (1973) designed a study to test for interhemispheric transfer in schizophrenics. The tasks included identification of letters and digits and matching of letters and digits with three groups—schizophrenics, psychiatric controls, and a normal nonpsychiatric patient group. In crossmatching of two pieces of information flashed simultaneously at 150 msec. to the two hemispheres, schizophrenics, as compared to psychiatric controls and normals, were significantly worse in matching letters and shapes.

Also, they were worse than normals in left-hemisphere matching of letters and worse than psychiatric controls in right-hemisphere matching of digits and shapes (normals occupied an intermediate position). The schizophrenic group's performance in matching was worse when stimuli were presented across hemispheres rather than matching stimuli to the same hemisphere. In fact, schizophrenics tended to do better than normals when simple identification was required rather than matching. The interpretation was that schizophrenics suffered from "partial brain disconnection." The decrement was in the ability to cross-match between the hemispheres, which was considered related to enlargement of the corpus callosum (Rosenthal & Bigelow, 1972). Unfortunately, the study did not distinguish between schizophrenic subgroups. Hence, the results are not informative about the specific patterns of paranoids and schizophrenics. What could be concluded, however, is that schizophrenics exhibit a deficit in integration of material across hemispheres.

Blau (1977) has recently reviewed the current evidence and presented some data that indicates that the schizophrenic could be characterized by problems in transcallosal transfer. Using a measure of the direction of circle drawing, Blau hypothesizes that the common hereditary link in schizophrenia may involve a defect in the corpus callosum: "The etiology of clinical schizophrenia may arise out of the effects of the neural integrative deficiency. These effects may prevent sufficient and/or appropriate language, cognition, and skill acquisition and socialization during the crucial developmental years [p. 1003]." His measure of circle drawing, called torque, is further hypothesized to reflect a corpus callosum deficit and is used as a measure of vulnerability toward schizophrenia. Blau recognizes the speculative nature of his inferences but is intrigued as we are with the possibilities for further research. The problem, of course, is that the integration process, whether it is localized in the corpus callosum or asserted as a higher order theoretical term, is difficult to study directly. Researchers tend to use the term in an ad hoc fashion after finding that there are not clear dominance effects.

Before concluding this section, one aspect of the Levy and Trevarthen (1976) study should be mentioned in order to suggest the exciting implications of hemispheric functioning and schizophrenia. They demonstrated the possibility of retraining to correct for inappropriate hemispheric dominance. One patient's demonstrated difficulty in getting right-hemisphere control of processing was overcome by instructions to use the contralateral hand. Left-hand pointing was effective in releasing the RH. Further testing revealed that this control was retained in subsequent trials requiring right-hand pointing. This result can be used as a model for and evidence for the possibility of retraining schizophrenics and paranoids to correct for improper hemispheric dominance. We offer such a possibility in the presentation of therapy methods in the last chapter. There also is data indicating that drug treatment may produce beneficial effects by affecting asymmetries. Gruzelier and Hammond (1976) and Hammond and Gruzelier (1978) found that chlorpromazine normalized hemisphere asymmetry in auditory performances of schizophrenics, and the increased symmetry was due to an improvement of left-hemisphere performance relative to right. However, these results were derived only from chronic patients. Serafetinides (1972) found that, with chlorpromazine treatment and improvement, EEG voltage increased on the left side. Itil (1977) has also confirmed the effect of chlorpromazine.

In the present chapter, we have argued that the paranoid and schizophrenic processes described in previous chapters may have a base in hemispheric functions or more specifically in the transfer of information between hemispheres. The schizophrenic and the paranoid prefer different hemispheres, but it is not clear whether or not any structural deficiencies exist. The data suggest but do not conclusively indicate transmission problems between hemispheres. But it does seem clear that processing strategies are central to hemispheric function and may in fact be the determining factor. It also seems that both hemispheres are necessary for an appropriate or "normal" performance on most tasks.

An excellent review by Shimkunas (1978) has developed this idea further to explain, what we have considered, V and K theories of the thought disorder. We present a rather long quote from Shimkunas (1978) to adequately describe what we think is an analysis that could readily summarize our own position:

Nevertheless, the present formulation is sufficient to consider the role of hemispheric asymmetry and interaction in schizophrenic thinking. Given the nature of the functions of the cerebral hemispheres, the schizophrenics' cognitive orientation toward similarity generalization appear best described as, primarily a left hemisphere operation. The left brain's focal directionality (Kinsbourne, 1974c) would be consistent with the active nature of cue selection inherent in categorical inclusion and progression through levels of abstraction. Overinclusion may be particularly salient as a left hemisphere activity inasmuch as Cohen (1973) found a distinct left hemisphere advantage for sameness judgments for both verbal and pictorial stimuli. The process of similarity generalization should rapidly seek resolution concerning incoming perceptual data. The processing of these data, however, is a right brain function as previously indicated. Hence it appears necessary to consider both hemispheres as ultimately interacting in the overall process which starts with perception and ends with some cognitive resolution. The verbal nature of the left hemisphere restricts it to conceptualizing largely in terms of words, concepts, names. These are the materials which form the substance of categorical inclusion and abstraction. But left brain focal conceptual processes should act in response to right hemisphere imagery, which forms the substance of its mediation of perceptual data. Images of the objects which have been perceived must be successfully communicated across the corpus callosum to the left hemisphere so that it can transform them into words. These words or names then enter into similarity/generalization continua for structuring and categorization. Preattentive structuring by the right hemisphere orients it toward pictorial/schematic representations of the external environment and cannot, in and of itself, do the verbal conceptual work of the left brain. It can only restructure cues which may not have been adequately conceptualized by the left brain. Thus poorly conceptualized images should be sent back to the right hemisphere for restructuring, followed by a return to the left hemisphere for another attempt at conceptualizing.

With the possible immobilization of the left hemisphere in acute schizophrenics (Gruzelier, 1973; Gruzelier & Venables, 1973, 1974) similarity generalization should be inefficient, resulting in return to the right brain for restructuring. If perceptual processing is still distorted, distorted imagery should be reprocessed to the left brain which can perform no better inasmuch as it is still immobilized by arousal. Repeated reversals between hemispheres may characterize schizophrenics' continued attempts to understand and communicate their perceptions of reality. The deficit observed in schizophrenic corpus callosum functioning (Beaumont & Dimond, 1973; Rosenthal & Bigelow, 1972) may either reflect an inherent defect in the structure or a result of excessive right/left brain approximations. If conceptual problems fail to resolve due to left brain immobilization, increased intercommunication between hemispheres should result. This may lead to a "jamming" of transcallosal fibers contributing to the interhemispheric transfer problems which have been observed (Beaumont & Dimond, 1973) [pp. 55–57].

Gestalt processing comparable to our automatic processing may be a right hemisphere function and as such seems to be preferred by the schizophrenic. Both of these hypotheses have yet to be tested. When we spoke of the formation and use of assemblies, we were referring to the conceptual activity that is deficient in the schizophrenic and is located in the left hemisphere. The encoding of the icon in a free, almost sensory, manner not biased by conceptual categories is the ability of the schizophrenic. That process seems to be centered in the right hemisphere. Previous hemispheric work, which speaks of a "weak left hemisphere" or a "disconnected left hemisphere," would be referring to both the schizophrenic's strength and weakness.

Analytic processing seems to be a dominant characteristic of the paranoid and, as with material requiring such a process, the preference is for the left hemisphere. The paranoid applies fixed assemblies to most perceptual data and in effect constructs information mainly with the overuse of the category. This conceptual biasing performed in a logical analytically controlled form of processing allows a definiteness to what is perceived. However, paradoxically it also distorts because the stimulus itself never receives a full hearing, so to speak. The right hemisphere is not used except to service the dominance of the left. As such, we would expect a weak hemisphere to exist for the paranoid but it would be the opposite of the schizophrenic.

It is intriguing to consider that this is a matter of preference and can be reversed with training. The following chapter offers some methods to produce such modifications in processing information, which could be the way to produce an effective therapy.

9

Treatment of Schizophrenia and Paranoia

INTRODUCTION

We have completed our interpretation of past research and presented our efforts to construct a new explanation of schizophrenic and paranoid task performance. We have consistently insisted on a return to a very specific operationalization of constructs and have offered an information theory strategy to meet previous methodological problems. The last chapter has attempted a "metaneurological" explanation of the behavioral data and, as such, has brought to a close our theoretical and empirical statement on the schizophrenic and paranoid condition. We will now conclude by moving further into theory by offering implications for therapy with schizophrenics and paranoids.

Discussion about therapy usually remains theoretical since it has so little alliance to empirical results and to what therapists do or say they do. In a previous work, we proposed that therapy as practiced reflects more about the culture than about successful treatment of individuals (Magaro, Gripp, & McDowell, 1978). We argued that treatment must move to a testable base. We now present a therapy with a definitive testable procedure. A reader who is not interested in implications but only hard facts would do best to skip this chapter. This chapter is for the reader who would like to follow us in speculating about what could be therapeutically done with the results produced in the laboratory.

One of the reasons we devote ourselves to research in schizophrenia is to discover a more effective treatment for the disorder. We strive to find the cause in order to modify the condition. In this chapter, we use our empirical understanding of schizophrenia and paranoia to propose treatment programs. Consistent with our thesis that the two conditions are not the same, we offer distinctively different treatments, addressing in a practical manner the problem of considering the two groups as separate ones rather than symptomatic variations of one condition. We will confine ourselves to using the perception and conceptualization terms used in the integration chapter to avoid the detail in the definition of terms presented in the information theory chapter. However, it should be kept in mind that perception refers to the encoding stage and conceptualization to the assembly stage. Integration will again be the "act of construction" that involves the combining of both processes. Ford and Urban (1963) state:

> Psychotherapists are frequently asked to proceed beyond the boundaries of verified knowledge about human behavior. The therapist may choose not to try, but if he does try, he may have to make the attempt on some basis other than verified knowledge. The most desirable basis other than verified knowledge to guide his attempts to deal with the new psychotherapeutic problem is a logically interrelated set of hypotheses about behavior—that is, a theory—which can be used as if they were verified [p. 24].

This passage expresses the need to use a theoretical framework in psychotherapy, regardless of the ultimate truth of the particular theory. Theories of psychotherapy serve to order and direct the actions of the therapist by proposing one or more theoretical constructs which are believed to be crucial in the maintenance of abnormality. Any theoretical framework specifies a particular conception of the central psychological processes acting within the individual. The modification of these processes is postulated to change behavior. Thus, therapy may be seen as attempts to modify a theoretical construct, which has been postulated to be the crucial element in the expression of the disorder.

Few therapeutic approaches have utilized or even considered the vast amount of literature that specifies the specific deficit in schizophrenia as found in laboratory tasks. In this chapter, we use our understanding of that literature to formulate a treatment program based on the performance deficit paradigm in general and the integration theory in particular. Our proposal is based on the relationship between the constructs that explain the schizophrenic condition and the performance on laboratory tasks that operationalizes the constructs. The treatment that we propose involves intensive training on laboratory tasks. We argue that improved performance on these tasks reflects a modification of construct, effectively eliminating the deficit. Thus, task improvement would be predicted to produce a general reduction in symptoms or in deviant behavior.

The same approach has been taken in a recent book devoted to the treatment of learning disabilities (Farnham-Diggory, 1978). The approach is to use an information-processing model to attempt the specification of the problem in different learning disabilities such as dyslexia. Hemisphere functioning in children is then examined to understand the processes invovled in reading. The theme is that the child with a learning disability functions as if he has "two right hemispheres and none left." If so, it may be that there is a similarity to schizophrenics and that the treatment for each should not be that different. We will pursue this thought in a moment. First we discuss an experimental treatment model in general.

TREATMENT OF
SPECIFIC COGNITIVE PROCESSES

We offer a therapeutic model which utilizes constructs reliably operationalized in laboratory research in schizophrenia. The general plan is to develop a treatment program designed to reduce the schizophrenic performance deficit on a certain set of tasks. With this performance orientation, it is similar to a behavior modification approach, which is also concerned with overt behavior or the improvement of performance on specified tasks rather than inner dynamics. But there are also two differences between our approach and behavior modification. First, we place a greater emphasis upon the nature of the tasks as they reflect an "inner" psychological process, the theoretical construct. Our choice of tasks is determined by the proposed construct such as perception, conceptualization, or integration. Therefore, although we are not concerned with psychoanalytic dynamics, we would attempt to modify an internal state through the modification of behavior. Second, although reinforcement is used in our treatment program, it is not viewed as the factor that modifes behavior. Reinforcement in our view is a motivational factor that is necessary to provide a sufficient level of drive to ensure performance, but not enough to interfere with what is conceptualized as the crucial element of the treatment—the performance of the tasks themselves.

We limit the scope of our proposed treatment program to acute paranoid and nonparanoid schizophrenics, because chronic schizophrenics apparently owe more of their deficit to the effect of hospitalization rather than the initial schizophrenic condition. We admit the speculative nature of our predictions about the effects of treatment on specific schizophrenic subgroups. The novelty of the approach precludes the applicability of a large body of previous therapeutic efforts. However, there have been similar attempts to utilize an experimental task approach as a treatment procedure.

Wagner (1968) attempted to train schizophrenics to improve their performance on laboratory tasks. A simple matching task using simple figures was utilized to train "attending" behavior, while a matching task using common attributes of stimuli was used to train "abstracting" behavior. Although he did not apply his findings to therapy for schizophrenics, Wagner concluded that reinforced practice not only increased schizophrenic attention and abstraction behavior, but results appeared to generalize to other measures given at a later date. Although the later measures did not reflect a large number of processes, the results indicated that the training tasks did not permit the solving of other tasks.

The only other work which has dealt directly with treatment of schizophrenics from a performance deficit approach is that of Broen and his students (Feeney, 1971; Meiselman, 1973). As previously discussed the Broen theory applied to chronics (Broen & Storms, 1977) is that the schizophrenic exhibits an inability to control a flood of external and internal stimulation that is terrifying and overwhelming. To deal with this flood, the schizophrenic restricts all stimulus input at a more peripheral or sensory level. Specifically, Broen hypothesizes that chronic schizophrenics restrict their monitoring more exclusively to one sensory channel than do acutes or normals. Meiselman (1973) developed a training procedure designed to alleviate the specific deficit of a narrowed range of cue utilization. Chronics were given training in a dual modality reaction time task in which they were required to monitor stimuli in different modalities. They were also given practice on a language master task which required attention to both auditory and visual stimuli. The conditions hypothesized to facilitate performance on these tasks were practice, explicitly stated expectations that performance would increase, and monetary reinforcement. Results indicated that the performance of those trained improved significantly over controls who received no training, but the improvement did not generalize to a different and more difficult task.

These studies demonstrate that it is possible not only to modify the specific performance deficit but also to produce generalization to other tasks. We will propose a greater variety of stimulus properties and training procedures to facilitate such generalization.

We hypothesize that the acute nonparanoid relies almost exclusively on perceptual processes in forming an adaptation to the environment. Cognitions are fleeting and transitory, being continually dissolved or distorted by the force of immediate perception. Described in Piagetian terms, the nonparanoid accommodates almost exclusively. That is, concepts are continuously transformed to fit incoming perceptual data. The nonparanoid deficit is thus seen as an inability to integrate perceptual and conceptual processes, with the compensation being one of an overreliance on perceptual processes to the exclusion of conceptual processes. The assemblies do not have the strength to maintain the conceptual consistency to impose enough order onto the world. In contrast, we describe the paranoid as having rigid conceptual sets that channel all information into schemata having strong associative assemblies. While the nonparanoid prefers accommodation, the paranoid prefers assimilation. That is, perceptions are altered to fit the existing conceptual structures. The paranoid deficit then is seen as a lack of integration between perceptual and conceptual processes, with the compensation being one of subjugation of perceptual to conceptual.

For these subgroups, there appear to be two possibilities. The first involves a strengthening of the already dominant process, similar to the "teaching the strengths" model used in special education. This method advocates teaching a child who cannot learn through visual channels to learn through other senses (such as auditory or tactile). For the paranoid, this would mean training in the use of conceptual processes to further compensate for perceptual inadequacies. The paranoid would be taught to recognize his distortion of perceptual information and a method of decreasing such distortion.

The second approach is that of "remediation." This involves intensive training in deficient areas. The child with a visual handicap would receive intensive visual training. For the paranoid, it would mean training to develop the perceptual process. He would be trained to encode the icon without a categorial set. The nonparanoid would be taught how to strengthen associations within an assembly.

We argue for the second approach. The deficit for the schizophrenic and paranoid is hypothesized to be primarily a lack of integration leading to a compensation of one process over another. In this situation, teaching the strengths would serve to increase the compensations, and reduce the possibility of integration, although it may lead to an easier adaptation. Remediating the less dominant process, on the other hand, would serve to decrease the reliance on compensation and facilitate integration.

While this approach is novel as a treatment for schizophrenia, it is not novel in the treatment of learning disabilities. Therefore, we will compare the needs of the schizophrenic and paranoid to the learning disabled, and briefly review some relevant empirical findings in that area in order to refine our concept of remediating the schizophrenic deficit.

LEARNING DISABILITIES
AND SCHIZOPHRENIA

Children with learning disabilities are described as having normal potential to learn, but disruptions of some sort in brain processing prohibit the realization of this potential (Bryan, 1974). Frequently cited problems include hyperactivity, perceptual-motor impairments, emotional lability, emotional impairment, general coordination deficits, disorders of attention (attention span, distractability, perseveration), impulsivity, disorders of memory and thinking, specific learning disabilities (reading, writing, spelling, arithmetic), disorders of speech and hearing, equivocal neurological signs, and electroencephalographic irregularities (Clements, 1966). But there is a paucity of basic research in this area resulting in knowledge gaps. Many studies that should have been done haven't been done, and replications are almost nonexistent (Bryan, 1974).

Using only data resulting from what are considered adequately controlled research, the following picture emerges: The learning disabled child only exhibits his deficit in a situation that requires integration at the sensory and/or perceptual-conceptual level. Visual and auditory processing mechanisms, which discriminate the learned disabled from comparison samples, are related to stimulus and response complexity, not to perception and discrimination of visual or auditory signals (Bryan, 1974; McReynolds, 1966; Monsees, 1968). Only in studies of cross-modal sensory integration does the learning-disabled child appear less sensitive to external input organization than normal comparison groups. Besides an inability to integrate contrasting sensory material, the learning disabled child's response to his integrational deficit tends to be an excessive reliance upon either perceptual or conceptual styles of organization. For example, nonretarded, learning-disabled children appear to impose insufficient organization on random material. Thus, external organization is nonfunctional (Simpson, King, & Drew, 1970). While normal children fall into groups that integrate along the whole range of possibilities (high conceptual–high perceptual, low conceptual–low conceptual, low conceptual–high perceptual, and high conceptual–low perceptual), learning-disabled children tend to fall into the latter two groups (Kirschner, 1975). Similarly, Levine and Fuller (1972) found, on the basis of 59 psychoneurological, psychological, and educational tests, that poor readers performed as extreme analytic conceptualizers (high conceptual–low perceptual), or without the benefit of analytic concepts (low conceptual–high perceptual).

This description of the two learning-disabled groups is remarkably similar to that of paranoid and nonparanoid schizophrenics offered by Integration Theory. Both the learning disabled and the schizophrenic demonstrate an integrational deficit by responding normally on tasks with little or no integrational demand and more poorly as integrational demand increases. Learning disabled children and schizophrenics demonstrate an inability to make use of external input organization to compensate for the integrational deficit (Preston & Drew, 1974). Moreover, both the learning disabled and the schizophrenic counter the deficit by an over-reliance on one type of organization to the exclusion of the other.

Given the theoretical similarity between the target populations, it is not unreasonable to hope that a treatment that benefits one will also benefit the other. Therefore we will briefly review the theory and practice of remedial instruction with learning disabled children. While there are many theories of psycholinguistic functioning, that presented by Osgood (1957) has had the greatest impact on the field of special education. The Osgood model encompasses two dimensions of language behavior: language processes and levels of organization. The process dimension includes decoding, association, and encoding (Hammill & Larson, 1975). Decoding is the same as our encoding and refers to the perceiving of stimuli (i.e., the recognition of what is seen or heard). Association has the same meaning as in Information Theory and refers to the ability to manipulate linguistic symbols (i.e., the inference of relationships from what is seen or heard). Encoding, which is the response end of the model, is the expression of linguistic symbols (i.e., the use of skills necessary to express thoughts). These processes are mediated at any one of three levels of neural organization (projection, integration, and representation). Projection relates receptor and muscle events to the brain, while integration provides for the sequencing and organization of incoming and outgoing messages, and representation is the employment of more sophisticated mediating organizations necessary for meaning symbolization (Hammill & Larson, 1975).

The educational applications of these particular psycholinguistic principles have generated both assessment techniques and remedial language programs. Kirk, McCarthy, and Kirk (1968) adapted and used this model to construct the Illinois Test of Psycholinguistic Abilities (ITPA), which has served as the basis of several remedial and developmental programs used extensively in schools (Bush & Giles, 1969; Dunn & Smith, 1966; Karnes, 1968; Minskoff, Wiseman, & Minskoff, 1972).

While there is a wide range of theoretical models that serve to specify the value of various remedial training therapies, the most common is presented by Hammill (1972). His division follows our distinctions presented in the last chapter. He notes (Hammill, 1972, p. 40) that perception is separated from conceptualization in the following manner: The processes that involve thinking, meaningful language, problem solving, etc., are assigned to cognition, while those dealing with nonsymbolic, nonabstract properties of the stimulus (e.g., size, color, shape, texture, sequence, etc.) are related to perception. Hammill notes that in psychometrics, almost all of the commonly used tests of visual perception adhere to this model. All of these devices include tasks which require matching geometric or nonsense forms, fine visual-motor coordination activities, and distinguishing embedded figures. Most of the visual-perceptual training programs (i.e., Frostig, Horne, & Kephardt; Fitchburg Plus; Winterhaven) attempt to develop these kinds of skills. Most, if not all, visual-motor programs are based upon the hypothesis that visual perception is an important factor, if not the most important factor, in the learning process.

The only empirical support, however, for the notion of unimodal instruction using the visual channel is offered by Raskin and Baker (1975), who report that vision is the dominant and superior modality for all populations, ages, and sexes. In selecting a learning strategy, they suggest that the therapist begin with visual presentation and proceed to add touch and other modalities, until the appropriate approach is found for the individual. In contrast, Friedrich (Friedrich & Fuller, 1973, 1974; Friedrich, Fuller, & Hawkins, 1969) has not found any support for the perceptual deficit that is used to explain the mentally retarded's poor performance on visual tasks. His results indicate that the perceptual deficit is more related to motor execution and higher-order integrative dysfunction. Hammill (1972) also reports that the correlational research does not support the view that reading comprehension and visual perceptual ability as a single process are related in any practical or meaningful degree. He notes that training in visual perception by itself does not positively affect reading. Thus, he suggests that training should proceed at the conceptual (representational) level.

In a comprehensive review of remedial training, which dealt only with studies using the ITPA or its subtests as a criterion for improvement in language behavior, and compared children who received special training with those who did not, the most encouraging finding pertained to training at the representational level, especially the expressive process. The most discouraging results were associated with training at the automatic level on receptive and organizing processes in both the auditory-vocal and the visual-motor modalities (Hammill & Larson, 1975). The authors noted, however, that instructional programs are uneven in that they emphasize training associative and expressive abilities to the comparative exclusion of training receptive and automatic skills. The positive findings regarding verbal expression suggest that at least one of the skills tapped by the ITPA may be responsive to training. However, as more skills are trained in conjunction with other skills, there is a greater possibility of successful effects of training. The teaching to the "weaknesses" must be combined with the use of the "strengths."

Ayres (1972) suggests an alternate approach, which is more similar to our interest. He designed an intervention program that encouraged sensory integration and produced significant changes in children with auditory language problems, as well as in children with more generalized problems on the WRAT reading and the SORT tests. By teaching how to combine processes, he modified a deficient process—in this case, auditory language comprehension. Unfortunately the design of the experiment makes it impossible to ascertain which aspects of the training were responsible for the changes.

To summarize, the state of the art of remedial training for integrational deficits, while receiving a great deal of financial support (and affirmation from hopeful teachers), is not especially refined (Bryan, 1974; Hammill & Larson, 1975). More basic research is urgently needed to refine treatment techniques. However, the work in developing means to modify an integration problem can serve as a basis for developing our treatment system.

TREATMENT TASKS FOR
PARANOIDS AND SCHIZOPHRENICS

There is precedent for using an approach developed with learning disorders for the treatment of schizophrenics. This interesting therapeutic approach for treating the chronic schizophrenic arose out of the occupational therapy efforts to treat children. King (1974) presents a sensory-integrative approach that trains the process schizophrenic to use proprioceptive feedback mechanisms through practice on a scooter board and other exercises designed to increase tactile stimulation and large tonic muscle activity. The increases in the sensori-perceptual activity are considered to increase integration of cognitive acuity. This approach, although coming from a very different area, views the schizophrenic as requiring practice in the basic sensory stimulation infants experience during the early stages of development. The therapy, therefore, attempts to duplicate the early motor actions that produce the stimulation, which must be integrated into an early schemata. While the little research in the method precludes evaluation, it is the theoretical basis of the therapy that interests us because it postulates an improvement in the conceptual process of schizophrenia. The emphasis is upon teaching to the perceptual weaknesses in order to improve the conceptual deficit. We will follow this strategy in devising our therapeutic approach.

There are several aspects of conceptualization and perception that must be specified in devising a treatment plan. First, they must be divided into small, manageable training units. The development of an adequate perceptual-conceptual integration requires certain processes which must be mastered before others are possible. Our training program is thus a step-by-step program, in which adequate performance at one level is a prerequisite for moving to the next.

Treatment of the Paranoid

Since the paranoid perceives only what fits into his conceptual framework, our treatment program will attempt to extend his perceptual input. Our aim is to increase the recognition of a greater number of stimuli. The first task in our program is a simple cue attendance task. The subject is shown a picture or a scene for a certain length of time and asked to describe a prescribed number of details within a specified time limit. Studies (Salomon & Suppes, 1971; Sieber & Lanzetta, 1966) using the same methodology employing tachistoscopic presentations have found that practice on such a task increases performance. That is, the person learns to be increasingly aware of cues in his environment. This training was also found (Sieber & Lanzetta, 1966) to generalize to other dissimilar information seeking tasks. In addition, these two studies indicate that performance improves with more intensive cue-attendance training, in terms of increasing the length of the icon and its encoding. In using this type of task with paranoids, our program would advocate beginning with low or simple levels of the three task dimensions (time of stimulus presentation, time of interval allowed for responding, and number of responses required) and gradually increasing task demands as performance reached a predetermined criterion. Other additions to the first series of tasks would ultimately include the use of multi-sensory stimuli to increase generalization. Reinforcement would be administered to maintain performance. Although it is not necessary for perceptual learning in normal children (Gibson, 1969), reinforcement has been found to help increase perceptual learning (Bijou & Baer, 1963). Thus, our first training task for the paranoid is designed to increase his awareness of his environment, beginning at low levels of difficulty and gradually increasing levels of difficulty and complexity until normal performance is reached.

After the paranoid has increased his awareness of stimuli to an acceptable level, the next step is a simple discrimination task to increase the focal attention process without the bias of the categorical set. A discrimination task forces the paranoid not only to be aware of stimuli, but also to recognize similarities and differences. One must possess broad enough attention to be aware of all relevant details, yet be able to narrow attention enough to distinguish relevant from irrelevant stimuli. For the paranoid, we are using this task to train the incorporation of a set of stimuli which are task relevant and not cogit determined. The importance of adequate discrimination has been pointed out by many authors, the most recent being the behavior modification approach of Salzinger and Salzinger (1973), who point out that stimuli must be adequately discriminated before acceptable levels of learning can occur. Performance on simple discrimination tasks is enhanced by the following conditions: (1) maximal differences between the two stimuli; (2) enhancement or exaggeration of differentiating features; (3) familiarity with the distinctive features of the stimuli; (4) gradually increasing the level of difficulty; and (5) practice (Fellows, 1968; Gibson, 1969). For the paranoid, training would involve beginning with easy, maximally different discrimination tasks and gradually increase in difficulty and complexity. Again, as in the cue attendance task, intensive practice, different sensory modalities, and reinforcement are the most important elements. Discriminations could begin with simple black–white discriminations and gradually work up to more complex discriminations such as fingerprints, hidden figures, etc. Familiarity with the objects would also be maximized on the early trials. For example, discriminations could initially be made between tables and chairs and later progress to distinguishing between doctors and aides or aides from FBI men. The emphasis is always on the character of the stimuli—the percept—rather than the interpretation of the percept.

The third series of training tasks begins to move away from primarily perceptual tasks to those requiring more of a construction of a percept and the integration of perceptual and conceptual processes. The next task, based upon the Hullian model of habit hierarchies, is a hypothesis generation task developed by Sieber and Lanzetta (1966). Maltzman (1960) and Mednick (1962) have argued that the ability to generate many response alternatives to a given stimulus is a function of the relative strength of the responses and their positioning in the response hierarchy. A person with a hierarchy that is broad and somewhat equally weighted is more likely to permit alternative responses than a person who has a great concentration of responses in one or two strong alternatives. It has been shown that the relative strength of responses within a hierarchy can be experimentally manipulated to produce changes in the ability to generate response alternatives (Maltzman, Bogartz, & Breger, 1958). Sieber and Lanzetta (1966) hypothesized that training to produce different hypotheses would generalize to other tasks as well.

The paranoid has a conceptual bias. That is, the concentration of strong associations automatically activate specific assemblies and prevent the recognition of discrepant perceptual stimuli. The purpose of the Sieber and Lanzetta hypothesis generation task is to increase the possible number of categories into which perceptual data can be fitted. Hypothesis generation training consists of administering a tachistoscopic presentation of a complex magazine picture. The subject is then told to generate as rapidly as possible ten guesses about the content of the slide. A signal light remains on whenever the subject produces different guesses, no more than 25 seconds apart, but goes out following long delays or separations. The criterion for completion of training is the production of ten or more guesses without the signal light going out for each of three different slides. On a similar task, in which subjects were asked to describe another set of tachistoscopic slides in as much detail as desired, this type of training produced increased amounts of information-searching behavior, greater levels of additional information given with each decision, greater numbers of correct responses, and an increased time span before reaching a decision. For the paranoid, this general procedure could be adopted to increase the number of conceptual categories that are used by demanding a greater attention to the variety of perceptual data which is presented.

To summarize the training plan for the paranoid, tasks would start at a low level and gradually become more difficult. The tasks would include all sensory modalities and would move toward multimodal tasks. Intensive practice with reinforcement for successful performance would be administered. The first step would be a series of cue awareness tasks designed to increase stimulus awareness. The next step would be a series of discrimination tasks designed to force awareness of gradually increasing perceptual subleties of differences and similarities. Finally, the last step would be a hypothesis generation task, in which the paranoid would be called upon to use his new perceptual skills to form new conceptual categories.

Treatment of the Schizophrenic

The nonparanoid has a perceptual compensation, continually disbanding concepts in the face of incoming perception. The principal focus of our treatment program would be to strengthen the nonparanoid's conceptual framework by creating stable and enduring associative structures. The first step is a graduated series of transposition tasks. A transposition task is any kind of transfer (of learning) that appears to result from responding to relations among stimuli, as opposed to absolute stimulus qualities (Reese & Lipsitt, 1970). The classic example of a transposition task is training subjects to respond to the larger of two circles. When an acceptable level of performance is reached, the subject is presented with two new circles. One circle is the original larger circle, while the other is a still larger circle. Transposition occurs when the subject responds to the larger circle rather than the circle originally reinforced. This type of task would train the nonparanoid schizophrenic to incorporate a more conceptual response style. On this task, responding solely on a perceptual basis is the incorrect approach. In order to respond correctly, the subject must discriminate between the two circles on the basis of a concept (i.e., "larger than") rather than the stimulus itself. The transposition task thus serves to force the nonparanoid to develop conceptual strategies instead of perceptual ones.

This program, like the paranoid program, would gradually increase task difficulty, stimulus modalities, and complexity. Simple practice has been found to improve performance significantly in transposition tasks (Gibson, 1969). Also, verbalizing hypothesized relations among stimuli has been found to improve performance (Pick, 1965) and could, therefore, be utilized in our training program. Thus, the first training task for nonparanoids would be a graduated series of transposition tasks in varying stimulus modalities. Intensive practice, coupled with reinforced verbalization of hypothesized relations among stimuli, would be used to facilitate acquisition of conceptual performance.

A more difficult conceptual task involves the use of feedback to increase conceptual consistency. Todd and Hammond (1965) used a multiple-cue learning task to compare the effects of different kinds of feedback upon cognitive performance. Each subject was given a series of cards with pictures of three triangles of different sizes. The task was to predict a number on the back of the card from the sizes of the three triangles on the front. The triangles on the front were related to the number on the back by different types of relationships. Multiple-cue learning tasks, such as this have been used with many different types of stimuli, including those dealing with interpersonal evaluation (Goldberg, 1970) and interpersonal conflict (Brehmer, Azuma, Hammond, Kostran, & Varomos, 1970). Todd and Hammond (1965) found that traditional feedback (correct or incorrect) had little positive and sometimes detrimental effects upon performance, while feedback concerning the category and logical properties of the task significantly increased performance. Hammond and Summer (1972) reanalyzed Todd and Hammond's (1965) data and concluded that a large degree of the increase in task performance was due to an increase in cognitive consistency. Thus, conceptually oriented feedback aimed at exposing relations or building relationships among stimuli can increase strength of associates and build stronger assemblies.

For the nonparanoid who is deficient in conceptual strategy, this task would provide training in several aspects of conceptual functioning. First, the task involves dealing with predictions from relationships between stimuli, rather than with the stimuli themselves. In this respect, it is similar to the transposition task discussed earlier. Second, the multiple-cue learning task enables the nonparanoid to practice modifying his conceptual categories by use of feedback from other cues. This procedure is a beginning step in integrating perceptual and conceptual processes. Third, conceptually oriented feedback increases the cognitive consistency of the nonparanoid.

In summary, the first step of the proposed treatment program for the schizophrenic is a graduated series of transposition tasks, coupled with intensive practice and reinforced verbalization of strategies. These tasks would train the nonparanoid to develop and utilize conceptual categories and relationships, instead of relying solely on perceptual ones. The next step is a series of multiple-cue probability learning tasks of increasing complexity, resembling normal living situations, and accompanied by feedback designed to increase awareness of the relational qualities of the task. Training with these tasks would augment the development of conceptual categories and relations by adding an additional element of consistent assemblies and schemata.

To conclude, this chapter has attempted to develop a treatment approach for the paranoid and the schizophrenic which is based upon the performance deficit model and Integration Theory. We have proposed a series of training tasks designed to eliminate the specific performance deficits of paranoids and schizophrenics. The recommended tasks for the paranoid center on improving his deficient perceptual skills, while the emphasis for the nonparanoid is on improving his conceptual skills.

It is not thought that a task improvement therapy is the only treatment procedure suggested in the present discussion of schizophrenic and paranoid cognitive processes. Possibly an equally beneficial procedure would be applying methods from our conceptions of hemispheric functioning. Rhead and Fischer (1977) applied the dual hemisphere conception to procedures in psychotherapy. They note that traditional therapy (by this they mean the talking-therapies) utilizes procedures that emphasize the left hemisphere by their focus on verbal transactions and logical reasoning. The newer humanistic therapies are considered to emphasize the right hemisphere, and as such, would seem to be indicated for certain types of disorders. There is also the suggestion that therapy may be most effective in altering the relationship between the hemispheres by surgical or other means such as biofeedback. Within the presently developed theoretical framework, it would seem advisable to give serious consideration, in treating paranoids and schizophrenics, to utilizing the nonpreferred hemisphere or to be trained in tasks that require the simultaneous action of both hemispheres. This type of therapeutic speculation does await some actual attempts, but it does seem appropriate to our current understanding of the processes active in both groups.

However, the definitive conclusions that can be drawn from both the research on the performance deficit and the recommended treatment are few. Although the position elaborated upon in the past few hundred pages does draw together may disparate positions and results, it is probably true that more questions have been raised than answered. That has been a prime purpose of the effort. Our desire is to create a paradigm shift. We hope that by asking new questions, answers more relevant to the condition will be offered.

Research and theory in schizophrenia are now moving in a new direction, with interest in information processing and hemispheric functioning. Our extensive review of the area should provide, at least, a detailed analysis of how we are traveling and what new sights we can expect to see. Possibly such sights may be seen in the therapy room, but this view seems a bit like science fiction at this point in time. We would be content to see the change in our scientific understanding, and that does seem to be occurring at present.

APPENDIXES

Appendix A:
Creativity and Schizophrenia
as a Semantical Construct Invention

The importance of analyzing research efforts in terms of theory structure, especially in relation to empirical constructs, cannot be better illustrated than in analyzing the issue of schizophrenia as an expression of creativity. Although there are strong opinions on this question supported by personal experience and anecdotes, there has been little empirical investigation directly comparing both processes. An analysis of the operations and theoretical terms applied to schizophrenia and creativity argues that on an empirical basis, they are the same process (Hasenfus & Magaro, 1976). Actual experimental procedures have produced equivalent empirical terms (Keefe & Magaro, 1978). Yet such a comparability has not been recognized in either area.

As we have attempted to demonstrate in Chapters 3 and 4, some theorists use a specific set of experimental tasks to operationalize a psychological process of interest, without recognizing that the same operation is being used to define a completely different process or theoretical term. We have labeled this process a "semantical construct invention." It occurs when the rules of theory building are not seriously observed in psychological research. Hence, we now explore and clarify at anecdotal, theoretical, and empirical levels the possibility that creativity and schizophrenia are two aspects of the same process or a semantical construct invention.

The philosophical and literary worlds are full of reference to the equivalence, as well as the difference, between madness and creativity. Plato wrote: "He who, without the Muses' madness in his soul, comes knocking at the door of poesy and thinks that art will make him anything fit to be called a poet, finds that the poetry which he indites in his sober senses is beaten hollow by the poetry of madmen" (Reed, 1972, p. 156). Nineteenth-century theorists such as Lombroso (1894) argued that both creative genius and insanity resulted from the same underlying cause, namely degeneration. The equivalence of madness and creativity has also been conceptualized in terms of more recent models of madness. Theorists now argue that the experience of the acute schizophrenic is actually a type of "peak experience," similar to that experienced by the creative or self-actualized person (Seigler, Osmond, & Mann, 1969).

Some psychological research has supported the contention that artistic creativity is madness. Cattel (1963) surveyed the biographies of famous scientists and writers and concluded that they tended to be schizothyme. He also found, with psychometric methods, that successful contemporary researchers were significantly more schizothymic than successful administrators and teachers. Barron (1972), in his psychometric study of student artists, found considerable evidence of what is usually considered pathology on their MMPI profiles with high scores on the "psychotic" scales, including that of schizophrenia.

The theoretical terms that tend to guide recent research in schizophrenia and creativity specify the same etiological process. Several theories of schizophrenia emphasize the disturbed nature of the schizophrenic's family during childhood, with the mother often thought to be particularly disturbed (Bateson, Jackson, Haley, & Weakland, 1956; Lidz, Cornelison, & Fleck, 1958). Similarly, Besdine (1968) claims that the biographies of eminent artists reveal a tendency toward a life history pattern characterized by an absent or weak father and an over protective, seductive mother. Goertzel and Goertzel (1962) also found that the families of "eminent" individuals tended to be maladjusted and the maternal relationship particularly was often abnormal. Thus, there is a long anecdotal history and some research results correlating Type 4 events which support the idea that creativity is madness.

The theories and research that are most important to us, however, are those derived from laboratory tasks. We first describe measures of creativity. Guilford (1970), who in the 1950's began the modern era of research into creativity, held that there are seven creativity factors. Wallach's (1970) review of the research on these tests established that some of Guilford's factors are not distinguishable from intelligence, and that the tests that do not measure intelligence all inter-correlate highly and are most appropriately considered to be measuring the single factor of ideational fluency.

Another aspect of creativity has been isolated by Barron with the Barron-Welsh Art Scale. He asserts that individuals who prefer complex asymmetrical designs are more creative. Wallach (1971), in his review of the literature, concludes that the Barron-Welsh Art Scale measures an aspect of creativity that is not significantly related to ideational fluency.

Another widely used test of creativity is the Remote Associates Test devised by Mednick (1962). This test is based on the idea that, given three remotely associated words, the creative individual is better able to supply the mediational association which connects the three words. Validity studies show that the Remote Associates Test can differentiate the more creative from the less creative (Mednick, 1962). Wallach (1970) concludes that although performance on the Remote Associates Test does depend to some degree on intelligence, it also depends on "breath of attention deployment" or in other words, on the ability to make wide associations. Wallach implies that the creativity factor measured by the Remote Associates Test is similar to ideational fluency, but its exact relationship is not described. Piers and Kirchner (1971) show that performance on the Remote Associates Test is unrelated to performance on the Revised Art Scale of the Welsh Figure Preference Test which correlates .90 with the Barron-Welsh Art Scale (Barron, 1972).

Therefore, the mainstream of creativity research suggests that there are at least two factors involved in creativity; ideational fluency and preference for complex and asymmetrical designs. Shouksmith (1970) found evidence supporting this conclusion in a factorial study of intelligence, reasoning, problem solving, and creativity. His measures included several ideational fluency tests plus a number of more obscure measures from the English psychological literature. Shouksmith reports finding two factors involved in creativity: creative associating, which he describes as similar to the ideational fluency of Wallach and Kogan (1965), and divergent flexibility of style, which is similar to receptivity to complex stimuli.

Now we will consider the operational definition of terms by examining the specific tasks creatives and schizophrenics are required to perform. We could not find a significant number of studies in which creatives and schizophrenics were given similar tasks. Therefore, we will compare the tests of creativity and the tasks used in the schizophrenic deficit literature to test the possibility that what is operationally defined as the schizophrenic "deficit" is, in some instance, equal to what is operationally defined as creativity.

The Alternate Uses Test has the subject list all the possible uses he can think of for a tin can, a shoe, and newspaper. Another test of ideational fluency requires the subject to name as many ways as possible in which two objects are similar, and a third test requires the subject to give as many objects as possible that belong to a given category (e.g., things that are round) (Wallach, 1971). Sometimes these tests are scored for originality of response, but since number of responses correlates highly with originality, usually the more creative individual is operationally defined as the individual who gives the greater number of responses.

The parallels between the ideational fluency tests used by some investigators to operationalize creativity and the sorting and object classification tasks on which schizophrenics manifest a "deficit" is striking.

The type of schizophrenic deficit supposedly manifested on these tasks is overinclusion. The object classification test used as a measure of overinclusion consists of asking the subject to sort 12 objects in as many ways as he can. The measure of overinclusiveness is the number of unusual (non-A) responses given (Payne & Friedlander, 1962). This task is very similar to the ideational fluency test, which requires the subject to give as many ways as possible in which two objects are alike. Both the creative and the overinclusive schizophrenic respond by giving more responses than the normal subject, but some researchers label this creativity, while the other group considers it a manifestation of schizophrenia. Another overinclusion measure is the Goldstein-Scheerer Object Sorting Test where the subject is asked to hand over one object of the many before him, and then he is asked to hand over all the other objects that he thinks could be grouped with the first object (Payne & Friedlander, 1962). The overinclusion score is the number of objects chosen in each group. The more objects chosen, the more overinclusive the individual is judged. This task is similar to the creativity test of giving as many instances as possible which exemplify a given category.

The comparisons described above strongly suggest that ideational fluency and overinclusion may be the same phenomenon. This conclusion is further supported in a study by Andreason and Powers (1975), showing that highly creative writers are overinclusive on the Goldstein-Sheerer Object Sorting Test. In this study, however, the schizophrenics were not found to be overinclusive, but this finding can be explained by the nature of the schizophrenic sample, which were chronic schizophrenics of various types. Payne, Caird, and Laverty (1964) demonstrated that overinclusion is exhibited more by acute schizophrenics.

Creativity may only relate to the broad behavioral overinclusion measure because of its incorporation of many different processes. There are many ways to sort on an overinclusion test, some creative and some idiosyncratic. When a total score is used, all of these processes are included. However, when the conceptual overinclusion measure is used, which, in effect, limits the definition of the process, a measure emerges which is distinct from creativity related more to idiosyncratic thinking and more unique to schizophrenia, and possibly to paranoid schizophrenia. This reasoning is somewhat conjectural, since all we know is that the schizophrenic who exhibits behavioral overinclusion also seems to exhibit rich or creative association. Idiosyncratic associations were given by those who exhibited a conceptual overinclusion (Harrow, Himmelhock, Tucker, Hersh, & Quinlan, 1972). The measure guarantees multiple processes that can produce the same score. Whether the score reflects creativity or a schizophrenic thought process is a matter of conjecture. What does seem clear is that the measure itself, in terms of its actual score value, measures creativity or overinclusion with one the semantical invention of the other.

The Barron-Welsh Art Scale or the Revised Art Scale are creativity measures, which have been administered to schizophrenics. They consist of approximately 60 different black and white designs. The subject indicates which designs he likes. The score is the number of designs preferred that are also preferred by a group of artists. Because artists tend to prefer the complex and asymmetrical, a preference for complex and asymmetrical designs results in a high creativity score. These scales to our knowledge have not been administered to schizophrenics, except by Lewis (1971). He gave the Revised Art Scale to 60 schizophrenics divided into process, reactive, and mixed groups. The mean scores for the mixed group (25.05) and the reactive group (18.50) were above the mean for men (17.33) given by Welsh (1959), and the process group (15.40) was below Welsh's mean for men. Thus, this study indicates that certain types of schizophrenics prefer the complex and asymmetrical more than normals.

The Remote Associates Test as a measure of creativity measures the ability to make wide associations. The characteristic, which is most often seen as establishing a link between creatives and schizophrenics, is their purported similar tendencies to emit unusual and abundant associations. Mednick's associative theory of creativity postulates that the creative should give a larger number of total responses and more original responses on a word association test. There is some support for this position (Mednick, 1962; Mednick, Mednick & Jung, 1964). The proposition that schizophrenics give more frequent and more unusual associations than controls is strongly supported by the literature. Johnson, Weiss, and Zelhart (1964) found that schizophrenics gave more idiosyncratic word associations than normal subjects, and Sommer, Dewar, and Osmond (1960) found the same results with the Kent-Rosanoff word association task. Buss (1966) reviews this literature and concludes that schizophrenics give uncommon associations and have difficulty learning common ones. Maher (1972) also reviews this literature and comes to the same conclusion.

A recent study in our laboratory by Jack Keefe (Keefe & Magaro, 1978) tested schizophrenics as defined by the Maine Scale of Schizophrenia and Paranoia on two traditional measures of creativity, the Barron-Welsh and the Alternate Uses Test. We found what would have been predicted if schizophrenia and creativity were equivalent empirical constructs. That is, schizophrenics, as compared to psychiatric controls, normals, and paranoids, were more creative. It could be argued that they were only more creative on these measures. However, that is the point of a semantic construct invention. Since creativity is usually operationally defined by these measures, the burden is upon the critic of such equivalence of constructs to demonstrate another operational definition of creativity that is distinct from the definition of schizophrenia. It is to be noted that this result only applied to nonparanoid schizophrenics. Paranoids performed similarly to normals and psychiatric controls. Hence, such equivalence only occurs when the operational definition of schizophrenia is refined.

In light of the evidence reviewed, it seems justifiable to conclude that there are substantial similarities between the operational definitions of creativity and some of the operational definitions of the schizophrenic "deficit." As measured by accepted tasks, the schizophrenic "deficit" does, in some instances, equal creativity. It seems probable that ideational fluency and over-inclusion are the same or are, at least, very similar. In terms of the word association literature, it is clear that schizophrenics emit remote and unusual associations, as some researchers conclude creatives do. Some aspects of schizophrenic performance seem to demonstrate a preference for the complex and asymmetrical, but admittedly the evidence on this point is meager. In terms of the production of remote associations, the evidence suggests this is most typical of some schizophrenics, but whether the production of such associations is a discrete factor in creativity is not yet established. What is of importance to us is the semantical equivalence of creativity and schizophrenia. The empirical reports seem to support the equivalence of madness and creativity. However, whether the empirical results are adequate to answer the question is possibly the relevant question. Obviously there has to be more to both schizophrenia and creativity than that measured by one test. Using such simplified definitions without a tie to other constructs seems to guarantee the type of confusion in which all that can be said, at this point, is that creativity is a semantical construct invention for schizophrenia. The empirical constructs and laws are identical. That we could reach such a conclusion and not necessarily accept it only demonstrates the problem that can occur with loose single construct theories.

Appendix B:
The Maine Scale of Paranoid and Nonparanoid Schizophrenia

PARANOID SUBSCALE

P1. Does he tend to suspect or believe on slight evidence or without good reason that people and external forces are trying to or now do influence his behavior, control his thinking?
1. No unjustified suspicions.
2. Will admit suspicion when pressed.
3. Easily admits suspicion.
4. Openly states others are trying to control him.
5. Has firm conviction that he is influenced or controlled.

P2. Does he tend to suspect or to believe on slight evidence or without good reason that some people are against him (persecuting, conspiring, cheating, depriving, punishing) in various ways?
1. No unjustified suspicions expressed.
2. When pressed expresses belief that he is conspired against.
3. Frequently inclined to suspect.
4. Frank inclination to believe in persecution.
5. Strongly expresses conviction of persecution.

P3. Does he have an exaggeratedly high opinion of himself or an unjustified belief or conviction of having unusual ability, knowledge, power, wealth, or status?
1. No expressed high opinion of himself.
2. When pressed expresses a high opinion of himself.
3. Frequently expresses a high opinion of himself.
4. Open conviction of unusual power, wealth, etc.
5. Strongly expresses conviction of grandiose or fantastic power, wealth, etc.

P4. Does he tend to suspect or believe on slight evidence or without good reason that some people talk about, refer to or watch him?
1. No unjustified suspicions.
2. Will admit suspicion.
3. Easily admits suspicion.
4. Openly states that he is watched.
5. Has firm conviction of being watched.

P5. Compared to others, how openly hostile is he? Does he show hostility or a high degree of ill will, resentment, bitterness, or hate?
1. No open hostility.
2. Relatively little hostility.
3. Some hostility.
4. Rather hostile.
5. Very hostile.

NONPARANOID

N1. Does he have perceptions (auditory, visual) without normal external stimulus correspondence?
1. None.
2. When pressed admits hallucinations.
3. Easily admits hallucinations.
4. Openly admits frequent hallucinations.
5. Openly hallucinates.

N2. On the basis of the integration of the verbal productions of the patient, does he exhibit thought processes that are confused, disconnected, or disorganized?
1. As normal.
2. Slight disorganization.
3. Mild disorganization.
4. Marked disorganization.
5. Complete disorganization.

N3. How incongruous are his emotional responses? (e.g., giggling or crying for no apparent reason or not showing any emotion when emotion would be appropriately shown)
1. As normal.
2. Slightly different from normal.
3. Responses somewhat incongruous.
4. Distinctly incongruous.
5. Very markedly incongruous.

N4. How well oriented is he as to time? For instance, does he know: (a) the season; (b) the month; (c) the calendar year; (d) the day of the week; (e) how long he has been in hospital?

1. As normal.
2. Occasional confusion.
3. Slight confusion.
4. Frequent confusion.
5. Marked continuous confusion.

N5. Does he assume or maintain peculiar, unnatural, or bizarre postures?

1. None.
2. On rare occasions.
3. For short periods.
4. Frequently.
5. All the time.

References

Chapter 1

Arieti, S. *Interpretation of schizophrenia.* New York: Brunner, 1955.

Bridgman, P. W. *The logic of modern physics.* New York: Macmillan, 1927.

Bridgman, P. W. Operational analysis. *Philosophy of Science,* 1938, *5,* 114–131.

Broen, W. E., Jr. *Schizophrenia research and theory.* New York: Academic Press, 1968.

Buss, A. H. *Psychopathology.* New York: Wiley, 1966.

Buss, A. H., & Lang, P. J. Psychological deficit in schizophrenia: I. Affect, reinforcement, and concept attainment. *Journal of Abnormal Psychology,* 1965, *70,* 2–24.

Chapman, L. J., Chapman, J. P. *Disordered thought in schizophrenia.* New York: Appleton-Century-Crofts, 1973.

Dallenback, K. The place of theory in science. In J. Vanderplas (Ed.), *Controversial Issues in psychology.* Boston: Houghton-Mifflin, 1966.

Garmezy, N. The prediction of performance in schizophrenia. In P. H. Hoch & J. Zubin (Eds.), *Psychopathology of schizophrenia.* New York: Grune & Stratton, 1966.

Hempel, C. G. Operationalism, observation, and scientific terms. In A. Danto & S. Morgenbosser (Eds.), *Philosophy of science.* Cleveland: World Publ. Co., 1960.

Hunt, J. McV., & Cofer, C. Psychological deficit in schizophrenia. In J. McV. Hunt (Ed.), *Personality and the behavior disorders* (Vol. 2). New York: Ronald Press, 1944.

Koch, S. The logical character of the concept of motivation: I, II. *Psychological Review,* 1941, *48,* 15–38; 127–154.

Kopfstein, J. H., & Neale, J. M. Size estimation in schizophrenic and nonschizophrenic subjects. *Journal of Consulting and Clinical Psychology,* 1972, *36,* 430–435.

Kuhn, T. S. *The structure of scientific revolutions* (2nd ed.). Chicago: University of Chicago Press, 1970.

Lang, P. J., & Buss, A. H. Psychological deficit in schizophrenia: II. Interference and activation. *Journal of Abnormal Psychology,* 1965, *70,* 77–106.

MacCorquodale, K., & Meehl, P. On a distinction between hypothetical constructs and intervening variables. *Psychological Review,* 1948, *55,* 95–107.

McGhie, A. Attention and perception in schizophrenia. In B. A. Maher (Ed.), *Progress in experimental personality research* (Vol. 5). New York: Academic Press, 1970.

Merriam, K. A. The experience of schizophrenia. In P. A. Magaro (Ed.), *The construction of madness*. New York: Pergamon Press, 1976.

Nagel, E. The formation of modern conception of logic in the development of geometry. *Osiris*, 1939, *8*, 142–222.

Neale, J. M., & Cromwell, R. L. Attention and schizophrenia. In B. A. Mahler (Ed.), *Progress in experimental personality research*. New York: Academic Press, 1970.

Neale, J. M., Held, J. M., & Cromwell, R. L. Size estimation in schizophrenics; a review and reanalysis. *Psychological Bulletin*, 1969, *71*, 210–221.

Pavy, D. Verbal behavior in schizophrenia; a review of recent studies. *Psychological Bulletin*, 1968, *70*, 164–178.

Payne, R. W. The measurement and significance of overinclusive thinking and retardation in schizophrenic patients. In P. H. Hoch & J. Zuben (Eds.), *Psychopathology of schizophrenia*. New York: Grune & Stratton, 1966.

Rodnick, E. A. Cognitive and perceptual response set in schizophrenics. In R. Jessor & S. Feshbach (Eds.), *Cognition, personality, and clinical psychology*. San Francisco: Jossey Bass, 1967.

Rodnick, E. H., & Garmezy, N. An experimental approach to the study of motivation in schizophrenia. In M. R. Jones (Ed.), *Nebraska Symposium on Motivation*. Lincoln: University of Nebraska Press, 1957.

Shakow, D. Segmental set. *Archives of General Psychiatry*, 1962, *6*, 1–17.

Silverman, J. The problem of attention in research and theory in schizophrenia. *Psychological Review*, 1964, *71*, 352–379.

Turner, M. B. *Philosophy and the science of behavior*. New York: Appleton-Century-Crofts, 1965.

Venables, P. H. Input disfunction in schizophrenia. In B. A. Maher (Ed.), *Progress in experimental personality research* (Vol. 1). New York: Academic Press, 1964.

Yates, A. J. Psychological deficit. *Annual Review of Psychology*, 1966, *17*, 111–144.

Chapter 2

Achinstein, P. Theoretical models. *British Journal of the Philosophy of Science*, 1965, *16*, 102–120.

Campbell, D. I. Stereotypes and the perception of group differences. *American Psychologist*, 1967, *22*, 817–829.

Cole, M., & Bruner, J. S. Cultural differences and inferences about psychological processes. *American Psychologist*, 1971, *26*, 867–876.

Hicks, R. G. Converging operation in the psychological experiment, *Psychophysiology*, 1971, *8*, 93–101.

Hull, C. L. *Principles of behavior*. New York: Appleton-Century-Crofts, 1943.

Hull, C.L. *A behavior system*. New Haven: Yale University Press, 1952.

Koch, S. The logical character of the concept of motivation: I, II. *Psychological Review*, 1941, *48*, 15–38; 127–154.

Koch, S., & Hull, C. L. In W. K. Estes, S. Koch, K. MacCorquodale, P. E. Meehl, C. G. Mueller, Jr., W. N. Shoenfeld, & W. S. Verplanck (Eds.), *Modern learning theory: A critical analysis of five examples*. New York: Appleton-Century-Crofts, 1954.

MacCorquodale, K., & Meehl, P. E. Edward C. Tolman. In W. K. Estes, S. Koch, K. MacCorquodale, P. E. Meehl, C. G. Mueller, Jr., W. N. Schoenfeld, & W. S. Verplanck (Eds.), *Modern learning theory: A critical analysis of five examples*. New York: Appleton-Century-Crofts, 1954.

Magaro, P. A. A theory of schizophrenic performance deficit. In B. Maher (Ed.), *Progress in experimental personality research.* New York: Academic Press, 1974.

Malmo, R. B. Activation: A neuropsychological dimension. *Psychological Review,* 1959, *66,* 367–386.

Marx, M. H. *Learning: Theories.* New York: Macmillan, 1970.

Nagel, E. *The structure of science.* New York: Harcourt, Brace, 1961.

Tecce, J. J., & Cole, J. O. Psychophysiologic responses of schizophrenics to drugs. *Psychopharmacologia (Berl.),* 1972, *24,* 159–200.

Turner, M. B. *Philosophy and the science of behavior.* New York: Appleton-Century-Crofts, 1965.

Walker, E. L. *Stimulus produced arousal patterns and learning.* Final Report, The University of Michigan, 1970.

Weiss, R. F., & Miller, F. G. The drive theory of social facilitation. *Psychological Review,* 1971, *78,* 44–57.

Chapter 3

Andreason, N. J. C., & Powers, P. S. Overinclusive thinking in mania and schizophrenia. *British Journal of Psychiatry,* 1974, *125,* 452–456.

Bannister, D. Conceptual structure in thought-disordered schizophrenics. *Journal of Mental Science,* 1960, *106,* 1230–1249.

Bannister, D. The nature and measurement of schizophrenic thought disorder. *Journal of Mental Science,* 1962, *108,* 825–842.

Bannister, D. Schizophrenia: Carnival mirror of coherence. *Psychology Today,* 1971, *4,* 66–84.

Berg, P. A., & Leventhal, D. B. The effect of distractor strength versus rate of item presentation on retention in schizophrenics. *British Journal of Social and Clinical Psychology,* 1977, *16,* 147–152.

Bjork, E. L., & Murray, J. T. On the nature of input channels in visual processing. *Psychological Review,* 1977, *84,* 472–484.

Bleuler, E. *Dementia praecox on the group of schizophrenics.* New York: International Universities Press, 1950.

Broen, W. E., Jr. *Schizophrenia research and theory.* New York: Academic Press, 1968.

Buss, A. H. *Psychopathology,* New York: Wiley, 1966.

Buss, A. H., & Lang, P. J. Psychological deficit in schizophrenia. I. Affect, reinforcement, and concept attainment. *Journal of Abnormal Psychology,* 1965, *70,* 2–24.

Cameron, N. S. Reasoning, regression, and communication in schizophrenia. *Psychological Monographs,* 1938, *50,* 1–33. (a)

Cameron, N. S. A study of thinking in senile deterioration and schizophrenic disorganization. *American Journal of Psychology,* 1938, *85,* 1012–1035. (b)

Cameron, N. S. Deterioration and regression in schizophrenic thinking. *Journal of Abnormal and Social Psychology,* 1939, *74,* 265–270.

Cameron, N. S. Perceptual organization and behavior pathology. In R. R. Blake & G. V. Ramsey (Eds.), *Perception: An approach to personality.* New York: Ronald, 1951.

Chapman, L. J. Intrusion of associative responses into schizophrenic conceptual performance. *Journal of Abnormal and Social Psychology,* 1958, *56,* 374–379.

Chapman, L. J., & Chapman, J. P. Interpretation of words in schizophrenia. *Journal of Personality and Social Psychology,* 1965, *1,* 135–146.

Chapman, L. J., & Chapman, J. P. *Disordered thought in schizophrenia.* New York: Appleton-Century-Crofts, 1973.

Chapman, L. J., Chapman, J. P., & Miller, G. A. A theory of verbal behavior in schizophrenia. In B. A Maher (Ed.), *Progress in experimental personality research* (Vol. I). New York: Academic Press, 1964.

Chapman, L. J., Chapman, J. P., & Miller, G. A. A theory of verbal behavior in schizophrenia. In B. A. Maher (Ed.), *Contribution to the psychopathology of schizophrenia.* New York: Academic Press, 1977.

Chapman, J., & McGhie, A. A comparative study of disordered attention in schizophrenia. *Journal of Mental Science,* 1962, *108,* 487–500.

Clark, W. C. The "psyche" in psychophysics: A sensory-decision theory analysis of the effect of instructions on flicker sensitivity and response bias. *Psychological Bulletin,* 1966, *65,* 358–366.

Cohen, B., Nachmani, G., & Rosenberg, S. Referent communication disturbances in acute schizophrenia. *Journal of Abnormal Psychology,* 1974, *83,* 1–13.

Craig, W. J. Objective measures of thinking integrated with psychiatric symptoms. *Psychological Reports,* 1965, *16,* 539–546.

Davis, K. M., & Blaney, P. H. Overinclusion and self-editing in schizophrenia. *Journal of Abnormal Psychology,* 1976, *85,* 51–60.

Dykes, M., & McGhie, A. A comparative study of attentional strategies of schizophrenic and highly creative normal subjects. *British Journal of Psychiatry,* 1976, *128,* 50.

Eliseo, T. S. Overinclusive thinking in process and reactive schizophrenics. *Journal of Consulting Psychology,* 1963, *27,* 447–449.

Epstein, S. Overinclusive thinking in a schizophrenic and a control group. *Journal of Consulting Psychology,* 1953, *17,* 384–388.

Foulds, G. A., Hope, K., McPherson, F. M., & Mayo, P. R. Cognitive disorder among the schizophrenias. I. The validity of some tests of thought-process disorder. *British Journal of Psychiatry,* 1967, *113,* 1361–1368. (a)

Foulds, G. A., Hope, K., McPherson, F. M., & Mayo, P. R. Cognitive disorder among the schizophrenias. II. Differences between the sub-categories. *British Journal of Psychiatry,* 1967, *113,* 1369–1374. (b)

Gamble, K. R. Paranoid integration and thought disorder. *Journal of Clinical Psychology,* 1975, *31,* 604–607.

Gathercole, C. E. A note on some tests of overinclusive thinking. *British Journal of Medical Psychology,* 1965, *38,* 59–62.

Goldberg, S. C., Schooler, N. R., & Mattson, N. Paranoid and withdrawal symptoms in schizophrenia: Relationship to reaction time. *British Journal of Psychiatry,* 1968, *114,* 1161–1165.

Goldstein, R. H., & Salzman, L. F. Proverb word counts as a measure of overinclusiveness in delusional schizophrenics. *Journal of Abnormal Psychology,* 1965, *70,* 244–245.

Goldstein, R. H., & Salzman, L. F. Cognitive functions in acute and remitted psychiatric patients. *Psychological Reports,* 1967, *21,* 24–26.

Goldstein, K., & Sheerer, M. Abstract and concrete behavior: An experimental study with special tests. *Psychological Monographs,* 1941, *53*(2, Whole No. 239).

Gonen, J. Y. Associative interference in schizophrenia as a function of paranoid status and premorbid adjustment. *Journal of Consulting and Clinical Psychology,* 1970, *34,* 221–225.

Hamsher, K. de S. Comments on "selection of subjects in studies of schizophrenic cognition" by Chapman and Chapman. *Journal of Abnormal Psychology,* 1977, *86,* 321–323.

Hamsher, K. de S., & Arnold, K. O. A test of Chapman's theory of schizophrenic thought disorder. *Journal of Abnormal Psychology,* 1976, *85,* 296–302.

Harrow, M., Harkavy, K., Bromet, E., & Tucker, G. J. A longitudinal study of schizophrenic thinking. *Archives of General Psychiatry,* 1973, *28,* 179–182.

Harrow, M., Himmelhoch, J., Tucker, G., Hersh, J., & Quinlan, D. Overinclusive thinking in acute schizophrenic patients. *Journal of Abnormal Psychology,* 1972, *79,* 161–168.

Harrow, M., & Quinlan, D. Is disordered thinking unique to schizophrenia? *Archives of General Psychiatry,* 1977, *34,* 15–21.

Hawks, D. V. The clinical usefulness of some tests of overinclusive thinking in psychiatric patients. *British Journal of Social and Clinical Psychology,* 1964, *3,* 186–195.

Hawks, D. V., & Payne, R. W. Overinclusive thought disorder and symptomatology. *British Journal of Psychiatry*, 1971, *118*, 663–670.

Haynes, E. T., Phillips, J. P. N. Inconsistency, loose construing and schizophrenic thought disorder. *British Journal of Psychiatry*, 1973, *123*, 209–217.

Hull, C. L. *Principles of behavior.* New York: Appleton-Century-Crofts, 1943.

Johnson, J. E., & Bieliauskas, L. A. Two measures of overinclusive schizophrenia: A comparative analysis. *Journal of Abnormal Psychology*, 1971, *77*, 149–155.

Klinka, J., & Papageorgis, D. Associative intrusions in the vocabulary of schizophrenics and other patients. *British Journal of Psychiatry*, 1976, *129*, 584–591.

Knight, R., Scherer, M., & Shapiro, J. Iconic imagery in overinclusive and nonoverinclusive schizophrenics. *Journal of Abnormal Psychology*, 1977, *86*, 242–255.

Knight, R. A., Sims-Knight, J. E., & Petchers-Cassell, M. Overinclusion, broad scanning, and picture recognition in schizophrenics. *Journal of Clinical Psychology*, 1977, *33*, 635–642.

Koh, S. D., Kayton, L., & Schwartz, C. The structure of word storage in the permanent memory of nonpsychotic schizophrenics. *Journal of Consulting and Clinical Psychology*, 1974, *42*, 879–887.

Korboot, P. J., & Damiani, N. Auditory processing speed and signal detection in schizophrenia. *Journal of Abnormal Psychology*, 1976, *85*, 287–295.

Lang, P. J., & Buss, A. H. Psychological deficit in schizophrenia: II. Interference and activation. *Journal of Abnormal Psychology*, 1965, *70*, 77–106.

Lawson, J. S., McGhie, A., & Chapman, J. Distractibility in schizophrenia and organic cerebral disease. *British Journal of Psychiatry*, 1966, *113*, 527.

Magaro, P. A. Theories of the schizophrenic performance deficit: An integration theory synthesis. In B. A. Maher (Ed.), *Progress in experimental personality research* (Vol. 7). New York: Academic Press, 1974.

Maher, B. The language of schizophrenia: A review and interpretation. *British Journal of Psychiatry*, 1972, *120*, 3–17.

Marshall, W. L. Cognitive functioning in schizophrenia. *British Journal of Psychiatry*, 1973, *123*, 413–423.

McGhie, A. Attention and perception in schizophrenia. In B. A. Maher (Ed.), *Progress in experimental personality research* (Vol 5). New York: Academic Press, 1970.

McGhie, A. Attention and perception in schizophrenia. In B. A. Maher (Ed.), *Contributions to the psychopathology of schizophrenia.* New York: Academic Press, 1977.

McGhie, A., & Chapman, J. Disorders of attention and perception in early schizophrenia. *British Journal of Medical Psychology*, 1961, *34*, 103.

McGhie, A., Chapman, J., & Lawson, J. S. The effect of distraction on schizophrenic performance. *British Journal of Psychiatry*, 1965, *111*, 383–391.

Miller, B. Semantic misinterpretations of ambiguous communications in schizophrenia. *Archives of General Psychiatry*, 1974, *30*, 435–440.

Neuringer, C., Fiske, J. P., Schmidt, M. W., & Goldstein, G. Adherence to strong verbal meaning definitions in schizophrenics. *The Journal of Genetic Psychology*, 1972, *121*, 315–323.

Neuringer, C., Kaplan, H. A., & Goldstein, G. Schizophrenic avoidance of strong meaning associations to emotional words. *The Journal of Genetic Psychology*, 1974, *124*, 123–129.

Pavy, D. Verbal behavior in schizophrenia: A review of recent studies. *Psychological Bulletin*, 1968, *70*, 164–178.

Payne, R. W. Thought disorder and retardation in schizophrenia. *Canadian Psychiatric Journal*, 1961, *6*, 75–78.

Payne, R. W. An object classification test as a measure of overinclusive thinking in schizophrenic patients. *British Journal of Social and Clinical Psychology*, 1962, *1*, 213–221.

Payne, R. W. The measurement and significance of overinclusive thinking and retardation in schizophrenic patients. In P. H. Hoch & J. Zubren (Eds.), *Psychopathology of schizophrenia.* New York: Grune & Stratton, 1966.

Payne, R. W. Cognitive defects in schizophrenia: Overinclusive thinking. In J. Hellmuth (Ed.), *Cognitive studies. Vol. 2: Deficits in cognition*. New York: Brunner/Mazel, 1971.

Payne, R. W., & Caird, W. K. Reaction time, distractibility, and overinclusive thinking in psychotics. *Journal of Abnormal Psychology*, 1967, *72*, 112–121.

Payne, R. W., Caird, W. K., & Laverty, S. G. Overinclusive thinking and delusions in schizophrenic patients. *Journal of Abnormal and Social Psychology*, 1964, *68*, 562–566.

Payne, R. W., & Friedlander, D. A short battery of simple tests for measuring overinclusive thinking. *Journal of Mental Science*, 1962, *108*, 362–367.

Payne, R. W., & Hewlett, J. H. G. Thought disorder in psychotic patients. In H. J. Eysenck (Ed.), *Experiments in personality*. London: Routledge & Kegan Paul, 1960.

Payne, R. W., Hochberg, A. C., & Hawks, D. V. Dichotic stimulation as a method of assessing disorder of attention in overinclusive schizophrenic patients. *Journal of Abnormal Psychology*, 1970, *76*, 185–193.

Piaget, J. *Judgment and reasoning in the child*. New York: Harcourt, Brace, 1928.

Reilly, F., Harrow, M., Tucker, G., Quinlan, D., & Siegel, A. Looseness of associations in acute schizophrenia. *British Journal of Psychiatry*, 1975, *127*, 240–246.

Royer, F., & Friedman, S. Scanning time of schizophrenics and normals for visual designs. *Journal of Abnormal Psychology*, 1973, *82*, 212–219.

Rutter, D. R., Wishner, J., & Callagher, B. A. The prediction and predictability of speech in schizophrenic patients. *British Journal of Psychiatry*, 1975, *126*, 571–576.

Salzinger, K. The immediacy hypothesis of schizophrenia. In H. M. Yaker, H. Osmond, & F. Cheek (Eds.), *The future of time: Men's temporal environment*. Garden City, N.Y.: Doubleday, 1971.

Salzinger, K., Portnoy, S., & Feldman, R. S. Verbal behavior in schizophrenics and some comments toward a theory of schizophrenia. In P. Hoch & J. Zubin (Eds.), *Psychopathology of schizophrenia*. New York: Grune & Stratton, 1966.

Scott, U. A. Structure of natural cognitions. *Journal of Personality and Social Psychology*, 1969, *12*, 261–278.

Scott, U. A. Cognitive correlates of maladjustment among college students in three cultures. *Journal of Consulting and Clinical Psychology*, 1974, *42*, 184–195. (a)

Scott, W. A. Varieties of cognitive integration. *Journal of Personality and Social Psychology*, 1974, *30*, 563–578. (b)

Shakow, D. Some psychological features of schizophrenia. In M. L. Reymert (Ed.), *Feelings and emotions*. New York: McGraw-Hill, 1950.

Shakow, D. Segmental set. *Archives of General Psychiatry*, 1962, *6*, 1–17.

Venables, P. H. Input dysfunction in schizophrenia. In B. A. Maher (Ed.), *Progress in experimental personality research* (Vol. 1). New York: Academic Press, 1964.

Vojtisek, J. E. *The influence of an interpolated stimulus on the size estimation performance of schizophrenic subgroups*. Unpublished doctoral dissertation, University of Maine, 1975.

Watson, C. G. Interrelationships of six overinclusion measures. *Journal of Consulting Psychology*, 1967, *31*, 517–520.

Weckowicz, T. E., & Blewett, D. B. Size constancy and abstract thinking in schizophrenic patients. *Journal of Mental Science*, 1959, *105*, 909–934.

Chapter 4

Asarnow, R. F., & Mann, R. Size estimation in paranoid and nonparanoid schizophrenics. *The Journal of Nervous and Mental Disease*, 1978, *166*, 96–103.

Ax, A. F., Banford, J. L., Beckett, P. G. S., Fretz, N. F., & Gottlieb, J. S. Automatic conditioning in chronic schizophrenia. *Journal of Abnormal Psychology*, 1970, *76*, 140–154.

Bergmann, G., & Spence, K. W. Operationism and theory in psychology. *Psychological Review*, 1941, *48*, 1–4.

Bernstein, A. S. The galvanic skin response orienting reflex among chronic schizophrenics. *Psychonomic Science,* 1964, *1,* 391–392.

Bernstein, A. S. Electrodermal base level, tonic arousal, and adaptation in chronic schizophrenics. *Journal of Abnormal Psychology,* 1967, *73,* 221–232.

Bible, G. H., & Magaro, P. A. Response hierarchy disorganization for chronic and acute schizophrenics. *Journal of Genetic Psychology,* 1971, *119,* 119–126.

Boland, T. B., & Chapman, L. J. Conflicting predictions from Broen's and Chapman's theories of schizophrenic thought disorder. *Journal of Abnormal Psychology,* 1971, *78,* 52–58.

Broen, W. E., Jr. Response disorganization and breadth of observation in schizophrenia. *Psychological Review,* 1966, *73,* 579–585.

Broen, W. E., Jr. *Schizophrenia research and theory.* New York: Academic Press, 1968.

Broen, W. E., Jr. Limiting the flood of stimulation: A protective deficit in chronic schizophrenia. In R. Solso (Ed.), *Contemporary issues in cognitive psychology: The Loyola Symposium.* New York: Wiley, 1973.

Broen, W. E., Jr., & Nakamura, C. Y. Reduced range of sensory sensitivity in chronic nonparanoid schizophrenics. *Journal of Abnormal Psychology,* 1972, *79,* 106–111.

Broen, W. E., Jr., & Storms, L. H. Lawful disorganization; the process underlying a schizophrenic syndrome. *Psychological Review,* 1966, *73,* 265–279.

Broen, W. E., Jr., & Storms, L. H. A theory of response interference in schizophrenia. In B. A. Maher (Ed.), *Progress in experimental personality research* (Vol. IV). New York: Academic Press, 1967.

Broen, W. E., & Storms, L. H. Postscript: Response disorganization and narrowed observation. In B. A. Maher (Ed.), *Contributions to the psychopathology of schizophrenia.* New York: Academic Press, 1977.

Bruner, J. S., & Postman, L. Symbolic value as an organizing factor in perception. *Journal of Social Psychology,* 1948, *27,* 203–208.

Bryant, A. R. *An investigation of process–reactive schizophrenia with relation to perception of visual space.* Unpublished doctoral dissertation, University of Utah, 1962.

Callaway, E. The influence of amobarbital (amylobarbitone) and methamphetamine on the focus of attention. *Journal of Medical Science,* 1959, *105,* 382–392.

Callaway, E., & Stone, G. Re-evaluating focus of attention. In L. Uhr & J. G. Miller (Eds.), *Drugs and behavior.* New York: Wiley, 1960, pp. 393–398.

Chapman, L. J., & Chapman, J. P. *Disordered thought in schizophrenia.* New York: Appleton-Century-Crofts, 1973.

Cicchetti, D. V. Critical review of the research relating mother dominance to schizophrenia. *Proceedings of the 77th Annual Convention of the American Psychological Association,* 1969, *4,* 557–558.

Crannell, C. W. The effect of interpolated stimuli on the time error in judgments of vertical distance. *Psychological Bulletin,* 1941, *38,* 609.

Culver, C. M. *The effect of cue value on size estimation in schizophrenic subjects.* Unpublished doctoral dissertation, Duke University, 1961.

Davies-Osterkamp, S., Rist, F., & Bangert, A. Selective attention, breadth of attention, and shifting attention in chronic nonparanoid schizophrenics. *Journal of Abnormal Psychology,* 1977, *86,* 461–469.

Davis, D., Cromwell, R. L., & Held, J. M. Size estimation in emotionally disturbed children and schizophrenic adults. *Journal of Abnormal Psychology,* 1967, *72,* 395–401.

DeVault, S. Physiological responsiveness in reactive and process schizophrenia. *Dissertation Abstracts,* 1957, *17,* 1387.

Easterbrook, J. A. The effect of emotion on cue utilization and the organization of behavior. *Psychological Review,* 1959, *66,* 183–202.

Ehrenworth, J. *The differential responses to affective and neutral stimuli in the visual–motor performance of schizophrenics and normals.* Unpublished doctoral dissertation, Boston University, 1960.

Epstein, S., & Coleman, M. Drive theories of schizophrenia. *Psychosomatic Medicine,* 1970, *32,* 113–140.

Fowles, D. C., Watt, N. F., Maher, B. A., & Grinspoon, L. Automatic arousal in good and poor premorbid schizophrenics. *British Journal of Social and Clinical Psychology,* 1970, *9,* 135–147.

Gardner, R. W. Scores for the cognitive control of extensiveness of scanning. *Perceptual and Motor Skills,* 1970, *31,* 330.

Gardner, R. W., Holzman, P. S., Klein, G. S., Linton, H. B., & Spence, D. P. Cognitive control: a study of individual consistencies in cognitive behavior. *Psychological Issues,* 1959, *1*(4).

Gardner, R. W., & Long, R. I. Control, defense, and centration effect: A study of scanning behavior. *British Journal of Psychology,* 1962, *53,* 129–140.

Garmezy, N. *Process and reactive schizophrenia: Some conceptions and issues.* Paper presented at the conference on the Role and Methodology of Classification in Psychiatry and Psychopathology, Washington, D.C., November 1965.

Garmezy, N. The prediction of performance in schizophrenia. In P. H. Hoch & J. Zobin (Ed.), *Psychopathology of schizophrenia.* New York: Grune & Stratton, 1966.

Gibeau, P. J. *Field dependency and the process-reactive dimenson in schizophrenia.* Unpublished doctoral dissertation, Purdue University, 1965.

Goffman, E. *Asylums.* New York: Doubleday, 1961.

Goldstein, M. J., & Acker, S. W. Psychophysiological reactions to films by chronic schizophrenics: II. Individual differences in resting levels and reactivity. *Journal of Abnormal Psychology,* 1967, *72,* 23–39.

Goldstein, M. J., Judd, L. J., Rodnick, E. H., & LaPolla, A. Psychophysiological and behavioral effects of phenothiazine administration in acute schizophrenics as a function of premorbid status. *Journal of Psychiatric Research,* 1969, *6,* 271–287.

Gruzelier, J. H., & Venables, P. H. Skin conductance actvity in a heterogeneous sample of schizophrenic: Possible evidence of limbic dysfunction. *Journal of Nervous and Mental Disease,* 1972, *155,* 277–287.

Gruzelier, J. H., & Venables, P. H. Skin conductance responses to tones with and without attentional significance in schizophrenic and non-schizophrenic patients. *Neuropsychologia,* 1973, *11,* 221–230.

Gruzelier, J. H., & Venables, P. H. Two-flash threshold, sensitivity, and B in normal subjects and schizophrenics. *Quarterly Journal of Experimental Psychology,* 1974, *26,* 594–604.

Guilford, J. P., & Park, D. G. The effect of interpolated weights upon comparative judgments. *American Journal of Psychology,* 1931, *43,* 589–599.

Hamilton, V. The size constancy problem in schizophrenia: A cognitive skill analysis. *British Journal of Psychology,* 1972, *63,* 73–84.

Hamsher, K. S., & Arnold, K. O. A test of Chapman's theory of schizophrenic disorder. *Journal of Abnormal Psychology,* 1976, *85,* 296–302.

Haronian, F. Anthropometric correlates of the size of the Müller–Lyer illusion. *Journal of Psychological Studies,* 1963, *14,* 161–171.

Haronian, F., & Sugerman, A. A. Field independence and resistance to reversal of perspective. *Perceptual and Motor Skills,* 1966, *22,* 543–546.

Harris, J. G. Size estimation of pictures as a function of thematic context for schizophrenic and normal subjects. *Journal of Personality,* 1957, *25,* 651–671.

Hock, P., Kubis, J. F., & Rourke, F. L. Psychogalvanometric investigations in psychoses and other abnormal states. *Psychosomatic Medicine,* 1944, *6,* 237–243.

Howe, E. S. GSR conditioning in anxiety states, normals, and chronic functional schizophrenic subjects. *Journal of Abnormal and Social Psychology,* 1958, *56,* 183–189.

Jackson, D. N. A short form of Witkin's Embedded-Figures Test. *Journal of Abnormal and Social Psychology,* 1956, *53,* 254–255.

Jacobson, G. R. Effect of brief sensory deprivation on field-dependence. *Journal of Abnormal Psychology,* 1966, *31,* 386–394.

Janucci, G. I. *Size constancy in schizophrenia: A study of subgroup differences.* Thesis abstract, Rutgers University, 1964.

Jurko, M., Jost, H., & Hall, T. D. Pathology of the energy system: An experimental clinical study of physiological adaptiveness capacities in a non-patient, a psychoneurotic, and an early paranoid schizophrenic group. *Journal of Psychology,* 1952, *33,* 183–189.

Kagan, J., Moss, L., & Sigel, I. E. Psychological significance of styles of conceptualization. In J. C. Wright & J. Kagan (Eds.), Basic cognitive processes in children. *The Monographs of Society Research in Child Development,* 1963, *28,* 86.

Karlin, L. The time error in the comparison of visual size. *American Journal of Psychology,* 1953, *66,* 564–573.

Klein, G. S. Need and regulation. In M. R. Jones (Ed.), *Nebraska Symposium on Motivation.* Lincoln: University of Nebraska Press, 1954.

Koester, T., & Schoenfield, W. N. The effect of context upon judgments of pitch differences. *Journal of Experimental Psychology,* 1946, *36,* 417–430.

Kopfstein, J. H., & Neale, J. M. Size estimation in schizophrenic and nonschizophrenic subjects. *Journal of Consulting and Clinical Psychology,* 1971, *36,* 430–435.

Lang, P. J., & Buss, A. H. Psychological deficit in schizophrenia: II. Interference and activation. *Journal of Abnormal Psychology,* 1965, *70,* 77–106.

Leibowitz, H. U. Multiple mechanisms of size constancy. *Hiroshima Forum of Psychology,* 1974, *1,* 47–53.

Leibowitz, H. W., & Pishkin, V. Perceptual size constancy in chronic schizophrenics. *Journal of Consulting Psychology,* 1961, *25,* 196–199.

Levinson, D. J., & Gallagher, E. B. *Patienthood in the mental hospital.* Boston: Houghton Mifflin, 1964.

Lovinger, E. Perceptual contact with reality in schizophrenia. *Journal of Abnormal and Social Psychology,* 1956, *52,* 87–91.

Lykken, D. T., & Venables, P. H. Direct measurement of skin conductance: A proposal for standardization. *Psychophysiology,* 1971, *8,* 656–672.

MacDorman, C. F., Rivoire, J. L., Gallagher, P. F., & MacDorman, C. F. Size constancy of adolescent schizophrenics. *Journal of Consulting Psychology,* 1962, *26,* 258–263.

Magaro, P. A. Size estimation in schizophrenia as a function of censure, diagnosis, premorbid adjustment, and chronicity. *Journal of Abnormal Psychology,* 1969, *74,* 306–313.

Magaro, P. A. Basal level and reactivity in schizophrenia as a function of premorbid adjustment, chronicity and diagnosis. *Journal of Genetic Psychology,* 1972, *120,* 61–73. (a)

Magaro, P. A. Form discrimination performance of schizophrenics as a function of social censure, premorbid adjustment, chronicity, and diagnosis. *Journal of Abnormal Psychology,* 1972, *80,* 58–66. (b)

Magaro, P. A. Skin conductance basal level and reactivity in schizophrenia as a fucntion of chronicity, premorbid adjustment, diagnosis, and medication. *Journal of Abnormal Psychology,* 1973, *81,* 270–281.

Magaro, P. A., & Vojtisek, J. E. Embedded figures performance of schizophrenics as a function of chronicity, premorbid adjustment, diagnosis, and medication. *Journal of Abnormal Psychology,* 1971, *77,* 184–191.

Malmo, R. B., & Shagass, C. Physiological studies of reaction to stress in anxiety states and early schizophrenia. *Psychosomatic Medicine,* 1949, *11,* 9–24.

Mandler, G., Mandler, J. J., Kreman, I., & Shelitan, R. D. The response to threat: Relations among physiological idices. *Psychological Monograph*, 1961, *75*(9).

McCormick, D. J., & Broekema, V. J. Size estimation, perceptual recognition, and cardiac rate response in acute paranoid and nonparanoid schizophrenics. *Journal of Abnormal Psychology*, 1978, *87*, 385–398.

McKinnon, T., & Singer, G. Schizophrenia and the scanning cognitive control: A reevaluation. *Journal of Abnormal Psychology*, 1969, *74*, 242–249.

Mednick, S. A. A learning theory approach to research in schizophrenia. *Psychological Bulletin*, 1958, *55*, 316–327.

Mednick, S. A., & McNeil, T. F. Current methodology in research on the etiology of schizophrenia: Serious difficulties which suggest the use of the high-risk group method. *Psychological Bulletin*, 1968, *70*, 681–693.

Mednick, S. A., & Schulsinger, F. Some premorbid characteristics related to breakdown in children with schizophrenic mothers. In D. Rosenthal & S. S. Kety (Eds.), *The transmission of schizophrenia*. Oxford: Pergamon, 1968, 267–291.

Meehl, P. E. Schizotoxia, schizotypy, schizophrenia. *American Psychologist*, 1962, *17*, 827–838.

Mehl, M. M. The effect of brief sensory deprivation and sensory stimulation on the cognitive functioning of chronic schizophrenics. *Journal of Nervous and Mental Disease*, 1969, *148*, 586–596.

Messick, S., & Fritzky, F. J. Dimension of analytic attitude in cognition and personality. *Journal of Personality*, 1963, *31*, 346–370.

Neale, J. M. & Cromwell, R. L. Size estimation in schizophrenics as a function of stimulus-presentation time. *Journal of Abnormal Psychology*,1968, *73*, 44–48.

Neale, J. M., Davis, D., & Cromwell, R. L. Size estimation in schizophrenia: Some additional controls. *Perceptual and Motor Skills*, 1971, *32*, 363–367.

Neale, J. M., Held, J. M., & Cromwell, R. L. Size estimation in schizophrenics: A review and reanalysis. *Psychological Bulletin*, 1969, *71*, 210–221.

Newbigging, P. L. The relationship between reversible perspective and embedded figures. *Canadian Journal of Psychology*, 1954, *8*, 204–208.

Oltman, P. K. Field dependence and arousal. *Perceptual and Motor Skills*, 1964, *19*, 441.

Paintal, A. S. A comparison of the GSR in normals and psychotics. *Journal of Experimental Psychology*, 1951, *41*, 425–428.

Perez, R. Size constancy in normals and schizophrenics. In W. H. Ittelson & S. B. Katush (Eds.), *Perceptual changes in psychology*. New Brunswick, N.J.: Rutgers University Press, 1961.

Phillips, L. Case history data and prognosis in schizophrenia. *Journal of Nervous and Mental Disease*, 1953, *17*, 515–525.

Piaget, J. *The Psychology of intelligence*. New York: Harcourt Brace, 1950.

Pishkin, V., & Hershiser, D. Respiration and GSR as functions of white sound in schizophrenia. *Journal of Consulting Psychology*, 1963, *27*, 303–337.

Pishkin, V., Smith, T. E., & Leibowitz, H. W. The influence of symbolic stimulus value on perceptual size in chronic schizophrenia. *Journal of Consulting Psychology*, 1962, *26*, 323–330.

Postman, L. Time error in auditory perception. *American Journal of Psychology*,1947, *59*, 193–219.

Pratt, C. C. Time errors in the method of single stimulus. *Journal of Experimental Psychology*, 1933, *16*, 798–814.

Pugh, L. A. The effects of praise, censure, and noise on electrodermal and reaction time measures in chronic schizophrenic and normal women (Doctoral dissertation, University of Oklahoma, 1965). *Dissertation Abstracts International*, 1966. (University Microfilms No. 65-1250)

Ray, T. S. Electrodermal indications of levels of psychological disturbance in chronic schizophrenia. *American Psychologist*, 1963, *18*, 393.

Raush, H. L. Perceptual constancy in schizophrenia. *Journal of Personality*, 1952, *21*, 176–187.

Rice, J. K. Disordered language as related to autonomic responsivity and the process–reactive distinction. *Journal of Abnormal Psychology*, 1970, *76*, 50–54.

Rodnick, E. H., & Garmezy, N. An experimental approach to the study of motivation in schizophrenia. In M. R. Jones (Ed.), *Nebraska Symposium on Motivation*. Lincoln: University of Nebraska Press, 1957, 109–183.

Sanders, R., & Pacht, A. R. Perceptual constancy of known clinical groups. *Journal of Consulting Psychology*, 1952, *16*, 440–444.

Schooler, C., & Silverman, J. Perceptual styles and their correlates among schizophrenic patients. *Journal of Abnormal Psychology*, 1969, *74*, 459–470.

Siegel, M. H. Discrimination of color. I. comparison of three psychophysical methods. *Journal of Optical Society of America*, 1962, *52*, 1067–1070.

Silverman, J. The problem of attention in research and theory in schizophrenia. *Psychological Review*, 1964, *71*, 352–379. (a)

Silverman, J. Scanning control mechanism and "cognitive filtering" in paranoid and nonparanoid schizophrenia. *Journal of Consulting Psychology*, 1964, *28*, 385–393. (b)

Silverman, J. Variations in cognitive control and psychophysiological defense in the schizophrenics. *Psychosomatic Medicine*, 1967, *29*, 225–251.

Silverman, J. Toward a more complex formulation of rod-and-frame performance in the schizophrenics. *Perceptual and Motor Skills*, 1968, *27*,1111–1114. (a)

Silverman, J. A paradigm for the study of altered states of consciousness. *British Journal of Psychiatry*, 1968, *114*, 1201–1218. (b)

Silverman, J., Berg, P. S. D., & Kantor, R. Some perceptual correlates of institutionalization. *Journal of Nervous and Mental Disease*, 1965, *141*, 651–657.

Silverman, J., & Goarder, K. Rates of saccadic eye movement and size judgments of normals and schizophrenics. *Perceptual and Motor Skills*, 1967, *25*, 661–667.

Solomon, A. P., Darrow, C. W., & Blaurock, M. Blood pressure and palmar sweat (galvanic) responses of psychotic patients before and after insulin and metrazol therapy. *Journal of Psychosomatic Medicine*, 1939, *1*, 118–137.

Stenn, P. G. *The relation between eye movement frequency and size estimation in schizophrenia and nonpsychiatric patients*. Presented at the meeting of the Eastern Psychological Association, Philadelphia, Pa., April 1969.

Storms, L. H., & Acosta, F. X. Effects of dynamometer tension on stimulus generalization in schizophrenic and nonschizophrenic patients. *Journal of Abnormal Psychology*,1974, *83*, 204–207.

Strauss, M. E. Thematic content and trials effects in the size estimation of meaningful stimuli. *Journal of Abnormal Psychology*, 1970, *76*, 276–278.

Strauss, M. E., Foureman, W. C., & Parwatikar, S. D. Schizophrenics' size estimation of thematic stimuli. *Journal of Abnormal Psychology*,1974, *83*, 117–123.

Syz, H. C., & Kinder, E. F. Electrical skin resistance in normal and in psychotic subjects. *Archives of Neurology and Psychiatry*, 1928, *19*, 1026–1035.

Tate, J. D., & Springer, R. M. Effects of memory time on successive judgments. *Psychological Bulletin*, 1971,*76*, 394–408.

Taylor, J. M. *A comparison of delusional and hallucinatory individuals using field dependency as a measure*. Unpublished doctoral dissertation, Purdue University, 1956.

Tecce, J. J., & Cole, J. O. Psychophysiologic responses of schizophrenics to drugs. *Psychopharmacologia (Berl.)*, 1972, *24*, 159–200.

Thayer, J., & Silber, D. E. Relationship between levels of arousal and responsiveness among schizophrenia and normal subjects. *Journal of Abnormal Psychology*, 1971, *77*, 162–173.

Venables, P. H. Input dysfunction in schizophrenia. In B. A. Maher (Ed.), *Progress in experimental personality research.* New York: Academic Press, 1964.

Venables, P. H. Input regulation and psychopathology. In M. Hammer, K. Salzinger, & S. Sutton (Eds.), *Psychopathology.* New York: Wiley, 1972.

Venables, P. H. Input dysfunction in schizophrenia. In B. A. Maher (Ed.), *Contributions to the psychopathology of schizophrenia.* New York: Academic Press, 1977.

Venables, P. H., & Wing, J. K. Level of arousal and the subclassification of schizophrenia. *Archives of General Psychiatry,* 1962, *7,* 114-119.

Vojtisek, J. E. *The influence of an interpolated stimulus on the size estimation performance of schizophrenic subgroups.* Unpublished doctoral dissertation, University of Maine, 1975.

Vojtisek, J. E., & Magaro, P. A. The two factors present in the embedded figures test and a suggested short form for hospitalized psychiatric patients. *Journal of Consulting and Clinical Psychology,* 1974, *42,* 554-558.

Wachtel, P. L. Field dependence and psychological differentiation: Re-examination. *Perceptual and Motor Skills,* 1972, *35,* 179-189. (a)

Wachtel, P. L. Cognitive style and style of adaptation. *Perceptual and Motor Skills,* 1972, *35,* 779-785. (b)

Wallach, M. A. Active-analytical vs passive-global cognitive functioning. In S. Messick & J. Ross (Eds.), *Measurement in personality and cognition.* New York: Wiley, 1962.

Webb, W. W., Davis, D., & Cromwell, R. L. Size estimation in schizophrenics as a function of thematic content of stimuli. *Journal of Nervous and Mental Disease,* 1966, *143,* 252-255.

Weckowicz, T. E. Size constancy in schizophrenic paients. *Journal of Mental Science,* 1957, *103,* 475-486.

Williams, M. Psychophysiological responsiveness to psychological stress in early chronic schizophrenic reactions. *Psychosomatic Medicine,* 1953, *15,* 456-462.

Witkin, H. A. Individual differences in ease of perception of embedded figures. *Journal of Personality,* 1950, *19,* 1-15.

Witkin, H. A. Psychological differentiation and forms of pathology. *Journal of Abnormal Psychology,* 1965, *70,* 317-335.

Witkin, H. A., Dyk, R. B., Faterson, J. F., Goodenough, D. R., & Karp, S. A. *Psychological differentiation.* New York: Wiley, 1962.

Witkin, H. A., Lewis, H. B., Hertzman, M., Machover, K., Meissner, P. B., & Wagner, S. *Personality through perception.* New York: Harper, 1954.

Zahn, T. P. Acquired and symbolic affective value as determinants of size estimation of schizophrenic and normal subjects. *Journal of Abnormal and Social Psychology,* 1959, *58,* 39-47.

Zahn, T. P. Autonomic reactivity and behavior in schizophrenia. *Psychiatric Research Report,* 1964, *19,* 156-173.

Zimet, N., & Fine, H. J. Perceptual differentiation and two dimensions of schizophrenia. *Journal of Nervous and Mental Disease,* 1959, 129, 435-441.

Zuckerman, M. Field dependency as a predictor of responses to sensory and social isolation. *Perceptual and Motor Skills,* 1968, *27,* 757-758.

Chapter 5

Abrams, L. *Reliability and validity of diagnostic rating scales for paranoid and nonparanoid schizophrenia.* Paper presented at Eastern Psychology Association, Washington, D.C., March 1978.

Abrams, G. M., Taintor, Z. C., & Lhamon, W. T. Percept assimilation and paranoid severity. *Archives of General Psychiatry,* 1966, *14,* 491-496.

Astrachan, B. M., Harrow, M., Adler, D., Brauer, L., Schwartz, A., Schwartz, C., & Tucker, G. A checklist for the diagnosis of schizophrenia. *British Journal of Psychiatry,* 1972, *121,* 529–539.

Bassos, C. A. Affective content and contextual constraint in recall by paranoid, nonparanoid, and nonpsychiatric patients. *Journal of Consulting and Clinical Psychology,* 1973, *40,* 126–132.

Bender, L. Childhood schizophrenia: Clinical study of one hundred schizophrenic children. *American Journal of Orthopsychiatry,* 1947, *17,* 40–56.

Bender, L. Child schizophrenia. *Psychiatric Quarterly,* 1953, *27,* 663–681.

Bender, L. Current research in childhood schizophrenia. *American Journal of Psychiatry,* 1954, *110,* 885–856.

Bender, L. Schizophrenia in chidhood: Its recognition, description, and treatment. *American Journal of Ortho-psychiatry,* 1956, *26,* 499–506.

Bender, L. The concept of pseudopsychopathic schizophrenia in adolescents. *American Journal of Orthopsychiatry,* 1959, *29,* 491–509.

Bennett, S., & Klein, H. Childhood schizophrenia: 30 years later. *American Journal of Psychiatry,* 1966, *112,* 1121–1124.

Binder, A. Personality variables and recognition response level. *Journal of Abnormal and Social Psychology,* 1958, *57,* 136–142.

Blashfield, R. An evaluation of the classification of schizophrenic as a nomenclature. *Journal of Abnormal Psychology,* 1973, *82,* 382–389.

Bleuler, E. *Dementia praecox or the group of schizophrenias.* New York: International Universities Press, 1950.

Bowers, M. B. *Retreat from sanity.* Baltimore: Penguin, 1974.

Bradley, C. Psychoses in children. In N. D. Lewis & B. L. Pacella (Eds.), *Modern trends in child psychiatry.* New York: International Universities Press, 1945.

Buss, A. H., & Lang, P. J. Psychological deficit in schizophrenia: I. Affect, reinforcement, and concept attainment. *Journal of Abnormal Psychology,* 1965, *70,* 2–24.

Calhoun, J. F. Comment on differentiating paranoid from nonparanoid schizophrenics. *Journal of Consulting and Clinical Psychology,* 1971, *36,* 104–105.

Cameron, N. Reasoning, regression, and communication in schizophrenia. *Psychological Monographs,* 1938, *50,* 1–33.

Cameron, N. S. *The psychology of behavior disorders.* New York: Houghton Mifflin, 1947.

Cameron, N. S. Perceptual organization and behavior pathology. In R. R. Blake & G. V. Ramsey (Eds.), *Perception: An approach to personality.* New York: Ronald Press, 1951.

Cameron, N. S. Paranoid conditions and paranoia. In S. Arieti (Ed.), *American handbook of psychiatry.* Vol. I. New York: Basic Books, 1959.

Cantrell, P. J., & Magaro, P. A. *Reliability and validity of interview rating scales for paranoid and nonparanoid schizophrenics.* Paper presented at the meeting of the Eastern Psychological Association, Washington, D.C., March 1978.

Cegalis, J. A., Leen, D., & Solomon, E. J. Attention in schizophrenia. An analysis of selectivity in the functional visual field. *Journal of Abnormal Psychology,* 1977, *86,* 470–482.

Chapman, A. H. *Management of emotional problems of children and adolescents.* Philadelphia: Lippincott, 1974.

Cohen, J., Gruel, L., & Stumpf, J. C. Dimensions of psychiatric symptoms ratings determined at thirteen timepoints from hospital admission. *Journal of Consulting Psychology,* 1966, *30,* 39–44.

Cohn, N. *The pursuit of the millenium.* New York: Harper Torchbooks, 1961.

Colby, K. M. Appraisal of four psychological theories of paranoid phenomena. *Journal of Abnormal Psychology,* 1977, *86,* 34–59.

Depue, R. A., & Woodburn, L. Disappearance of paranoid symptoms with chronicity. *Journal of Abnormal Psychology,* 1975, *84,* 84–86.

Despert, L. Schizophrenia in children. *Psychiatric Quarterly*, 1938, *12*, 366–371.

Eiduson, B. T. *Scientists: Their psychological world*. New York: Basic Books, 1962.

Esman, A. H. Childhood psychosis and childhood schizophrenia. *American Journal of Orthopsychiatry*, 1960, *30*, 391–396.

Farina, A., Garnezy, N., Zalusky, M., & Becker, J. Premorbid behavior and prognosis in female schizophrenic patients. *Journal of Consulting Psychology*, 1962, *26*, 56–60.

Forgus, R. H., & DeWolfe, A. S. Coding of cognitive input in delusional patients. *Journal of Abnormal Psychology*, 1974, *83*, 278–289.

Foulds, B. A. *Personality and personal illness*. London: Tavistock Publ., 1965.

Foulds, G. A., & Owen, A. Are paranoids schizophrenics? *The British Journal of Psychiatry*, 1963, *109*, 674–679.

Freud, S. The defense neuropsychoses. Reprinted in *Collected papers* (Vol. 1). London: Hogarth Press, 1946. (Originally published, 1894.)

Fromm-Reichmann, F. Notes on the development of treatment of schizophrenics by psychoanalytic psychotherapy. *Psychiatry*, 1946, *11*, 263–273.

Goldfarb, W. An investigation of child schizophrenia. *Archives of General Psychiatry*, 1964, *11*, 620–634.

Goldfarb, W., Goldfarb, N., Braunstein, P., & School, H. Speech and language faults of schizophrenic children. *Journal of Autism and Childhood Schizophrenia*, 1972, *2*, 219–233.

Goldstein, M. J. Premorbid adjustment, paranoid status, and patterns of response to phenothiazine in acute schizophrenia. *Schizophrenia Bulletin*, 1970, *3*, 24–37.

Goldstein, M. J., Held, J. M., & Cromwell, R. L. Premorbid adjustment and paranoid-nonparanoid status in schizophrenia. *Psychological Bulletin*, 1968, *70*, 382–386.

Gordon, A. V., & Gregson, R. M. The symptom-sign inventory as a diagnostic differentia for paranoid and nonparanoid schizophrenics. *British Journal of Social and Clinical Psychology*, 1970, *77*, 90–96.

Guertin, W. H. A factor analytic study of schizophrenic symptoms. *Journal of Consulting Psychology*, 1952, *16*, 308–312.

Ham, H. W., Spanos, N. P., & Barber, T. X. Suggestibility in hospitalized schizophrenics. *Journal of Abnormal Psychology*, 1976, *85*, 550–557.

Heilbrun, A. B. Tolerance for ambiguity in late adolescent males: Implications for a developmental model of paranoid behavior. *Developmental Psychology*, 1972, *1*, 288–294.

Heilbrun, A. B. *Aversive maternal control: A theory of schizophrenic development*. New York: Wiley, 1973.

Heilbrun, A. B., & Heilbrun, K. S. Content analysis of delusions in reactive and process schizophrenics. *Journal of Abnormal Psychology*, 1977, *86*, 597–608.

Henderson, D. K., & Gillespie, R. D. *Textbook of psychiatry* (8th ed.). London: Oxford University Press, 1956.

Hoffstadter, R. *The paranoid style in American politics and other essays*. New York: Knopf, 1965.

Jenkins, R. M., Stauffacher, F., & Hester, R. A symptom rating scale for use with psychotic patients. *Archives of General Psychiatry*, 1959, *1*, 197–204.

Johansen, W. G., Friedman, S. H., Leitschuh, T. H., & Ammons, H. A study of certain schizophrenic dimensions and their relationship to double alternation learning. *Journal of Consulting Psychology*, 1963, *27*, 375–382.

Jordan, K., & Prugh, D. G. Schizophreniform psychosis of childhood. *American Journal of Psychiatry*, 1971, *128*, 323–329.

Kanner, L. *Child psychiatry* (3rd ed.). Springfield, Ill.: Charles Thomas, 1960.

Kant, I. *The classification of mental disorders* (C. T. Sullivan, ed. and trans.). Doylestown, Pa.: Doylestown Foundation, 1964. (Originally published, 1798.)

Katz, M. M., Cole, J. O., & Lowery, H. A. Nonspecificity of diagnosis of paranoid schizophrenia. *Archives of General Psychiatry*, 1964, *11*, 197–202.

Kelm, H. The figural after-effect in schizophrenic patients. *Journal of Nervous and Mental Disease,* 1962, *135,* 338–345.

Klein, M. *Contribution to psychoanalysis.* London: Hogarth, 1948.

Kowalski, P. A., Daley, G. D., & Gripp, R. F. Token economy: Who responds how? *Behavior Research and Therapy,* 1975, *14,* 372–374.

Kraepelin, E. *Dementia praecox and paraphrenia.* Chicago: Chicago Medical Book Co., 1919.

Kraepelin, E. *Manic-depressive insanity and paranoia.* New York: Anno Press, 1976.

Landauer, A. A., Singer, C., & Day, R. H. Correlation between visual and kinesthetic spatial after-effects. *Journal of Experimental Psychology,* 1966, *72,* 892–894.

Lang, P. J., & Buss, A. H. Psychological deficit in schizophrenia: II. Interference and actuation. *Journal of Abnormal Psychology,* 1965, *70,* 77–106.

London, L. S. Mechanisms in paranoia with report of a case. *Psychoanalytic Review,* 1931, *18,* 39–412.

Lorr, M. Multidimensional scale for rating psychiatric patients. Hospital form. *Veteran's Administration Technical Bulletin,* 10–507, Nov. 1953.

Lorr, M. Factors descriptive of psychopathology and behavior of psychotics. *Journal of Abnormal and Social Psychology,* 1955, *50,* 78–86.

Lorr, M. A simplex of paranoid projection. *Journal of Consulting Psychology,* 1964, *28,* 378–380.

Lorr, M. *Explorations in typing psychotics.* London: Pergamon Press, 1966.

Lorr, M., Jenkins, R. L., & O'Connor, J. P. Factors descriptive of psychopathology and behavior of hospitalized psychotics. *Journal of Abnormal and Social Psychology,* 1955, *50,* 78–86.

Lorr, M., O'Connor, J. P., & Stafford, J. W. The psychotic reaction profile. *Journal of Clinical Psychology,* 1960, *16,* 241–245.

Lorr, M., McNair, D., Klett, C. J., & Lasky, J. J. Evidence of ten psychotic syndromes. *Journal of Consulting Psychology,* 1962, *26,* 185–189.

Lorr, M., Klett, C. J., & McNair, D. M. *Syndromes of psychosis.* New York: Pergamon Press, 1963. (a)

Lorr, M., Klett, C. J., McNair, D. M. & Lasky, J. J. *Inpatient multidimensional psychiatric scale manual.* Palo Alto: Consulting Psychologists Press, 1963. (b)

Lorr, M., Klett, C. J., & Cave, R. Higher-level psychotic syndromes. *Journal of Abnormal Psychology,* 1967, *72,* 74–77.

Lothrop, W. W. A critical review of research on the conceptual thinking of schizophrenics. *Journal of Nervous and Mental Disease,* 1961, *132,* 118–126.

Magaro, P. A. Size estimation in schizophrenia as a function of censure, diagnosis, premorbid adjustment, and chronicity. *Journal of Abnormal Psychology,* 1969, *74,* 306–313.

Magaro, P. A., Gripp, R., & McDowell, D. J. *The mental health industry: A cultural phenomenon.* New York: Wiley, 1978.

Magaro, P. A., & Vojtisek, J. E. Embedded figures performance of schizophrenics as a function of chronicity, premorbid adjustment, diagnosis, and medication. *Journal of Abnormal Psychology,* 1971, *77,* 184–191.

Maher, B. *Principles of psychopathology.* New York: McGraw-Hill, 1966.

Maher, B. A. Delusional thinking and perceptual disorder. *Journal of Individual Psychology,* 1974, *30,* 98–113.

McConaghy, N. Modes of abstract thinking and psychosis. *American Journal of Psychiatry,* 1960, *117,* 106–110.

McDowell, D. J., Reynolds, B., & Magaro, P. A. The integration defect in paranoid and nonparanoid schizophrenia. *Journal of Abnormal Psychology,* 1975, *84,* 629–636.

McGhie, A. Attention and perception in schizophrenia. In B. A. Maher (Ed.), *Progress in experimental personality research* (Vol. 5). New York: Academic Press, 1970.

McReynolds, P., Collins, B., & Acker, M. Delusional thinking and cognitive organization in schizophrenia. *Journal of Abnormal and Social Psychology,* 1964, *69,* 210–212.

Meissner, W. W. *The paranoid process*. New York: Jason Aronson, 1978.

Mosse, H. L. The misuse of the diagnosis childhood schizophrenia. *American Journal of Psychiatry*, 1958, *114*, 791–794.

O'Neil, P., & Robins, L. N. Childhood patterns predictive of adult schizophrenia: A 30-year follow-up study. *American Journal of Psychiatry*, 1958, *115*, 385–391.

Overall, J. E., & Gorham, D. R. The brief psychiatric rating scale. *Psychological Reports*, 1962, *10*, 799–812.

Payne, R. W. The measurement and significance of overinclusive thinking and retardation in schizophrenic patients. In P. H. Hock & J. Zubin (Eds.), *Psychopathology of schizophrenia*. New York: Grune & Stratton, 1961.

Payne, R. W., Caird, W. K., & Laverty, S. G. Overinclusive thinking and delusions in schizophrenic patients. *Journal of Abnormal and Social Psychology*, 1964, *68*, 562–566.

Phillips, L. Case history data and prognosis in schizophrenia. *Journal of Nervous and Mental Disease*, 1953, *117*, 515–525.

Piggott, L. R., & Gottlieb, J. S. Childhood schizophrenia—What is it? *Journal of Autism and Childhood Schizophrenia*, 1973, *3*, 95–105.

Rapaport, D., Gill, M. M., & Schafer, R. *Diagnostic psychological testing*. New York: International Universities Press, 1968.

Rappaport, M., Hopkins, H. K., Silverman, J., & Hall, K. Auditory signal detection in schizophrenics. *Psychopharmacologia*, 1972, *24*, 6–28.

Reiss, D., & Elstein, A. S. Perceptual and cognitive resources of family members: Contrasts between families of paranoid and nonparanoid schizophrenics and nonschizophrenics. *Archives of General Psychiatry*, 1971, *24*, 121–134.

Rimland, B. *Infantile autism*. New York: Appleton-Century, 1964.

Ritzler, B. A., & Smith, M. The problem of diagnostic criteria in the study of the paranoid subclassification of schizophrenia. *Schizophrenia Bulletin*, 1976, *2*, 209–217.

Ryan, E. D., & Foster, R. Athletic participation and perceptual augmentation and reduction. *Journal of Personality and Social Psychology*, 1967, *6*, 472–476.

Saucer, R. T. A further study of the perception of apparent motion by schizophrenics. *Journal of Consulting Psychology*, 1958, *22*, 256–258.

Saucer, R. T. Chlopromazine and apparent motion perception by schizophrenics. *Journal of Consulting Psychology*, 1959, *23*, 134–136.

Saucer, R. T., & Deabler, H. L. Perception of apparent motion in organics and schizophrenics. *Journal of Consulting Psychology*, 1956, *20*, 385–389.

Schafer, R. *The clinical application of psychological tests*. New York: International Universities Press, 1948.

Schafer, R. *Psychoanalytic interpretation in Rorschach testing: Theory and application*. New York: Grune & Stratton, 1954.

Schmidt, H. O., & Fonda, C. P. The reliability of psychiatric diagnosis: A new look. *Journal of Abnormal and Social Psychology*, 1956, *52*, 262–267.

Searles, H. The effort to drive the other person crazy—an element in the aetiology and psychotherapy of schizophrenia. *British Journal of Medical Psychology*, 1959, *32*, 1–18.

Shakow, D. Segmental set: A theory of the formal psychological deficit in schizophrenia. *Archives of General Psychiatry*, 1962, *6*, 1–17.

Shakow, D. Psychological deficit in schizophrenia. *Behavioral Science*, 1963, *8*, 272–305.

Shapiro, D. *Neurotic styles*. New York: Farrar, Strauss, & Giroux, 1965.

Silverman, J. The problem of attention in research and theory in schizophrenia. *Psychological Review*, 1964, *71*, 352–279. (a)

Silverman, J. Scanning-control mechanism and "cognitive filtering" in paranoid and nonparanoid schizophrenia. *Journal of Consulting Psychology*, 1964, *28*, 385–393. (b)

Silverman, J. Variations in cognitive control and psychophysiological defense in the schizophrenia. *Psychosometic Medicine*, 1967, *29*, 225–251.

Silverman, J. Stimulus intensity modulation and psychological disease. *Psychopharmacologia,* 1972, *24,* 42–80.

Silverman, J., Buchsbaum, M., & Henkin, J. Unpublished data cited in J. Silverman, Stimulus intensity modulation and psychological disease. *Psychopharmacologia,* 1972, *24,* 42–80. (Data completed, 1969.)

Singh, M. M., & Kay, S. R. *Psychobiological significance of schizophrenia subtypes.* Paper presented at the Second World Congress of Biological Psychiatry, Barcelona, Spain, 1978.

Strauss, M. E. Behavioral differences between acute and chronic schizophrenia. Course of psychosis, effects of institutionalization, or sampling biases? *Psychological Bulletin,*1973, *79,* 271–279.

Sullivan, H. S. *The interpersonal theory of psychiatry,* New York: Norton, 1953.

Tustin, F. *Autism and childhood psychosis.* New York: Science House, 1972.

Venables, P. H., & O'Conner, N. A short scale for rating paranoid schizophrenia. *Journal of Mental Science,* 1959, *105,* 815–818.

Vojtisek, J. E. Signal detection and size estimation in schizophrenia (Doctoral dissertation, University of Maine, 1975). *Dissertation Abstracts International,* 1976, *36,* 5209B–5291B.

Weiner, J. *Psychodiagnosis in schizophrenia.* New York: Wiley, 1966.

Young, M. L., & Jerome, E. A. Problem-solving performance of paranoids and nonparanoid schizophrenics. *Archives of General Psychiatry,*1972, *26,* 442–444.

Zilboorg, G., & Henry, G. W. *A history of medical psychology,* New York: Norton, 1941.

Chapter 6

Abrams, G. M., Taintor, Z. C., & Lhamon, W. T. Percept assimilation and paranoid severity. *Archives of General Psychiatry,* 1966, *14,* 491–496.

Bannister, D. Schizophrenia: Carnival mirror of coherence. *Psychology Today,* 1971, *4,* 66–84.

Bauman, E., & Kolisnyk, E. Interference effects in schizophrenic short-term memory. *Journal of Abnormal Psychology,* 1976, *85,* 303–308.

Bauman, E., & Murray, D. J. Recognition versus recall in schizophrenics. *Canadian Journal of Psychology,* 1968, *22,* 18–25.

Bernback, H. A. A multiple-copy model for post-perceptual memory. In D. A. Norman (Ed.), *Models of human memory.* New York: Academic Press, 1970.

Bjork, R. A. Repetition and rehearsal mechanisms in models for short-term memory. In D. A. Norman (Ed.), *Models of human memory.* New York: Academic Press, 1970.

Boring, E. G. Attention research and beliefs concerning the conception in scientific psychology before 1930. In D. I. Mostofsky (Ed.), *Attention: Contemporary theory and analysis.* New York: Appleton-Century-Crofts, 1970.

Broadbent, D. E. *Perception and communication.* London: Pergamon Press, 1958.

Broadbent, D. E. *Decision and stress.* London: Academic Press, 1971.

Bruner, J. S. Personality dynamics and the process of perceiving. In R. R. Blake & G. V. Ramsey (Eds.), *Perception: An approach to personality.* New York: Ronald Press, 1951.

Bruner, J. S. *Toward a theory of instruction.* Cambridge, Mass: Harvard University Press, 1966.

Bruner, J. S., Goodnow, J. J., & Austin, G. A. *A study of thinking.* New York: Wiley, 1956.

Bruner, J. S., & Minturn, A. L. Perceptual identification and perceptual organization. *Journal of General Psychology,* 1955, *53,* 21–28.

Bugelski, B. R., & Alampay, D. ·A. The role of frequency in developing perceptual sets. *Canadian Journal of Psychology,* 1961, *15,* 205–211.

Calhoun, J. F. Effects of performance payoff and cues on recall of hospitalized schizophrenics. *Journal of Abnormal Psychology,* 1970, *76,* 485–491.

Carini, L. Explanations of percepts and concepts in schizophrenia. *Psychiatria Neurologia Neurochirurgia,* 1973, *76,* 129–138.

Cash, T. F., Neale, J. M., & Cromwell, R. L. Span of apprehension in acute schizophrenics full-report technique. *Journal of Abnormal Psychology*, 1972, *79*, 322–326.

Chapman, L. J., & Chapman, J.P. *Disordered thought in schizophrenia*. New York: Appleton-Century-Crofts, 1973.

Chase, W. G., & Simon, H. A. The mind's eye in chess. In W. G. Chase (Ed.), *Visual information processing*. New York: Academic Press, 1973.

Clooney, J. L., & Murray, D. J. Same–different judgments in paranoid and schizophrenic patients: A laterality study. *Journal of Abnormal Psychology*, 1977, *86*, 655–658.

Cohen, B. D., & Camhi, J. Schizophrenic performance in a word-communication task. *Journal of Abnormal Psychology*, 1967, *72*, 240–246.

Cohen, B. D., Nachmani, G., & Rosenberg, S. Referent communication disturbances in acute schizophrenia. *Journal of Abnormal Psychology*, 1974, *83*, 1–13.

Craik, F. I. M., & Lockhart, R. S. Levels of processing: A framework for memory research. *Journal of Verbal Learning and Verbal Behavior*, 1972, *11*, 671–684.

Davidson, G. S., & Neale, J. M. The effects of signal-noise similarity on usual information processing of schizophrenics. *Journal of Abnormal Psychology*, 1974, *83*, 683–686.

Deutsch, J. A., & Deutsch, D. Attention: some theoretical considerations. *Psychological Review*, 1963, *70*, 80–90.

De Groot, A. D. *Thought and choice in chess*. The Hague: Mouton, 1965.

De Groot, A. D. Perception and memory versus thought: Some ideas and recent findings. In B. Kleinmuntz (Ed.), *Problem solving*. New York: Wiley, 1966.

DeWolfe, A. S. Cognition structure and pathology in association of process and reactive schizophrenics. *Journal of Abnormal Psychology*, 1971, *78*, 148–153.

DeWolfe, A. S., & Youkillis, H. D. Stress and the word associations of process and reactive schizophrenics. *Journal of Clinical Psychology*, 1974, *30*, 151–153.

Erickson, C. W., & Collins, J. F. Backward masking in vision. *Psychonomic Science*, 1964, *1*, 101–102.

Estes, W. K. A technique for assessing variability of perceptual span. *Proceedings of the National Academy of Science*, 1965, *54*, 403–407.

Foulds, G. A. *Personality and personal illness*. London: Tavistock, 1965.

Gamble, K. R. Paranoid integration and thought disorder. *Journal of Clinical Psychology*, 1975, *31*, 604–607.

Gibson, J. J. *The perception of the visual world*. Boston: Houghton Mifflin, 1950.

Gibson, J. J. *The senses considered as perceptual systems*. Boston: Houghton Mifflin, 1966.

Goldstein, G., & Halperin, K. M. Neuropsychological differences among subtypes of schizophrenia. *Journal of Abnormal Psychology*, 1977, *86*, 34–40.

Gregson, R. A. M., & Fearnley, H. Atypical relation similarity judgments in schizophrenia. *British Journal of Clinical and Social Psychology*, 1974, *13*, 80–90.

Grodin, M., & Brown, D. R. Multivariate stimulus processing by normal and paranoid schizophrenic subjects. *Psychonomic Science*, 1967, *8*, 525–526.

Haber, R. N. The nature of the effect of set on perception. *Psychological Review*, 1966, *73*, 335–350.

Hayes-Roth, B. Evolution of cognitive structures and processes. *Psychological Review*, 1977, *84*, 260–278.

Hebb, D. O. *The organization of behavior*. New York: Wiley, 1949.

Hemsley, D. R. Attention and information processing in schizophrenia research. *British Journal of Social and Clinical Psychology*, 1976, *15*, 199–209.

Hirt, M., Cuttler, M., & Genshaft, J. Information processing by schizophrenics when task complexity increases. *Journal of Abnormal Psychology*, 1977, *86*, 256–260.

Kantowitz, D. A., & Cohen, B. D. Referent communication in chronic schizophrenia. *Journal of Abnormal Psychology*, 1977, *86*, 1–9.

Klinka, J., & Papageorgis, D. Associative intrusions in the vocabulary of schizophrenics and other patients. *British Journal of Psychiatry*, 1976, *129*, 584–591.

Knight, R. A., Sims-Knight, J. E., & Petchers-Cassell, M. Overinclusion, broad scanning, and picture recognition in schizophrenics. *Journal of Clinical Psychology*, 1977, *33*, 635–642.

Knight, R., Scherer, M., & Shapiro, J. Iconic imagery in over-inclusion and nonoverinclusion schizophrenics. *Journal of Abnormal Psychology*, 1977, *86*, 242–255.

Koh, S. D., & Kayton, L. Memorization of "unrelated" word strings by young nonpsychotic schizophrenics. *Journal of Abnormal Psychology*, 1974, *83*, 14–22.

Koh, S. D., Kayton, L., & Berry, R. Mnemonic organization in young nonpsychotic schizophrenics. *Journal of Abnormal Psychology*, 1973, *81*, 299–310.

Koh, S. D., Kayton, L., & Schwarz, C. The structure of word storage in the permanent memory of nonpsychotic schizophrenics. *Journal of Consulting and Clinical Psychology*, 1974, *42*, 879–887.

Koh, S. D., Szoc, R., & Peterson, R. A. Short-term memory scanning in schizophrenic young adults. *Journal of Abnormal Psychology*, 1977, *86*, 451–460.

Kopfstein, J. H., & Neale, J. M. A multivariate study of attention dysfunction in schizophrenia. *Journal of Abnormal Psychology*, 1972, *80*, 294–298.

Kornetsky, C. The use of a simple test of attention as a measure of drug effects in schizophrenic patients. *Psychopharmacologia*, 1972, *24*, 99–106.

Larsen, S. F., & Fromholt, P. Mnemonic organization and free recall in schizophrenia. *Journal of Abnormal Psychology*, 1976, *85*, 61–65.

Leeper, R. A study of a neglected portion of the field of learning—The development of sensory organization. *Journal of Genetic Psychology*, 1935, *46*, 41–75.

Lindsay, P. N., & Norman, D. A. *Human information processing*. New York: Academic Press, 1972.

Lisman, S. A., & Cohen, B. D. Self-editing deficits in schizophrenia: A word-association analogue. *Journal of Abnormal Psychology*, 1972, *79*, 181–188.

MacKinnon, T., & Singer, C. Schizophrenia and the scanning cognitive control: a reevaluation. *Journal of Abnormal Psychology*, 1969, *74*, 242–249.

McCormick, D. J., & Broekema, V. J. Size estimation, perceptual recognition, and cardiac rate response in acute paranoid and nonparanoid schizophrenics. *Journal of Abnormal Psychology*, 1978, *87*, 385–398.

McIntyre, C., Fox, R., & Neale, J. Effect of noise similarity and redundancy on the information processed from brief visual displays. *Perception & Psychophysics*, 1970, *7*, 328–332.

McReynolds, P. Anxiety, perception, and schizophrenia. In D. Jackson (Ed.), *The etiology of schizophrenia*. New York: Basic Books, 1960.

McReynolds, P., Collins, B., & Acker, M. Delusional thinking and cognitive organization in schizophrenia. *Journal of Abnormal and Social Psychology*, 1964, *69*, 210–212.

Miller, G. A. The magical number five, plus or minus two: Some limits in our capacity for processing information. *Psychological Review*, 1956, *63*, 81–97.

Nachmani, G. & Cohen, B. D. Recall and recognition free learning in schizophrenics. *Journal of Abnormal Psychology*, 1969, *74*, 511–516.

Neale, J. M. Perceptual span in schizophrenia. *Journal of Abnormal Psychology*, 1971, *77*, 196–204.

Neale, J. M., & Cromwell, R. L. Size estimation in schizophrenics as a function of stimulus presentation time. *Journal of Abnormal Psychology*, 1968, *73*, 44–49.

Neale, J. M., & Cromwell, R. L. Attention and schizophrenia. In B. A. Maher (Ed.), *Contributions to the psychopathology of schizophrenia*. New York: Academic Press, 1977.

Neale, J. M., McIntyre, C. W., Fox, R., & Cromwell, R. C. Span of apprehension in acute schizophrenics. *Journal of Abnormal Psychology*, 1969, *74*, 593–596.

Neisser, U. Decision time without reaction time. Experiments in visual scanning. *American Journal of Psychology*, 1963, *76*, 376–385.

Neisser, U. *Cognitive psychology*. New York: Appleton-Century-Crofts, 1967.

Neisser, U. *Cognition and reality*. San Francisco: Freeman, 1976. (a)

Neisser, U. General, academic, and artificial intelligence. In L. B. Resnick (Ed.), *The nature of intelligence*. Hillsdale, N. J.: Lawrence Erlbaum Associates, 1976. (b)

Neisser, U., & Becklen, R. Selective looking: Attending to visually-specified events. *Cognitive Psychology*, 1975, *7*, 480–494.

Neufield, R. W. J. Simultaneous processing of multiple stimulus dimensions among paranoid and nonparanoid schizophrenics. *Multivariate Behavioral Research*, 1976, *4*, 425–442.

Neufield, R. W. J. Components of processing deficit among paranoid and nonparanoid schizophrenics. *Journal of Abnormal Psychology*, 1977, *86*, 60–64.

Nolan, J. D. With-in subjects analysis of discrimination shift behavior of schizophrenics. *Journal of Abnormal Psychology*, 1974, *83*, 497–511.

Norman, D. A. Acquisition and retention in short-term memory. *Journal of Experimental Psychology*, 1966, *72*, 369–381.

Oltmanns, T. F. Selective attention in schizophrenic and manic psychosis: The effect of distraction on information processing. *Journal of Abnormal Psychology*, 1978, *87*, 212–225.

Pic'l, A. K., Magaro, P. A., & Wade, E. A. Hemispheric functioning in paranoid and nonparanoid schizophrenia. *Journal of Biological Psychiatry*, 1979, in press.

Polyakov, V. F. The experimental investigation of cognitive functioning in schizophrenia. In M. Cole & I. Maltzman (Eds.), *Handbook of contemporary soviet psychology*, New York: Basic Books, 1969.

Russell, P. N., Bannatyne, P. A., & Smith, J. F. Association strength as a mode of organization in recall and recognition: A comparison of schizophrenic and normals. *Journal of Abnormal Psychology*, 1975, *84*, 122–128.

Russell, P. N., & Beekhuis, M. E. Organization in memory: A comparison of psychotics and normal. *Journal of Abnormal Psychology*, 1976, *85*, 527–534.

Russell, P. N., & Knight, R. G. Performance of process schizophrenics on tasks involving visual search. *Journal of Abnormal Psychology*, 1977, *86*, 16–26.

Saccuzzo, D. P., Hirt, M., & Spencer, T. J. Backward masking as a measure of attention in schizophrenia. *Journal of Abnormal Psychology*, 1974, *83*, 512–522.

Saccuzzo, D. P., & Miller, S. Critical interstimulus interval in delusional schizophrenics and normals. *Journal of Abnormal Psychology*, 1977, *86*, 261–266.

Sarbin, T. R., Juhasz, J. B., & Todd, P. The social psychology of "hallucinations." *Psychological Record*, 1971, *21*, 87–93.

Schneider, S. J. Selective attention in schizophrenia. *Journal of Abnormal Psychology*, 1976, *85*, 167–173.

Schneider, S. J. Speculating about cognitive experiments using schizophrenics. *Schizophrenia Bulletin*, 1978, *4*, 483–487.

Schneider, W., & Shiffrin, R. M. Controlled and automatic human information processing: I. Detection, search, and attention. *Psychological Review*, 1977, *84*, 1–66.

Shiffrin, R. M. Memory search. In D. A. Norman (Ed.), *Models of human memory*. New York: Academic Press, 1970.

Shiffrin, R. M., & Schneider, W. Controlled and automatic human information processing: II. Perceptual learning, automatic attending and a general theory. *Psychological Review*, 1977, *84*, 127–190.

Smith, E. E. Association and editing processes in schizophrenic communication. *Journal of Abnormal Psychology*, 1970, *75*, 182–186.

Spelke, E., Hirst, W., & Neisser, U. Skills of divided attention. *Cognition*, 1977, *4*, 215–230.

Sperling, G. The information available in brief visual presentation. *Psychological Monographs*, 1960, *74*(11, Whole No. 498).

Spohn, H., Thetford, P. E., & Woodham, F. L. Span of apprehension and arousal in schizophrenics. *Journal of Abnormal Psychology*, 1970, *75*, 113–123.

Sternberg, S. Memory scanning: New findings and current controversies. *Quarterly Journal of Experimental Psychology*, 1975, *27*, 1–32.

Steronko, R. J., & Woods, D. J. Impairment in early stages of visual information processing in nonpsychotic schizotypic individuals. *Journal of Abnormal Psychology*, 1978, *87*, 481–490.

Szekely, L. Knowledge and thinking. *Acta Psychologia*, 1950, *7*, 1–24.

Traupmann, K. L. Effects of categorization and imagery on recognition and recall by process and reactive schizophrenics. *Journal of Abnormal Psychology*, 1975, *84*, 307–314.

Traupmann, K. L., Berzofsky, M., & Kesselman, M. Encoding of taxonomic word categories by schizophrenics. *Journal of Abnormal Psychology*, 1976, *85*, 350–355.

Triesman, A. M. Strategies and models of selective attention. *Psychological Review*, 1969, *76*, 282–299.

Yates, A. J. Psychological deficit. *Annual Review of Psychology*, 1966, *17*, 111–114.

Yates, A. J., & Korboot, P. Speed of perceptual functioning in chronic nonparanoid schizophrenics. *Journal of Abnormal Psychology*, 1970, *76*, 453–461.

Young, M. L., & Jerome, E. A. Problem solving performance of paranoid and nonparanoid schizophrenics. *Archives of General Psychiatry*, 1972, *26*, 442–444.

Zubin, J. Problem of attention in schizophrenia. In M. L. Kietzman, S. Sutton, & J. Zubin (Eds.), *Experimental approaches to psychopathology*. New York: Academic Press, 1975.

Chapter 7

Abrams, G. M. Taintor, Z. C., & Lhamon, W. T. Percept assimilation and paranoid severity. *Archives of General Psychiatry*, 1966, *14*, 491–496.

Barthell, C., & Holmes, D. High school yearbooks: A nonreactive measure of social isolation in graduates who later become schizophrenic. *Journal of Abnormal Psychology*, 1968, *73*, 313–316.

Bell, R. Q. Retrospective and prospective view of early personality development. *Merrill-Palmer Quarterly*, 1959–1960, *6*, 131–144.

Binder, A. Personality variables and recognition response level. *Journal of Abnormal and Social Psychology*, 1958, *57*, 136–142.

Blatt, S. J., & Wild, C. M. *Schizophrenia: A developmental analysis*. New York: Academic Press, 1976.

Bogoch, S., Belval, P. C., Dussik, K. J., & Concan, P. C. Psychological and biochemical syntheses occurring during recovery from psychosis. *American Journal of Psychiatry*, 1962, *119*, 128–135.

Bridger, W. H. Sensory habituation and discrimination in the human neonate. *American Journal of Psychiatry*, 1961, *117*, 991–996.

Carini, L. *An experimental investigation of perceptual behavior in schizophrenics*. Unpublished doctoral dissertation, Clark University, 1955.

Carini, L. The theory of symbolic transformations. *Acta Psychologica*, 1961, *31*, 1–44. (Mimeo)

Carini, L. Explanations of percepts and concepts in schizophrenia. *Psychiatria Neurologia Neurochirugia*, 1973, *76*, 129–138.

Chapman, L. F., Hinkle, L. E., & Wolff, H. G. Human ecology, disease, and schizophrenia. *The American Journal of Psychiatry*, 1960, *117*, 193–204.

Cole, M., & Maltzman, I. *Handbook of contemporary soviet psychology*. New York: Basic Books, 1969.

Despert, J. L. *Schizophrenia in children*. New York: Brunner, 1968.

Escalona, S. K. The differential impact of environmental conditions as a function of different reaction patterns in infancy. In G. C. Westman (Ed.), *Individual differences in children*. New York: Wiley Interscience, 1973.

Feffer, M. Symptom expression as a form of primitive decentering. *Psychological Review*, 1967, *74*, 16–28.

Feigenberg, I. M. Probabilistic prognosis and its significance in normal and pathological subjects. In M. Cole & I. Mattzman (Eds.), *Handbook of contemporary soviet psychology.* New York: Basic Books, 1969.

Fisher, S. Body image and psychopathology. *Archives of General Psychiatry,* 1964, *10,* 519–529.

Fisher, S. Body image in neurotic and schizophrenic patients. *Archives of General Psychiatry,* 1966, *15,* 90–101.

Flavell, J. H. *The developmental psychology of Jean Piaget.* New York: Van Nostrand, 1963.

Friedman, H. Perceptual regression in schizophrenia: An hypothesis suggested by the use of the Rorschach Test. *Journal of Genetic Psychology,* 1952, *81,* 63–98.

Grossman, J. J., & Greenberg, N. H. Psychosomatic differentiation in infancy. *Psychosomatic Medicine,* 1957, *19,* 293–306.

Heath, R. G. A biochemical hypothesis on the etiology of schizophrenia. In D. D. Jackson (Ed.), *The etiology of schizophrenia.* New York: Basic Books, 1960.

Inhelder, B., & Piaget, J. *The growth of logical thinking from childhood to adolescence.* New York: Basic Books, 1958.

Jeri, F. R., & Sanchez, C. Psicosis en la ninez de comiemzo Tardio, *Neuro-Psiquiatria,* 1971, *34*(2), 91–109.

Johannsen, W. J. Responsiveness of chronic schizophrenics and normals to social and nonsocial feedback. *Journal of Abnormal and Social Psychology,* 1961, *62,* 106–113.

Kanner, L., & Eisenberg, L. Early infantile autism and childhood schizophrenia symposium. *American Journal of Arthopsychiatry,* 1956, *26,* 556–564.

Kitamura, S. Integrative regulation of psychological functions. *Tohoku Psychologica Folia,* 1974, *33,* 1–12.

Kolvin, I., Garside, R. F., & Kidd, J. S. Studies in the childhood psychoses: IV. Parental personality and attitude and childhood psychoses. *British Journal of Psychiatry,* 1971, *118,* 403–406. (a)

Kolvin, I., Garside, R. F., & Kidd, J. S., III. The family and social background in childhood psychosis. *British Journal of Psychiatry,* 1971, *118,* 396–402. (b)

Letourneau, J. E. The Oppel-Kundt and the Muller-Lyer illusions among schizophrenics. *Perceptual and Motor Skills,* 1974, *39,* 775–778.

Lipsitt & Levy, L., & Levy, N. Pain threshold in the human neonate. *Child Development,* 1959, *30,* 547–554.

Magaro, P. A., Miller, I. W., & McDowell, D. J. Autism childhood schizophrenia, and paranoid and nonparanoid adult schizophrenia: An integration theory synthesis. In D. V. Siva Sankar (Ed.), *Mental health in children* (Vol. II). Westbury, N.Y.: PJD Publ., 1976.

Mahler, M. S. *On human symbiosis and the vicissitudes of individuation* (Vol. 1). New York: International Universities Press, 1968.

McDowell, D. J. Integration of perceptual and conceptual processes. In R. H. Woody (Ed.), *Encyclopedia of clinical assessment.* San Francisco: Jossey-Bass, in press.

McDowell, D., Reynolds, B., & Magaro, P. A. The integration defect in paranoid and nonparanoid schizophrenia. *Journal of Abnormal Psychology,* 1975, *84,* 629–636.

McReynolds, P. Anxiety, perception, and schizophrenia. In D. Jackson (Ed.), *The etiology of schizophrenia.* New York: Basic Books, 1960.

McReynolds, P., Collins, B., & Acker, M. Delusional thinking and cognitive organization in schizophrenia. *Journal of Abnormal and Social Psychology,* 1964, *69,* 210–212.

Meehl, P. E. Schizotaxia, schizotypy, schizophrenica. *American Psychologist,* 1962, *17,* 827–838.

Mook, B. *Causal thought in schizophrenic children.* Johannesburg, South Africa: Rand Afrikaans University, 1973.

Namache, G. F., & Ricks, D. F. *Life patterns of children who became adult schizophrenics.* Presented at the annual meeting of the American Orthopsychiatry Association, San Francisco, April 1966.

Piaget, J. *The psychology of intelligence.* New York: Harcourt Brace, 1950.

Piaget, J. *The origins of intelligence in children.* New York: International Universities Press, 1952.

Piaget, J. *The construction of reality in the child.* New York: Basic Books, 1954.

Piaget, J. Development and learning. In C. S. Lavatelli & F. Stendler, (Eds.) *Readings in child behavior and development* (3rd ed.). New York: Harcourt, Brace, Javanovich, 1972.

Polyakov, U. F. The experimental investigation of cognitive functioning in schizophrenia. In M. Cole & I. Maltzman (Eds.), *A handbook of contemporary Soviet psychology.* New York: Basic Books, 1969.

Rado, S., Buchenholz, B., Dunton, H., Karlen, S. H., & Senescu, R. A. Schizotypical organization: Preliminary report on a clinical study of schizophrenia. In S. Rado & G. Daniels (Eds.), *Changing concepts of psychoanalytic medicine.* New York: Grune & Stratton, 1956.

Robbins, L. N. *Deviant children grow up.* Baltimore: Williams & Witkins, 1966.

Sarbin, T. R., Juhasz, J. B., & Todd, P. The social psychology of "hallucinations." *Psychological Record,* 1971, *21,* 87–93.

Siegel, E. L. Genetic parallels of perceptual structuralization in paranoid schizophrenia: An analysis by means of the Rorschach technique. *Journal of Projective Techniques,* 1953, *17,* 151–161.

Silverman, J. The problem of attention in research and theory in schizophrenia. *Psychologial Review,* 1964, *71,* 352–379.

Sommer, R., & Whitney, G. The chain of chronicity. *American Journal of Psychiatry,* 1961, *118,* 111–117.

Szekely, L. Knowledge and thinking. *Acta Psychologica,* 1950, *7,* 1–24.

Wapner, S., & Werner, H. *Perceptual Development.* Worcester: Clark University Press, 1957.

Watt, N. F. Longitudinal changes in the social behavior of children hospitalized for schizophrenia as adults. *Journal of Nervous and Mental Diseases,* 1972, *155,* 42–54.

Werner, H. *Comparative psychology of mental development* (rev. ed.). Chicago: Follet, 1948.

Young, M. L., & Jerome, E. A. Problem solving performance of paranoid and nonparanoid schizophrenics. *Archives of General Psychiatry,* 1972, *26*(5), 442–444.

Zigler, E., & Levine, J. Premorbid adjustment and paranoid–nonparanoid status in schizophrenia: A further investigation. *Journal of Abnormal Psychology,* 1973, *82*(2), 189–199.

Zigler, E., & Phillips, L. Psychiatric diagnosis: A critique. *Journal of Abnormal and Social Psychology,* 1961, *63,* 607–618.

Chapter 8

Alpert, M., Rubinstein, H., & Kesselman, M. Asymmetry of information processing in hallucinators and nonhallucinators. *Journal of Nervous and Mental Disease,* 1976, *162,* 258–265.

Bakan, P. Hypnotizability, laterality of eye-movements and functional brain asymmetry. *Perceptual Motor Skills,* 1969, *28,* 927–932.

Bakan, P. The eyes have it. *Psychology Today,* 1971, *4,* 64–69.

Bazhin, E. F., Wasserman, L. I., & Tonkonogii, M. Auditory hallucinations and left temporal lobe pathology. *Neuropsychologia,* 1975, *13,* 481–487.

Beaumont, J. G., & Dimond, S. J. Brain disconnection and schizophrenia. *British Journal of Psychiatry,* 1973, *123,* 661–662.

Berlucchi, G. Anatomical and physiological aspects of visual functions of corpus callosum. *Brain Research,* 1972, *37,* 371–392.

Berlucchi, G. Cerebral dominance and interhemispheric communication in normal man. In F. O. Schmitt & F. G. Worden (Eds.), *The neurosciences third study program*. Cambridge, Mass.: MIT Press, 1974.

Bever, T. G., & Chiarello, R. J. Cerebral dominance in musicians and non-musicians. *Science,* 1974, *185,* 537–539.

Blau, T. H. Tongue and schizophrenic vulnerability: As the World Turns. *American Psychologist,* 1977, *32,* 997–1005.

Bowers, D., & Heilman, K. M. Material specific hemispherical arousal. *Neuropsychologia,* 1976, *14,* 123–127.

Bruce, R., & Kinsbourne, M. *Orientational model of perceptual asymmetry.* Paper presented at the 15th annual convention of the Psychonomic Society, Boston, November 1974.

Bryden, M. P. Tachistoscopic recognition, handedness, and cerebral dominance, *Neuropsychologia,* 1965, *3,* 1–8.

Caplan, D., Homes, J. M., & Marshall, J. C. Word classes and hemispheric specialization. *Neuropsychologia,* 1974, *12,* 331–337.

Clooney, J. L., & Murray, D. J. Same–different judgments in paranoid and schizophrenic patients: A laterality study. *Journal of Abnormal Psychology,* 1977, *86,* 555–658.

Cohen, G. Hemispheric differences in serial versus parallel processing. *Journal of Experimental Psychology,* 1973, *97,* 349–356.

Corballis, M. C., & Beale, I. L. *The psychology of left and right.* New York: Wiley, 1976.

Davidson, R. J., Schwartz, G. E., Pugash, E., & Bromfield, E. Sex differences in patterns of EEG asymmetry. *Biological Psychology,* 1976, *4,* 119–138.

Davis, R., & Schmit, V. Visual and verbal coding in the interhemispheric transfer of information. *Acta Psychologia,* 1973, *37,* 229–240.

Day, M. E. An eye-movement phenomenon relating to attention, thought and anxiety. *Perceptual and Motor Skills,* 1964, *19,* 443–446.

Day, M. E. An eye-movement indication of individual differences in the physiological organization of attentional processes and anxiety. *Journal of Psychology,* 1967, *66,* 51–62.

Day, M. E. Attention, anxiety, and psychotherapy. *Psychotherapy: Theory, research, and practice,* 1968, *5,* 146–149.

Dee, H. L., & Fontenot, D. J. Cerebral dominance and lateral difference in perception and memory. *Neuropsychologia,* 1973, *11,* 167–173.

DeSisto, M., Rice, A. P., & Magaro, P. A. *Lateral eye movements in paranoid and nonparanoid schizophrenics.* Paper presented at the meeting of the Eastern Psychological Association, Washington, D.C., April 1978.

Doyle, J. C., Ornstein, R., & Galin, D. Lateral specialization of cognitive mode: II. EEG frequency analysis. *Psychophysiology,* 1974, *11,* 567–578.

Dumas, R., & Morgan, A. EEG asymmetry as a function of occupation, task, and task difficulty. *Neuropsychologia,* 1973, *13,* 219–228.

Dunford, M., & Kimura, D. Right hemisphere specialization for depth perception reflected in visual field differences. *Nature,* 1971, *231,* 394–395.

Egeth, H. Laterality effects in perceptual matching. *Perception and Psychophysics,* 1971, *9,* 375–376.

Ellis, H. D., & Shepherd, J. W. Recognition of abstract and concrete words presented in left and right visual fields. *Journal of Experimental Psychology,* 1974, *103,* 1035–1036.

Flor-Henry, P. Psychiatric syndromes considered as manifestations of lateralized temporal-limbic dysfunction. In L. V. Laitenen & K. E. Livinston (Eds.), *Surgical approaches in psychiatry.* Lancaster, England: Medical and Technical Publ. Co., 1973.

Flor-Henry, P. Lateralized temporal–limbic dysfunction and psychopathology. *Annals of the New York Academy of Sciences,* 1976, *280,* 777–795.

Fontenot, D. J. Visual field differences in the recognition of verbal and nonverbal stimuli in man. *Journal of Comparative and Physiological Psychology,* 1973, *85,* 564–569.

Furst, C. J. EEG alpha asymmetry and visuo-spatial performance. *Nature,* 1976, *226,* 254–255.

Galin, D. Implications for psychiatry of left and right cerebral specialization. *Archives of General Psychiatry*, 1974, *31*, 572–583.

Galin, D., & Ellis, R. R. Asymmetry in evoked potentials as an index of lateralized cognitive processes: Relation to EEG alpha asymmetry. *Neuropsychologia*, 1975, *13*, 45–50.

Galin, D., & Ornstein, R. Individual differences in cognitive style: I. Reflective eye movements, *Neuropsychologia*, 1974, *12*, 367–376.

Gazzaniga, M. S. Changing hemisphere dominance by changing reward probability in split-brain monkeys. *Experimental Neurology*, 1971, *33*, 413–419.

Geffen, G., Bradshaw, J. L., & Nettleton, N. C. Attention and hemispheric differences in reaction time during simultaneous audio-visual tasks. *Quarterly Journal of Experimental Psychology*, 1973, *25*, 404–412.

Gruzelier, J. H. Bilateral asymmetry of skin conductance orienting activity and levels in schizophrenics. *Biological Psychology*, 1973, *1*, 21–41.

Gruzelier, J., & Hammond, N. Schizophrenia: A dominant hemisphere temporal–limbic disorder. *Research Communications in Psychology, Psychiatry, and Behavior*, 1976, *1*, 33–72.

Gruzelier, J. H., & Venables, P. H. Skin conductance responses to tones with and without attentional significance in schizophrenic and nonschizophrenic psychiatric patients. *Neuropsychologia*, 1973, *11*, 221–230.

Gruzelier, J., & Venables, P. Bimodality and lateral asymmetry of skin conductance orienting activity in schizophrenics: Replication and evidence of lateral asymmetry in patients with depression and disorder of personality. *Biological Psychiatry*, 1974, *8*, 55–73.

Gur, R., & Gur, R. C. Defense mechanisms, psychosomatic symtomatology, and conjugate lateral eye movements. *Journal of Consulting and Clinical Psychology*, 1975, *43*, 416–420.

Gur, R., Gur, R. C., & Harris, L. J. Cerebral activation, as measured by subjects' lateral eye movements, in influenced by experimenter location. *Neuropsychologia*, 1975, *13*, 35–44.

Gur, R. C., & Gur, R. E. Handedness, sex, and eyedness as moderating variables in the relation between hypnotic susceptibility and functional brain asymmetry. *Journal of Abnormal Psychology*, 1974, *83*, 635–643.

Gur, R. E. Motoric laterality imbalance in schizophrenia: A possible concomitant of left hemisphere dysfunction. *Archives of General Psychiatry*, 1977, *44*, 33–37.

Gur, R. E. Left hemisphere dysfunction and left hemisphere overactivation in schizophrenia. *Journal of Abnormal Psychology*, 1978, *87*, 226–238.

Gur, R. E., & Reyher, J. The relationship between style of hypnotic induction and direction of lateral eye movement. *Journal of Abnormal Psychology*, 1973, *82*, 499–505.

Hammond, N. V., & Gruzelier, J. H. Laterality, attention, and rate effects in the auditory temporal discrimination of chronic schizophrenics: The effect of treatment with chlorpromazine. *Quarterly Journal of Experimental Psychology*, 1978, *30*, 91–103.

Hannay, H. J., & Malone, D. R. Visual field effects and short-term memory for verbal material. *Neuropsychologia*, 1976, *14*, 203–209. (a)

Hannay, H. J., & Malone, D. R. Visual field recognition memory for right-handed females as a function of familial handedness, *Cortex*, 1976, *12*, 41–48. (b)

Harmon, L. D. The recognition of faces. *Scientific American*, 1973, *229*, 70–82.

Hecaen, H., & Angelergues, R. Agnosia for faces (porsopagnosia). *Archives of Neurology*, 1962, *7*, 19–48.

Hellige, J. B. Hemispheric processing differences revealed by differential conditioning and reaction time performance. *Journal of Experimental Psychology General*, 1975, *104*, 309–326.

Hellige, J. B., & Cox, P. J. Effects of concurrent verbal memory on recognition of stimuli from the left and right visual fields. *Journal of Experimental Psychology, Human Perception and Performance*, 1976, *2*, 210–221.

Hines, D. Recognition of verbs, abstract nouns, and concrete nouns from the left and right visual half-fields. *Neuropsychologia*, 1976, *14*, 211–216.

Itil, T. M. Qualitative and quantitative EEG findings in schizophrenia. *Schizophrenia Bulletin,* 1977, *3,* 61–79.

Kimura, D. Dual functional asymmetry of the brain in visual perception. *Neuropsychologia,* 1966, *4,* 275–285.

Kimura, D. Spatial localization in left and right visual fields. *Canadian Journal of Psychology,* 1969, *23,* 445–458.

Kimura, D., & Dunford, M. Normal studies on the function of the right hemisphere in vision. In S. J. Dimond & J. G. Beaumont (Eds.), *Hemisphere function in the human brain.* New York: Wiley, 1974.

Kinsbourne, M. The cerebral basis of lateral asymmetries in attention. *Acta Psychologia,* 1970, *33,* 193–201.

Kinsbourne, M. Direction of gaze and disturbance of cerebral thought processes. *Neuropsychologia,* 1974, *12,* 279–281. (a)

Kinsbourne, M. Lateral interactions in the brain. In M. Kinsbourne & W. L. Smith (Eds.), *Hemispheric disconnection and cerebral function.* Springfield, Ill.: Charles C. Thomas, 1974. (b)

Kinsbourne, M. Mechanisms of hemispheric interaction in man. In M. Kinsbourne & W. L. Smith (Eds.), *Hemispheric disconnection and cerebral function.* Springfield, Ill.: Charles C. Thomas, 1974. (c)

Klein, D., Moscovitch, M., & Vigna, C. Attentional mechanisms and perceptual asymmetries in tachistoscopic recognition of words and faces. *Neuropsychologia,* 1976, *14,* 55–65.

Leiber, L. Lexical decisions in the right and left cerebral hemispheres. *Brain and Language,* 1976, *3,* 443–450.

Levy, J. Possible basis for the evolution of lateral specialization of the human brain. *Nature,* 1969, *224,* 614–615.

Levy, J. *Cerebral asymmetries as manifested in split-brain man.* In M. Kinsbourne & W. L. Smith (Eds.), *Hemispheric disconnection and cerebral function.* Springfield, Illinois: Charles C. Thomas, 1974.

Levy, J., & Trevarthen, C. Meta-control of hemispheric function in human split-brain patients. *Journal of Experimental Psychology: Human Perception and Performance,* 1976, *2,* 299–312.

Levy, C., Trevarthan, C., & Sperry, R. W. Perception of bilateral chimeric figures. *Brain,* 1972, *95,* 61–78.

Mackavey, W., Curcio, F., & Rosen, J. Tachistoscopic word recognition performance under conditions of simultaneous bilateral presentation. *Neuropsychologia,* 1975, *13,* 27–33.

Marshall, J. C. Some problems and paradoxes associated with recent accounts of hemispheric specialization. *Neuropsychologia,* 1973, *11,* 463–470.

McGlone, J., & Davidson, W. The relation between cerebral speech laterality and spatial ability with special reference to sex and hand preference. *Neuropsychologica,* 1973, *11,* 105–113.

McKeever, W. F., & Huling, M. D. Left-cerebral hemisphere superiority in tachistoscopic word-recognition performance. *Perceptual and Motor Skills,* 1970, *30,* 763–766.

Mintz, S., & Alpert, M. Imagery vividness, reality testing, and schizophrenic hallucinations. *Journal of Abnormal Psychology,* 1972, *79,* 310–316.

Mishkin, M., & Forgays, D. G. Word recognition as a function of retinal locus. *Journal of Experimental Psychology,* 1952, *43,* 43–48.

Morgan, A., McDonald, P. G., & Macdonald, H. Differences in bilateral alpha activity as a function of experimental task, with a note on lateral eye movements and hypnotizability. *Neuropsychologia,* 1971, *9,* 459–469.

Nebes, R. D. Hemispheric specialization in comissurotomized man. *Psychological Bulletin,* 1974, *84,* 1–14.

Patterson, K., & Bradshaw, J. L. Differential hemispheric mediation of nonverbal visual stimuli. *Journal of Experimental Psychology: Human Perception and Performance,* 1975, *1,* 246–252.

Pic'l, A. K., Magaro, P. A., & Wade, E. A. Hemispheric functioning in paranoid and nonparanoid schizophrenia. *Journal of Biological Psychiatry,* 1979, in press.

Ray, W. J., Morell, M., Frediani, A. W., & Tucker, D. M. Sex differences and lateral specialization of hemispheric functioning. *Neuropsychologia,* 1976, *14,* 391–394.

Rizzolatti, G., Umilta, C. A., & Berlucchi, G. Opposite superiorities in the right and left cerebral hemispheres in discriminative reaction time to physiognomical and alphabetical material. *Brain,* 1971, *94,* 431–442.

Robbins, K., & McAdam, D. W. Interhemispheric alpha asymmetry and imagery mode. *Brain and Langauge,* 1974, *1,* 189–193.

Rosenthal, R., & Bigelow, L. B. Quantitative brain measurements in chronic schizophrenia. *British Journal of Psychiatry,* 1972, *121,* 259–264.

Schwartz, G. E., Davidson, R. J., & Maer, F. Right hemisphere lateralization for emotion in the human brain: Interactions with cognition. *Science,* 1975, *190,* 286–288.

Schweitzer, L., Becker, E., & Welsh, H. Abnormalities of cerebral lateralization in schizophrenic patients. *Archives of General Psychiatry,* 1978, *35,* 982–985.

Semmes, J. Hemispheric specialization: A clue to mechanism. *Neuropsychologia,* 1968, *6,* 11–26.

Serafetinides, E. A. Laterality and voltage in the EEG of psychiatric patients. *Diseases of the Nervous System,* 1972, *33,* 622–623.

Shaw, J. C., O'Connor, K., & Ongley, C. The EEG as a measure of cerebral functional organization. *British Journal of Psychiatry,* 1977, *130,* 260–264.

Shimkunas, A. Hemispheric asymmetry and schizophrenic thought disorder. In S. Schwartz (Ed.), *Language and cognition in schizophrenia.* Hillsdale, N.J.: Lawrence Erlbaum Associates, 1978.

Sherman, J. L., Kalhavy, R. W., & Burns, K. Cerebral laterality and verbal processes. *Journal of Experimental Psychology: Human Learning and Memory,* 1976, *2,* 720–727.

Sperry, R. W. Lateral specialization of cerebral function in the surgically separated hemispheres. In F. J. McGuigan & R. A. Schoonover (Eds.), *The psychophysiology of thinking.* New York: Academic Press, 1973.

Trevarthen, C. Functional relations of disconnected hemispheres with the brain stem, and with each other: Monkey and man. In M. Kinsbourne & W. L. Smith (Eds.), *Hemispheric disconnection and cerebral function,* Springfield, Ill.: Charles C. Thomas, 1974.

Tucker, D. M. Sex differences in hemispheric specialization for synthetic visuospatial functions. *Neuropsychologia,* 1976, *14,* 447–454.

Warren, L. R., Peltz, L., & Haueter, E. S. Patterns of EEG alpha during word processing and relations to recall. *Brain and Language,* 1976, *3,* 283–291.

Warrington, E. K., James, M., & Kinsbourne, M. Drawing disability in relation to laterality of cerebral lesion. *Brain,* 1966, *89,* 53–82.

Young, M. J. *Hemispheric specialization and bilateral integration of cognitive processes in schizophrenia.* Unpublished doctoral dissertation, University of Missouri, 1974.

Chapter 9

Ayres, A. J. Improving academic scores through sensory integration. *Journal of Learning Disabilities,* 1972, *5,* 338–343.

Bijou, S. W., & Baer, D. M. Some methodological contributions from a functional analysis a child development. In L. P. Lipsitt & C. C. Spiker (Eds.), *Advances in child development and behavior* (Vol. 1). New York: Academic Press, 1963.

Brehmer, B., Azuma, H., Hammond, F. R., Kostran, L., & Varomos, D. A cross-national comparison of cognitive conflict. *Journal of Cross-Cultural Psychology,* 1970, *1,* 5–20.

Broen, W. E., & Storms, L. H. Postscript: Response disorganization and narrowed observation. In B. A. Maher (Ed.), *Contributions to the psychopathology of schizophrenia.* New York: Academic Press, 1977.

Bryan, T. H. Learning disabilities: A new stereotype. *Journal of Learning Disabilities,* 1974, *7,* 48–51.

Bush, W. J., & Giles, M. T. *Aids to psycholinguistic teaching.* Columbus, Ohio: Charles E. Merrill, 1969.

Clements, S. Minimal brain dysfunction in children. *NINDB Monograph,* No. 3, Public Health Service Bulletin No. 1415, Washington, D.C.: U.S. Department of Health, Education, and Welfare, 1966.

Dunn, L. M., & Smith, J. O. *The Peabody language kits.* Circle Pines, Minn.: American Guidance Service, 1966.

Farnham-Diggory, S. *Learning disabilities.* Cambridge, Mass.: Harvard University Press, 1978.

Feeney, S. *Breadth of cue utilization and ability to attend selectively in schizophrenics and normals.* Unpublished doctoral dissertation, University of California, Los Angeles, 1971.

Fellows, T. *Discriminative process and learning.* Oxford: Pergamon Press, 1968.

Ford, D. H., & Urban, H. B. *Systems of psychotherapy: A comparative study.* New York: Wiley, 1963.

Friedrich, D., & Fuller, G. B. Visual-motor performance: Delineation of the "perceptual deficit" hypothesis. *Journal of Clinical Psychology,* 1973, *29,* 207–209.

Friedrich, D., & Fuller, G. B. Visual-motor performance: Additional delineation of the "perceptual deficit" hypothesis. *Journal of Clinical Psychology,* 1974, *30,* 30–33.

Friedrich, D., Fuller, G. B., & Hawkins, W. F. Relationship between perception (input) and execution (output). *Perceptual and Motor Skills,* 1969, *29,* 923–934.

Gibson, E. J. *Perceptual learning and development.* New York: Appleton-Century-Crofts, 1969.

Goldberg, L. R. Man versus model of man. A rationale, plus some evidence for a method of improving clinical inferences. *Psychological Bulletin,* 1970, *73,* 422–432.

Hammill, D. Training visual perceptual processes. *Journal of Learning Disabilities,* 1972, *5,* 552–559.

Hammill, D., & Larson, S. The effectiveness of psycholinguistic training. *Exceptional Children,* 1975, *41,* 5–14.

Hammond, K. R., & Summer, D. A. Cognitive control. *Psychological Review,* 1972, *79,* 58–67.

Karnes, M. B. *Helping young children develop language skills: A book of activities.* Washington, D.C.: The Council for Exceptional Children, 1968.

King, L. J. A sensory-integrative approach to schizophrenia. *The American Journal of Occupational Therapy,* 1974, *28,* 529–536.

Kirk, S. A., McCarthy, J. J., & Kirk, W. D. *Illinois test of psycholinguistic abilities.* Urbana: University of Illinois Press, 1968.

Kirshner, J. R. Visual-spatial organization and reading: Support for a cognitive–developmental interpretation. *Journal of Learning Disabilities,* 1975, *8,* 30–36.

Levine, M., & Fuller, C. Psychological, neuropsychological, and educational correlates of reading deficit. *Journal of Learning Disabilities,* 1972, *5,* 363–371.

Magaro, P. A., Gripp, R., & McDowell, D. J. *The mental health industry: A cultural phenomenon.* New York: Wiley, 1978.

Maltzman, I. On the training of originality. *Psychological Review,* 1960, *67,* 229–242.

Maltzman, I., Bogartz, W., & Breger, L. A. A procedure for increasing word association originality and its transfer effects. *Journal of Experimental Psychology,* 1958, *56,* 392–398.

McReynolds, L. V. Operant conditioning for investigating speech sound discrimination in aphasic children. *Journal of Speech and Hearing Research,* 1966, *9,* 519–528.

Mednick, S. A. The associative basis of the creative process. *Psychological Review,* 1962, *69,* 220–232.

Meiselman, K. Broadening dual modality cue utilization in chronic nonparanoid schizophrenics. *Journal of Consulting and Clinical Psychology,* 1973, *41,* 447–453.

Minskoff, E., Wiseman, D.E., & Minskoff, J. G. *The MWM program for developing language abilities.* Ridgefield, N.J.: Educational Performance Associates, 1972.

Monsees, E. Temporal sequence and expressive language disorders. *Exceptional Child,* 1968, *35,* 141–147.

Osgood, C. E. Motivational dynamics of language behavior. In M. R. Jones (Ed.), *Nebraska Symposium on Motivation.* Lincoln: University of Nebraska Press, 1957.

Pick, A. D. Improvement of visual and tactual form discrimination. *Journal of Experimental Psychology,* 1965, *69,* 331–339.

Preston, C. W., & Drew, C. J. Verbal performance of learning disabled children as a function of input organization. *Journal of Learning Disabilities,* 1974, *7,* 424–428.

Raskin, L. M., & Baker, G. P. Tactual and visual integration in the learning processes: Research and implications. *Journal of Learning Disabilities,* 1975, *8,* 51–55.

Reese, A. W., & Lipsitt, L. P. *Experimental child psychology.* New York: Academic Press, 1970.

Rhead, J. C., & Fischer, R. Complementarity of consciousness: Man's two cerebral hemispheres and their duplications for psychotherapy. In O. L. McCabe (Ed.), *Changing Human Behavior.* New York, Grune & Stratton, 1977.

Salomon, G., & Suppes, J. S. Learning to generate subjective uncertainty: Effects of training, verbal activity and stimulus structure. *Journal of Personality and Social Psychology,* 1971, *18,* 163–175.

Salzinger, K., & Salzinger, S. Behavior theory for the study of psychopathology. In M. Hammer, K. Salzinger, & S. Sutton (Eds.), *Psychopathology: Contribution from the social, behavioral, and biological sciences.* New York: Wiley, 1973.

Sieber, J. E., & Lanzetta, J. T. Some determinants of individual differences in predecision information processing. *Journal of Personality and Social Psychology,* 1966, *4,* 561–571.

Simpson, R. L., King, J. D., & Drew, C.J. Free recall by retarded and non-retarded subjects as a function of input organization. *Psychonomic Science,* 1970, *19,* 334.

Todd, F. J., & Hammond, K. R. Differential feedback in two multiple-cue learning tasks. *Behavioral Science,* 1965, *10,* 429–435.

Wagner, B. R. The training of attending and abstracting responses in chronic schizophrenics. *Journal of Experimental Research in Personality,* 1968, *3,* 77–88.

Appendix A

Andreason, N. J. C., & Powers, P. S. Creativity and psychosis. *Archives of General Psychiatry,* 1975, *32,* 70–73.

Barron, F. *Artists in the making.* New York: Seminar Press, 1972.

Bateson, G., Jackson, D. D., Haley, J., & Weakland, J. Toward a theory of schizophrenia. *Behavioral Science,* 1956, *1,* 251–264.

Besdine, M. The Jocusta Complex, mothering, and genius. *Psychoanalytic Review,* 1958, *55,* 2.

Buss, A. H. *Psychopathology.* New York: Wiley, 1966.

Cattel, R. B. The personality and motivation of the researcher from measurements of contemporaries and from biography. In C. W. Taylor & F. Barron (Eds.), *Scientific creativity.* New York: Wiley, 1963.

Goertzel, V., & Goertzel, M. *Cradles of Eminence.* Boston: Little, Brown, 1962.

Guilford, J. P. Traits of creativity. In P. E. Vernon (Ed.), *Creativity.* Baltimore, Md.: Penguin Education, 1970.

Harrow, M., Himmelhock, J., Tucker, G., Hersh, J., & Quinlan, D. Overinclusive thinking in acute-schizophrenic patients. *Journal of Abnormal Psychology,* 1972, *79,* 161–168.

Hasenfus, N., & Magaro, P. Creativity and schizophrenia: An equality of empirical constructs. *British Journal of Psychiatry,* 1976, *129,* 346–349.

Johnson, R. C., Weiss, R. L., & Zelhart, P. F. Similarities and differences between normal and psychotic subjects in response to verbal stimuli. *Journal of Abnormal and Social Psychology,* 1964, *68,* 221–226.

Keefe, J., & Magaro, P. A. *An empirical investigation of creativity in schizophrenia.* Paper presented at the meeting of the Eastern Psychological Association, Washington, D.C., March 1978.

Lewis, N. P. *Cognitive style, cognitive complexity, and behavior prediction in process and reactive schizophrenia.* Unpublished doctoral dissertation, Fordham University Library, 1971.

Lidz, T., Cornelison, A. R. T. D., & Fleck, S. The intrafamiliar environment of the schizophrenic patient. VI. The transmission of irrationality. *Archives of Neurology and Psychiatry,* 1958, *79,* 305–316.

Lombroso, C. *The man of genius* (6th ed.). New York: Scribner, 1894.

Maher, B. The language of schizophrenia: A review and interpretation. *British Journal of Psychiatry,* 1972, *120,* 3–17.

Mednick, S. A. The associative basis of the creative process. *Psychological Review,* 1962, *69,* 220–232.

Mednick, M. T., Mednick, S. A., & Jung, C. C. Continual association as a function of level of creativity and type of verbal stimulus. *Journal of Abnormal and Social Psychology,* 1964, *69,* 511–515.

Payne, R. W., Caird, W. K., & Laverty, S. G. Overinclusive thinking and delusions in schizophrenic patients. *Journal of Abnormal and Social Psychology,* 1964, *68,* 562–566.

Payne, R. W., & Friedlander, D. A short battery of simple tests for measuring overinclusive thinking. *Journal of Mental Science,* 1962, *108,* 362–367.

Piers, E. V., & Kirchner, E. P. Productivity and uniqueness in continued word association as a function of subject creativity and stimulus properties. *Journal of Personality,* 1971, *39,* 264–276.

Reed, J. L. Schizophrenic thought disorder: A review and hypothesis. In R. Cancono (Ed.), *Annual review of the schizophrenic syndrome.* New York: Brunner/Mazel, 1972.

Shouksmith, G. *Intelligence, creativity and cognitive style.* New York: Wiley, 1970.

Siegler, M., Osmond, H., & Mann, H. Laing's models of madness. *British Journal of Psychiatry,* 1969, *44,* 947–958.

Sommer, R., Dewar, R., & Osmond, H. Is there a schizophrenic language? *Archives of General Psychiatry,* 1960, *3,* 665–673.

Wallach, M. A. Creativity: In P. H. Mussen (Ed.), *Carmichael's Manual of Child Psychology.* New York: Wiley, 1970.

Wallach, M. A. *The intelligence/creativity distinction.* New York: General Learning Press, 1971.

Wallach, M. A., & Kogan, N. *Modes of thinking in young children: A study of the creativity-intelligence distinction.* New York: Holt, Rinehart & Winston, 1965.

Welsh, G. *Welsh figure preference test.* Palo Alto, Calif.: Consulting Psychologists Press, 1959.

Author Index

Italics denote pages with complete bibliographic information.

Subject Index